THE COLUMBIA GUIDE TO

American Women in the Nineteenth Century

THE COLUMBIA GUIDES TO AMERICAN HISTORY AND CULTURES

Columbia Guides to

American History and Cultures

Michael Kort, *The Columbia Guide to the Cold War*

THE COLUMBIA GUIDE TO

American Women in the Nineteenth Century

Catherine Clinton
Christine Lunardini

COLUMBIA UNIVERSITY PRESS

NEW YORK

Columbia University Press
New York

Columbia University Press
Publishers Since 1893
New York   Chichester, West Sussex
Copyright © 2000 Columbia University Press
All rights reserved

Library of Congress Cataloging-in-Publication Data

Clinton, Catherine, 1952—
    The Columbia guide to American women in the Nineteenth Century / Catherine Clinton,
Christine Lunardini.
        p.   cm. — (Columbia guides to American history and cultures)
        Includes bibliographical references and index.
        ISBN 0–231–10920–2
        1. Women—United States—History—19th century.   I. Lunardini, Christine A., 1941–
II. Title. III. Series.
HQ1418.C58   1999   98—50373

∞

Casebound editions of Columbia University Press books are printed on permanent and durable
acid-free paper.
Printed in the United States of America
c 10 9 8 7 6 5 4 3 2 1

For
Agatha P. Colbert
and
Patsy Cavanaugh Ferriter

CONTENTS

INTRODUCTION

When we began our careers as graduate students together at Princeton in the fall of 1975, little did we know what an ambitious, diverse, and burgeoning field nineteenth-century American women's history would become—but we both knew we wanted to be a part of this exciting and expanding enterprise. Over the next few years one of us would go on to complete her dissertation on plantation mistresses in the Old South and the other would finish her thesis on Alice Paul and Paul's role in the woman suffrage movement (each publishing her study as a book in the 1980s). Then, as now, we were swept away by the dynamic scholarship and the heady sense of anticipation and expectations for work on American women's past.

When asked to undertake the challenge of a Columbia Guide covering American women in the nineteenth century, we leaped at the opportunity—to revisit, to renew acquaintance, to rise to the occasion of the tide of new and exciting studies rushing into print. Charting the course of progress in our fields has been exciting, and we wanted to expand our collective readings to explore new and diverse areas of ongoing inquiry. Subjects are being explored in sensitive and creative ways, employing new data and research techniques that have only become available in recent years.

Naturally, we were daunted at the prospect of trying to cover all the existing materials and incorporating every aspect of nineteenth-century women's experience. Thus our task has been to emphasize those areas in which scholars have highlighted important changes (such as suffrage and reform), to illuminate those areas in which scholars are now making great strides (such as racial, ethnic, religious, and regional diversity), and to incorporate those innovative and relatively recent explorations (for example, work on female friendships and female sexuality) into a compact yet inclusive format.

To make the volume as accessible as possible for readers and in keeping with the overall format of the series, the book is divided into four distinct parts. Each part is designed to be used independent of the other three, but we intend them to be interlocking and to reinforce each other.

Part I begins with a historiographical essay intended to inform or refresh the reader regarding the development of topical interests within women's history in the past century. With our exploration of the themes, ideas, and concerns of scholars during the twentieth century we provide the broad brushstrokes of change for the field and focus in more closely on the research and writing of the past three decades. Our abbreviated discussions of groundbreaking work show how not only women's history but American history in general have been recast by feminist scholarship. Our survey demonstrates the way in which nuanced analysis of gender can reshape our view of the past and provide new approaches for historical periodization. This essay draws the reader's attention to important publications on a multitude of issues comprising the study of gender and American women, issues that continue to expand our knowledge and reconfigure our notions of America's past.

The historiographical essay is followed by a narrative overview of the century, comprised of ten chapters that describe the conditions affecting women's lives and their historical experiences. This narration is meant to convey a fluid picture of the changes that took place between 1800 and 1900, although important discontinuities such as war and peace, slavery and emancipation, and other major shifts are also given extensive analysis. These ten chapters include discussions of families and households, labor and the workforce, religion and morality, immigration and westward expansion, race, ethnicity and class, literacy and education, reform and voluntarism, feminism and equal rights, sexuality and relationships, industrialization and urbanization, pioneering previously male professions and carving out careers—in short, a cornucopia of issues central to people's lives over the course of the century.

In discussing these issues, we have attempted to pay particular attention where appropriate to how race and class altered and informed experience, how ethnic identity or minority status might have diverse impact on gender status. Finally, each of the ten narrative chapters in part I is preceded by an abstract—introductory paragraphs that summarize the themes and issues discussed within the chapter.

In many cases topics are introduced in specific chapters (such as education in chapter 3), or by chapter titles (such as religion in chapter 4), but many issues are also discussed in later chapters. Chapters are both chronological and thematic, which creates some overlapping analysis within our narrative. We have composed each chapter so that it might be read separately, to extract information on specific topics contained within it. Yet it was also our hope that readers would digest these ten chapters all together in the order in which they appear, thus absorbing the full sweep of women's historical experience in the nineteenth century and following historical developments as they evolve.

Chapter 1, "Post-Revolutionary America," focuses on the struggles white female colonists endured and their transformations within the recently United States, and also looks at American Indian women and women of African descent. The chapter outlines the emergence of republican motherhood and the way in which American Indian women, slave women, and immigrant women had dramatically differing experiences within the new American nation.

Chapter 2, "The Economy, Households, and Labor," charts the dramatic transformations within the household economy during the first half of the nineteenth century, as well as the changes taking place within the plantation economy in the South and with the rise of the factory system in the North. Changing notions of labor and "women's work" are outlined.

Chapter 3, "Education and Reform," traces the way in which the tenets of the Founding Fathers translated into improved educational opportunities for American women, creating a revolution for American daughters by the middle decades of the century. This improvement in women's education encouraged women's increasing role in moral reform, which led to female temperance movements, purity campaigns, and, eventually, antislavery agitation.

Chapter 4, "Church and State," explores women's unique role in many Protestant revivals and especially in religious sects, such as Shakers, Quakers, and among the Mormons. The chapter examines Catholic women and Jewish women as well. With the "feminization" of American religion, women began to explore roles outside the church, beyond the hearth, which could and did lead to public campaigns. As women wanted to shore up the moral foundations of their culture, they sought a larger role in the world outside the home and began to advocate on behalf of legal protection. For some women this even translated into crusades for gender equality, especially in the area of family law. Women's campaigns in this arena are traced through the middle decades of the century.

Chapter 5, "Natives and Immigrants," looks at demographic changes for American women, beginning with the precipitous decline of American Indian women and the decimation of their indigenous culture, often through "acculturation." The flood of European immigrants, transforming both cities and the frontier, is outlined. The roles of religious affiliation and ethnic identity provide additional insight into the female immigrant experience in nineteenth-century America.

Chapter 6, "The Civil War and Reconstruction," might perhaps appear to privilege this event as pivotal for women. But since all American women's lives were so dramatically transformed by the traumatic onset of war and by its devastating effects, the Civil War has a central role in this narrative. Further, since the emancipation of slaves and the transformations wrought by freedpeople, especially the emergent status and struggles of freedwomen, were so central to subsequent changes within American society, this era and women's crucial roles are given extensive and detailed analysis.

Chapter 7, "Commerce and Culture," looks at the ways in which post–Civil War America launched a new era of massive westward expansion, a dramatic influx of immigrants, the exponential growth of industry and manufacturing, and, finally, the rise of the cities. Women's experiences were manifold and their responses varied. Many of the postwar generation of women made dramatic inroads into the professions, with increasing influence on civic culture through clubs and the literary arts. Women also pioneered urban reform and the settlement house movement, putting their college degrees and collective experience to work among the laboring poor in overcrowded and corrupting cities. Women's networks flourished and provided a firm foundation for turn-of-the-century American reform.

Chapter 8, "Sexuality, Reproduction, and Gender Roles," examines a host of transforming issues—marital ages, spousal choices, limiting childbearing, abortion, and "voluntary motherhood"—and how all these changes were reflected in nineteenth-century women's lives. Campaigns against vice and the rise of prostitution throughout the century are reviewed. Attitudes toward the bonds of womanhood, romantic friendships, and women's sexual identities are also explored in this chapter. Women's increasing interest in choice—in all matters but especially in regard to their own bodies—is examined at length.

Chapter 9, "Suffrage and Reform Politics," looks at the way in which women reformers tackled a wide range of critical issues at the end of the nineteenth century. Although campaigns for women's equality and demands for the vote increased (with a newly reunited suffrage organization), most suffragists did not limit themselves to gender battles alone. Many women struggled against segregation and the increasing threat of lynching within the American South. Women of all classes took an increasing interest in women's roles within industry and agitated for improved working conditions and humanitarian reforms. Women were not only pushing for improvements in the cities; farm women also launched their own campaigns. Women's activism at the end of the century is developed in full.

Finally, chapter 10, "Epilogue: The Turn of the Century," recapitulates the themes and struggles over women's status and roles, the parade of progress and prohibitions evolving from 1800 to 1900. This epilogue places gender issues within the context of change for American society as a whole during this crucial period.

For the purposes of our narrative, many important events and major figures are mentioned only briefly in part I. However, expanded information on significant people, places, and events is provided in part II, an alphabetical listing of concise entries. The majority of these entries are brief biographical descriptions of women who made important and noteworthy contributions to nineteenth-century history, but included as well are brief descriptions of significant events and organizations that affected women's lives or in which women played a major role. This section also provides cross-references in bold type, so that individual topics and issues can be followed up in additional entries providing expanded or more detailed information.

Part III is an extended annotated chronology, intended to allow the reader to easily place a particular event in its historical context. Most of the entries in the chronology appear within part I or part II, but several provide some sense of the struggles and landmarks of ordinary women whose everyday triumphs and achievements transformed American life.

Part IV is an extensive yet accessible list of resources. We knew we would not be able to provide complete information on all the topics and issues now covered in monograph and article literature on nineteenth-century women, with databases numbering in the hundreds and entries multiplying into the thousands every year. Nevertheless, our bibliography provides the opportunity to point readers to insightful and in-depth analyses, as well as to sources for further research on those myriad topics we were forced either to omit or address only in brief. It also offers an annotated route through those very important works that have shaped and influenced the field. It was not our intention to privilege certain topics or areas of concern, but our guide—and even the topical listings—reveals those prevailing concerns reflected in the most accessible and available literature taught and cited in American women's history today.

Part IV includes standard bibliographical references covering all of the themes and issues discussed within the historiographical essay and the narrative overview. Most of these references are annotated, which again provides the reader with more information regarding both historical context and directions for further research. We employed more than one hundred specific categories, and our bibliography of publications is a compilation of classic studies, influential and groundbreaking works, and a sense of the emerging literature being published at the turn of the twenty-first century.

Part IV also contains a listing of important academic journals, both historical and contemporary, to review both primary and secondary sources in women's history. We have also prepared a list of novels chosen for their insight, descriptive prowess, and/or historical importance. These may provide newcomers to the field with vivid portraits to stimulate further reading.

A brief selection of university, public, and private archives is also included, along with representative lists of their most important collections. Although it may not be possible to visit all these archives with relative ease at the present time, as electronic frontiers are being pioneered, we may be able in future to delve into resources around the world via computers in our own homes or offices.

We have been simultaneously stimulated and stunned by the challenges of the computer revolution. With readily available Internet access, online connections, and increasingly shrinking attention spans—our own and those we face in the classroom—how can we keep up in a world of list-servers and e-mail, where paperless catalogues and virtual libraries are creeping into use?

Our resource guide attempts to tackle some of these important contrivances. Search engines, indexes, and a listing of websites have been included, all of which we think will enhance and expand our appreciation of the lives of women in nineteenth-century America.

Our volume does not include any illustrative material, so we provide limited guidance to this particular source. Visual literacy remains an increasing challenge for twenty-first-century scholars in women's history, as well as American historians in general. Part IV does, however, include a readily available and important resource—an annotated list of the ten best films (mainly available on video, although some can be found in DVD format) depicting the lives of nineteenth-century American women.

Trying to shape all the complex and, in some cases, competing categories of substantive analysis into a compressed narrative framework was no easy task. We hope our mini-encyclopedia entries provide enough additional information on the topics and people we have treated in an abbreviated fashion within chapters. In addition, the chronology created an opportunity to highlight some of the events and issues that do not fit smoothly into our narrative. It is, however, impossible to be comprehensive, considering the leaps and bounds our field is making every day, with twenty-four-hour online databases, with theses and conference papers pouring forth unabated. We have used our collective interests and those of the leading scholars and historians publishing in the field to shape our volume. We all make choices in our work—and we know that this volume reflects our choices, for better or worse.

We hope that the worst is over, now that we have been through the agony of deletion and pruning. And we trust that the best is yet to come—hearing from those who demand more, who wanted less, who offer constructive critiques.

As this guide was designed to be useful to specialists as well as readers and students of any age, we do not apologize for its compact and accessible format. We hope we have made it as jargon-free and user-friendly as possible. It remains our goal that many of you picking up and picking over this guide will find glaring omissions—and make it your business that subsequent editions of *The Columbia Guide to American Women in the Nineteenth Century* include important new work, in vibrant new areas. We look forward to the next generation of scholars who will be delving into American women's past. We will profit from their work as well as from their recognition of the debt owed to those who have come before.

Catherine Clinton, Riverside, Connecticut
Christine Lunardini, New York City
November 1998

THE COLUMBIA GUIDE TO

American Women in the Nineteenth Century

PART ONE

Narrative Overview

Nineteenth-Century Women's History:
A Historiographical Essay

The lives of nineteenth-century American women were circumscribed by those dramatic forces that shaped all Americans: politics, economics, social upheaval, wars, depressions, disease, protest movements, migrations are among the dozens of influential factors. We have only recently become aware of the significant ways in which women were able to shape their times as well. The interpretation of their experiences remains an ongoing process, an unbroken chain of literature from the nineteenth century to the present and onward—an impressive body of material that constitutes American women's history, especially the scholarship of the last few \decades, and that provides us with a valuable map of this past. Some of the milestones and landmarks, detours and rest stops along this journey are traced in this essay.

PIONEERS

Many of the pioneers in the field of nineteenth-century American women's history were themselves women born in the nineteenth century—such as Annie Nathan Meyer, who published her *Woman's Work in America* in 1891, Lucy Maynard Salmon, author of *Domestic Service* (1897), and Edith Abbott, whose *Women in Industry* (1913) was extremely influential. Eighteenth-century women were also coming into focus at the turn of the twentieth century through important research being published by scholars such as Elisabeth Dexter and Alice Morse Earle, leading the way for Mary Sumner Benson's impressive study, *Women in Eighteenth-Century America: A Study of Opinion and Social Usage* (New York: Columbia University Press, 1935). Bur perhaps the most influential scholar of her generation, Mary Beard, began her long and impressive career in women's history with the publication of *Women's Work in Municipalities* (New York: D. Appleton, 1915). Her most intellectually daring book, *Woman as a Force in History*, was published in 1946 and provided impressive analysis of women's contributions in the past. However, Beard did not concentrate on the accomplishments of the few, nor did she lament the subordination of the many. Rather, this book was a pointed departure, a call for new ways of looking at culture and civilization, ways that put women more at the center of historical theory and discourse. It presaged the outpouring of feminist scholarship that would appear in the 1960s. Beard's work foreshadowed Gerda Lerner's 1979 call for a "woman-centered" history.

Prior to the 1960s most literature on women's role in American history was confined to biographical treatments of famous women, and the fame of women was most often determined by their relationships to famous men—for example, the wives of American presidents. This is not to say that prior to the 1960s there were no excellent studies on female roles in America, but this work was very limited in its scope and influence. Many fine studies were the result of funded research, such as Katherine Anthony's *Mothers Who Must Earn* (1914) and Louise Odencrantz's *Italian Women in Industry* (1919), which were sponsored by the Russell Sage Foundation.

The role of American women was also considerably neglected in historical overviews of the nineteenth century. Any survey of textbooks prior to the 1970s would indicate that schoolchildren might become familiar with only a handful of women's names, as opposed to the scores of male role models offered to them. And those women most often discussed ranged from the patriotic Betsy Ross and her folkloric sewing skills to the disreputable Peggy Eaton, the subject of scandal during Andrew Jackson's presidency.

Slowly but surely, a small group of scholars began to reexamine those historical movements within which women played dynamic roles. This growing body of literature revived an interest in women's neglected and unheralded achievements. Pioneering books such as Caroline Ware's *Early New England Cotton Manufacture* (Boston: Houghton Mifflin, 1931) integrated women's experiences where they belonged, at the center of key transformations. Alice Felt Tyler's *Freedom's Ferment* (New York: Harper and Row, 1944) revisited social reformers and placed women more prominently within abolitionism and other important movements. Eleanor Flexner's heroic volume, *Century of Struggle: The Woman's Rights Movement in the United States* (1959; reprint, Cambridge: Harvard University Press, 1996), illuminated a vast network of events and grassroots activity, highlighting leaders but underscoring the crucial role of followers as well. Not surprisingly, much of this important and pathbreaking research was undertaken by women scholars, both those within and those excluded from the academy.

In 1943 the Women's Archives at Radcliffe College (initiated by a gift of the papers of suffragist and alumna Maud Wood Parker) was launched. This repository of material on American women's history grew, especially under the sponsorship of Professor Arthur Schlesinger Sr. and his wife, Elizabeth. In 1967 the archives were renamed the Schlesinger Library in honor of these benefactors; with more than two thousand collections and fifty thousand images, the Schlesinger Library is now acknowledged as the finest collection of research material available on American women's past. While teaching history at Harvard, Arthur Schlesinger Sr. was a guiding light for a number of projects in the field of women's history. Many decades of work led to the publication of the three-volume *Notable American Women, 1607–1950*, coedited by Edward James, Janet James, and Paul Boyer (Cambridge, Mass.: Belknap, 1971), which created considerable interest in the reclaimed lives of hundreds of American women.

But the grassroots movement in women's history did not just concentrate on the great lives of exemplary women; rather, it began to broaden the boundaries of historical inquiry. Scholars in women's history began to reject the categories and language that kept women's issues imprisoned in archival listings as "of no political interest." They began to redefine politics and shift emphasis away from the public arena—where relatively fewer women ventured—to survey the complex and interesting stories that remained anchored within households, where the majority of nineteenth-century women spent most of their lives.

This revolution in sensibilities sparked new interest and new debates, creating a whole new category of topics for eager young scholars to pursue in the 1960s and 1970s. It is important to point out that many previously all-male bastions—history graduate programs at Ivy League schools and other major research institutions—were at the same time beginning to admit women, which resulted in a generation with new scholarly interests and agendas.

WOMEN'S "CULTURE"

One of the most influential early articles in the field of women's history was an essay by Barbara Welter, "The Cult of True Womanhood, 1800–1860" (1966). Welter outlined the prescriptive boundaries within which most nineteenth-century women were judged, focusing on piety, sexual purity, domesticity, and submissiveness. Further, she argued that women were expected to internalize these idealized values of "femininity" (often prescribed by men—ministers, editors, and statesmen), and either demonstrate loyalty to this cult or suffer serious consequences. They might be shunned and ostracized for "deviant" behavior, such as using their own intellects and talents in contradiction of a socially decreed female inferiority. Welter's description of the period's rigid set of values and behavior and her rich analysis of the literature initiated important debate within the field about "gender."

Men and women of course manifested distinct biological differences, but nineteenth-century American society was obsessed with maintaining gender differences through regulation of behavior, and, if possible, of attitudes and ideals. These attitudes and ideals were not transhistorical but shifted dramatically over time.

Barbara Welter's work on Victorian ideals of self-sacrifice and repression was challenged by many scholars who argued that women's behavior could not be extrapolated from prescriptive literature. Further, other scholars have suggested that middle-class women might have subverted the intent of the notion of "true womanhood," accepting this caricatured "means" only to justify the "ends" of increased empowerment for literate, privileged women.

The growth of domesticity studies was swift and powerful in the 1970s. The empowerment of women through shifting definitions of "femininity" and the cultivation of a female consciousness was an important subtext of Kathryn Sklar's exemplary *Catharine Beecher: A Study in Domesticity* (New Haven: Yale University Press, 1973). Certainly, Nancy Cott's *The Bonds of Womanhood: "Woman's Sphere" in New England, 1780–1835* (New Haven: Yale University Press, 1977) was one of the first volumes within this historical renaissance to look closely at the daily lives of ordinary white, literate women. Cott was, in some sense, looking at those women who were the targets of Beecher's mission and philosophy. Her study of New England woman posited that females in the nineteenth century created their own "women's culture" and that this culture formed a foundation upon which these women might build an expanding platform for their activities and interests. The bonds of womanhood became an important theme for scholarly discussion: Joan Jensen moved beyond Cott's New England with her *Loosening the Bonds: Mid-Atlantic Farm Women, 1750–1850* (New Haven: Yale University Press, 1986)—as did Mary Ryan in her *Cradle of the Middle Class: The Family in Oneida County, New York, 1790–1835* (New York: Cambridge University Press, 1981), and Nancy Hewitt in *Women's Activism and Social Change, Rochester, New York, 1822–1872* (Ithaca, N.Y.: Cornell University Press, 1984). Along these same ideological lines, Suzanne Lebsock examined the southern urban setting in *The Free Women of Petersburg: Status and Culture in a Southern Town, 1784–1860* (New York: Norton, 1984) and Julie Roy Jeffrey illuminated women in the West with her *Frontier Women: "Civilizing" the West?, 1840–1880* (1979; reprint, New York: Hill and Wang, 1998). The bonds of womanhood was also an important motif in the work of Deborah Gray White, whose *Ar'n't I a Woman? Female Slaves in the Plantation South* (New York: Norton, 1985) was one of the first monographs to look closely at the lives of black American women.

LABORING WOMEN

Even as this diverse work on gender and female consciousness was blossoming, a very different approach to work on nineteenth-century American women was being undertaken by a group of scholars who chose to focus on the crucial distinctions that kept women segregated—most especially class distinctions. This revisionism was prodded by Gerda Lerner in her influential 1969 article, "The Lady and the Mill Girl: Changes in the Status of Women in the Age of Jackson, 1800–1840." Several important monographs would follow, examining the critical role of women as laborers, including Thomas Dublin's *Women at Work: The Transformation of Work and Community in Lowell, Massachusetts, 1826–1860* (New York: Columbia University Press, 1979) and Faye Dudden's *Serving Women: Household Service in Nineteenth-Century America* (Middletown, Conn.: Wesleyan University Press, 1983). Dublin and many others looking at industrial labor demonstrated the ways in which women were drafted into the industrial work force from the beginnings of the factory system. Dudden's work pointed out how common paid domestic work was for the majority of rural American women throughout the century, and the critical fact that most American women remained in rural communities until the twentieth century.

But even more interesting is the way in which this new group of historians of American women began to challenge conventional wisdom about women's work roles and began to reconfigure the terms of analysis. Women's labor historians have exploded the myth that American women did not "work." Although the majority of American women in the nineteenth century did not earn wages, they were part of the productive economy. By examining their significant roles in the farm economy, for example, such books as Nancy Grey Osterud's *Bonds of Community: The Lives of Farm Women in Nineteenth-Century New York* (Ithaca, N.Y.: Cornell University Press, 1991) provide a broadening appreciation of "women's work." Many of these scholars examined the intersections of both class and race, and even region, as in Dolores Janiewski's *Sisterhood Denied: Race, Gender, and Class in a New South Community* (reprint, Philadelphia: Temple University Press, 1985).

Certainly childcare and housework are significant contributions to the household economy, as outlined in Susan Strasser's *Never Done: A History of American Housework* (New York: Pantheon, 1982). How and in what way "women's" work became "invisible" is an important issue, both for women's history and for understanding construction of gender. That this transformation was neither spontaneous nor accidental is explored in depth in Jeanne Boydston's *Home and Work: Housework, Wages, and the Ideology of Labor in the Early Republic* (New York: Oxford University Press, 1990).

Further, labor historians appreciate that wage-earning women were an important part of the industrial economy when it was being jump-started in the early decades of the nineteenth century. The low wages of single, young women contributed to the growth and prosperity of the factory system at its outset. The decline of female labor in the American industrial workforce can be attributed to multiple causes.

Throughout the nineteenth century craft unions were a force for discrimination against women and created the lowest proportion of unionization among female wage earners in an industrialized nation. Alice Kessler-Harris's *Out to Work: A History of Wage-Earning Women in the United States* (New York: Oxford University Press, 1982) detailed the pervasive masculine character of nineteenth-century unions, and the "clubby" milieu that kept women from "men's jobs."

Despite this discrimination within the culture and among unions, women began to slowly and steadily move into wage earning, a shift imaginatively traced in Lynn Wiener's *From Working Girl to Working Mother: The Female Labor Force in the United States, 1820–1980* (Chapel Hill: University of North Carolina Press, 1985). Although the average female wage earner at the beginning of the nineteenth century was most likely an unmarried white girl, perhaps even born into the middle class, by the end of the century the average female wage earner was a mother, most likely an immigrant or the wife of a working-class husband. Scholars in women's history have been able to demonstrate that the "living wage," the amount a male breadwinner could earn to allegedly support his family when working an hourly rate, was always a fiction. From the very beginnings of the wage economy, women's productive work remained invisible—as it was conducted in the household. During the first decades of the nineteenth century, for example, nearly three times as much cloth was produced in households—for market consumption—as was produced in cotton mills.

By the 1990s innovative, more complex appreciations of the contours of women's lives as workers were emerging.

FEMINIST ORIGINS

Certainly the parameters of domesticity continued to expand, with new and interesting ways of discussing this phenomenon. Dolores Hayden's *The Grand Domestic Revolution: A History of Feminist Designs for American Homes, Neighborhoods, and Cities* (Cambridge: MIT Press, 1981) looked at the ways in which women expanded definitions of the domestic sphere to provide more "housekeeping" for neighborhoods, or even towns. Women reformers began to exert "maternalism," to try to take larger and larger roles within social reform. Soon "social housekeeping" became as much a part of the vocabulary of nineteenth-century history as it was of women's lives in the nineteenth century. Women's pioneering roles in reforms other than woman suffrage began to be explored.

Of course, woman suffrage was still an important component of appreciating nineteenth-century women, and Ellen DuBois's *Feminism and Suf-*

frage: The Emergence of an Independent Women's Movement in America, 1848–1869 (Ithaca, N.Y.: Cornell University Press, 1978) provided a significant revisionist view of women's complex struggles to forge a unified movement for the vote. Most scholars who revisited suffrage in the 1970s and 1980s would produce biographies of suffragists, such as Ruth Barnes Moynihan's *Rebel for Rights: Abigail Scott Duniway* (New Haven: Yale University Press, 1983). Essentially, there was relatively little redefining of the field until the 1990s when important new work appeared, such as Marjorie Spruill Wheeler's *New Women of the New South: The Leaders of the Women's Suffrage Movement* (New York: Oxford University Press, 1993) and Dubois's own study of Harriot Stanton Blatch (New Haven: Yale University Press, 1998).

At the same time, many other avenues for looking at women's political activism were pursued. Mary Jo Buhle's *Women and American Socialism, 1870–1920* (Urbana: University of Illinois Press, 1982) was not merely a treatise on women's involvement in socialism; rather, it was a wide-ranging analysis of their roles in interlocking movements, including temperance, labor activism, suffrage, and other crusades. Buhle's is but one of several examples of feminist scholarship expanding the definitions of women's public roles in nineteenth-century American life.

Another important study with a similarly innovative approach, Christine Stansell's *City of Women: Sex and Class in New York, 1789–1860* (New York: Knopf, 1986), was not meant merely as a look at women in antebellum Manhattan; it was a scholarly embrace of the entanglement of politics, reform, and feminism in the metropolis—a metaphor for the larger changes going on in American life. Stansell emphasized that gender was being redistricted in the American urban landscape. Women's historians were redefining the shifting boundaries for men and women in this tempestuous era.

FEMINIZATION AND BEYOND

Scholars from a variety of disciplines began to explore the complex, layered permutations of American women's cultural contributions. Ann Douglas's influential *The Feminization of American Culture* (New York: Knopf, 1977) limned the world of the antebellum upper- and middle-class elites whose ideals shaped the moral and literary economy of early nineteenth-century America. Douglas's descriptions of both ministerial influence and the women over whom that influence was wielded provided a textured portrait of nineteenth-century women's culture in its infancy.

Literate middle-class white women built on their spiritual training, making educational and intellectual inroads into the culture. Many women took advantage of the significance of their role within the family to expand their educational opportunities, making a transition from tutors at the hearthside to instructors in the classroom. Sklar's 1973 biography of Catharine Beecher chronicled this transition, and Anne Firor Scott's influential article, "The Ever-Widening Circle: The Diffusion of Feminist Values from the Troy Female Seminary" (1979), tracked the way in which women's academies, such as Emma Willard's school in upstate New York, created a ripple effect throughout the country, as women pupils became teachers and spread the gospel of female education. This work charted a new course, and several important studies followed, including Helen Lefkowitz Horowitz's *Alma Mater: Design and Experience in the Women's Colleges from Their Nineteenth-Century Beginnings to the 1930s* (New York: Knopf, 1984) and Barbara Miller Solomon's *In The Company of Educated Women: A History of Women and Higher Education* (New Haven: Yale University Press, 1985).

The expansion of educational opportunities created more and more opportunities for white middle-class women. Certainly women's talents in the literary domain were considerable. Mary Kelley's *Private Woman, Public Stage: Literary Domesticity in Nineteenth-Century America* (New York: Oxford University Press, 1983) examined women writers of the period, demonstrating the empowerment of both the process and the product of female literary consciousness.

REFORMERS

While labor scholars focused on wage-earning women in the lower rungs of the American economy, other historians rediscovered the important role played by female pioneers in the professions. Rosalind Rosenberg's study of women social scientists, *Beyond Separate Spheres: Intellectual Roots of Modern Feminism* (New Haven: Yale University Press, 1982), was an important case study with implications for the examination of larger cultural shifts. Equally significant was Margaret Rossiter's heroic *Women Scientists in America: Struggles and Strategies to 1940* (Baltimore: Johns Hopkins University Press, 1981), which sheds light on pathbreaking women in the sciences.

Medicine was also a crucial area for research. Mary Walsh's focus on women doctors in Boston, *"Doctors Wanted: No Women Need Apply": Sexual Barriers in the Medical Profession 1835–1975* (New Haven: Yale University Press, 1977) provided a pioneering case study. Regina Markell Morantz-Sanchez's authoritative survey, *Sympathy and Science: Women Physicians in*

American Medicine (New York: Oxford University Press, 1987), analyzed the challenges for women in the medical profession and their progress in establishing standards and the opening of training institutions.

Nineteenth-century women also had to negotiate the challenge of discriminatory laws. Norma Basch's *In the Eyes of the Law: Women, Marriage, and Property in Nineteenth-Century New York* (Ithaca, N.Y.: Cornell University Press, 1982) offered an exemplary case study, outlining the reforms pushed by feminists in the nineteenth century and the legal responses to those reforms. Other scholars began to look at the important role of family law in shaping women's lives and choices, such as Michael Grossberg's *Governing the Hearth: Law and Family in Nineteenth-Century America* (Chapel Hill: University of North Carolina Press, 1985) and Peter Bardaglio's *Reconstructing the Household: Family, Sex, and the Law in the Nineteenth-Century South* (Chapel Hill: University of North Carolina Press, 1995). A comprehensive and authoritative volume by Joan Hoff, *Unequal Before the Law: A Legal History of U.S. Women* (New York: New York University Press, 1991), provides a sweeping, critical analysis of the legal status of women in the United States since the American Revolution. Hoff persuasively demonstrates that women have struggled against prejudice and that this prejudice dictated that women were never deemed full citizens before the law. The history of women's entrance into the legal profession was also being recorded, although most of this work, except for a few biographical studies, concentrates on the twentieth century.

REPRODUCTIVE STRATEGIES

While all this important research was uncovering women's progress in the public realm, a significant body of scholarly inquiry focused on the private lives of American women, on family and sexual concerns. Perhaps the most important pioneering book on this topic was Linda Gordon's *Woman's Body, Woman's Right: A Social History of Birth Control in America* (New York: Penguin, 1976), where she argued that women began to assert their rights within marriage by refusing to submit to male sexual prerogatives and by limiting their family size. Marital fertility was cut in half during the nineteenth century without the benefit of modern scientific information or technology. Feminist scholarship in the 1970s came to focus on questions of sexuality and reproduction. James Mohr's *Abortion in America: The Origins and Evolution of National Policy* (New York: Oxford University Press, 1978) and Carl Degler's *At Odds: Women and the Family in America* (New York: Oxford University Press, 1980) demonstrated patterns of change. Both chronicled the criminalization of abortion, and Mohr demonstrated how nineteenth-century mothers used abortions to limit family size. Degler outlined the ways in which women's role in the family evolved during the nineteenth century. His work also provided some contradiction of the thesis that nineteenth-century women embraced "passionlessness," as he chronicled educated women's progressive attitudes toward their own sexual pleasure.

Other feminist scholarship pioneered new analysis of women's roles in family life, such as Elizabeth Pleck's *Domestic Tyranny: The Making of American Social Policy Toward Family Violence* (New York: Oxford University Press, 1987) and Linda Gordon's *Heroes of Their Own Lives: The Politics and History of Family Violence* (New York: Viking, 1988).

SEXUALITY

Carroll Smith-Rosenberg's 1975 article, "The Female World of Love and Ritual," published in the first issue of a new feminist scholarly journal, *Signs: A Journal of Women in Culture and Society,* made an enormous impact on the field of women's history. Her research suggested that women manipulated the doctrine of separate spheres to forge communities of women, whose intense bonds provided fulfilling relationships. Many female friendships revealed intense intimacy and some perhaps had erotic components as well. Homosocial relationships, Smith-Rosenberg speculated, might have superseded the marital bond for many middle- and upper-class white women in the nineteenth century.

Smith-Rosenberg's work stimulated a groundswell of research among scholars in search of homosocial relationships—in the field of the history of women's education and the field of reform and Progressivism, but most important, in the newly emergent literature on the history of sexuality. Lillian Faderman's *Surpassing the Love of Men: Romantic Friendship and Love between Women from the Renaissance to the Present* (New York: Morrow, 1981) and John D'Emilio and Estelle Freedman's *Intimate Matters: A History of Sexuality in America* (New York: Harper and Row, 1988) were illuminating and comprehensive works.

At the same time, however, both Ellen Rothman, in her *Hands and Hearts: A History of Courtship in America* (New York: Basic Books, 1984) and Karen Lystra, in *Searching the Heart: Women, Men, and Romantic Love in Nineteenth-Century America* (New York: Oxford University Press, 1989), provide ample evidence of the richness of relationships between men and women, and the primacy of heterosexual attachment for women.

Scholars also began to look at other aspects of sexuality by reexamining the politics of prostitution. Ruth Rosen's *The Lost Sisterhood: Prostitution in America, 1900–1918* (Baltimore: Johns Hopkins University Press, 1982) launched important debate over the role of women in the sex trade and reformers who attacked the sexual double standard in America. Lucie Cheng Hirata's important case study, "Free, Indentured, Enslaved: Chinese Prostitutes in Nineteenth-Century America" (*Signs: A Journal of Women in Culture and Society* 5 [1] [Autumn 1979]) demonstrated the various ethnic and racial issues at play when exploring this topic. Timothy Gilfoyle's *City of Eros: New York City, Prostitution and the Commercialization of Sex* (New York: Norton, 1992) shows the broad range of recent work.

REGIONAL VARIATIONS

During the 1970s and into the 1980s scholars began to develop paradigms for appreciating nineteenth-century women's experiences. Almost as soon as scholars began to develop their models, a generation of revisionists began to develop alternative views and countertheses. Certainly Anne Scott's *The Southern Lady: From Pedestal to Politics, 1830–1930* (Chicago: University of Chicago Press, 1970), a survey of white southern women, challenged conventional views of "American women," as did Catherine Clinton's attack on the "New Englandization" of American women's history, *The Plantation Mistress: Woman's World in the Old South* (New York: Pantheon, 1982) and Elizabeth Fox-Genovese's treatment of antebellum plantation life, *Within the Plantation Household: Black and White Women of the Old South* (Chapel Hill: University of North Carolina Press, 1988). Many of these pioneering works have been challenged by new and exciting books in the 1990s, volumes such as Stephanie McCurry's *Masters of Small Worlds: Yeoman Households, Gender Relations, and the Political Culture of the Antebellum South Carolina Low Country* (New York: Oxford University Press, 1995) and Laura Edwards's *Gendered Strife and Confusion: The Political Culture of Reconstruction* (Urbana: University of Illinois Press, 1997).

At the same time, pioneering historians of women in the West broadened our appreciation of nineteenth-century women's history with John Faragher's *Women and Men on the Overland Trail* (New Haven: Yale University Press, 1981) and Glenda Riley's *Frontierswomen: The Iowa Experience* (Ames: Iowa State University Press, 1981). After this 1980s regional renaissance, a 1990s phenomenon emerged—whereby the revisionists were almost immediately revisited by revisionism. For example, Peggy Pascoe's important study, *Relations of Rescue: The Search for Female Moral Authority in the American West,*

1874–1939 (New York: Oxford University Press, 1993) provided an impressive investigation of both ethnicity and gender within the American West—a leap forward over the single focus of previous analysis.

RACE, GENDER, AND ETHNICITY

Clearly some of the most important revisionist work in the 1980s was the explosion of interest in and research on race, especially work on African American women. The vitality of scholarship on African American culture in the past quarter century has spawned an important intersection of fields—as dynamic work in black women's history has grown exponentially over the past three decades. (However, it is important to note that African American women's history had its first-wave pioneers as well, such as Hallie Q. Brown, whose *Homespun Heroines and Other Women of Distinction* can be found in Oxford University Press's thirty-volume set, *The Schomburg Library of Nineteenth-Century Black Women Writers*, edited by Henry Louis Gates, Jr.)

Ironically, modern research on slave women was launched by Angela Davis when she published an article she had initiated while incarcerated in a California jail: "Reflections on the Black Woman's Role in the Community of Slaves" (*Black Scholar* 3 [December 1971]). This theoretical tour de force laid down the gauntlet to scholars in slavery studies. Gerda Lerner's *Black Women in White America* (New York: Pantheon, 1982), an heroic documentary collection, appeared the next year. Herbert Gutman's impressive *The Black Family in Slavery and Freedom, 1750–1925* (New York: Pantheon, 1976) challenged conventional wisdom concerning the weakness of the family under slavery, a theme echoed in Jacqueline Jones's magisterial survey, *Labor of Love, Labor of Sorrow: Black Women, Work, and the Family from Slavery to the Present* (New York: Basic Books, 1985). Jones's work also moved the field forward by leaps and bounds, offering a challenge to both scholars in women's history and historians of African Americans to put black women's experience at the vital center of American history. Elsa Barkley Brown, Nell Painter, and others joined Jones in demanding that the exploration of issues of both race and gender as well as their interaction transform our perspective on the American past. Paula Giddings, in *When and Where I Enter: The Impact of Black Women on Race and Sex in America* (New York: Bantam, 1984), and Angela Davis, in *Women, Race, and Class* (New York: Random House, 1982), advanced the need for a reevaluation of American history in its entirety, as well as of American women's history.

The important work that was produced in the 1980s was a virtual renaissance, looking at black women in slavery, in freedom, in reform, and in separate, even segregated spheres. Vibrant research was undertaken, for example Rosalyn Terborg-Penn's 1977 Howard University Ph.D. thesis, "Afro-Americans in the Struggle for Woman Suffrage." Exemplary volumes appeared, such as Cynthia Neverdon-Morton's *Afro-American Women of the South and the Advancement of the Race, 1895–1925* (Knoxville: University of Tennessee Press, 1989) and Adele Logan Alexander's *Ambiguous Lives: Free Women of Color in Rural Georgia, 1789–1870* (Fayetteville: University of Arkansas Press, 1991).

In the 1990s a very exciting body of work on black women has gained recognition, such as Brenda Stevenson's *Life in Black and White: Family and Community in the Slave South* (New York: Oxford University Press, 1996) and Glenda Elizabeth Gilmore's *Gender and Jim Crow: Women and the Politics of White Supremacy in North Carolina, 1896–1920* (Chapel Hill: University of North Carolina Press, 1996).

Equally innovative has been the pioneering work in the field of American Indian women's history. Rayna Green's important article, "The Pocahontas Perplex: The Image of Indian Women in American Culture" (1975), helped to launch debate, and her 1980 review essay in *Signs: A Journal of Women in Culture and Society* charted fertile areas for investigation. The many germinal articles of Theda Perdue have kept the field alive for the past two decades, culminating with her splendid *Cherokee Women* (Lincoln: University of Nebraska Press, 1998). Other scholars, including Sarah Hill, in her *Weaving New Worlds: Southeastern Cherokee Women and their Basketry* (Chapel Hill: University of North Carolina Press, 1997), are beginning to emerge. Nevertheless, work on other women of color and ethnic women has far outstripped the academic output on American Indian women.

Immigrant women began to receive scholarly attention from the 1980s onward, in significant studies such as Hasia Diner's *Erin's Daughters in America: Irish Immigrant Women in Nineteenth-Century America* (Baltimore: Johns Hopkins University Press, 1983). From Scandinavian women in the upper Midwest to Creole women on the Louisiana frontier, nineteenth-century immigrant women have stimulated an outpouring of articles. Although important essays have appeared on Asian American women (whose numbers were small) and Hispanic women (whose numbers were large) in nineteenth-century America, most of the research in this field has concentrated on the twentieth-century experiences of women in minority groups. A welcome exception to this rule is Deena J. Gonzales's *Refusing the Favor: The Spanish-Mexican Women of Santa Fe, 1820–1880* (New York: Oxford University Press, 1999). Many excellent pieces can be found in Ellen DuBois and Vicki Ruiz's *Unequal Sisters: A Multicultural Reader in U.S. Women's History* (New York: Routledge, 1994). This research is part of an ongoing process of historical recovery. For example, work on the complex and hybrid mix of cultures in nineteenth-century Hawaii and on the unique experience of Inuit women in Alaska remains to be done.

GENDER AND THE CIVIL WAR

The feminist scholarship of the 1970s reexamined both the role of women in World War II and their contributions to the conflicts during the era of the American Revolution, producing new interpretations. Historians of American women were slow to tackle questions of the American Civil War, despite its dominant position in popular historical work and its central role in the nineteenth century. Although Mary Elizabeth Massey's *Bonnet Brigades* (New York: Knopf, 1966) had been commissioned by a U.S. Civil War Centennial project, and although C. Vann Woodward's *Mary Chesnut's Civil War* (New Haven: Yale University Press, 1981) won him a Pulitzer prize, interest in women's role in the American Civil War failed to thrive until the 1990s. The role of southern women then began to be explored extensively, beginning with George Rable's *Civil Wars: Women and the Crisis of Southern Nationalism* (Urbana: University of Illinois Press, 1989), LeeAnn Whites's *The Civil War as a Crisis in Gender: Augusta, Georgia, 1860–1900* (Athens: University of Georgia Press, 1995), Catherine Clinton's *Tara Revisited: Women, War, and the Plantation Legend* (New York: Abbeville, 1995), and Drew Faust's *Mothers of Invention: Women of the Slaveholding South in the American Civil War* (Chapel Hill: University of North Carolina Press, 1996). Elizabeth Leonard's collection of biographical studies, *Yankee Women: Gender Battles in the Civil War* (New York: Norton, 1994) is one of the few comparable studies of northern women during the era. A survey of emerging work in the field appeared in Catherine Clinton and Nina Silber's influential anthology, *Divided Houses: Gender and the Civil War* (New York: Oxford University Press, 1992).

It is perhaps a tribute to the tenacity of scholars in American women's history that finally even the Civil War, the great male bastion of nineteenth-century scholarship, has fallen prey to feminist interpretations. Most of American women's history in the nineteenth century is militant rather than military in character, however, within the third wave of feminist scholarship, even the subject of women soldiers has become both intriguing and acceptable. For example, in the 1990s the advanced degree program at the University of Wisconsin has graduated historians with double concentrations in women's history and military history.

Scholars examining the nineteenth century, feminists argue, have for too long regarded historical agency as men's domain and victimization as the female preserve. Historians for the last decades of the twentieth century have challenged and reconfigured these shopworn formulas. In attempting to right past wrongs, flaws have doubtless appeared.

Yet even flaws might be cherished—for as scholars paint women as victims of male power, a revisionist literature emerges to celebrate women's heroic resistance. As women's heroic resistance is celebrated, a rising generation of scholars disputes "heroine" worship and attempts to portray women's choices as more complex and difficult. Even a complex web of women's collaboration with their own oppression might evolve, or perhaps the argument that gender cannot continue to be privileged in our research agendas. The endless debates over shadings and nuances, analyses and interpretations, "isms" and other objectives, keep academic discourse enlivened with disagreements, keep the field of nineteenth-century women's history ever alive—on the threshold of the twenty-first century and the beginning of a new millennium.

CHAPTER ONE

Post-Revolutionary America

From the first settlements in the early 1600s to the American Revolution nearly two centuries later, in 1776, the American colonies witnessed a slow but steady growth in both population and stability. The fragile nature of early settlements depended upon the resourcefulness of their inhabitants, who faced a combination of isolation, disease, harsh climate, and, in some instances, their own ineptness in dealing with American Indians. By the Revolution, with the exception of relations with Indians, these issues no longer obtained. Strengthened by the success that came with permanence, and especially by the transformation of their primarily male-populated society to a family-dominated one, American colonists had evolved socially and politically into a force that ultimately sought autonomy from British rule.

Women had helped to stabilize the colonies and to ensure their continued success. They influenced the social and political transformation and were, in turn, influenced by the Revolution and by the actuality of the new nation. By 1800 their status in the new American nation, never static by any means, was constantly being modified by a variety of issues and events, the effects of which were never absolute for all women. These issues and events included the concept of republican motherhood, economic and social standing, a lack of Constitutional protection, inadequate education, religious expectations, westward expansion, separate spheres, and health and child-bearing issues. The relative effect on ind--ividual women depended on their fundamental identities as American Indians, slaves, indentured servants, original settlers or descendants, or recent immigrants. Ethnic identities also informed group and individual experience.

This chapter establishes the prevailing conditions for women at the beginning of the nineteenth century. It discusses the evolving status of women and seeks to define the historical, social, and political themes that continued throughout the nineteenth century, including race, immigration, labor, reform, education, women's rights, and women's place and role in society.

The post-Revolutionary generation faced great challenges on the eve of a new century. The new American nation had been born during a period of unprecedented transformation. While North American British colonies threw off the yoke of the British empire, native peoples along the Atlantic seaboard had been divided during the battle for American independence, and African Americans, slave and free, joined in struggles for liberty.

By 1800 Americans were committed to their program of continual westward migration—by the thousands. Settlers might enlist Indians as allies, or play one native nation off against another, when they could. Equally often, white migrants were content to sweep the native peoples out of their way, by force if necessary. These restless settlers were determined to carve white communities out of the wilderness and to eliminate any obstacles, human or otherwise, that blocked their path.

Slaves were disheartened by the setbacks they suffered after the Revolution had been "won." Although many enslaved Africans fought for and with their masters, too few were rewarded for loyalty or made significant gains during the early national era. Slave women especially found themselves in difficult straits when the government closed the international slave trade in 1808: the only means of expanding the slave population was through natural increase, and the only way to increase the number of slaveholders was the domestic slave trade. This placed a strong burden on women. Both women's field labor and their reproductive capacities became even more crucial to the plantation economy in the South. While the cotton revolution was transforming the southern frontier, several economic and social factors were working against African Americans' efforts to secure more freedom and more rights within the new American nation.

On the eve of the Revolution, white colonists were 60 percent English, 15 percent Scotch (and Scotch-Irish), nearly 10 percent German, 6 percent Dutch, and 4 percent Irish. Roughly 38 percent of the population of these British colonies was African-born or African American. In South Carolina, blacks were a majority.

Nearly a quarter of a century later, African slaves were a substantial minority within the American population. Their numbers far outstripped those of native Americans, a reversal that had taken place over nearly a two-hundred-year period of settlement. The proportion of the population of African descent was dwindling in the North and growing steadily in the South. Black American females, especially enslaved women, maintained one of the highest birth rates recorded at the time. Meanwhile, the white population of the United States diversified and grew exponentially in the period from the Revolution to the turn of the new century. America remained a beacon for settlers seeking autonomy. The new nation enjoyed in-migration from Europe as well as westward expansion into adjacent territories—as the country doubled in size in 1803 with the acquisition of the Louisiana Purchase.

REPUBLICAN MOTHERHOOD

Many women had demonstrated their commitment to the patriotic ideals of the Revolution and sacrificed much to gain the victory of independence. In recognition of their importance to the new country being forged, statesmen embraced the notion of republican motherhood. Ministers and statesmen alike celebrated the bearing and rearing of "liberty-loving sons" as a top priority. This was mainly a rhetorical gesture, and many women rejected this highly stylized role in favor of something more substantial. They preferred not to be merely the cultural icons of liberty; rather, they wanted to be active and respected citizens in the new experiment of democracy. The protracted and shared battle for independence as well as women's post-Revolutionary struggles for autonomy created distinctive cultural differences for American women.

As early as 1783 a New Jersey law gave women who met property requirements the vote. This was a tribute to Quaker legislators who hoped their state might adopt the more egalitarian views their faith upheld. Women's role at the polls led to acrimonious debates within the state legislature, to recall elections, and to many frauds and abuses. Finally in 1807 a new statute was enacted to deny New Jersey women and other "undesirables" the right to vote. Even though women had only been granted this right during a twenty-year experimental period, this nevertheless demonstrated how revolutionary the attempts at democracy were in the emerging United States, even, upon rare occasion, including gender equality.

Although women were denied the franchise, many argued successfully for improvement in women's education. Daughters of the post-Revolutionary generation demanded education not just as a privilege but as a necessity. True, most shaped their arguments to highlight women's roles as mothers and the "first teachers" of their children, but even so, female academies became a central feature of the American landscape.

American women's position and influence were distinctive, according to French writer Alexis de Tocqueville, who noted in his *Democracy in America*: "I have nowhere seen women occupying a loftier position; and if I were asked, now that I am drawing to the close of this work, in which I have spoken of so many important things done by the Americans, to what the singular prosperity and growing strength of that people ought mainly to be attributed, I should reply: To the superiority of their women."[1]

Nevertheless, within the United States gender roles were rigorously maintained. Indeed, there were developments that seemed to rigidify even more the conventions that maintained differences between the sexes. This was a natural response to the lessening of gender definition during the war. But other shifts, slow but significant, were also taking place.

SEPARATE SPHERES

Within the post-Revolutionary American economy, production was increasingly shifted out of the household and into separate manufacturing establishments. Scholars have suggested that the "division of spheres"—public versus private, work versus home, male versus female—stemmed from this shift within the economy, from home-based to factory-based production. This was primarily a northern phenomenon during the half century following the Revolution—but it slowly spread southward and westward. This restructuring of the economy did have a universal and permanent effect within society as a whole. According to this new social ideology, the household became the female domain, as hearth and home reflected a women's role, while the marketplace—and the consequent expansion of manufacturing and the rise of urban culture—reflected male prerogative and patriarchal concerns. The new mythology confined women to the comforts of home, while men went out into the workplace and what was increasingly perceived as "the real world."

Manufacturers began to restructure the workplace in significant ways. Workers were paid for their time with an hourly wage—rather than for their skills or for the items they produced. The concept of a "living wage"—the amount a male head of household would need to support a family—ushered in a new era.

As women's roles became even more isolated and segregated, their contributions certainly continued to be or became even more devalued. Even today housework generally remains women's unpaid responsibility, a figure left out of family budget calculations. From the beginning of the nineteenth century onward, although wage-earning women labored the same sixty minutes as a man's hour, their pay was often half what men earned. The abstract division into gendered "spheres" had very concrete and damaging consequences for American women.

Some scholars have suggested that within an agrarian economy, women's domestic labor was more fully acknowledged as producing part of the family income. Also, female labor was regarded as being on a more equal footing with men's work when family income was derived from a family farm. This has been characterized as a "golden age" theory. It also suggests that with the development of commercial and industrial enterprises, the value of women's labor was subsequently diminished. The boom in factories for cloth- and shoe-making created a shift of manufacturing out of the household, and the perceived value of women's work suffered as a result.

Critics of this theory argue that women's labor was always regarded as a separate and devalued category, even within the farm and household economies.

They also argue that the growth of manufacturing and industry simply enhanced men's status, thus greatly increasing the difference between the perceived value of women's economic contribution as opposed to men's.

The expansion of industrial markets during the second quarter of the nineteenth century may have affected only a minority of women as wage earners, but this development had a powerful impact in the nation as a whole, shaping patterns of consumption and redefining domesticity for all classes. And as the century progressed, the division between household and workplace would widen and produce even more profound changes.

WESTWARD EXPANSION

The nineteenth century saw an unprecedented boom in immigration and westward migration. This trend continued steadily throughout the century. Even the American Civil War did not slow down the flow of foreign settlers into the country. Between 1815 and the beginning of the American Civil War, more than five million people immigrated to the United States (nearly 50 percent of them English speaking, and almost 40 percent of these from Ireland). Between 1865 and 1890 ten million immigrated, mainly from northwestern Europe, and during the next twenty-five years another fifteen million immigrants entered the country.

The huge westward expansion that took place at the opening of the nineteenth century had very direct and different consequences for American women, depending upon their color and status. For white women, especially those who were immigrants, the westward migration offered unprecedented opportunities. Large numbers of European women found the trail westward both exhausting and exhilarating. Although women settlers moving onto the frontier might be isolated and unhappy to lose family connections and female companionship, they nevertheless found that the fact that women were in the minority also allowed them greater freedoms. Many younger women found rigid gender conventions relaxed when their small numbers in a newly settled region required that the talents of every individual be exploited regardless of age, gender, and status.

Many African Americans found their status enhanced on these western frontiers, as whites looked to them for skills and for solidarity against, for example, American Indians. Women as well as men benefited from the "bucksaw equality" extended in sparsely populated western settlements. (When clearing the frontier, white settlers granted partial equality, if only by allowing slaves an equal role at the other end of the bucksaw—or when the fort came under attack by Indians, etc.) It was also the case that enslaved African American women might be midwives or herbal healers for owners and other whites on the rural

[handwritten margin note: As has been argued about original Virginian settlement]

frontier. But this "equality" also meant that women might be equally exploited as laborers, treated harshly as field workers clearing the wilds and planting previously untilled soil. And, of course, slave women were more frequently exploited for their sexual and reproductive capacities than were male slaves.

AMERICAN INDIANS

Charles Brockden Brown observed that during the Revolution large numbers of people lived through "reversals of fortune, encounters with strangers and physical dislocation." No group suffered more from this than the Indian peoples of eastern North America. The victory of the independence movement did not automatically mean peace to Indians; rather, for certain nations it signaled a new round of warfare. Those Indians branded as loyalists, who had sided with the English king, paid a steep price by being forced off their homelands and into Canada. Other tribes knew the westward stampede of Americans would mean forced migration for them as well, regardless of the side on which they had served. For the women of those Indian nations that had sided with the victors, the American ascendancy ironically heralded rapid decline. For example, women within the Catawba nation looked forward to a return to *status quo antebellum*. But the Catawba's support of the Revolution translated into an increasing adaptation of English values—most especially those ideals regarding gender. For example, Catawba women had been managers of land and active within commerce prior to the Revolution, and a Catawba child might take the family name of its mother. Choctaw women had long been a visible force in town markets. Women might sell vegetables or cane baskets, moccasins, and other goods they made. These and other patterns of female parity were stifled by the onset of "Americanization."

Indian women were increasingly pressed to adopt the gender roles of their white sisters. In 1802 President Thomas Jefferson told Handsome Lake, a Seneca leader, the expectations of his countrymen: "Go on, then brother, in the great reformation you have undertaken. Persuade our red men to be sober and to cultivate their lands; and their women to spin and weave for their families."[2] In attempting to spin and weave their gender roles to suit European standards, Indian women were forced to unravel their own cultural heritage. They paid a high and perhaps unwanted price for Americanization. Subsequent to the "civilizing influence" of European culture, the voices of Iroquois women were no longer welcome at tribal councils. Cherokee women were expected to adopt more English, and indeed more discriminatory marital practices, giving up the serial monogamy they had enjoyed and the relative ease of divorce, which had been a female prerogative within their tribal customs. The Catawba women were increasingly hemmed in by their new status as self-sacrificing wives and mothers. Thus the overall consequence of Americanization for Indian women was a decline in their status within their individual nations and tribes. Indian women were forced into the equivalent, and correspondingly diminished, status of their "civilized" counterparts.

LITERACY AND RELIGION

Meanwhile, white women within American society were struggling to raise their own social and political status—through literacy and religious evangelicalism. Parents welcomed the advent of academies for daughters that replaced "dame schools," run by any matron who hung out a shingle and called herself an educator and where girls were only taught ornamental arts—dancing and embroidery. While most female schools remained at the colonial dame school level, a handful of new female seminaries afforded young women a more rigorous training, offering a "traditional English education." The curriculum might include geography, history, mathematics, and other demanding subjects. Very few women of the middle and upper classes benefited from this new educational environment, however. And, while those fortunate few may not have had an immediate outlet for the educations they received, the foundation of these academies helped to pave the way for future gains. Beginning in the 1820s, the move toward an enriched and meaningful education for girls began to grow and never stopped.

Additionally, following the drastic decline of religion in the wake of the American Revolution, women's proportionate numbers and influence in Christian congregations began to rise after 1800. Religious enthusiasm blossomed into what became known as the Second Great Awakening. Ministers struck a chord with women hungry for a spiritual revival. Evangelical opposition to the ideas flourishing after the French Revolution, most especially deism, created a political backlash that fueled American evangelicals. This cultural movement resulted in sweeping revivals, cresting in upstate New York (which became known as the "Burnt-Over District"), where Charles Grandison Finney, an itinerant minister, preached the power of individual conversion. Finney won his listeners over with the power of his strong religious medicine and urged his followers to repent, join churches, and recruit more converts to the faith. The active practice of Christian principles had dramatic consequences for all Americans. In 1831 alone, the peak year of the movement, church membership grew by more than 100,000 members. Women were a potent part of this boom, and many became missionaries and lay preachers in the wake of the call to faith.

The effect on young, literate white women in the New England and Middle Atlantic states was quite profound. Religious conversion could and did offer young women of varying backgrounds the element of choice. They might publicly proclaim their faith—and that proclamation was often an affirmation of their adulthood. Just as often, however, a girl's conversion augured rebellion, as many pious and impassioned daughters might affiliate with a sect to which their parents objected. In addition, some women's zealous religious bent disaffected them from husbands who did not accept or embrace their faith. Religion was clearly an area in which individual conscience was respected, as well as a window of opportunity for autonomy that women eagerly seized.

Increasingly, women began to exert more choice in secular as well as spiritual matters, fighting for their preferences in the "private" sphere that had been designated their domain. This manifested itself primarily by women having more influence over their choice in spouses. The rise of companionate marriage (a union of two individuals rather than a family merger) was an outgrowth of women's struggle to enhance their domestic spheres. Simultaneously, females attempted to play a larger role in limiting or perhaps even planning their pregnancies. American women as a group, and especially white literate women, steadily reduced the birth rate over the course of the nineteenth century, without modern medical information or devices. They battled for increased autonomy in this crucial area of motherhood.

After the Revolution, a number of women also extended their arguments about "political tyranny" to include a broader spectrum of domestic politics, as Abigail Adams reminded her husband when he was working on the Constitution: "Remember, all men would be tyrants if they could."[3] In northern states, women began to find the pathway to divorce eased by legislative remedy, and marital dissolutions became easier to obtain than during the colonial era. By contrast, white women in the South still labored under severe legal disabilities. For example, in South Carolina until the 1830s the only way for a woman to free herself from a spouse, no matter how abusive or aberrant, was by petitioning the legislature to grant her a divorce. The improvement of women's status continued to be very circumscribed not only by her status and race but also by the region in which she lived.

As literacy increased and slaveowning declined for the majority of New England middle-class women, literary and reform pursuits came into greater prominence during the first quarter of the nineteenth century. The rise of consumer culture led to the growth of new and stimulating publications during the antebellum era, and more and more magazines and journals were directed at homemakers. At the same time, an explosion of religious tracts competed with sentimental novels for their attention.

Both these literary products confronted women with tales highlighting the evils of sin. The corruptions of the outside world were perceived as a threat to domesticity, and society had decreed that it was mothers' sworn duty to serve and protect their families. Ironically, this led large numbers of women out into the world, venturing into the public sphere to battle the creeping corruptions seeping into their precious households.

REFORM

Aided by ministers from their pulpits, moral reformers began to decry drunkenness, licentiousness, and impiety as enemies of any "true woman," the moral exemplar that was American women's inheritance and destiny. Even though they expected only to rule by the hearthside and to demonstrate their value by attendance in the church pew, true women also became active outside the household, invoking the protection of the home as their excuse. As society became more urbanized, more secular, and more complex, it became harder for women to make their male kin obey even simple religious tenets. Women redoubled their efforts to keep their families safe from polluting influences, to use charity and reform to browbeat and beckon men back into the fold.

Such female campaigns might have undermined male authority, but they were designed to be mere extensions of female preoccupation with morality. In the eighteenth century the term "virtue" was employed most often in political discussions, but by the early decades of the nineteenth century this label was more often attached to a female, most likely a model churchwoman, rather than employed as an appellation for a man. Virtue as a concept increasingly reflected social or moral considerations.

The rise of charitable institutions was a direct outgrowth of female benevolence. Some of women's most virtuous enterprises were directed to solving the problems they faced as women, such as asylums for widows and orphans. Families might find themselves unable to take on the added burdens of those who fell by the wayside. When mobility and urbanization let many slip through the cracks, the rise of public institutions was meant to assuage this growing social concern. The Sunday school movement and "penny-a-week" campaigns for missions on the frontier were also designed to lay the groundwork for a fundamental revitalization of American morals, a campaign championed and in some cases led by women.

So this new American woman was expected to step outside her sphere to protect those within it. At the same time women battering away at this artificial division of spheres confronted ironies for which their educations had not prepared them. White middle-class women in the North confronted a slew of social ills that required a complex system of dissemblance if they were to maintain their ladylike demeanor while trying to counter the corrosive effects of vice and immorality. Indifference was a plague that many women opposed: how could the plight of the poor, the plight of the slave, the plight of the heathen be forgotten? And as women became involved in the various campaigns to reform and improve society, many came to believe that their own plights were not much better. Even a handful of slaveowners' wives began to question a system that held white women as chattel, in legal liability similar to the restrictions imposed on those who were so unfortunate as to be of African descent.

Immigrants to America found a world of opportunity, but even within the nation's earliest years, a "nativist" movement festered and blossomed into righteous religious bigotry and ethnic prejudice. Subsequently, Americans witnessed the rise of the Know Nothing party during the antebellum era and the American Protectionist League during the latter part of the nineteenth century. The American government even began to severely restrict immigration, banning Chinese women from immigrating during the period when railroad bosses were importing Chinese "coolies" to build the transcontinental and other railways in an attempt to prevent the permanent settlement of immigrant laborers.

It was a constant struggle for Asian immigrants as well as other racial minorities to obtain fair and just treatment. Equality of opportunity was nothing but a dream for the millions who sought a new life in America. Most wanted simply to survive and to have their children lead better lives. They may have traversed the ocean in steerage, but they wanted to enjoy the privileges to which their triumph over adversity entitled them.

The entire nineteenth century was an era of struggle, during which women as well as men shook society by its very foundations and tried to build a nation upon the genuine articles of freedom for which they believed their Revolutionary forefathers had fought. Women, black and white, rich and poor, native born, American Indian, or immigrant, fought for the values for which their foremothers had made their own sacrifices. At times women from different classes and races were pitted against one another. Also at times, certain women were willing to seize their gains at the expense of others. This era of dynamic transformation would be the real test of America's revolutionary and radical roots, as women throughout the century battled to create new definitions of womanhood and to remedy its discontents.

CHAPTER TWO

The Economy, Households, and Labor

In the first half of the nineteenth century all Americans experienced profound changes that were a consequence of the economic shifts that reorganized household and market labor. Since the Revolution, the groundwork had been laid for an independent economic infrastructure promoting a mature economy able to support the industrialization taking root. In the face of continued westward migration, immigration as well as natural increase contributed to rapid economic expansion of the industrial sector along the eastern seaboard.

With the introduction of the factory system and with the growth of piecework, more and more Americans were finding alternatives to traditional roles in family households. The concept of "separate spheres" determined new family roles and responsibilities in the young nation. The factory system changed household labor for both men and women in both rural and urban economies. This corresponded to an increasing reliance on wage labor as factories grew and new markets boomed.

This chapter examines the changes affecting household structures as more and more men engaged in wage labor and young rural women ventured into factories in droves. The role of women as both native-born and immigrant wage earners is explored, as well as the attitudes that prevailed regarding working-class and middle-class sensibilities. A comparison of the experiences of frontier and rural women with those of their eastern and urban counterparts reveals the broadening range of expectations both for and by women as the century progressed.

The impact of cotton on the American economy at the turn of the nineteenth century was momentous and dramatic. It had a profound effect on all Americans, and women would find themselves undergoing dramatic transitions. During the eighteenth century the rise and fall of the tobacco boom had been followed by the rise of rice planters and indigo planters, a trend that was still increasing by the onset of the American Revolution. Planters along the southern Atlantic seaboard were able to cultivate sea island cotton, which fetched a high price in London, but this cotton could only be grown in a narrow strip along the coast. Since rice and indigo could also only be cultivated in specific climatic areas, the expansion of slavery on southern plantations was still limited. When Yale-trained tutor Eli Whitney came to the South Carolina plantation of Catharine Greene in 1792 to teach her children, he also took an interest in the problems of separating the cotton seeds from the bolls. In 1793 Whitney revolutionized this time-consuming process with the development of the "gin," which he patented and sold to southern legislatures. This relatively simple mechanism revitalized the plantation system in the South.

THE PLANTATION ECONOMY

Once planters were able to separate the seeds from the cotton by machine rather than by hand, in a cheap and efficient method, they could grow short staple cotton (with less silky bolls) at a tremendous profit. Short staple cotton provided a robust crop that could be grown inland—indeed all over the South from North Carolina to northern Louisiana, and eventually into the Texan wilderness. This rejuvenated the slave trade, as settling on southwestern lands in Georgia, Alabama, and other regions could now be made tremendously profitable by growing cotton. By the 1820s southern planters introduced a new strain of cotton, known as Mexican cotton, which was even more hardy than the standard cotton. This doubled the output per acre, increasing profits even more. The planter class invested in vast tracts of land, and individuals often possessed multiple estates for cotton cultivation.

The demand for cotton had been increasing exponentially with changes in the northern economy, especially the development of textile mills throughout the Middle Atlantic and New England states. In 1813 Francis Cabot Lowell's Boston Manufacturing Company (in Waltham, Massachusetts) became the first cotton factory in America. The production of standardized cotton cloth was a development with limitless possibilities, as consumers and garment makers could not seem to get enough.

Planters were exporting cotton at unprecedented rates, and with the boom in the demand for cotton, the demand for slaves seemed limitless. Spreading southward and westward, slaveowners headed for the agriculturally rich regions of the Mississippi Delta and the Black Belt (a large swath of fertile land stretching across central Alabama and Mississippi, named for its rich black soil).

The increasing dependence on slave labor by landowners placed growing demands on the planters' wives. The management of estates, in which women were deeply involved, became more complex and burdensome throughout the first half of the nineteenth century. The plantation mistress was expected to re-create domestic havens on the frontier, all the while providing for her husband's slaves in four important areas: food, clothing, shelter, and medicine. She was also charged with the religious supervision and spiritual well-being of all on the plantation, a role that varied from estate to estate. Rather than being the mere decoration the rhetoric of chivalry proclaimed, the plantation mistress was the linchpin in the enterprise of gaining a foothold in the southwestern wilds. She made the entire operation possible, and her efficient management made estates profitable.

The popular image of a plantation mistress was a distortion of reality carefully cultivated and embraced by southern culture. She was meant to embody the grace and ease to which white southerners aspired. Of course the majority of white women in the South throughout the century were far removed from the life of grandeur afforded by wealthy estates. At the beginning of the antebellum era fewer than 2,500 families in the Old South (out of a white population of 3 million) constituted the planter elite, a minority that did not grow appreciably in the years leading up to Confederate independence. Even the wives of great planters did not live the life of luxury described in legend. After the Civil War, planter-daughter Susan Dabney Smedes claimed that "the mistress of the plantation was the most complete slave on it." This lament stemmed in large part from the gulf between the myth and the reality of plantation life in the Old South.

But whether or not the women of the planter class were comfortable or content, the men of the region were eager to move to the frontier, taking their wives, children, and slaves in tow. The cry "Cotton is King" rallied planters to strike out for parts unknown by the thousand.

THE RISE OF THE MILLS

Francis Lowell recruited girls off New England farms to fill his factories. The term "spinster" originated from the fact that unmarried females in the household might be drafted to spin, and now factories were drawing these women into their economic web. First in Britain and then in America, textile industries jump-started industrialization on a massive scale.

In rural New England white single women flocked to the newly opened mills. By 1831 females made up nearly 70 percent of the 58,000 millworkers in the North. Despite an influx of male immigrants—into the country and into the wage economy—women maintained a strong presence in the textile industries. On the eve of the Civil War, women were nearly one quarter of the country's industrial work force, due to the predominance of female laborers in cotton manufacturing. As new land on the frontier lured young single men westward, the northeastern factories gave young women economic opportunity and some measure of autonomy.

Women of the working classes were encouraged to earn money outside the home as a temporary measure—to support themselves or supplement the family income before marriage. Limited by gender discrimination, women had very few employment avenues they might pursue. If they were educated, they might try to become teachers, although wages were extremely low and prospects poor until women were allowed to teach in the public schools in the 1830s. Uneducated women had few opportunities to earn money outside the home, except as domestic servants. Especially in rural New England the majority of farmer's daughters were servants in other families' homes for a temporary period before marriage. Before the textile mills sprang up and drew the young unmarried females from the countryside into mill towns, very few young women escaped from farm labor or family dependence.

Working in factories was celebrated as a means by which females could contribute to their families and their own sense of selfhood. Alexander Hamilton commented that industry would create for farmers "a new source of profit and support from the increased industry of his wife and daughters."[1] Early factories were heralded as a model institutions.

Factory owners were expected to play the role of surrogate father to the young women entering the mills, and they embraced this role with relish. For example, the Lowell Company required all female employees to inform them of "the place where they board" and threatened workers with being fired if they broke curfew, were caught smoking, or engaged in other improprieties. The regulations, designed to create model workers, shaped the culture in factory towns. Throughout New England workers were required to board in company boardinghouses and to observe the Sabbath — company scrutiny extended well beyond the worker's shift. Workers' reform associations organized lyceums and lectures, trying to improve the circumscribed lives of factory employees. Despite the restrictions instituted by mill owners, young women were drawn to factory work by the opportunity for female community, for educational opportunities, and for the cultural programs they were offered.

Lucy Larcom, a teacher and writer who in 1889 published her memoir of her early life, including her years as a mill girl, emphasized the sense of female community women gained by their wage-earning experience in the factories. Harriet Robinson, the daughter of a poor carpenter, also left a memoir of her years in the mill (1830s). Robinson had a very critical perspective, having led a strike (called a turnout in the antebellum era) against mill owners in 1836. She left factory work in 1840 to marry and involve herself in antislavery agitation and women's rights. Robinson reported that some wives assumed false names when they ran away from husbands to work in the mills: "I have seen more than one poor woman skulk behind her loom or her frame when visitors were approaching the end of the aisle where she worked."[2] Husbands could seize their wives' wages until married women's property acts, passed later in the century, allowed women a separate legal status after they wed. Before such legislation, the *femme couvert* status of the married woman stripped her of legal standing and made her little more than her husband's ward or property.

Although mill workers had little independence and were forced into a strict regimen, women, with few alternatives, still flocked to the mills. Most females spent less than three years—nonsequential—in the mills: a year of work and a year off was the most common pattern. As a result most factory girls were slow to focus on the difficulty and hardships textile work imposed. Commitment to long-range improvements was also slow in coming.

By the 1830s, however, factory conditions had declined to the point that many women were willing to organize and strike for better conditions, for the next generation if not their own. "Speedups" (forced increases in productivity) were introduced, and wage cuts further demoralized women workers. Many complained of the "wage slavery" imposed by factory owners.

At the same time the influx of foreign labor made it easier for factory owners to exploit workers, offering lower wages and fewer benefits. Between 1840 and 1860 more than 4 million immigrants poured into the country, nearly six times more than America had seen in the previous quarter century. Nearly 40 percent of these immigrants were Irish, refugees from the potato famine, eager to accept work at rock-bottom wages. Domestic service, with its low pay and comparative lack of freedom, was the only alternative to factory work for the uneducated daughters of the foreign-born poor.

Large numbers of free blacks lived near factory towns and sought work as well. Mill owners usually refused to employ blacks in cotton manufacturing. This restricted poor black women to wage-earning roles as maids, cooks, laundresses—demeaning echoes of slavery's legacy. Some black women might be able to raise their status by becoming milliners, dressmakers, or perhaps seamstresses. But many more were reduced to becoming "scabs": when white workers went out on strike, black women took their jobs in order to secure a foothold in the factory labor force.

LABOR PROTEST

Protests against "wage slavery" led large numbers of white workers into labor agitation. Factory girls at Lowell created their own paper, *The Lowell Offering* (where Lucy Larcom got her literary start), with financial support from the company. Not only was this journal full of poems and other creative writing, it also allowed women to express themselves in new ways, as they published pieces offering political opinions. **The Lowell Female Labor Reform Association** was founded in 1845. When these labor militants wanted their views aired in the company magazine, the *Offering* was censored. The company refused to allow editors to print a letter indicting the mill owners: "Will you sit supinely down and let the drones of society fasten the yoke of tyranny, which is already fitted to your necks. . . . Shall we not hear the response from every hill and vale, 'EQUAL RIGHTS, or death to the corporations'?"[3]

A petition for a ten-hour day was submitted to the Massachusetts state legislature in 1845 by reform association leader **Sarah Bagley**. The petition failed, but legislators organized hearings, which uncovered deplorable conditions. The Lowell labor militants abandoned the *Offering* and published their views in the *Voice of Industry*, a leading labor weekly.

During the decades leading up to the Civil War, factories became increasingly dangerous and unhealthy for workers. Testimony before the 1845 Massachusetts legislative committee reported twelve-hour shifts from 5 A.M. to 7 P.M. Because work started while it was still dark, nearly 300 lamps lit a vast workroom for the more than 100 workers jammed into its stifling space. Meal breaks were brief and dictated by bosses. Women were not allowed to bring reading material to the workplace. Women's wages of twenty-five dollars a month were docked for absences due to sickness. This kind of severe regimen induced workers to threaten a boycott over such issues as moving the lunch hour from noon to one P.M. (so that women might work six instead of five hours before being allowed any sustenance). Female operatives were desperate for some measure of control over their meager lives. In 1836 women activists argued: "As our fathers resisted unto blood the lordly avarice of the British ministry, so we, their daughters, never will wear the yoke which has been prepared for us."[4]

Lowell women were not alone in their pleas for labor justice. Their agitation reflected and reinforced campaigns throughout the northern states in favor of raising the conditions for workers. In 1824 mill girls in Pawtucket, Rhode Island, protested reductions in wages. As early as 1828 more than 300 women working in mills in Dover, New Hampshire, launched a strike when their pay was cut. In 1834 the women operatives of Dover formed a union, and 800 joined to improve wages and standards. However, the company would only hire back those workers who pledged not to be "engaged in any combination," which destroyed the neophyte organization. Companies continued to work against labor organization by forcing returning workers to pay fines, by keeping blacklists, and by docking pay for "troublemakers."

Wage-earning women across the northern states were involved in dozens of protests and labor actions. In 1831 women and children in Paterson, New Jersey, staged a walkout to try to keep their lunch hour unaltered by company rules. In October 1836, when the Lowell company raised its boarding-house rates without offering any equivalent raise in pay, 1,500 female operatives left their jobs in protest. In 1844 mill women in the towns of Allegheny and Pittsburgh, Pennsylvania, protested against declining labor conditions. In September 1845 women in the Manchester, New Hampshire, mills threatened a boycott unless their demands for a ten-hour day were met. Workers who called for reduced workdays were blackballed by employers. When a riot broke out in a Pittsburgh mill in October 1845, operatives were able to take over the plant and temporarily win the fight: they were granted a ten-hour day. Owners took their revenge, however, by reducing pay by one sixth, creating another setback.

By the 1850s women mill workers had gained a strong foothold in the textile industry. In the 1830s women worked an average of 1.8 years in the mills, but by 1860 the mean had risen to 3.6 years. And Irish women, entering the mills in large numbers, were less than 5 percent of the workforce in 1845 but nearly 25 percent by 1860. Increasingly, poor and immigrant married women were unable to leave wage earning once they wed or had children. The family economy kept them in the factories.

Women who took in sewing at home during the antebellum era were in a weak and exploited position, rarely able to bargain. Male tailors organized in New York City as early as 1825, trying to create a solid front. Women seamstresses in Philadelphia created a fixed list of prices in 1833, to improve their situation. But it was an uphill battle for both male and female workers within the nascent garment industry.

In 1835 fifteen thousand women were involved in the New England shoe trade. Most were doing "piecework" (pay by the item rather than the hour). In the beginnings of industrialization, daughters and wives did the binding for male shoemakers, who were the heads of their households. But in towns such as Lynn, Massachusetts, a shoe and boot center in New England, shop bosses began to collect piecework (or "outwork") from women throughout the town, not just from the homes of male shoemakers, in order to accelerate the manufacturing process. This moved the industry out of the household and into a more competitive market economy. One woman pieceworker described her day's work, which consisted of binding four to five pairs of shoes; one shoe might require more than seven hundred stitches. Women remaining in the home could undertake this outwork without leaving their household and child-tending responsibilities. As a result of women's entry into this home work force, the pay for "pieces" declined precipitously during the antebellum era, and with the introduction of the sewing machine in the 1850s, women in the hand-sewing trades lost even more ground.

Piecework and outwork allegedly allowed women more time to be with their families. This false image of domesticity was nurtured by middle-class women who worried about working-class women and maternal neglect. Middle-class women could persuade themselves that piecework and outwork were actually beneficial to family stability since, in theory, mothers could better supervise their homes and children. In fact, regardless of the venue, working-class women had little time for anything that distracted from the task at hand. When they did work at home, mothers often had to impress the help of even their youngest children beyond the toddler stage in order to earn the meager wages promised. Poor women, especially widows, trying to earn a living by collecting piecework were in a devastating cycle of powerlessness and poverty. The indigent women of New York City often showed up in the courts complaining, for example, "I am the mother of the baby and I can't earn a living for myself and the other four children I have beside this one."[5] Their isolation in the household was unlikely to lead to labor solidarity, another bonus for manufacturers trying to keep the workforce docile, productive, and uncomplaining.

FAMILY FARMS

While women in urban and industrial settings found their lives dominated by the clock, women on family farms, the overwhelming majority of white women in America before the Civil War, found their lives dominated by the seasons. Women's work, like men's, was largely confined to daylight hours. Spring thaws created the beginning of the planting season: clearing, draining, plowing, and sowing seeds. Women planted and tended the vegetable gardens that supplied the household with food all year long. Summer was a season of watering, weeding, and replanting, anticipating the fall harvest. The processing of harvested food for cold storage engaged women all summer long and into the fall. Winter was the season for butchering animals, heavy labor for farm wives.

Family farms were supported by the labor of young and old, male and female, all pitching in to do whatever needed to be done. Conventional gender roles were observed, but a husband's illness might lead to a woman hitching the oxen and doing the plowing and other work usually designated for males only. On the other hand, most men did not take up the work an absent or ill female created within the household (except for cooking) but hired temporary help or waited until a woman returned or recovered for many of the "female" chores to be completed.

However, it might be argued that women were more essential to family farm subsistence than men were. The U.S. Department of Agriculture published a study in 1862, which argued that "a farmer's wife, as a general rule, is a laboring drudge. . . . It is safe to say that on three farms out of four the wife works harder, endures more, than any other on the place."[6] Fathers and sons might be in charge of the cash crops, but wives and daughters supervised the dairy barn, grew the vegetables, and cured the meat consumed by the family. Women usually tended the henhouses, and removing shovel-loads of manure was an especially thankless task.

The sheer amount of labor farm women performed in the nineteenth century was prodigious. Hired help and farmhands had less work than did the farmer's own wife. Farm wives had to make their own soap, make their own candles, and throughout the century were producers more than consumers. Doing the laundry was a lengthy, tedious process. Ironing was an equally labor-intensive task. Women might slaughter and strip geese and ducks, collecting feathers for pillows. After husbands slaughtered the pigs, it was the women's job to cure the animals in brine. Women harvested flax, and "scutching" (beating the flax into a silky fiber) was tough and grueling. Shearing sheep and turning wool into yarn was another ongoing female chore. The linsey-woolsey produced on household looms was a family wardrobe staple. The dying of cloth and cutting out and sewing of garments was a yearlong process for most women, like knitting and darning socks. Until the American Civil War, most farm families were clothed in homespun.

Clothing too ragged to be mended might be torn up into scraps and used for patches or for quilting. As one Kentucky woman recalled: "The Lord sent in the pieces, but we can cut 'em out and put 'em together pretty much to suit ourselves."[7] Some women in farm families even enjoyed needlework enough to move beyond the basics required. Taught embroidery by their mothers, girls might prepare a needlepoint sampler, or crochet or appliqué or create a counterpane. These delicate ladies' preoccupations were in stark contrast to the travail of their everyday chores.[8]

Within an agricultural society, the political divisions between work and home were lessened. This did not mean that gender conventions were necessarily blurred or that class divisions disappeared, however. And certainly within southern rural culture, racial boundaries were rigidly maintained.

THE DOMESTIC SPHERE

The rise of "domesticity" was a powerful cultural trend in the early decades of the nineteenth century. Theoretically, with the onset of industrialization and the expansion of capitalism, the world of commerce and the household would be expected to drift apart. But as the home began to be perceived as women's domain, and as production shifted away from the household, commerce directed its attentions to these new "domestic" consumers. Indeed, advice literature and the role of "domestic science" in the nineteenth century signaled women's new role as protector of family morality and upholder of cultural ideals. Individualism, competitiveness, and success were rampant in the marketplace. Men found mobility and choice within the wider world. Women needed to influence men to adhere to religious and community values and to support the family, economically and emotionally. Under these changing circumstances, homemaking became professionalized.

Antebellum ideologues harped on female inferiority and confinement, arguing that whenever a woman went out to mingle in the public realm, she was deserting the station God and nature intended. Home was her designated arena. More than a hundred magazines directed at ladies blossomed from the first decades of the century, none more popular than **Godey's Lady's Book**, edited by **Sarah Josepha Hale**. Hale and other women writers and editors, such as **Catharine Beecher** and **Lydia Maria Child** (who edited a children's magazine before she became an antislavery activist), paved the way for a "grand domestic revolution," whereby women glorified and exalted their roles as homemakers and mothers.

Many women took their segregated status not as a badge of inferiority but as an opportunity to be exploited. Some might even be called "domestic feminists" for the way in which they celebrated distinctive female traits and activities, contrasting them favorably with the standards and behaviors of men. Some of these women championed the protection of women, especially poor and dependent women, who were not being well served by the gender conventions designed to confine them to the home, "the haven in a heartless world." Many took their campaigns on women's behalf onto the public platform, using skills honed in voluntary and religious associations to advance their goals in the larger social arena. The opening decades of the nineteenth century witnessed a transformation in women's education and their expanding roles in reform that was nothing short of a revolution.

CHAPTER THREE

Education and Reform

Education had been important to the founders of the new nation, but well into the nineteenth century education for women remained highly rudimentary, with notable exceptions that only served to underscore the inadequate norm. Between 1810 and 1870, however, a true revolution in education for women took place. Beginning with the theories and actions of the visionary **Emma Willard**, notions of what constituted a proper education for future wives and mothers began to give way in the face of a growing desire that quickly became a demand for more meaningful education and training for young women.

This chapter traces the transformation of female education, discussing the early dame schools, the quest for a more rigorous curriculum, the early public school system, the beginning of female higher education and the founding of the first women's colleges, and the dominant role of women in the teaching profession. The chapter also highlights the relationship between education and those reform movements of the 1820s and onward in which women began to play a larger and more active role, including abolitionism, temperance, and, by the 1840s, women's rights.

SETTING THE STAGE

From the beginning, the uniquely American form of democracy put forward by the Founding Fathers and incorporated into the Declaration of Independence and the American Constitution placed a premium on the value and necessity of an educated populace. While most Americans overtly viewed formal education as a male prerogative, there was enough positive sentiment in favor of female education that the idea grew and expanded in the first decades of nationhood. Even in the earliest years of settlement, there had been evident support for female education, albeit for often dubious reasons. Cotton Mather, a seventeenth-century Puritan clergyman, advocated female education as a necessity to help women better navigate the paths of righteousness and thus avoid the wildness that Mather believed was a woman's more natural state. Mather was not advocating education for the benefit of women. In a society where women's opportunities and actions were highly constrained, it was convenient to favor ideas—such as Mather's conception of what education could accomplish—that would enlist women's aid in maintaining the constraints. In the eighteenth century, well-known women such as Abigail Adams consistently supported female education. While Adams believed in the necessity of an educated female population, she placed the argument squarely in the realm of rights as opposed to convenience.

The rationale for female education would continue to elicit strong arguments throughout the nineteenth century. On the one hand were those who viewed female education as a means to preserve the republican ideal of the home as the launch pad for the nation's leaders, sons who would eventually enter government and politics, law and medicine, commerce and farming. On the other hand were those who credited women with the ability and the right to pursue education, not necessarily for the sole purpose of enhancing family life.

In 1784 essayist Judith Sargent Murray published "Desultory Thoughts Upon the Utility of Encouraging a Degree of Self-Complacency, Especially in Female Bosoms," in *Gentlemen and Ladies Town and Country Magazine*. Murray's advocacy of female education continued in a series of essays published under the pseudonym "Constantia," in *Massachusetts Magazine* almost a decade later. Murray had by now found support for her views in Mary Wollstonecraft's *A Vindication of the Rights of Woman*, published in the United States in 1792, which argued forcefully that women would better serve their family, community, and nation if they were afforded rights and opportunities, not the least of which was an equal education.

A notable example of the education advocated for women by Murray and others already existed in a unique institution founded in 1787, the Philadelphia Young Ladies Academy. The academy was founded by the male professional, commercial, and political elites of Philadelphia, many of whom had themselves attended college. They oversaw the building and growth of the school and advocated a rigorous course of study. The all-male teaching staff instructed students in reading, writing, composition, geography, arithmetic, and rhetoric. With the exception of the classics and the sciences, it was a curriculum very much like those offered to most male students. While the founders had no doubt that such an education was appropriate for their daughters, who were fully capable of exposure to knowledge without being damaged in any measurable way, they nevertheless insisted that the ultimate goal of a serious education for women was to imbue them with the "rational, well-informed piety" necessary for successful wife- and motherhood. The education provided for women at Philadelphia Young Ladies Academy was an exception, however. The educational experiences of most females remained far removed from that example for several decades.

The changes in the social fabric concomitant with the realization of nation-hood promoted and supported the emerging role being carved out for women in the new republic and helped to make desirable and acceptable the idea of female education. In the wake of the Revolution, to which they had contributed so much, white women became the dispensers of values, morals, and character. As designated conservators within the family of the republican ideology upon which the nation was built, women had not so much a right as a necessity to acquire at least a rudimentary education that would allow them to carry out their responsibilities with a sufficient degree of competence and confidence. Mothers had always taught their daughters the homemaking skills necessary to their future families' well-being. From cooking and cleaning to weaving and sewing, from candle- and soap-making to child and health care, women began their apprenticeships at a tender age, either in the bosom of their birth families or as indentured servants.

Intellectual stimulation was mostly a function of class in Revolutionary America. The daughters of northern merchants and southern planters frequently had tutors or perhaps even attended a local finishing school. The teachers were most likely no better educated than the students, but since the emphasis was on acquiring desirable social skills, including dance, needlepoint, drawing, music, and, occasionally, conversational French, the intellectual preparation of teachers was not an issue. Very few female students were taught reading and writing. When Protestant church elders began to counsel reading as an appropriate pursuit for women, it was not because they were persuaded that women ought to be afforded the same opportunities as men. Rather, in keeping with the ideal of republican motherhood, the clergy wanted women to be better positioned to teach scripture to their children. (More than a century later, in Margaret Mitchell's sentimentalized version of the Old South, *Gone With the Wind* [1936], the image of Mrs. O'Hara reading to her children from the Bible and leading them in prayer was precisely what nineteenth-century clergy had had in mind when they began to support literacy for women.)

To be sure, the nature of education for both males and females was a matter of concern primarily for those who could afford it. Most children received no formal education at all throughout the eighteenth century. But even among the wealthy classes, the literacy rates for women lagged far behind those for men. When the means existed within families to educate their children, boys were given priority both in quantity and quality. Available secondary education for boys at the end of the eighteenth century was more substantial and advanced than that available for girls. Nevertheless, as the nineteenth century approached, the growing number of literate women had an enormous impact on the future education of all American women.

Many of the early female readers had parents willing to expose their daughters to the world of books and of ideas beyond those found in the Bible. There was virtually no expectation—or desire—that their newfound knowledge would be used anywhere except within the confines of their families. In retrospect, even this limited exposure to knowledge carried far more influence in shaping the values of future generations than might have been imagined, for it came at the critical time when women assumed the *de facto* role as arbiters within the domestic/private sphere and men claimed public life for themselves.

THE RISE OF THE ACADEMY

By the first decade of the nineteenth century, female academies—sometimes called seminaries—were springing up in both the North and the South. Between 1790 and 1830 as many as four hundred such schools were established. More would open their doors before the Civil War. Many remained little more than finishing schools for the daughters of middle- and upper-class families who hoped to enhance the girls' marriage opportunities by equipping them with the skills necessary for social success. At the same time, however, the new century brought with it a new desire to improve the quality of female education. Thus historians have marked the opening of the "age of the academy" at 1800. Schools, single-sex as well as coeducational, began to offer a more rigorous curriculum (the classic English education: Latin, geography, history, mathematics, and composition). With Harvard and Yale already established, along with a smattering of other college-level institutions, the opportunity for higher education, while limited, did exist for males. There were no advanced educational opportunities for women, however, until **Emma Willard** opened her seminary for females in Troy, New York, in 1821. **Mary Lyon**, a Willard student, established **Mount Holyoke Seminary** in western Massachusetts in 1837 as the first women's college in the United States. And Oberlin College, the first coeducational institution of higher learning, opened its doors to both men and women in early 1837. But Emma Willard's role in female education is exemplary. Her institution became a training school for female educators throughout the country.

Willard held a lifelong belief in the ability of women to accomplish far more than society thought them capable of. Forced by circumstance to support herself and her children, she turned to teaching, first opening a school in Connecticut and later one in New York. Her experience quickly led Willard to the conclusion that the major advantage enjoyed by schools for young men was funding. Communities funded boys' schools but did not provide similar support for girls' schools. Determined to address the issue at its source, Willard sent an appeal to the Connecticut legislature, requesting funding for her school. Denied there, Willard approached the New York State legislature, but her *An Address to the Public, Particularly to Members of the Legislature of New York, Proposing a Plan for Improving Female Education* (1818) met with little more success. The city of Troy, however, offered to fund Willard's school if she would relocate to Troy, which she did in 1821.

Willard was indefatigable. In 1846 she traveled nearly eight thousand miles conducting workshops and lecturing on behalf of education. Willard's Troy students were stamped for life with a sense of women's equal ability and set on a course of intellectual achievement. Willard never advocated anything other than "true womanhood" for her students—the belief that they would go on to become wives and mothers. So profound was her belief in education for women, however, that after being educated at her Troy academy, Willard students were more likely to pursue careers, less likely to marry, and if they did, were likely to have fewer children than women of their class with less education. Feminist **Elizabeth Cady Stanton** fondly remembered Willard's "profound self-respect," which doubtless made a favorable impression on her young student. But Willard's contribution was greater perhaps in the difference she made in the lives of the average rather than the outstanding among her pupils.

Willard graduates were known for high standards and capable talents. The school provided teachers for institutions throughout the country. Caroline Livy's academy in Rome, Georgia, trained more than 5,000 young women; Urania Sheldon went on to head the Utica Female Academy; Almira Lincoln Phelps founded the Patapsco Female Institute in Maryland; and Mary Lyon, of course, founded Mount Holyoke College. A survey of antebellum female education reveals that the "Troy ideal" became the model for more than two hundred schools in nineteenth-century America. Willard played an enormous role in this improvement and expansion of women's education in both the North and the South.

Another major contributor to the female academy movement was a great promoter of domesticity, **Catharine Beecher**, a prominent reformer and distinguished author of, among other well-known works, *Domestic Economy* (1841), the housewife's Bible for the antebellum period. Her father was Lyman Beecher, an influential clergyman, and her siblings included Henry Ward Beecher, also a notable clergyman in his own right; **Harriet Beecher Stowe**, the author of *Uncle Tom's Cabin* (1852); and Isabella Beecher Hooker, a women's rights activist. Ironically, Catharine Beecher spent most of her life outside the domestic circle, demonstrating the ways and means for women to remain confined to this sphere.

Beecher founded the Hartford Female Seminary in 1823, listening to her father's admonishments not to let it become "only a commonplace, middling sort of school." In 1845, in an article entitled "The Duty of American Women to Their Country," Beecher argued that ignoring the nearly two million children who were growing up uneducated posed an enormous threat to the future well-being of the nation. Beecher also established educational institutions throughout the country, especially in needy frontier areas. She was adept at coaxing funds from backwoods communities, making sure the money she raised was earmarked for the building of academies to be staffed by her protégées. Through teaching careers, young, unmarried middle-class females could achieve some measure of independence and mold a new life for themselves as well as for future generations.

The number of female teachers—and the number of schools—continued to accelerate throughout the century. By 1870 more than half the 200,000 primary and secondary school teachers in America were women. In the early years of the republic, teaching was not a common vocation for women. By the end of the nineteenth century, however, women were the mainstay of the teaching profession. Moreover they were beginning to move up the ladder into administration and as elected members of school boards. Not surprisingly, the early women educators met with resistance. But domestic feminists, such as Catharine Beecher, argued that teaching was a "natural extension" of women's maternal role. In truth, it was an argument that was easy to accept because of the underlying assumption held by many Americans that women were purer and more virtuous, less susceptible to the evils of the "outside world," and therefore better suited to work with young, impressionable minds.

Once their basic educational options were increased, women began to develop greater expectations almost immediately. This was reflected in the success of efforts to open a variety of advanced education opportunities to women. For example, when Catharine Beecher tried to enlist the aid of educator Zilpah Grant as director of religious studies at the Hartford Seminary in 1834, Grant declined. She was already advancing the idea of a boarding school for female students, a notion so radical that the board of directors at Ipswich Academy, where Grant was the administrator, refused even to consider the proposal. Grant remained at Ipswich for another five years until her retirement in 1839, continuing to develop a rigorous academic curriculum for her students that caused one observer to remark that "the primary objective of the school seems to be to provide faithful and enlightened teachers, but the course of instruction is such to prepare the pupil for any destination in life."[1]

At about the same time Mary Lyon, Grant's teaching colleague at Ipswich Academy, moved forward on her own desire to establish a school. Lyon was ready to proceed with Grant's boarding school idea. Lyon believed that future statesmen, rulers, ministers, and missionaries would inevitably be molded in some degree by women, and her intent was to prepare those women for the greater social roles that would be demanded of them. Just as the city of Troy, New York, offered economic inducement to Emma Willard, the town of South Hadley, Massachusetts, was willing to pledge $8,000 if Lyon opened her school in that community. By 1836, with money raised from Ipswich house-wives and the South Hadley pledge, Lyon obtained a charter for her school. The following year the first class of 80 boarding students entered Mount Holyoke Seminary. Students and faculty occupied a four-story red Georgian building that served as both dormitory and academic facility.

Although it did not officially become a college until 1888, Mount Holyoke holds the distinction of being the first women's college in the United States. It offered the rigorous academic curriculum—ranging from Greek and Latin to human anatomy—advocated by Willard and Grant, as well as attention to the domestic concerns that Beecher had long championed as integral to female education. Lyon always professed great hopes for her students, encouraging them to go out into the world prepared to make positive changes. As the 1839 catalogue noted, Mount Holyoke students were expected to be efficient auxil-iaries in the "great task of renovating the world."

Meanwhile Oberlin College in Ohio, founded in 1833, was the first char-tered college to accept women and African Americans as well as white males. To be sure, women did not hold a position equal to males, either as students or teachers. Most women elected to follow the "ladies" literary program rather than a full bachelor's degree. While the first woman finished the full course in 1841, when **Elizabeth Brown Blackwell** expressed her desire to pursue a degree in theology in 1847, the college balked. Blackwell was finally allowed to take the theology course, but she was denied a theology degree. On the eve of the Civil War there were more than 300 female graduates of Oberlin, including Blackwell, **Lucy Stone**, and the first African American female grad-uate, **Anna Julia Cooper**.

A few state universities and private schools in addition to Oberlin began to open their doors to women in the years before the Civil War. The first women's school to call itself a "college," the Georgia Female College, opened its doors in Macon, Georgia, in 1836. Still in existence as Wesleyan College, the school offered a finishing-school education to its students in its early years. In the 1850s Milwaukee Female College, Bowdoin College (Maine), Mary Sharp College (Tennessee), Antioch College (Ohio), Western Reserve (Ohio), Hollins College (Virginia), and the universities of Wisconsin and Michigan all began to accept women students or were founded as women's schools.

Despite the groundswell of support for female education, those women determined to pursue a college degree did not always find acceptance easily. Women at coeducational institutions were frequently prohibited from taking any classes in some departments. They often found themselves relegated to seats at the very back of the class, ignored—and worse, ridiculed—by professors, and taunted by male students. Many of these early women college students actually arrived on campus with several years of teaching experience. But neither age nor experience provided protection against the daily slights and insults that followed them from the classroom to living quarters and dining halls. Indeed, living arrangements were frequently difficult to obtain because of the attitudes shared by faculty, students, and local residents. Despite the difficulties visited upon women who chose to pursue education, both the concept and the reality of female education continued to grow.

EDUCATION AND TEACHING

The first census that measured literacy was conducted in 1850 and revealed that women were as likely to be literate as men even though they still had fewer opportunities for formal education. Taking on the role of "teacher" within the home even before they were provided with educational opportunities had helped to develop a basic level of literacy that women were then able to pass on to their children and sometimes even their husbands. With the proliferation of dame schools in the early nineteenth century, teaching for women became an easily accessible means of supplementing family income. Fully 25 percent of all native-born white women were involved in some aspect of formal teaching in the second quarter of the nineteenth century, according to some estimates. The amount of time that these women spent as teachers varied, but by midcentury, teaching had become a profession into which single women entered in significant numbers, largely in private, tuition-based schools.

Catholic nuns were another source of teaching professionals. Although parochial schools were just beginning to spring up in areas with large Catholic constituencies, for example in Maryland and Louisiana, Catholic schools soon became commonplace, especially in larger urban areas with growing immigrant populations. A number of Catholic boarding schools for young women also attracted non-Catholics, who took comfort in the belief that their daughters would receive an education that stressed piety and would, therefore, better prepare them for the responsibilities of family.

As a profession, teaching proved to be a mixed blessing for women. On the one hand it provided the Willard-Beecher-Lyon students a natural avenue, for those who wished to pursue it, to use their educations to expand horizons for themselves, other women, and the nation. It helped to create an enormous network that spread throughout the country. Teachers sometimes became respected members of the community, more so in rural areas and in the frontier West where they tended to be higher profile. At the same time, the youth of many teachers and the minuscule wages paid them prevented respect from growing into influence in the community, particularly prior to the Civil War. They were often participants, if not initiators, of local voluntary associations and groups concerned about a range of issues that affected women both directly and indirectly.

On the other hand, female teachers were paid very little and always less than male teachers in similar positions. The fact that teaching was such a low-paid occupation paved the way for women since men sought out jobs with higher wages or moved to areas where free land for farming and ranching was still abundant. Low pay and inequitable pay scales characterized the teaching profession for women throughout the nineteenth century. In addition, women were generally passed over for administrative positions, while male teachers with similar educations and often less experience could and did secure administrative posts quite routinely. Particularly in public education, women teachers entered and left the system at roughly the same level.

Most women who went into teaching were not graduates of the more rigorous schools such as Mount Holyoke, nor of any school of higher education. Most women teachers in fact had educations only slightly more advanced than the students they were charged with teaching, and very often they were not much older than their students. Teaching as a profession was still in its infancy and therefore not yet encumbered with minimum requirements. At the same time, education levels, experience, and age were not impediments that prevented some women from working their way up. The rules of conduct for women teachers were determined by male administrators and school board members, who could and did micromanage teachers' daily existence, including dictating the color of clothing considered appropriate for classroom wear. And, of course, once a woman married she was no longer allowed to hold a teaching position.

As time went on and more women entered the profession, teaching became stigmatized as poorly paid women's work. Female teachers were also expected to possess an uncommon amount of endurance and to accept without question a life of self-sacrifice in order to remain molders of the nation's youth. Despite these drawbacks, women continued to enter the profession. By the end of the century education had become a largely female domain and a feminized mission.

Education for women and teaching as a profession open to women did not progress at the same rate and at the same time across the board. In the sparsely settled areas of the West and the Midwest, public schools became the norm. But it was not until after the passage of the Morrill Land Act (1862) and the end of the Civil War that land grants for settlement required of communities that they set aside parcels of land for colleges and public schools. By the 1870s, for most settlers, accessible schools were a desirable priority. The one-room schoolhouse that ministered to the needs of children of all ages became a common fixture. Most communities had to import teachers, generally young women, willing to live with the families of their students—a system called "boarding round"—and teach for two or three dollars a week. But by the last quarter of the nineteenth century, except for the South, there were more female students in public and private schools than there were male students. Particularly in frontier, farming, and rural areas, boys tended to dispense with formal schooling after they reached an age where they could be usefully employed to work on the family farm or ranch.

In the South different forces were at work. Prior to the Civil War, a significant proportion of the school-age population was prohibited by law from attending school. It was illegal to teach reading and writing to slaves of any age. The daughters of planters and merchants received home instruction either from their mothers or from tutors, or they attended one of the many finishing schools founded for the express purpose of broadening their cultural, if not intellectual, horizons as preparation for marriage. But regardless of race, the literacy rate in the South lagged behind the literacy rate in the North.

Women Schoolteachers in the South

Following the Civil War, women educators faced major challenges. Immediately after the war, the South demanded a special campaign to combat widespread illiteracy, especially among freed slaves. Women argued that education was an important tool in the effort to make the nation whole again, to improve conditions in the backward states of the former Confederacy.

Nearly four thousand women engaged in the work of setting up schools for the Freedmen's Bureau throughout the South, an endeavor W. E. B. DuBois called "the Tenth Crusade." The Freedmen's Bureau was established by the Reconstruction government to assist former slaves in their transition to full citizenship. Hundreds of schools in countless communities were opened in the immediate aftermath of war. Many of the teachers came from the North and brought with them the hope and expectation that they could mold the newly freed slaves in their own image, one complete with a Puritan work ethic that would enable the former slaves to build lives as free citizens. Those who returned to the North helped to spread the gospel of the Reconstruction campaign, in some cases writing memoirs of their years in the South, including **Charlotte Forten**'s "Life on the Sea Islands," published in the *Atlantic Monthly* in 1864.

For many teachers in the South, the atmosphere in which they had to carry out their tasks was one of bitterness and opposition and, on occasion, violence. More than one had to watch helplessly while her school burned down, the victim of local vigilantes unwilling to accept the consequences of the Confederate defeat. Many of the schoolteachers who stayed on in the South, witnessing at first hand the virulence of racism, became involved in political activism as a result of their careers as educators. Women agitated for an increase of state funding for black schools in the South and pressed for black land claims, black suffrage, and other radical issues. Women educators found themselves drawn into the concerns of southern blacks, not just in the schoolroom but also in society at large. Thus, the educators were being educated.

These female schoolteachers did not revolutionize black education in the South, however, despite their enormous sacrifices and important contributions. The 1870 census revealed that although whites throughout the country had an illiteracy rate of only 12 percent (with a disproportionately higher number of white illiterates in the South), illiteracy among blacks was nearly 80 percent. Schools for freedpeople made some headway during Reconstruction, but progress slackened with the end of federal rule in 1877. Despite the loss of momentum, educators provided an important beginning for that first free generation of ex-slave children. Black southerners cherished this legacy of learning as they struggled in the last quarter of the nineteenth century to build their own schools. In addition, the partnership between southern blacks and northern philanthropy blossomed as a result of the strong bonds initially forged by the women educators who went to the South.

MORAL REFORM

Fueled by the emotionally charged religious revivals of the Second Great Awakening in the 1820s, women turned their attention to the ills of prostitution and poverty, and to the quest for moral purity. Their organizational experience was grounded in church membership, with its reliance on volunteers to help conduct the business of running a congregation. Ladies' groups met regularly in most churches to, for example, discuss and share ideas about raising pious children, study the Bible, and raise money for missions. Local groups were often linked into statewide networks. Moreover, informal discussion groups often led to formal programs that extended beyond the original boundaries of the congregations. For example, an informal charitable group established in

New York at the beginning of the century had, by 1816, grown into the Society for the Relief of Widows with Small Children, providing relief and food for more than two hundred widows and five hundred children. And by the 1820s nearly fifty thousand Sunday schools had been established and staffed by churchwomen acting out of a concern for the children of immigrants and the needy who might otherwise not be exposed to spiritual values.

The increasing urbanization and immigration of the 1830s brought with them an array of social problems—including prostitution and the possible danger that could befall unsupervised young women working and living away from home—that were alarming to many middle-class women. Early attempts to reform New York City prostitutes and save young men from corruption led in 1834 to the formation of the New York Female Moral Reform Society. Led by the wife of evangelist Charles Finney, its members were in fact more interested in saving fallen women than in rescuing corrupted young men. The rapidity with which the movement grew and spread to other cities as well as smaller communities revealed the extent of the concern, not only among middle-class women but among immigrants as well, who feared that their children would go astray in an unfamiliar environment. The Boston Female Moral Reform Society, organized in 1835, started with seventy women and very quickly claimed hundreds of members in chapters throughout the state. By 1840 the New York State group, with more than 500 auxiliary chapters and thousands of members, became national in scope as the **American Female Moral Reform Society**.

The movement publicized its cause in periodicals such as the *Advocate of Moral Reform*, but it mainly relied heavily on the direct involvement of its members to engage in high-profile activities that would, they hoped, discourage immoral behavior. It was not unusual to see small groups of women singing hymns and praying at the doors of brothels, visiting almshouses to preach to the inmates, and threatening to publicize the names of men who frequented brothels. They also lobbied state legislatures for laws that would prohibit seduction or solicitation. Both Massachusetts (1846) and New York (1848) passed antiseduction laws. Moral purity crusaders were also responsible for opening up homes that accommodated former prostitutes, female transients, and young girls in need of refuge. Often, these homes also served as employment agencies for their residents.

TEMPERANCE

Drinking and alcoholism was another issue that went hand-in-hand with the moral purity movement. During the early nineteenth century reformers grew increasingly alarmed at the rise in per capita consumption of alcohol. Alcohol, especially rum, was an important trade commodity. Moreover, ale had long been a part of the daily diet not only for adults but for children as well. And, with little access to medicines, such as they were, alcohol was a common substitute. By 1810 per capita alcohol consumption was approximately seven gallons per adult per year. Over the next decade consumption increased by almost 50 percent, to ten gallons per adult per year. This posed a problem that went beyond the nuisance of public drunkenness. The majority of alcohol abusers were male, and with few legal protections in place, women and children often bore the brunt of men's excessive drinking. The sanctity of the home appeared to be at risk. The work of the **American Society for the Promotion of Temperance**, founded in 1826, became immediately attractive, especially to women, who were the majority of its members. In 1833 the first national temperance convention was held in Philadelphia. The movement attracted both middle-class reformers intent on imposing a set of moral values and practical reformers more concerned with the immediate problems associated with alcoholism. The goal of both was the same, however: the prohibition of alcoholic beverages.

In 1834 Congress passed a law prohibiting the sale of alcoholic beverages to American Indians. It was an instructive piece of legislation for two reasons. First, it demonstrated the cultural biases against Indians; there was no existing factual evidence that they were more likely to fall victim to alcoholism than any other group. Second, Congress could appease reformers while not unduly antagonizing alcohol producers. Temperance advocates continued to lobby their cause, and in 1836 several temperance organizations joined together as the American Temperance Union. It took more than a decade for temperance supporters to gain their first significant victory. In 1851 Maine became the first state to pass a prohibition law. Several other states followed suit, and others passed more liberal legislation in the form of "local option" laws that gave municipalities the right to determine their own alcohol policies.

By midcentury the moral reformers began to lose some of their zeal for imposing uniform standards for purity and morality. They found that they could not eradicate prostitution by either moral suasion or threats of exposure and punishment. Consequently, they began to change their focus, urging more attention to ensuring that the family environment was one in which uplifting values predominated. The movement also placed moral reform on the agenda of women's issues, where it would remain throughout the nineteenth century and into the twentieth. Temperance remained a viable issue that, while it would always be dominated by women, increasingly attracted male supporters as well. And although advocates ultimately succeeded in banning the use of all alcohol, like the purity crusade, temperance was doomed to failure. But the experience of organizing on such a grand scale was an invaluable one for women. The movements for moral purity and temperance were coexistent with abolition, and many women were involved in more than one cause. They transferred and added to one movement the skills they had developed in another, which contributed to the development of a women's rights movement in the years following the Civil War.

ABOLITION AND WOMEN'S RIGHTS

For many women religious enthusiasm led to an opposition to slavery because slavery represented a system that, by its nature, eroded spiritual values. By the 1830s antislavery sympathies in the North had escalated from spiritual concern to full-fledged political activism. The efforts of women abolitionists in particular, who were indispensable to the antislavery network, helped to raise the consciousness of millions of Americans who up till then had paid little attention to the issue of the morality of slavery. Female abolitionists gathered thousands of signatures on petitions supporting abolition, since, as **Angelina Grimké** noted, "the right of petition is the only political right that women have." Abolition escalated into a national campaign, and southern defenders of the system of slavery became more vocal. When Massachusetts Representative John Quincy Adams introduced those petitions into Congress, it produced a firestorm of abuse from members of the Virginia delegation, some of whom expressed the wish that women in Massachusetts would "swing from a lamppost."

A generation of dynamic women leaders grew with the abolition movement—women such as Maria Weston Chapman, one of the founders of the Boston Female Antislavery Society in 1832 and William Lloyd Garrison's right hand; **Abby Kelley Foster**, an antislavery lecturer, **Sojourner Truth**, a former slave and a preacher; **Lydia Maria Child**, an abolitionist editor; and the **Grimké sisters**, Angelina and Sarah, authors and activists. The Grimkés derived at least part of their strength as abolitionists from the fact they were daughters of a slaveholder and could address the evils of slavery with an intimacy that few other abolitionists possessed. Raised to take their places as southern ladies, the sisters went north instead, became Quakers, and joined the abolitionist cause. Angelina spoke before mixed audiences of males and females, an audacious act that marked her as an oddity. Both sisters collected thousands of signatures on antislavery petitions, and Angelina became the first woman to testify before a government committee.

In Philadelphia **Lucretia Mott** helped to found the **Philadelphia Female Antislavery Society** in 1833. A Quaker minister and the mother of six children, she served as president of the organization for more than twenty-five years. Mott earned a reputation as a dedicated, effective abolitionist and was selected as a delegate to the World Antislavery Convention, to be held in London in 1840. Her selection brought out long-standing resentment from male abolitionists who objected to women taking anything more than a supportive role in the abolition movement. The **American Antislavery Society** had been seriously divided earlier that same year over the issue of women's role in the movement. Half the society's members favored the exclusion of women from any decision-making position and the other half, the Garrison wing, supported women as equal participants.

The split in the abolitionist movement did not heal, and many male members blamed women for causing the rift rather than the men who had initiated it. Even so, the role women played in the abolitionist crusade was crucial to the success of the movement. Thousands of women held weekly prayer vigils to protest slavery. They continued to gather petitions, sending Washington an avalanche of paper for Congress to handle. They held rallies and fund raisers, and subscribed to antislavery periodicals. Women's efforts made abolition one of the most successful grassroots movements in American history.

Abolition also helped, indirectly, to launch another grassroots movement, one that would prove to be as successful as abolition. When the first rumblings of secessionist talk drifted northward from the South, it was for Thomas Jefferson like a "firebell in the night." Just so, when Lucretia Mott was denied her delegate's seat at the World Antislavery Convention, it was for her an unmistakable wake-up call. With **Elizabeth Cady Stanton**, who had accompanied her delegate husband to the convention, Mott discussed the precarious nature of women's status in America. A women's rights movement was conceived in London in 1840. It would take eight years to become a reality in Seneca Falls, New York, in July 1848.

CHAPTER FOUR

The Church and the Law

The separation of church and state formally established religious freedom if not religious tolerance in the new American nation. The majority of the population subscribed to some form of Protestantism, drawing heavily on British religious traditions. At the same time, within the new nation religious dissenters were given freedom of expression and room to grow. Throughout the nineteenth century, immigrant groups brought with them their own distinctive religious beliefs—and a conviction that they should be allowed to worship without interference.

This chapter explores women's roles within their religious communities and the feminization of religion in nineteenth-century America. The expansion of religious freedoms in the United States and a climate of toleration allowed new ideas and religious practices to flourish. At the same time it was perhaps in large part the abundance of land and the lure of the West that allowed fringe communities to prosper, some in exile. Within several of these emerging religious communities, women sought and secured more egalitarian status. And within some groups, such as the Mormons, women had a unique role.

Just as many church leaders looked to British tradition for their tenets of religious authority, so too did secular leaders look to British common law to provide a basis for legal doctrine in America. As the moral welfare of the family became the responsibility of the female sphere, women increasingly exerted their influence to improve households, neighborhoods, and—eventually—communities. Many women sought legal protection in court—looking to the state to ensure more equitable treatment. They wanted the law to conform to feminist demands. Women reformers became involved in politics directly through their campaigns for judicial equality, especially in the area of family law.

Feminists made great strides during the nineteenth century in the areas of religious practice and legal doctrine, as they struggled against male tradition in order to secure more just treatment for all women. As they battled against the powerful institutions of the church and the state, women fought for their improved social and political status. These powerful institutions may have been separated by the Constitution, but they remained linked in ideological terms throughout the century and continued to operate as strong interlocking forces within women's lives.

Many of those who emigrated to the American colonies came seeking religious freedom, especially those hardy Pilgrim women who settled New England. Among the early settlers, most subscribed to some form of Protestantism.

At the same time the predominant religious sects, such as the Puritans, proved inhospitable to religious dissenters. Anne Hutchinson was banished from the Massachusetts Bay Colony in 1638 after repeated warnings that she was over-stepping her bounds in her desire to preach and to publicly disagree with pre-vailing religious tenets. Such warnings to other would-be dissenters failed to halt the spread of religious diversity, however. Dissenting Protestant sects began springing up even before the Revolution, and in 1788 the Constitution codified the separation of church and state. Methodists, Presbyterians, and Baptists were all solidly established Protestant sects by 1800. In the Early National period before 1820, the majority of churchgoing Americans were attending the Protestant churches of their choice. With increased immigra-tion, America became fertile soil for other religious groups.

THE FEMINIZATION OF AMERICAN RELIGION

At the beginning of the nineteenth century women's participation in religious activities was on the increase. The rise of deism during the American Revolu-tion and the loss of influence of organized churches that came with the sepa-ration of church and state advocated by Jefferson, among others, caused a spir-itual and organizational decline within American religion. Because of this decline, women stepped into the breach. Male clergy recognized women's supportive role, and felt that a woman with a missionary spirit could be as valu-able as her husband, perhaps even more so.

By the second decade of the century ministers depended on women to help them spark a revival in western New York—the Second Great Awakening—that quickly spread to surrounding areas. In 1810 New England clergyman John Buck-minister preached to his flock: "We look to you, ladies, to raise the standard of character in our own sex. We look to you for the continuance of domestick purity, for the revival of domestick religion, for the increase of our charities, and the sup-port of what remains of religion in our private habits and public institutions."[1] Women responded with fervor and eagerly embraced these new responsibilities.

Presbyterians and Congregationalists flourished in New England. In camp meetings on the frontier, Baptists and Methodists made great gains. Women's active support of these revivals resulted in strong bonds between women and male clergy, who were willing to acknowledge and celebrate women's special role in maintaining Protestantism.

By 1815, in Utica, New York, for example, women outnumbered men in church membership. When a woman converted within a household, her con-version might bring the larger circle of her family into the fold. Women demanded that the Sabbath be observed, that the Bible be read, that church charities be donated to, and that the faith be kept strong within families. In 1838, when the attendance at a Baptist revival in Utica was only 50 percent female, more than 70 percent of the converts were women.

As women still had few occasions for autonomy, they used their growing presence in maintaining religious faith as one of the first steps toward a more equal status in the world outside their homes. Their growing consciousness contributed to what scholars have labeled "the feminization of American religion" during the early decades of the nineteenth century. Indeed, women's enlarged and increasingly equitable role in religious revivals threatened many ministers. Lyman Beecher, Catharine and Harriet's father, passed a resolution "that in social meetings of men and women for religious worship, females are not to pray."[2] This kind of objection fell on deaf ears, and women's prominence in evangelical situations continued, creating a challenge to male domination in the religious domain.

Many women pioneered important religious firsts: **Antoinette Blackwell** attended Oberlin College and completed her work in theology in 1850, but was denied her divinity degree (it was finally granted honorarily in 1878). Blackwell was nevertheless ordained by a sympathetic Congregational church in 1853, thus becoming the first woman to be ordained in America. She struggled with Congregationalist church hierarchy and eventually converted to Unitarianism. Her marriage and seven children curtailed the preaching career of this pioneer theologian. Feminist **Anna Howard Shaw** was ordained as a United Methodist minister in 1880. Although the church revoked her ordination on account of her sex in 1884, Methodists today revere her as an important spiritual leader.

Ellen Gould White became a member of William Miller's Adventist sect, which later became known as the Seventh-Day Adventists. In the 1860s White became a spiritual leader of this movement and founded the Western Health Reform Institute in Battle Creek, Michigan.

African American Women

Women from all walks of life took the opportunity to play larger and larger roles within their religions. **Jarena Lee**, a free black woman, was so moved after her religious conversion that in 1809 she petitioned her Philadelphia church, the Bethel African Methodist Episcopal (AME) Church, requesting to preach, a request that was denied. Following her widowhood in 1817, which left her with two children, Lee again petitioned to hold "prayer meetings in my own hired house." This time AME bishop Richard Allen granted her request, and Lee not only preached in her hometown of Philadelphia but became an itinerant evangelical speaker, traveling throughout New England and publishing *Life and Religious Experience of Jarena Lee, A Colored Lady, Giving an Account of Her Call to Preach* (1836). Lee was but one of dozens of such women called to speak who became itinerant women preachers, mainly in the New England and Middle Atlantic regions.

The overwhelming majority of female preachers were white—and many, if not most, had been reared within the Society of Friends before they went out on the road. However, Christianity was perhaps the key component of black women's entrance onto the public platform, venturing into the public realm— and it played a crucial role in the emergence of the most notable African American woman of the century, **Sojourner Truth**. Her early involvement in a religious cult in New York City in the 1830s eventually led to her abiding conversion experience in the 1840s and the adoption of the name Sojourner Truth. Her extraordinary career as a speaker and reformer originated with her religious regeneration. Her spiritual stories and trademark hymns (which she offered at the beginning of each engagement) stemmed from her unshakable religious faith. She later became a powerful advocate for antislavery and women's rights, but her speaking career began with her itinerant Christian ministry.

Amanda Smith, a disciple of Phoebe Palmer, was an outstanding lay preacher in the AME church and an advocate of women's ordination. She became a powerful force within the AME church after the Civil War, preaching the gospel from Maine to Tennessee in the 1870s. She took her ministry to England, India, and even Africa in the 1880s.

Quakers

Members of the Society of Friends, known as Quakers, were disproportionately female. The Quakers believed that the restrictions imposed on women by St. Paul could be ignored if females had been blessed by an "inner light." So each and every woman within the Society of Friends might have access to witness, to offer her voice, to testify to her beliefs. Within Quaker meetings, women were allowed to exert extraordinary authority—including being allowed to prophesy. This last issue was a sore point with the Quakers' Puritan hosts, who felt such subversion would lead to impiety or worse.

Some Quakers were persecuted for their radical beliefs, and some, like Mary Dyer, even died. Dyer was hanged on Boston Common in 1660, after being repeatedly banished from the colony and after she refused to curb her campaign to preach.

Shakers

Despite these incidents of intolerance, the American colonies were a magnet for religious groups. In 1776 Mother Ann Lee settled in upstate New York, with her followers who were know as "Shakers," a Christian sect who lived in celibate, sex-segregated communes. Ann Lee asserted God's dual nature—male and female—and believed that at the second coming Christ would appear as a female. Following her death in 1784, the Shakers continued to flourish. Their greatest period of growth was during the late antebellum era, by which time they were scattered into several communities across New England, having collected nearly 6,000 souls. Orphans were frequently taken in by the Shakers, and more adolescent females than males elected to remain within the community when they reached the age of eighteen. The separation of the sexes and the communitarian approach to work appealed to many converts, despite the disparaging comments of Abba Alcott, wife of **Transcendentalist** Bronson Alcott (whose colleagues included **Margaret Fuller**, Nathaniel Hawthorne, and Ralph Waldo Emerson), who argued after a visit to a Shaker farm that she saw women "yoked" at every turn.

Shaker eldresses were figures of authority within their sex-segregated communities, and their sister Shakers seemed to value the harmony their community afforded. If the celibate community was thrown into chaos upon the rare occasion of a sister's pregnancy, the Shakers wisely decided to label the pregnancy as the result of an "angel visit" rather than to exile or punish any mothers-to-be.

Moravians

A German Protestant sect, the Moravians created model communities in both the North and the South, notably in rural Pennsylvania at Bethlehem in 1741 and in North Carolina in a region known as Wachovia in 1753. Women played an important role in congregations, as the church was divided into "choirs" (nothing to do with our modern notion of a chorus), or groups segregated according to age and marital status. The solidarity of these female choirs within the Moravian church provided women with strong bonds of sisterhood within their small farming communities. In the southern Moravian communities of Bethabara and Salem, African Americans as well as Europeans were welcomed into the Moravian church in the late eighteenth century. At first black converts, or African Americans born into the faith, were accorded equal status. But with the increase of slaveholding among the brethren of Bethabara and Salem (from 25 slaves in 1780 to 300 in 1830), whites began in the early years of the nineteenth century to erect racial barriers to isolate Afro-Moravians and diminish their role within these religious communities.

Catholics

Maryland was the first colony to welcome Catholics, and Baltimore became a stronghold for the faith. Pope Pius VI created the Diocese of Baltimore, appointing John Carroll as its first Bishop (1789–90). Later, in 1808, the diocese became the Archdiocese of Baltimore, with dominion over other dioceses ultimately established in Boston, New York, and Philadelphia until they too reached sufficient size and strength to support an archdiocese status. Ursuline nuns established a convent and academy in New Orleans in 1727, and Catholicism flourished throughout the eighteenth and into the nineteenth century in port cities dotting the Gulf of Mexico. Catholic colleges and schools, beginning with Georgetown (1789) and St. Mary's Seminary for Girls (1791), were established to help the sons and daughters of wealthy Catholics receive the religious-specific education that the Church supported. (St. Mary's began as a typical finishing school that also provided the religious education deemed appropriate for Catholic wives.) African American as well as white nuns ministered to the needs of their urban flocks in racially segregated religious communities such as Baltimore and New Orleans.

Elizabeth Seton, a convert to Catholicism, founded the Sisters of Charity of St. Joseph in rural Maryland in 1809. Mother Seton, as she became known, attracted postulants and pupils to her community, spreading her religious order to Philadelphia in 1814 and New York in 1817. For her lifelong work and devotion to Catholicism (she died of tuberculosis in 1821 at the age of forty-six), Seton was beatified and given the title "blessed" by the Vatican in 1963, the first American nun to be so honored.

Catholicism was not especially bothersome to the predominantly Protestant population until large-scale immigration began in the mid-nineteenth century. The first wave of Irish immigrants, beginning in the 1840s, were predominantly Catholic, poor, urban, and working-class. The influx of a new labor pool that would potentially work for lower wages than the "native" workers did not sit well with citizens who feared that their own futures and well-being would henceforth be held hostage to inferior laborers. Nativist objections to the new immigrants swelled or receded with the economic fortunes of the country. When work was plentiful and the economy was good, there were fewer objections. When times were hard, the immigrants became the target for nativists. For the Irish—and later, the Italians, Slavs, and other Catholic European immigrants—their Catholicism became a target of nativist hatred. Catholics, it was widely believed, were all bound to follow the dictates of Rome, the seat of the Roman Catholic Church. Catholics were loyal first to Rome and only second to secular authority. Frequently, the anti-Catholic sentiment in America was linked to outbursts of anti-Catholicism in England. Anti-Catholic sentiment spilled over into politics with the rise of parties such as the Order of the Star-Spangled Banner (1869) and the American Party (1884). Until the end of the century many Irish-Catholic immigrants were routinely greeted by signs advertising NO IRISH NEED APPLY, especially in urban areas, and it was not always clear whether it was their ethnicity or their religion that was the bigger handicap. Women were not as affected by the boycott since they mostly worked as domestics and were not competing for factory jobs.

Jews

Jews founded Touro synagogue in Newport, Rhode Island, in 1763, and subsequent congregations sprang up as far afield as Port Gibson, Mississippi, and Charleston, South Carolina. The latter city had a large Jewish population well into the nineteenth century. In 1801 Charleston Jews organized the Hebrew Orphan Society, which offered charity to motherless Jewish children as well as providing Jewish widows with relief. In 1833 the society was able to fund the purchase of an imposing structure to house Jewish orphan children.

Philanthropy was an important part of Judaism, and there were many exemplary Jewish women philanthropists in the nineteenth century. During the early years of the century, Rebecca Gratz of Philadelphia was a prime mover in the establishment of the Female Association for the Relief of Women and Children in Reduced Circumstances (1801), the Hebrew Sunday School (1818), and the Jewish Foster Home and Orphanage (1855). By the end of the century, hundreds of thousands of Eastern European Jewish immigrants were pouring into ports along the eastern seaboard. Many second- or third-generation women of Sephardic or German Jewish origins formed relief societies to help these newest Americans during the rough period of adjustment to a new country. Their efforts were especially helpful during an era of heightened prejudice against "foreign hordes" and of rising anti-Semitism. Emma Lazarus, who wrote "The New Colossus," a poem with a stanza inscribed on the base of the Statue of Liberty and was the cousin of Supreme Court Justice Benjamin Cardozo, was a member of the New York circle of philanthropic Jewish women.

Christian Science

Several alternative religious movements gave women an enhanced leadership role, most prominently Christian Science. Mary Baker Eddy was born in New Hampshire in 1821 and raised in her parents' Congregational faith. After marriage and widowhood, Eddy embarked on a spiritual quest and in 1875 produced a manuscript, *Science and Health*, which became a Bible to her followers. In 1876 Eddy formally launched her Christian Science Association, which eventually grew into a new and powerful American religion, the Church of Christ Science.

Eddy's movement reflected a broad spectrum of religious dissent that focused on the "power of positive thinking" and other Christian liberal philosophy. This religious movement attracted an extremely high proportion of educated, urban, female adults. Christian Scientists also had a higher per capita income than members of any other faith throughout the nineteenth century—and into the twentieth. In the twentieth century this faith has been associated with the spurning of traditional medical care, but during its early years the training of doctors was one of Eddy's major concerns as she advocated physician care rather than a reliance on pharmaceuticals.

Spiritualism

Spiritualism was another important movement in the nineteenth century, one that attracted many well-educated women. Catherine (Kate) and Margaret Fox were not yet teenagers, living in a farming community near Rochester, New York, with their parents, when their bedroom was disturbed by mysterious rappings. The local community concluded these rappings were communications from the dead, and in 1849 the sisters began to perform for the public, giving rise to the popularity of "spirit circles." These young girls were exploited by male managers, put on tour, and forced to constantly conduct séances. Both turned to alcohol to dull the stress of their lives.

The Fox sisters represented the popular craze for spiritualism that swept the country and nearly invaded the White House during Mary Todd Lincoln's mourning for her son Willie, who died at the age of twelve in 1862. Those who joined spirit circles and subscribed to spiritualism included leading literary figures such as James Fenimore Cooper, George Bancroft, and Horace Greeley. In 1855 the Society for the Diffusion of Spiritual Knowledge was founded, and Kate Fox could be booked for séances. Kate migrated to England, married a lawyer, and gave birth to two sons. After her husband's death she returned to

America—and her role as a medium. She was losing her battle with alcohol and in 1888 was arrested, jailed, and denied custody of her sons. Fox and her sisters blamed prejudice against Spiritualism for her sad decline. During the 1880s, the decade leading up to their deaths, the sisters alternately claimed the movement was fraudulent and demonstrated their sham techniques in public exhibitions or repudiated those who "forced" them to expose spiritualism. Despite this behavior, the lives of these women and other mediums demonstrate women's central role in spiritual revivals throughout the nineteenth century.

Mormonism

Women have played a complex role within the extraordinarily patriarchal Church of Jesus Christ of Latter-Day Saints, also known as Mormonism. This faith, founded by Joseph Smith in 1830, simultaneously promoted an egalitarian religious ethos yet forced women to play subordinate roles within the church. Smith and his successor, Brigham Young, who led the faithful to the Utah territory during the 1840s, supported women's right to vote, and warmly greeted **Susan B. Anthony** when she visited Salt Lake City during the 1860s. (Scholars have suggested that Mormons supported the vote for women—and indeed Utah in 1870 was the *second* state to grant women the franchise—only as a means of protecting Mormon political ascendancy, not as a means of expanding or advancing women's status within society at large.)[3]

At the same time, within the Latter-Day Saints, women were barred from the priesthood, which is the prerogative of all "worthy males" over the age of twelve. When the Mormons founded their Utah community, they practiced "plural marriage," under which husbands took multiple wives. Some women saw this as a means of bonding, as one Mormon woman on the western frontier commented: "We acted as nurses for each other during confinement, we were too poor to hire nurses. One suit or outfit for new babies and confinement did for us all, and when one piece wore out, it was supplied by another. For many years we lived thus, working together." A dissenting view was expressed by Lucinda Lee Dalton, who complained, "Only for the sake of its expected joys in eternity, could I endure its trials through time."[4]

Estimates suggest that as many as two thirds of all Mormon marriages were polygamous before 1894, when Congress finally legislated against this practice. The existence of these plural-marriage households created hostility to the Mormons, and after Utah was refused admission as a state due to the Mormon church's support for polygamy, the church (by divine revelation) ordered the revocation of the practice. However, polygamy among the conservative faithful reportedly continues well into the present in an underground or "outlaw" fashion.

FEMINIST DISSENT

Many women's rights advocates voiced strong opposition to traditional religious institutions and Christian doctrine. In the 1870s **Victoria Woodhull** and her sister, Tennessee Claflin, created a national scandal by publishing an article in their *Woodhull and Claflin's Weekly* exposing the hypocrisy of Brooklyn minister Henry Ward Beecher, who was sexually involved with the wives of his parishioners while preaching purity and monogamy. Woodhull advocated a doctrine of free love and attacked male sexual double standards. She was labeled "Mrs. Satan" by her critics in the popular press for her explicit sexual language and liberal views.

Between 1895 and 1898 **Elizabeth Cady Stanton,** in conjunction with other women scholars, produced *The Woman's Bible,* a commentary critiquing those passages within the Old and New Testaments that denigrated female equality in the spiritual realm. One of the most vehement critics of Christianity and its effects was **Mathilda Jocelyn Gage,** coauthor with Stanton and Anthony of the monumental *History of Woman Suffrage* (1881–86). By 1890 Gage had been alienated by the slow pace of women's progress and blamed the teachings of Christianity, which, she argued, preached women's inferiority. In 1893 Gage published *Woman, Church, and State,* which portrayed Christian doctrine as debilitating for women. Her radical and outspoken views on religion alienated her from more mainstream feminists.

WOMEN'S LEGAL STATUS

From the very founding of the nation, women's legal status has been problematic. Women were not even mentioned in the Constitution, in stark contrast to the inclusion of American Indians (granted a special role) and slaves (accorded the mythical "three fifths" of a person status for Congressional apportionment). The Tenth Amendment to the Constitution in 1791 gave the states authority over matters not assigned to the federal government, so the states individually passed statutes to govern family law, property law, and the franchise. Only Indian women—governed by tribal or federal law—were exempt from these rules. Enslaved women were further legally disabled by being treated as property under southern slave codes, rather than as people.

Most states adapted the principles of English common law for their civil codes. From common law, states derived the concept of *coverture*. A married woman (*feme covert*) was to be represented in public matters by her husband. The doctrine of spousal unity meant that wives were not able to enter into contracts on their own or control their own earnings.

Coverture was quick to earn women's enmity and was continually eroded by women's steady assertion of individual rights. Many married women in the colonial period, hampered by marital unity, declared themselves *feme sole* traders, freeing themselves legally from insolvent husbands and declaring economic independence in newspaper advertisements.

Prenuptial agreements, favored by wealthy elites, kept a married woman's property under the control of a kinsman rather than within reach of her husband. Also, women of property began to exert more control over their own disposable goods. For example, women began to write their own wills. In 1810 in one Massachusetts county, women wrote only 2 percent of the wills filed, but by 1850 this proportion had risen to 22 percent. In Baltimore County, Maryland, during this same period, the number of women writing their wills rose from 15 percent to nearly 40 percent. Consequently a number of female beneficiaries began to reap profit from this trend of females naming their own heirs and willing goods to favored intimates.

The first Married Women's Property Act within the United States was passed in Mississippi in 1839. This legislation was not inspired by feminist demands for parity, however; rather, the disastrous panic of 1837 triggered the desire of bankrupt husbands to keep their assets in their wives' names and out of the hands of creditors. Alabama passed a similar statute in 1848.

The first state law endorsing women's separate ownership of real and personal property prompted by feminist advocacy was passed in New York in 1848. Women activists had lobbied long and hard against women's legal invisibility and married women's inferior status. Susan B. Anthony argued, "We have every qualification required by the Constitution, necessary to the legal voter, but one of sex. We are moral, virtuous, and intelligent, and in all respects equal to the proud white man himself, and yet by your laws we are classed with idiots, lunatics and negroes."[5] Anthony and her followers wanted to guarantee that the law would reflect a shift in the status of women, although critics would argue that these middle-class reformers favored property rights that brought bourgeois benefits only to a narrow female elite. In fact, feminists also campaigned for women's right to keep their own wages—definitely not an issue for middle-class women at that time. They were able to win this concession in New York State in the 1860s.

Constitutional Crises

The American Civil War brought about a new legal crisis with the passage of new amendments. Most feminists celebrated the passage of the Thirteenth Amendment in 1865, which abolished slavery. But women were on both sides of the battle during subsequent legislative debates. Some women's rights advocates wanted to push for the rights of former slaves only if those rights were linked to women's rights, while others believed votes for women would follow in the wake of votes for freedmen. The Fourteenth Amendment, passed in 1868, guaranteed the rights of citizenship to all persons born or naturalized in the United States. Further, the federal government claimed the right to interfere with those state laws that violated due process. But the Fourteenth Amendment was also the first time the Constitution used the term "male" (referring to male citizens for the purpose of Congressional apportionment).

Regardless, feminist Victoria Woodhull argued that suffrage was a right of citizenship and as such should be granted to women under the Fourteenth Amendment. Claiming they were already entitled to the vote, women went to the polls in 1871 and 1872 to pledge their support for Woodhull's position. Susan B. Anthony was arrested for her role in this "vote-in." The merits of her case were rejected by the U.S. Supreme Court in **Minor v Happersett** in 1875, when the court ruled that suffrage was not a right conferred upon citizens but a privilege granted by individual states.

Divorce and Custody

Prior to the American Revolution, divorce was rare in the colonies. Indeed marriage was viewed as indissoluble and annulments were granted only occasionally. But following the Revolution, the courts allowed for "fault divorce" under which one partner could provide proof of innocence and charge the other partner with guilt. Such a divorce might be granted, with alimony and property provided as part of the settlement. Adultery and desertion were the most common "faults" claimed. During the Early National Era (1787–1810), the legal dissolution of marriages was on the rise, primarily in New England and Middle Atlantic states—and more frequently the divorce was sought by the female partner. This new liberal attitude did not extend to the South, where divorce remained rare. Divorces were obtained in the South by petitioning the state legislature. In North Carolina in 1813, for example, forty-one petitions were submitted: twenty-eight from women, twelve from men, and one jointly. Only twenty-one of the divorces were granted. Only eight divorce petitions appear in the records of South Carolina from its statehood in 1788 to 1830.

Many women took a grim view of their limited opportunities, as did the southern matron who claimed, "Marriage is such a lottery, there are so many blanks to a prize."[6] Many women remained in abusive or intolerable situations for a variety of reasons: women had few economic alternatives, and even though opportunities increased by the end of the century, divorced mothers continued to face hardships raising children and supporting themselves.

Primarily, many women did not want to divorce if it meant they were forced to surrender their children. A father had an obligation to support his children, and until the Civil War custody was almost always granted solely to the father following a divorce, so children might not lose either his affection or his financial support. Fathers might not wish to keep custody of their children, but it was paternal prerogative.

It was only during the second half of the nineteenth century that feminists began to argue in favor of maternal custody, claiming that a father's obligations could be fulfilled by child-support payments. During the 1870s "the best interest of the child" became a matter of judicial inquiry, and the issue of custody was no longer a purely pecuniary matter between parents.

Courts began to shift away from exclusively granting paternal custody, and by the early twentieth century mothers were viewed as primary and essential caretakers for children following a divorce. Mothers were especially able to obtain custody of children under the age of seven, and by 1900 this extended to all offspring under the age of consent. This transformation was a major triumph for women's rights advocates, shifting children out of the realm of property and allowing them a legal status of their own, with rights recognized by the courts.

Feminists pushed long and hard during the nineteenth century to win legal improvements for women. By 1900 married women could maintain their earnings in two thirds of the states, and they were able to make contracts and bring suit in half the states. In addition, in many states maternal rights to legal guardianship were guaranteed by law. Nevertheless, the legal disabilities faced by women in the courts continued to be viewed by feminists as an impediment to their equality—an obstacle to be overturned through female suffrage.

CHAPTER FIVE

Natives and Immigrants

The demographic changes that transformed the United States during the nineteenth century were unprecedented. Hardship, economic deprivation, political oppression, starvation, and despair all helped to drive Europeans away from their homelands—and onto America's shores. The availability and relative cheapness of land, a booming market growth, the lure of industrial expansion—all conspired to draw newcomers to the United States, with hopes for freedom, success, wealth, and adventure. These population movements and growth were significant developments that contributed to changing female populations in the country.

As the population of the United States increased and moved westward, American Indians struggled to preserve their lands and cultures. U.S. policy makers insisted that Native people transform their ways of life and reduce their landholdings. Disease, war, and dislocation deci-mated the Native population; land cessions and allotments shrank their territories; and by the end of the nineteenth century the situation of the Native peoples had ceased to concern most other Americans. Nevertheless, Indians adapted to these profound changes and man-aged to sustain their ancient cultural traditions and values. Women played a major role in that process.

The arrival of ethnic minorities from Europe flooded cities and peopled the expanding fron-tier. Religion and ethnicity each shaped the immigrant experience. This chapter examines the effects of immigration on established neighborhoods and the impact of the influx of newer immigrants in already established ethnic communities, as well as the impact of the new arrivals on industrialization and the market economy. These dramatic transformations had a direct influ-ence on women's socioeconomic opportunities.

AMERICAN INDIANS

Cultural diversity characterized Native peoples in North America. Native lan-guages, religious beliefs and practices, social and political organizations, and economies varied substantially among the different societies.

Nevertheless, some generalizations can be made about the ways in which Native peoples constructed gender. Native cultures based their worldview on a system of opposites, in which men balanced women instead of having dominion over them. Myths often attributed the creation of the world and human beings to females, and religions permitted women as well as men to have access to the spiritual world and its powers. A rigid sexual division of labor gave women in most Native societies control over their labor and its product. Indians east of the Rockies grew corn, and in most of these societies women did the farming. The privileges of tribal membership, or "citizenship," to use a European concept, traditionally derived from kin ties rather than from property ownership and military service, which meant that women did not suffer civil liabilities. Native peoples generally had a concept of common or tribal ownership of property that gave women as well as men access to economic resources and a right to property. Finally, most Indian cultures in the United States, but not all, practiced matrilineal kinship—that is, they traced kin ties through women only, and children belonged solely to their mother's family.

U.S. Indian policy sought fundamental changes in Native culture. The "civilization" program was intended to transform Native men from hunters into farmers so that the United States could acquire their hunting grounds for white settlement. Policy makers also promoted the concept of private property and the idea that land was a commodity that individuals should buy and sell. The implications for Native gender roles were profound. If male hunters became farmers, what would women do? If tribes carved up common land holdings and embraced individual ownership like whites, how would women retain access to economic resources?

George Washington provided an answer in a letter he wrote Cherokee men (in northern Georgia, northeastern Alabama, southeastern Tennessee, and western North Carolina) in 1796: "By using the plow you can vastly increase your crops of corn. You can also grow wheat as well as other useful grain. To these you will easily add flax and cotton which you may dispose of to the White people, or have it made up by your own women into clothing for yourselves. Your wives and daughters can soon learn to weave and sew."[1] Washington intended women to become subservient to men. Like all subsequent presidents, he learned that Native people preferred their own ways of doing things and that they often resisted or modified policies developed in the nation's capital. Most Cherokee women, for example, continued to farm while the men tended livestock, engaged in commerce, operated ferries and toll roads, and tended to political matters. Cherokee law recognized patrilineal inheritance to accommodate intermarried whites and their descendants, but it also protected descent through the mother's line and a married woman's right to own property separate from her husband.

The economic roles of women among the Mesquakies (eastern Iowa), Saukies (northwestern Illinois), and Winnebagos (southern Wisconsin) led them to market participation. They raised corn, made maple sugar, harvested beeswax for candles, and plucked feathers for bedding, and they sold these products as well as handcrafted mats and other objects to white Americans. They even became involved in commercial mining. An American explorer near Dubuque, Iowa, observed in 1820 that "the lead ore at these mines is now exclusively dug by the Fox [Mesquakie] Indians, and as is usual among savage tribes, the chief labor devolves upon the women."[2] Women's economic autonomy had social consequences. In 1827 a U.S. Indian agent who had traded among the Saukies for more than thirty years commented: "It is a maxim among the Indians that every thing belong[s] to the woman or women except the Indians hunting and war implements . . . the Indians seldom make their wives feel their authority, by words or deeds."[3]

Although the United States did not succeed in converting economically productive Native women into subservient housewives, it did mange to obtain enormous tracts of Native land. The Mesquakies and Saukies resisted white efforts to push them off their land in the Black Hawk War of 1832, and their defeat resulted in their expulsion from their homeland. Most ultimately resettled in what is today Kansas. The Cherokees fought a judicial battle against dispossession and won a victory in the U.S. Supreme Court in 1832, but the ruling had little practical effect. During 1838 and 1839 the United States forced the Cherokees west to what is today eastern Oklahoma. Throughout the nineteenth century the United States ejected Indians from their homelands, reduced the acreage they owned, and demanded that they adopt individual ownership of land. The loss of land had a profound effect on Indian women as well as men. As the farmers, they had a special connection to the fields and orchards they tended and an appreciation for equitable economic opportunities that common ownership provided.

Even under the most difficult circumstances, however, Native women helped preserve cultural traditions. In 1864 and 1865 the U.S. army defeated the Navajos of northern New Mexico and Arizona. Intending to impose acculturation on these people, the army forcibly relocated 8,000 of them to a desolate region 250 miles away in southeastern New Mexico. The commanding general intended to construct barracks for his captives, but the Navajos refused to occupy them and instead settled "in scattered and extended camps, unorganized by bands or otherwise."[4] Their chief told the general that this settlement pattern stemmed from their practice of abandoning a house where someone had died, but equally significant was the strong Navajo tradition of matrilocal residence in which a husband lived with his wife in her hogan (house). In 1868 the Navajos secured their release by signing a treaty in which they accepted a reservation and agreed to stop raiding their white and Indian neighbors.

Like most treaties of the nineteenth century, this agreement imposed far greater restrictions on Native men than on women. Native men posed a more serious physical threat to white U.S. citizens than women, and hunting and war demanded a far greater expanse of land than did the farming, gathering, herding, and domestic chores of women. As the United States forced men to give up important aspects of their culture, the things that women did increasingly defined Native culture for most Americans. By the end of the nineteenth century many white Americans were beginning to decorate their homes with the rugs, baskets, and pottery of Native women. They also began to feminize their views of Indians, and these less threatening images prompted easterners to board trains to western tourist destinations and seek a glimpse of American exotica.

What these tourists saw often shocked them. The reservations on which Native people had been confined were dismal places characterized by idleness, poverty, sickness, and alcoholism. Philanthropists and policy makers, however, believed that they had a solution to the "Indian problem": divide up tribal domains, allot land to individual owners, and promote economic competition. In 1887 Congress passed the General Allotment (or Dawes) Act that provided for the division of reservations into individual tracts ranging from 160 acres for the head of household to 40 acres for small children. Upon negotiation of an allotment agreement (Congress no longer permitted treaties with Indians), tribal governments ceased and tribe members came under the laws of the state or territory in which they lived. The goal, according to philanthropists, was the assimilation of Native people, but the opening to white settlement of "surplus" acreage left over after allotment points to white land hunger as a primary motivation for allotment. The use of the term "head of household" to distinguish sizes of allotments implied discriminatory treatment for women, whom U.S. agents did not normally consider as "heads of household," even in matrilocal tribes, unless they were widows or married to someone outside the tribe. In the allotment of the Southern Ute reservation (southwestern Colorado), for instance, husbands received allotments; wives received no land separately. Most had married under tribal custom, and in the event they parted from their husbands, they did not seek legal divorces. This situation left a number of Ute women with no legal claim to an allotment. Daisy Spencer Baker's outrage is palpable in her letter complaining to the Ute agent that her husband has taken her land and slandered her: "Jim Baker says with his own tongue I was not his wife, he says he just lived with me like any lose [*sic*] animal. . . . If I was a lose animal what does he want my land for."[5]

In practice, most tribes negotiated an equal allotment for adults regardless of gender, but U.S. agents used allotment to restructure families among tribes that practiced polygamy—the marriage of a man to more than one wife at a time. Whites regarded such practice as contrary to Christian principles and demeaning to women. The former was certainly the case; the second, however, may not have been. Multiple wives fostered the development of a distinct women's culture, one that sometimes even included a somewhat different language for women and men, and women often preferred the presence of several wives to provide companionship and share the labor. Few U.S. agents waged war against plural marriage with more passion than Major A. E. Woodson of the Cheyenne-Arapaho reservation in western Oklahoma. In 1897 he succeeded in getting the Oklahoma territorial government to enact a law that prohibited polygamy among Indians and required men to choose among their wives. Most refused. Left Hand, an Arapaho chief, told Woodson: "I will not part with any of my wives, but will obey the law and not marry any more. Those whom I have got I will protect for my children's sake."[6] Woodson relented, limiting further prosecution to those who took multiple wives after the law was passed.

Nevertheless, enforcement threatened to erode women's culture, and Woodson's insistence that people live on their allotments undermined community. Men no longer hunted, and they refused to farm; a lone adult woman in a household could not produce enough to sustain her family; Indians increasingly depended on government rations; and dependency, in a vicious cycle, permitted greater federal intrusion into their lives. Agents demanded that parents send children to boarding school and prohibited public ceremonies and rituals. When Native people refused to obey, U.S. officials blamed the Indians for their own misfortunes. While Native people lost much in these years other than their land—for example, an Arapaho women's priesthood and much of the ceremonial life that these women directed disappeared—such resistance promised cultural survival. With the formal revocation of the Dawes Act in the 1930s, Native people began a cultural revival that continues today.

Native women have preserved their cultural traditions in a host of ways. Navajos, for example, continue to mark a young woman's transition into adulthood through an elaborate ceremony that links modern Navajos to an ancient past. The Arapahos honor elderly women who conduct important rituals, such as the Paint Ceremony that promotes tribal unity. The survival of other traditions concerning women is apparent from the analysis of historical documents. Among the Yakima of south-central Washington, for example, ledgers from trading posts reveal that women continued to make most purchases long after allotment, an indication that they retained their traditional control of the economy. Among the Cherokees, women maintained a political ethic of community service that surfaced at the end of the twentieth century with the election of Wilma Mankiller, a community organizer, as chief of the Oklahoma Cherokees and Joyce Dugan, a teacher, as chief of the North Carolina Cherokees. Native women helped their people survive both physically and culturally, and they provided the foundation for the dynamic Native cultures that still exist in the late twentieth century.

WESTWARD MIGRATION: 1840–60

When James Marshall made his legendary discovery of gold at Sutter's Mill in California in 1848, it touched off a new wave of westward migration. More than 100,000 migrants, known as Forty-Niners, traveled from the East to the West over the next few years, in search of fortunes. Previously, with little trailblazing to assist travelers and no guarantee that they would find opportunity in a still dangerous environment, only the hardiest of souls had left civilization for the lands west of the Mississippi. The potential to strike it rich, combined with the advent of trailblazing, made westward migration a more attractive option for both adventurers seeking fortunes and families in search of homesteads.

The gold seekers created a whirlwind of activity. Towns sprang up almost overnight around mining areas, bringing with them a retinue of people hoping to make their fortunes off those who mined the gold. Merchants, cooks, gamblers, and prostitutes were among those who peopled the mining towns. The communities themselves tended to be lawless and violent. The accoutrements of family life, such as churches and schools, were either missing entirely or were significantly outnumbered by saloons and brothels. Women were also vastly outnumbered by men in the mining communities. Indeed, one observer noted that miners in a particular isolated area paid to see women's clothing on display, so infrequently did they see real live women. Nevertheless, women did live and work in mining towns, although most were not part of a family unit. Some of them worked in the saloons and bars as dancehall girls. These occupations helped to promote an image of women who lived in the mining towns as loose, if not prostitutes. Whether the stereotype had a basis in reality or grew out of a fantasy kept vivid in popular imagination is difficult to determine. Most of them eventually married, and some even became pillars of the community, making it all the more unlikely that they would speak freely about a previous lifestyle that, were it true, would surely have been frowned upon.

By the 1870s states and territories were already beginning to pass legislation that would help curb what they viewed as wanton behavior by outlawing places such as dancehalls. Resorting to legal imperatives proved unnecessary, however. As the potential for striking it rich diminished, the gold fever subsided, bringing fewer people into the mining towns and ultimately causing people to move on to less glamorous but more realistic enterprises elsewhere.

In the wake of the boom-or-bust mentality that had dominated the period, ghost towns littered the landscape from Colorado to California.

The vast majority of women who participated in the westward movement did so as members of a family unit. Over 350,000 men and women traveled to distant lands in the West over the Oregon Trail. Thousands more headed southwest via the Santa Fe Trail. Thousands more settled en route. Frontier life, for most women, was pure drudgery with very little opportunity for improvement or advancement. At the same time, the West offered women new and important challenges that were met with resolve if not always with enthusiasm.

The overland journey west in many ways paralleled the transoceanic odysseys of the European immigrants. Moving west meant packing up belongings, leaving home, and bidding adieu to family and friends with the expectation of never seeing them again. It meant leaving behind everything familiar and therefore comforting, in exchange for a long and rigorous journey through an often inhospitable environment and without a network to fall back on should disaster strike. Although some women were eager to head west, most did not make the decision. Wives were, for the most part, bound by the choices made by their husbands. Children were bound by their fathers' choices. Because of the uncertainty of what lay ahead, women faced the journey with trepidation, fearing especially for the health and welfare of themselves and their children. The journey itself was an exercise in resourcefulness, as women faced the daily chores of housekeeping—child care, cooking, mending, laundering, and nursing—all within the confines of a wagon in an expansive wilderness. And, because the wagon trains had to keep to a schedule in order to avoid the serious dangers of winter travel, there were few opportunities to stop and rest for more than a day.

Once the destination was reached, life did not immediately improve. Building a home, often out of sod because wood was not available, and getting used to life on the prairie or the plains where neighbors were separated by miles, required every bit as much perseverance and courage as the journey itself. Homesteading with only what a family had been able to pack into a wagon, provided that supplies had not been lost on the journey, presented its own challenge. Replacements for things broken or worn out were not easy to come by, and all of the chores associated with keeping a home and raising children had to be performed every day. And if equipment did not fail, supplies did not run out, water remained plentiful, children remained healthy, weather cooperated, crops did not fail, animals did not die, locusts did not invade, and dust storms did not overwhelm, frontier women still had to deal with the almost oppressive isolation of the prairie and with not seeing another human being apart from family members for months or even years on end.

While women often had no say in the decision to move west, and in almost every case paid some price—from leaving family behind to losing a child to illness on the journey to the backbreaking rigors of living on the frontier—at the same time, they gained something positive from the experience. Because they had to shoulder responsibility for survival equally with their husbands, and in some instances totally, they gained a new sense of confidence in their abilities and resourcefulness. Eventually, many women also gained a sense of entitlement, of their right to be treated as equals. It was no coincidence that women in the West won suffrage long before their sisters in the East.

IMMIGRANTS

The original New World **immigrants** arrived on American shores in the same fashion that all subsequent immigrants would arrive. Once the Revolutionary War had been fought and the new American nation established, the early immigrants were referred to as "colonists." The combination of their Old World culture, tradition, and values and their New World experiences defined to a large extent the idealized American identity. People who arrived after the Revolution—no longer colonists but immigrants—for better or worse were measured against that ideal. While it is incontrovertible that the waves of immigration throughout the nineteenth century shaped the American experience and even changed it profoundly, the standard against which the new immigrants were measured and judged helped to create equally profound stresses during that experience. The further they were from the ideal, the greater the conflict that was generated.

In the early decades of the nineteenth century, relatively little immigration took place. Between 1820 and 1840 the annual rate of immigration grew slowly from about 8,000 to about 84,000. Conditions in Europe propelled greater numbers westward after 1840. Most of those who did immigrate in those early years came from northern Europe, including England and Scotland. Dutch immigrants established sizable strongholds in New York. French settlers, drawn to the fur trade, moved along the Hudson River and up toward Canada, as well as settling along the Gulf Coast and the Mississippi Delta.

At the same time these early decades were years of unprecedented demographic and economic growth. The population almost doubled between 1820 and 1840, but the growth was due primarily to natural increase. The large percentage of people who had reached childbearing age and a decrease in infant mortality, among other factors, more than offset the declining birth rate.

Beginning in 1840, the rate of immigration accelerated, and over the next twenty years 4.2 million immigrants reached American shores. The vast majority still came from northern Europe. Five hundred thousand immigrants came from England, Scotland, and Wales. Because they were very similar, ethnically and culturally, to resident American citizens and held the same traditional values and religious beliefs, they experienced very few impediments to an almost seamless acculturation. Other major ethnic groups often found the transition to American life significantly more complicated.

The first major wave of Irish immigration began in the mid-1840s when a serious failure of potato crops set off a chain of events that led to large-scale famine and starvation, eviction, and homelessness. The 1.5 million Irish who immigrated before 1860 included families as well as single men and women. Because the Irish were relatively poor when they arrived in America, they remained in the cities of debarkation—mostly along the East Coast and the Gulf Coast. The first real ghettos in America were the Irish ghettos in cities such as New York, Boston, and Philadelphia. Most Irish immigrants came from agricultural backgrounds and consequently possessed few skills with which to find reasonable employment. They were in big demand, however, as day laborers, digging canals and building railroads. Since the majority were Catholics, they experienced severe discrimination, and even unskilled jobs were difficult to come by if there was any alternative labor pool upon which to draw.

Unlike any other ethnic group, a large percentage of Irish immigrants were single women. The laws of inheritance in Ireland kept many single men at home, and young single women had fewer opportunities (since the average marriage age tended to be relatively high). So young single women left Ireland, traveling on their own, and worked in America primarily as servants and domestics. Moreover, unlike women in other ethnic groups, Irish women were more likely to remain single, sending their wages home in order to support parents and siblings. Irish maids, cooks, and nannies were commonplace in the families of the well-to-do throughout the Northeast. The Irish dominated domestic service for the remainder of the century. Even as late as 1920, when African Americans began moving into domestic work in large numbers, the Irish still constituted 43 percent of all domestic workers. They also found employment in textile mills and other industries that required few or no skills.

Germans also migrated in large numbers after 1840. Unlike Irish women, German women tended to immigrate in family units. But the nearly one million German immigrants did not remain in eastern cities. Arriving with greater wealth than the Irish, the Germans continued their journey to the cities and farmlands of the Midwest. Resuming the agricultural life they had left behind in the old country, many German women were not readily identifiable in the labor market. For the same reasons, many German Jews did not face the same levels of discrimination visited upon the much more visible Irish.

By the time the Civil War began, immigration had slowed down, reflecting the uncertainty that accompanied the approaching war. When immigration resumed in earnest after the war, there were new—and to many Americans unsettling—changes in the demographics of the new immigrants, who increasingly came from southern and eastern Europe. Millions of Russian and Polish Jews, Italians and Scandinavians, Slavs and Hungarians, among others, joined the English, Scotch, and Irish who also continued to immigrate. Like the Irish before them, many of the new arrivals from southern and eastern Europe settled in large cities that offered some hope for employment for unskilled laborers.

Most immigrant women from non-English speaking countries, regardless of their ethnicity, followed their husbands and families. Ethnic communities, identified by language, custom, and culture, became commonplace in most cities. That, as much as anything, determined immigrant women's experience. For many women, family defined their world, and work was determined by their family roles. Most married immigrant women did not become wage laborers. They worked at home, although it was unusual for an immigrant family to be able to survive on the income of the male head of household alone. Consequently, many women took in boarders and performed housekeeping services for them, a necessity in an environment containing a surplus of single men. And, because the male breadwinner was likely to be an unskilled laborer with little guarantee that his job would exist from week to week, women often took in home piecework as well. While this could be shared by women and their children—and sometimes even their husbands—home piecework was far from an ideal solution to economic shortfalls. The garment industry, in particular, needed the services of home workers to perform the finishing work of sewing on buttons, making buttonholes, and hemming garments. While it was true that women could watch over their children and earn money at the same time, the work consumed long hours—sometimes more even than actual work in the factories—and the wages paid were abysmally low, sometimes no more than pennies a week.

Whether women sought work outside or inside the home often depended on their ethnic background as well as their fluency—or lack of it—in English. Italian tradition, for example, was quite conservative where women were concerned. Married women did not work outside the home. But young single Italian women could and did become part of the labor force out of economic necessity. Toward the end of the century, fully half of all Italian women in Chicago between the ages of fifteen and nineteen worked outside the home. Even so, the types of industries in which a young Italian woman could seek work with the blessing of her family were restricted, by and large, to those where there were few, if any, male employees. Factories that provided feathers and flowers to milliners, or manufactured candy, frequently had a high percentage of Italian employees.

On the other hand, it was not unusual to find Slavic women, both married and single, employed in heavy industries, including foundries. In steel-making regions in Pennsylvania, immigrant women rarely worked outside the home because there were no opportunities for them. They were, however, employed in jobs that routinely required heavy lifting in Pittsburgh metal-working foundries. Indeed, by 1900 the foundries were the third-largest employers of women, most of them immigrants who spoke little or no English.

Jewish women tended to immigrate alone, much like Irish women. But any similarities stopped there. For one thing, most Jewish women eventually married. For another, very few went into domestic service, preferring instead to work in industry, particularly the garment industry, and in retail trades. The garment industry was especially harsh on employees. Often crowded into airless rooms, working elbow to elbow, it was not unusual for garment workers to put in twelve- to fourteen-hour days, six days a week, for a pittance. Some shops required that the women employees buy their own needles and scissors, despite the fact that these tools were necessary to do the job. Women who used electric sewing machines were sometimes even charged for the electricity that they used while operating the machines. Finally, there was no guarantee that the tasks performed in the course of a week's work would meet the "standard" imposed by the factory owners. If their work was rejected, employees would go home empty-handed. Those who objected would be told not to return at all.

In the last decades of the nineteenth century, after the Civil War, approximately fifteen million immigrants came to America. Fully one-third were women. Some of them became wage laborers until they married. Most married women remained at home, and many of those engaged in some form of at-home wage labor. Most immigrants remained in the cities in which they landed, but others migrated west. Very few immigrants settled in the South, primarily because there were fewer economic opportunities available and because they did not want to compete with free black laborers who would, out of necessity, work for even smaller wages than the immigrants.

While the so-called "melting pot" was more myth than reality, the diversity of the immigrants nevertheless left an indelible imprint on American life and culture. The variety of languages, traditions, and values they brought into the country remained almost intact in ethnic ghettos. At the same time, however, parts of each ethnic culture were cannibalized and expropriated by the larger American culture, transforming over time what was accepted as genuinely "American."

Because the history of immigration is most frequently viewed through the prism of the male immigrant experience, it remains difficult to construct a completely accurate picture of the ways in which immigration affected women and the distinctive impact that women immigrants had on society and social change. It is, however, reasonable to assume that the experiences of the specific immigrant women about whom information is available reflect in large part the variety of experiences of most immigrant women during the nineteenth century.

CHAPTER SIX

The Civil War and Reconstruction

If there is a single defining event in American history in the nineteenth century, it is the Civil War. Between 1860 and 1865 the nation engaged in a life-and-death struggle to determine the fate of the nation, especially the fate of the slaves. The debate over slavery had been from the founding of the nation a divisive issue. By the second decade of the century an abolitionist movement exerted disproportionate influence within society and grew in size and scope for the next thirty years. A series of political crises over the admission of territories into the Union exacerbated sectionalism, often accompanied by outbreaks of violence. These tensions finally erupted into a full-scale civil war when southern states seceded and shots were fired on Fort Sumter, South Carolina, in April 1861.

This chapter traces the rise of sectionalism and the role of slavery and abolitionism in the years leading up to the Civil War. It explores both the influence that women exerted in shaping events and the effects of those issues on the lives of different groups of women. The experiences of female slaves and white southern women before, during, and after wartime are discussed, as well as how the institution of slavery shaped women in both the North and the South. The chapter highlights the emergence of a women's rights movement that arose out of the radical abolitionist movement. It reveals the tensions and conflicts that sprang up between women fighting against slavery and women fighting for women's equality, as the Civil War divided women on the issue of their priorities. Finally, the chapter discusses the successes and failures of Reconstruction and women's roles in the postwar era.

SLAVERY

Before the Louisiana Purchase (1803), the Mason-Dixon line and the Ohio River formed a boundary between northern and southern states. When territories from west of the original thirteen colonies began to apply for statehood, conflicts erupted. Congress settled disputes with the Missouri Compromise in 1820: Missouri would be admitted as a slave state, and Maine would break off from Massachusetts and form a separate free state. Any future states applying for admission from the Louisiana Territory would be free if they were north of Missouri's southern boundary and slave if they were south of it.

After the U.S.-Mexican War (1846–48), America acquired a large chunk of the continental Southwest. Congress again fought over what was to be done with these new lands. With the Compromise of 1850 Congress decided to admit California into the Union as a free state and to abolish the slave trade in the District of Columbia. Congress also created two new territories: Utah and New Mexico. And the new, tough Fugitive Slave Law of 1850 allowed the federal government to provide assistance to slaveholders searching for runaway slaves.

The consequences of westward expansion for slaves in the plantation South were devastating. Life for black families, especially black women, was already difficult. The westward stampede encouraged the internal slave trade, as more children were sold away from their parents and droves of young African American men were shipped off the frontier. There were far fewer black women than black men on the southwestern frontier until the late antebellum era.

Many slave children, deprived of their birth kin, developed deep and long-lasting relationships with "fictive kin," unrelated adults who stood in for the loved ones from whom they were separated. Half of all slave marriages in which both spouses were alive in 1865 had been broken up by masters. Many slave women were forced to marry "abroad," off the plantation, and owners controlled visits between spouses. Slaves might celebrate their unions with or without their masters' approval—often using the African folk custom of "jumping the broom."

Few dispensations from fieldwork were granted to pregnant female slaves. High rates of miscarriage prevailed, especially for those women who worked in the rice fields of South Carolina or the cane fields of Louisiana, where backbreaking work was the standard. Most new mothers were sent into the fields within weeks of giving birth, forced either to take their children with them or wean them prematurely.

On large plantations an older slave might be designated to oversee a nursery where as many as fifty slave children from twelve weeks to eight years old were tended. Slave children were not provided with even rudimentary educations; rather, they were prepared for lives of drudgery. Some young women might be trained to work in the master's household, as cooks or housemaids, but the vast majority of slaves—both women and men—were drafted as field hands.

Slave women were frequently subjected to the unwanted sexual advances of white men, especially masters and overseers. Under the law, a slave woman could not be raped. Also under the law, the child of a slave mother inherited its mother's not its father's status—which enabled white men to fornicate with slave women without fear that their illicit offspring might gain freedom.

Slavery's legacy was a burden for free blacks, in both the North and the South. Free people of color, as they were known in the South, were circumspect, and a surprising number even owned slaves themselves. In early Charleston, South Carolina, the Brown Society was established so the elite among the emancipated or freeborn—usually African Americans of "mixed blood" and/or with "lighter skin"—could create a separate and distinct cultural clique. The free black community in the North was more diverse and overwhelmingly against slavery. These African Americans joined abolitionist societies, established newspapers, and championed the cause of immediate emancipation. Black women, as well as men, created antislavery enclaves. "Colored females" formed separate abolitionist organizations and advocated rights and education for emancipated slaves.

ANTISLAVERY RADICALS

Radical abolitionists defied the law in larger and larger numbers—especially following passage of the Fugitive Slave Law in 1850—and continued to take their campaigns "underground." The Underground Railroad was perhaps the most elaborate system of extralegal activity ever organized in the United States. Perhaps as many as 100,000 African Americans were spirited to freedom between 1780 and 1860. Although many of the "conductors" on this railroad were men, women assisted their efforts and endangered themselves by allowing homes to become "depots" or "safe houses" for runaways making their way north.

Runaways often used elaborate disguises, including wigs and mustaches. Ellen Craft, a light-skinned slave, dressed up and pretended to be a white man, accompanied by a slave, William—really her husband—in order to escape to freedom. One of the most famous conductors on the Underground Railroad was former slave **Harriet Tubman**, who became known as the Moses of her people, leading more than 300 of them to freedom in her years of activity before the Civil War.

Harriet Beecher, daughter of the Reverend Lyman Beecher and sister of **Catharine Beecher**, grew up in a family steeped in intellectualism and reform. In Cincinnati, where Beecher's father became head of a seminary in 1832, Harriet met many runaway slaves and was moved by their stories. After she married Calvin Stowe, her husband encouraged her to write, despite the burdens of their family, which by 1850, when the couple moved to Maine, had grown to seven children. When antislavery sentiment flared over the Compromise of 1850, catapulting the fierce debates over slavery into the headlines, Harriet began to write a serial story for an antislavery journal, drawing on her experiences in Ohio. In 1852 she published the completed novel,

Uncle Tom's Cabin, feeling that "I had written some of it almost with my heart's blood."[1] Stowe's book became an immediate bestseller. More than 300,000 copies were sold in America during its first year of publication, and sales in England reached more than a million and a half copies by 1860.

SECTIONALISM AND WESTWARD EXPANSION

Congressional attempts to settle sectional debates over the expansion of slavery in the West resulted in the Compromise of 1850 and the Kansas-Nebraska Act of 1854. The latter led to a westward stampede to settle the Kansas frontier.

Abolitionist families moved to Kansas carrying rifles supplied by Emigrant Aid societies. These guns were nicknamed "Beecher's Bibles," after antislavery spokesman Henry Ward Beecher, Harriet Beecher Stowe's brother. When the U.S. Supreme Court declared the Missouri Compromise unconstitutional because under it slaveowners had been denied their property rights in the 1857 Dred Scott decision, all western lands became available to slaveholders.

In 1859 radical abolitionist John Brown led a raid at Harper's Ferry, Virginia, hoping to stimulate slaves to rise up in rebellion and defeat slaveowners. But after all the smoke had cleared, Brown and his surviving conspirators were sentenced to hang. Brown became a hero to abolitionists in the North. **Lydia Maria Child** wanted to write his biography, and black abolitionist **Frances Harper** went to live with Brown's wife and spent time helping her through her husband's trial and execution.

Conflicting responses to Brown's attack on Harper's Ferry deepened the sectional divide between North and South, and when November 1860 arrived, four major candidates entered the race for the presidency. The Republican candidate, Abraham Lincoln, only won 39 percent of the popular vote, but he won in the electoral college and became president-elect.

With the threat of war looming, when southern radicals gathered in Charleston to endorse an Ordinance of Secession on December 20, 1859, women in both the North and the South feared the consequences. Lincoln and his supporters believed the North had the industrial might to win a war. It also had a population of more than 20 million, compared to the South's population of 9 million, which included more than 3.5 million slaves. But while men seemed eager for war, most women hoped that secession might be a means for maintaining peace and that the South might gain independence without bloodshed. Following the Confederate attack on Fort Sumter in Charleston's harbor on April 12, 1861, however, those hopes were shattered as the nation mobilized for war.

MOBILIZING FOR WAR

Lincoln's call to arms drew a strong, positive response. Mary Livermore, a staunch Unionist from Boston, described the scene of soldiers in her home-town: "They were escorted by crowds cheering vociferously. Merchants and clerks rushed out from stores, bareheaded, saluting them as they passed. Windows were flung up; and women leaned out into the rain, waving flags and handkerchiefs . . . cheer upon cheer leaped forth from their thronged doors and windows. . . . I had never seen anything like this before."[2]

After Fort Sumter, more than three thousand New Yorkers turned out to rally to the Union cause, to form a huge relief society that would provide bandages, clothing, and other supplies for the soldiers at the front. Women were the mainstay of this and most other Union relief organizations. All across the North these organizations joined together to form the Sanitary Commission. Many of these groups held "Sanitary Fairs," auctions and sales to raise money for the Union cause. A two-week fundraiser in Chicago brought in nearly one hundred thousand dollars for the Union treasury.

Hundreds of northern women volunteered to become nurses, although nursing had been a male occupation before the war. Now women rushed to fill the void. Many women were exposed to harrowing scenes, such as those described by Sophronia Bucklin, writing about the conditions where she served in Washington, D.C.: "About the amputating tent lay large piles of human flesh—legs, arms, feet and hands. They were strewn promiscuously about—often a single one lying under our very feet, white and bloody—the stiffened members seeming to be clutching of times at our clothing. . . . We grew callous to the sight of blood."[3]

Dorothea Dix became the Union Superintendent of Nurses. She demanded that volunteers be over thirty and "plain in appearance," rules that earned her the nickname "Dragon Dix." But her skilled and efficient nurses boosted her reputation throughout the Union. Nurse Mary Anne Bickerdyke wore her Quaker bonnet as she sought to comfort wounded men close to battlefields. Rather than waiting for men to be transported to hospitals, she went out to the field, braving danger so that soldiers would not die before getting the medical care they needed.

As many as 2,000 northern women served, officially and unofficially, as nurses over the course of the war. One of these nurses was **Louisa May Alcott**, who spent time in a Washington, D.C. hospital before she returned home to Concord, Massachusetts, to write her first book, *Hospital Sketches*, in 1863. This was followed by her classic, *Little Women* (1867), a fictionalized story of her family life during and after the Civil War. More men in the army died of disease than in battle, and a Sanitary Commission supervisor, Frederick Law Olmsted, praised women volunteers: "God knows what we should have done without them, they have worked like heroes night and day."

Clara Barton was working in the U.S. Patent Office in the District of Columbia when the Civil War broke out. She returned to her native Massachusetts to coordinate private relief efforts to help the soldiers. She enlisted volunteers to form an independent nursing corps and took oxcarts of supplies to the battlefront. She raised thousands of dollars and nursed thousands of men. Near the end of the war Barton spent time and money trying to help families reunite with loved ones. She received more than 60,000 letters from families seeking information on prisoners of war and other missing soldiers. After the war Barton went on to become the founder of the American Red Cross.

Southern women also played an important role during wartime. An Atlanta newspaper warned when the war broke out: "If we are defeated, it will be by the people at home." Southern white women on the home front were expected not only to keep the "home fires burning" but to chop the wood as well. They would have to handle the axe, also the plow, the pitchfork, even a gun to keep family farms running. The army required enormous amounts of food, and farms were expected to raise extra crops to sell to the government. In the South especially, this was a great sacrifice. Confederate leaders warned planters they could "plant corn and be free or plant cotton and be whipped." Cotton production was cut in half in the war's first year, as southerners planted beans and corn, vegetables and grain to keep the Confederacy fed.

Women throughout the South, like their northern counterparts, formed hospital auxiliaries and soldier's relief societies. Following the first Battle of Bull Run, twenty-eight-year-old Sally Tompkins commandeered the Richmond home of Judge Robertson and created an exemplary hospital. Her talents were so extraordinary that she became the single woman awarded a Confederate military rank—that of captain. Phoebe Pember, a wealthy society widow, also worked in Richmond, as a matron at the Chirimborazo Hospital. Juliet Hopkins, wife of the chief justice of Alabama, performed such feats that she became known as the "Angel of the Confederacy"; in May 1862 she sustained injuries while nursing on the battlefield.

Women in both the North and the South were drafted for labor that would have been both unsuitable and unthinkable for them before the war. Females filled positions in the Treasury Office for both the Union and Confederate governments, as women clerks were thought to be doing their patriotic duty by serving the government so men might enlist. Young and single women found themselves working in government factories, not just producing uniforms but also doing dangerous and difficult work in arms factories. Females were maimed and wounded while working with explosives, and many women died on both sides of the war in munitions explosions. Although they were expected to remain true women, patriotically serving on the home front, women found gender conventions were suspended during the difficulties of wartime.

WOMEN SPIES AND SOLDIERS

During the Civil War some of the most celebrated spies on both sides were women. After Confederate agent Belle Boyd was captured by the Union government, she was able to flee to Canada and avoid prosecution when her Union jailor fell in love with her and allowed her to escape. **Rose Greenhow**, a well-known Washington society hostess, was arrested after the Confederate victory at Bull Run, when it was learned she had smuggled information to southern generals that had contributed to the victory. Greenhow was eventually released and ran the blockade to Europe. She was smuggling funds and documents back to President Jefferson Davis when her ship ran into a Union patrol. Greenhow tried to row ashore to avoid capture, but her boat capsized, and she drowned, weighed down by the gold coins sewn into her gown.

Elizabeth Van Lew, a Richmond woman loyal to the Union, was able to place her former slave, a free black woman, Mary Elizabeth Bowser, as a spy within the home of Jefferson Davis. Bowser was able to sneak out information she gathered from Davis's desk at the Confederate White House. Van Lew scribbled messages in code on dress patterns and smuggled them north.

Pauline Cushman, an actress born in New Orleans, was a double agent. She played the role of a Confederate sympathizer but passed along secrets to Union officers. These women are just a handful of the scores of agents who passed vital information along during the war. Their bravery behind enemy lines was patriotic and exemplary.

Some women were so patriotic that they even decided to defy gender conventions and serve their country in a more direct fashion. For example, in the summer of 1862 Sarah Rosetta Wakeman, just twenty-one years old, left her upstate New York home and disguised herself as a man in order to enlist in the army. She assumed a false identity as Private Lyon Wakeman and served with the 153d New York Regiment. The army was so desperate for soldiers that few recruiting officers bothered with serious physical exams—instead, they took anyone who looked able-bodied. Wakeman served in the Red River campaign in Louisiana, but later died in an army hospital.

Although information is scarce, there are more than a hundred documented cases of women dressing in men's clothing and playing the role of a soldier during the Civil War. There are more reported cases of northern women in uniform, including a single reported case of a black woman who masqueraded as a man in the Union army.

Women went to war for a variety of reasons. Even very young girls might be found in army camps. When a male relative joined up, occasional female children accompanied the troops, becoming adopted as mascots and known as "daughters of the regiment" or "viviandieres." Sarah Taylor accompanied her southern relations with the Confederacy's First Tennessee regiment, while Lucy Ann Cox was adopted by the Thirteenth Virginia Regiment. With their innocence and patriotic spirit, these young girls were meant to cheer men marching into battle.

Scores of adult women accompanied sweethearts or husbands, or went searching for loved ones. Some were independent spirits, not willing to obey society's rules and wait out the war. Many saw the war as a golden opportunity to seek adventure. A few of the women who succeeded in assuming a male identity wrote memoirs about their wartime adventures. Sarah Emma Edmonds wrote *Nurse and Spy in the Union Army*, describing her contributions to the Union cause as "Frank Thompson," and *The Woman in Battle*, by Loreta Janeta Velasquez, told the story of her identity in disguise, Lieutenant Henry Buford, who raised a Confederate cavalry company and was wounded twice in battle.

CONTRABANDS AND EMANCIPATION

War brought the promise of freedom and hope of deliverance from slavery to thousands of African Americans. Within weeks of the war's first official battle, the first Battle of Bull Run in June 1861, Union commanders faced a perplexing dilemma. Slaves were escaping by the thousands behind enemy lines. Some Union officers gave runaway slaves refuge, while others let slaveowners reclaim their property. Mary Barbour remembered her father taking his family behind Union lines: "One of the first things that I 'members was my pappy waking me up in the middle of the night, dressin' me in the dark, all the time telling me to keep quiet. . . . I reckon that I will always remember that walk. . . . I was half asleep an' skeered stiff, but in a little while we passed the plum thicket and there were the mules and wagon."[4] Those slaves who escaped successfully or were brought behind Union lines became known as "contrabands."

The Reverend Sella Martin of the Joy Street Baptist Church in Boston, himself a former slave, attacked the return of runaways and warned that this kind of action would make runaway slaves determined to fight for the South, betting that their masters might set them free after the war. Finally, on August 6, 1861, Congress passed the First Confiscation Act authorizing seizure of "all property in aid of rebellion"—including human property, slaves. Union quartermasters and engineers rapidly put the African American refugees to work as manual laborers—ditch diggers and dike builders. Ex-slave women were drafted into roles as cooks and washerwomen. The war was less than six months old, but an increasingly black labor force demonstrated its vitality to the Union. **Harriet Tubman**, who had been in Canada when the Civil War broke out, went to Fortress Monroe in Virginia to help with the contrabands. Before long, she was sent to Beaufort, South Carolina, where she helped Union commanders liberate slaves on Confederate plantations. Nearly 800 slaves found their way behind Union lines during the war, with her intrepid assistance. Tubman also served as a scout and spy for the Union cause.

When the Yankee troops poured into the sea islands of South Carolina, they discovered that planters on Hilton Head, St. Helena, Paris, Phillips, and Daw islands had abandoned their plantations, leaving behind thousands of African Americans who were eager to assist the conquering Union force.

The military had an especially challenging task caring for slaves when they occupied southern territory. Northern teachers, black and white, many with the **American Missionary Society**, volunteered on a crusade to help the freedpeople during the chaotic era of war. Some, such as Bostonians Mary Ames and Mary Bliss, who spent two years on Edisto Island tutoring 150 students, adults and children, went south without their families' approval. The majority of the 4,000 women who set up freedmen's schools in the South had returned north by the 1870s. However some, such as Laura Towne of Philadelphia, spent a lifetime dedicated to black education. Towne established her Penn School in September 1862 on St. Helena Island. She later added a normal school (a training academy for teachers) and involved herself in temperance and public health as well as education during her 40 years in South Carolina. Towne was but one of the dozens of devoted Yankee reformers whose contributions made a permanent difference to the African Americans emancipated by war.

By September 1862 Lincoln decided to shift Union policy to include the emancipation of the slaves. Although radical abolitionists charged that protecting slavery in the border states was not enough, Lincoln's Emancipation Proclamation (January 1, 1863) dealt southern slavery a stunning blow. The proclamation also allowed for the enlistment of African American soldiers in the Union army.

Slave women and families left behind while men went off to war were thrown into precarious situations. One wife left behind in Missouri confided,

"They are treating me worse and worse every day. Our child cries for you. Send me some money as soon as you can, for me and my child are almost naked."[5] One Kentucky woman spirited her several children away, only to be halted on the road by her master's son-in-law, who drew a pistol and forced her to return to her situation of slavery at gunpoint. He then held her seven-year-old child hostage to ensure she would not run away again.

DEFEAT, VICTORY, AND WOMAN SUFFRAGE

The emancipation of slaves on January 1, 1863, was a blow that struck deep into the heart of the Confederacy. Two months later, an accident in a Richmond munitions factory on March 16, 1863, killed more than fifty workers—mainly young girls—and injured twenty more. Two weeks later, women in Richmond staged a bread riot to highlight worsening conditions in the besieged South. The twin Union victories on July 4, 1863, in Gettysburg and Vicksburg, spelled Confederate doom, but it took nearly two more years of fighting before the war ended. Especially hard on planter women in the southern interior was the infamous "March to the Sea," during which Union General William T. Sherman sacked and scorched his way from Atlanta to Savannah. He turned his sights northward to South Carolina, and his name became an epithet in Confederate families.

With the Confederate surrender at Appomattox in April 1865, the nation was hardly reunited, but the process of restoration could at least begin. During the chaotic early years of Reconstruction, many feminists, notably **Elizabeth Cady Stanton** and **Susan B. Anthony**, were willing to join forces with any group willing to advocate **woman suffrage**—even those that might be openly racist and opposing black rights. Such alliances appeared unholy to many women abolitionists. The battle for votes for women erupted in an especially ugly episode, the "Kansas Campaign" of 1867. In Kansas separate referenda on the vote for black men and the vote for women were introduced. During critical postwar campaigns white feminists lost elections in both Kansas and New York. Black leaders, even such a staunch champion of women's rights as Frederick Douglass, argued that the tumultuous era was "the Negro's hour," and that women would have to wait their turn for franchise reform.

Thus many women turned to a single-purpose movement. Stanton and Anthony launched publication of *The Revolution* with the motto "Men their rights and nothing more, women their rights and nothing less." At the end of the Civil War, women political reformers were divided over their battle for woman suffrage. In 1865 most Republicans were overwhelmed with the issue of freedpeople and were willing to put woman suffrage on the back burner.

However, many feminists decided the woman's movement would have to focus entirely on the fight for woman suffrage.

POSTWAR DEVELOPMENTS

The American Civil War created unique tensions and opportunities for women. The central event of the mid-nineteenth century, the war, exploded at a time when gender was being transformed in both the North and the South. Northern society had witnessed the rise of a new middle-class culture that emphasized separate spheres and female domesticity. White southerners shared these sensibilities but were preoccupied with male dominance and issues of honor specific to a slaveholding society. Men and women alike found their notions about gender challenged and their lives reconfigured after the war.

Although Confederate women might have gained a sense of independence from male authority and even exerted assertiveness in the wake of male absence, questions remained concerning the long-term effects of this wartime experience. When men came marching home, seeking a return to "normalcy" and/or the women they had left behind, what would be the personal as well as social consequences for those women? Some white women recommitted themselves to male hegemony in response to men's alarm concerning this issue. Some women challenged and berated men over this male notion of honor and victory. However, women looked back wistfully to the glory days of the "Lost Cause" and solicited funds for the building of memorials and the formation of veteran's societies, as well as the development of one of the most powerful postwar legacies, the United Daughters of the Confederacy.

Following the war, freedwomen were now able to assert their choice over family and personal matters, in a way that had been systematically denied them as slaves. At the same time the postwar economy offered women of color few opportunities to move ahead within society. Black southern women clung more ferociously to educational opportunities—seeing education as their one slim chance of advancement. Black women also used their churches and separate clubs as a means for social improvement.

Saddled with stereotypes of inequality and inferiority, African American men welcomed the chance to go to war to prove their manhood. Part of that manhood was tied up with the ex-slave male's concern for protection—and perhaps subordination—of his blood family, which had previously been dominated by white owners. After Confederate surrender white males attempted to reassert their authority over blacks by continuing their sexual harassment and exploitation of black women, a long-standing practice under the slave regime.

This despicable syndrome led to racial and sexual mistrust and escalating violence. It also led some black women to support their men's raised positions within the black community, as an antidote to white emasculation. Class, culture, and region, as well as strategies for racial advancement, divided African Americans in the postwar South.

The gender fallout from the war may have been quite different for black northern women, many of whom asserted their independence by undertaking what W. E. B. DuBois has called "the Tenth Crusade," referring to the brave women who moved south to work in freedpeople's schools. Many of these black schoolmarms found themselves at odds with the culture of slavery, as they tried to impose their values as "Ebony Yankees" on African Americans in the South.

For most Yankee women, however, the war provided an unprecedented opportunity to display the talents they had honed in secular reform organizations during the antebellum era. Some historians have suggested that the expansion of prewar female networks and the remarkable achievements of this generation of women laid the groundwork for the great wave of feminism that followed the war and led to women's rise in the professions, in education, and within the Progressive reform movement at the turn of the century.

CHAPTER SEVEN

Commerce and Culture

The end of the Civil War in 1865 signaled a renaissance in industrial development in the United States. With the Reconstruction government in place in the South, federal and state development, postponed at the beginning of the war, resumed with renewed vigor as a direct result of the increase in mobilization that had taken place during the war.

The complex system of rail delivery that had moved troops and supplies during the war now became the means of expanding urban development, giving rise to new cities in the process. For women, urban growth provided new opportunity as the first and second generations of college-educated females sought to utilize their new status. Women began to make some inroads into the professions, including religion, academics, law, and medicine. Female writers and artists contributed to the new cultural growth in the last half of the century. All these endeavors were supported by a growing network of women's organizations that eventually culminated in the women's club movement. Women were also the prime movers in the settlement house movement that aimed to ease the transition of new immigrants into city life.

This chapter examines the multiple developments in the urban growth, immigration, and rapidly expanding industrialization of the second half of the nineteenth century. It discusses women's changing status; the growth of women's networks and their consequences; and women's forays into the professions, including their involvement in the development of the profession of social work.

THE RISE OF THE CITIES

Massive economic growth (fueled by expanded agricultural production, the beginnings of industrialization, and a transportation revolution) characterized the first half of the nineteenth century in the United States. This growth was reflected in the changes in size, number, and populations of the nation's cities. In 1790, 5 percent of the population lived in 24 American cities, with cities defined as communities with 2,500 or more residents. By 1840, 11 percent of the population lived in cities, and New York, the nation's largest city, had a population of more than 250,000. In the same year Chicago boasted a population of about 3,000.

The latter half of the century was characterized by rampant industrialization and accelerating urbanization, both of which transformed America fundamentally. Around midcentury and particularly after the **Civil War**, cities continued to grow at a rapid rate, both in size and in numbers. In the 1850s alone, the proportion of urban dwellers increased from 15 to 20 percent. This growth was shaped by ongoing demographic changes that included both **immigration** and internal migration.

Not all regions developed at the same pace. Wagon trains carried thousands of people westward, as they searched for cheap land. From Kansas to California, from Texas to Minnesota, new settlers arrived, slowly at first and then with increasing speed. This expansion began spawning new cities, such as Los Angeles, whose population reached three thousand by 1880. Southern life remained largely rural and agricultural at the same time that the Northeast was growing by leaps and bounds. In 1860 more than 50 percent of the populations of Massachusetts and Rhode Island lived in either cities or towns. Older Northeast cities, including New York and Philadelphia, also flourished during this period. An ever-accelerating migration from rural communities to urban communities, along with the influx of post–Civil War immigrants, combined to provide a new look and shape for America.

While the urban population would not eclipse the rural population until 1920, the growth of all cities in the last half of the nineteenth century indicated that future economic opportunity would be increasingly found in the cities and not on the farms. Between 1860 and 1910 the total population of the nation nearly tripled. In the cities, however, populations doubled every decade.

Expanding cities required a variety of "social" services, the need for which carried with them a sense of urgency. Construction, heat, food and water distribution, sanitation facilities including sewage and garbage disposal, transportation, communication, police, fire control, education, and recreational facilities—the provision of all of these had to be dealt with. At the same time, most cities were faced with one or more of the same set of impediments that made required services difficult to secure. These impediments included restrictive state charters that limited bond indebtedness and tax rates; improper legislative apportionment; and a sense of competition among the diverse ethnic, cultural, and socioeconomic groups pouring into urban centers. These combined to result in a high level of poverty, slum development, crime, and vice, especially in the older and larger cities. Moreover, job opportunities did not always keep pace with the available labor pool.

URBAN WORKING WOMEN

Despite all of the drawbacks, inconveniences, and even dangers associated with rapidly growing cities, **immigrants** and natives alike were still drawn to them for a variety of reasons, including economic opportunity. Women came to cities not only for economic reasons but also because cities offered them more opportunity to pursue equality with their male counterparts. Cities were increasingly the places where women exercised their leadership in the newly flourishing women's movements, and they also provided new opportunities for women in the professions and in nontraditional creative fields.

In addition, the city offered cultural attractions not generally available in rural communities. Women not only enjoyed the theater as members of the audience, but over the course of the nineteenth century increasingly took to the stage, becoming a more visible part of the urban landscape.

New work opportunities that were more stimulating and that offered both autonomy and anonymity attracted young, single women to cities. Better, more efficient machinery for manufacturing reduced the need for skilled labor and benefited women, who most often fell into the unskilled and therefore cheaper labor category. The vast majority of women in both rural and urban settings were still contributing to the family economy through traditional, nonwage, domestic labor. But the number of wage-earning women increased dramatically in the middle decades of the century, and mostly in the cities. In 1860, 10 percent of the female population over the age of ten made up 10 percent of the country's labor force. By 1870, 15 percent of the work force was female. Between then and the turn of the new century, the number of working women would triple. Gradually, women wage earners moved away from domestic work to take jobs in factories as well as in offices, stores, and, of course, classrooms.

Women in industry would continue to work in unskilled and semiskilled jobs throughout the century and were usually confined to specific industries, including clothing manufacturing. White collar workers were also limited in the types of employment they could find. Women white collars worked as teachers, nurses, in offices as file clerks, and eventually as typists and on switchboards. And increasingly, the "working girl" was really a working girl. The Bureau of Labor study concluded in 1880 revealed that women urban workers were overwhelmingly single (90 percent), young (75 percent were between the ages of fourteen and twenty-four), and native-born (90 percent), although that would change very rapidly with the onslaught of immigration over the next decades. By the 1890s New York City's garment district relied heavily on young, single, and poorly paid immigrant women. Women of color who worked broke most of those stereotypes, however: African American women worked at almost any age, and they continued to work after they married.

VICE AND MORAL REFORM

Many women wage earners, especially the young and single but including older women who were widowed or divorced, had no family ties in the cities where they lived and worked. They often lived in boarding houses and lodges. In some cases, women formed peer groups, pooling their money in order to enhance their living conditions and in the process developing an elaborate network of peer culture observances that substituted for family values and parental guidance. Others preferred living independently without the trappings of surrogate families. It was this group that tended to worry moral reformers. Many middle-class women feared that the apparent lack of structure would leave such women defenseless to prevent a decline into risky behavior and worse, prostitution.

The moral reformers of the late nineteenth century based their fears on the growing prevalence of the female prostitution that was one of the by-products of urbanization. In background, prostitutes had much in common with the working girls. They too were predominantly young and single and were often former servants. Young, white, native-born or immigrant women became the targets of numerous investigations and remedial efforts to deter or extract them from the "white slave trade." Investigators blamed a variety of conditions for prostitution, including the low quality of city life and its accompanying perils, seducers and recruiters, and a low threshold for resistance on the part of some women. But, despite the conclusions of moral reformers, studies indicated that it was in fact the low wages paid to women that led directly to vice of all kinds. The Massachusetts Labor Bureau argued in 1870 that until wages were high enough to allow women to support themselves honorably, prostitution would not disappear.

Not quite as threatening as the fall into a life of degradation posed by prostitution, another small subset of women kept moral reformers on their toes. Acting and the theater was a borderline profession in the eyes of most people, and women were entering it and other creative professions, including singing, writing, and painting. Women's growing economic and cultural independence from families created social tensions.

REFORMERS AND ORGANIZERS

Growing cities and their problems became fertile grounds for innovative solutions from a most unlikely segment of the population: club women and first- and second-generation women college graduates.

In the early 1870s the country was in the midst of an economic depression. Women in Hillsboro, Ohio, building on pre–Civil War efforts to curb alcohol use and after attending a temperance meeting in 1873, rose up against what they viewed as men's wasteful spending in bars and saloons. Families could ill afford either the expenditure or the emotional turmoil visited upon women and children when husbands and fathers drank too much. The Hillsboro women posted themselves outside the drinking establishments, shaming the male customers and eventually causing owners to close shop. Remarkably, this anti-alcohol campaign spread rapidly even without an organized plan or identifiable leadership. As the movement spread from town to town, more than 60,000 women joined in, leading to the shutdown of more than 1,000 saloons and bars. Capitalizing on this success, the **Women's Christian Temperance Union** (WCTU) was organized in 1874, and the following year, a group of Chicago women persuaded veteran educator **Frances Willard** to become president of their branch. Within four years Willard was elected national president.

Willard was a supreme organizer and motivator. During her twenty-year tenure in office, Willard built the WCTU into a massive organization with branches in every state and nearly every city across the nation. By 1890 there were 160,000 members, and the organization embraced both a single-minded quest to curb or eliminate alcohol use and a broad-based reform movement that addressed a range of social ills from prostitution and political corruption to child welfare and health care. This was made possible by Willard's organizing principle—"Do Everything"—a flexible strategy that invited individual branches to remain conservatively dedicated to the temperance cause or to become as broadly involved in social reform as the sensibilities of its members dictated. The Chicago WCTU, for example, ran two Sunday schools, two day nurseries, an industrial school, a homeless shelter, and a free medical dispensary, while the Springfield, Illinois branch concentrated on temperance.

Women's clubs had existed since before the Civil War. Initially, most clubs were founded for the purpose of promoting cultural activities. After the Civil War new women's clubs often had a much vaguer mission statement and, like Sorosis founded in New York in 1868, were organized to be "helpful" to women and "benevolent in the world." The New England Woman's Club, also founded in 1868, by Julia Ward Howe and others, was organized as a social center for "united thought and action." Clubs routinely held discussions and seminars on issues as diverse as ancient history and current literature and, in the process, exposed their members to new ideas.

Women's clubs continued to proliferate throughout the 1880s and 1890s, enabling middle-class women to participate in public life without the stigma of associating directly with suffragists and temperance advocates. In 1892 the **General Federation of Women's Clubs** was organized, with more than 500 affiliates and 100,000 members. And with the clout of an umbrella organization, club women began raising money for and supporting libraries, hospitals, playgrounds, colleges, settlement houses, and beautification programs. They also began to use their combined membership to lobby for other civic reforms, particularly education and clean water. Finally, club women endorsed and supported child labor laws, food and drug reform, and protective laws for women wage earners.

Women were able to realize their abilities fully within the club movement in part because of decades of exposure to a growing body of literature available to them, much of which was written specifically for women. From the 1820s on the values these club women embraced were extolled in magazines such as *The Ladies Magazine* and *Godey's Lady's Book*. A rising tide of literature by and about women became available throughout the antebellum period. With technological advances aiding in the production and distribution of books and female literacy advancing to meet the challenge that availability presented, annual book production rose from 2,000 volumes in 1820 to more than 12,000 volumes in 1850. Women were exposed to advice literature on personal topics, including such books as *The Young Wife* (1836), a marriage guide; *Home* (1835), Catherine Sedgwick's treatise idealizing middle-class life; Sedgwick's *Letters to Young Ladies* (1835) and her *Letters to Mothers* (1838), both of which offered advice and direction; and *The Frugal Housewife* (1829), **Lydia Maria Child's** guide to household management. Women writers also dominated the market in fiction by midcentury. Novels, particularly those by women writers,were especially attractive to women readers. A favorite topic was a heroine triumphing over adversity and succeeding in a hostile world. And while these romantic novels had their literary failings, they did in fact expose women to conditions of class and race with which they would otherwise have remained unfamiliar.

While most bestselling authors stayed away from political issues, **Louisa May Alcott's** *Work* (1873) told the story of an independent working girl who refused to settle for and marry the first man who promised to deliver her from the rigors of wage labor. This and other novels and magazines helped middle-class women to understand the need for social reform.

Exposure to ideas did not help white club women and female social reformers overcome the boundaries of race, however. Helping African Americans through activism did not translate into the acceptance of African American women, regardless of their class standing, into white women's clubs and associations. Josephine Ruffin, a black Bostonian whose husband was a Harvard graduate and a judge, was an exception among women of color and belonged to the exclusive New England Women's Club, but eventually, in 1893, she organized the New Era Club for African American women, and in 1895 she organized the **National Conference of Colored Women**. Another African American woman, Fannie Barrier Williams, left the prestigious, largely white Chicago Women's Club and chose instead to become active in the **National Association of Colored Women**, an umbrella organization for black women's clubs. These clubs also dealt with social issues, including the establishment of day care, health, and education facilities, but they were much more inclined to focus on issues specific to African Americans, including antilynching campaigns, race leadership, home training, and moral uplift.

WOMEN AND THE PROFESSIONS

Educational opportunities for women continued to expand after the Civil War. Admission to land grant colleges and the founding of **women's colleges** raised expectations for all women. After 1861, when Vassar College was founded, several more prestigious women's colleges were established: Radcliffe (1874), Smith (1871), Wellesley (1875), Bryn Mawr (1880), and, finally, Barnard in 1889, all of which followed the **Mount Holyoke College** curriculum model. Although the overall percentage of American students who attended colleges and universities was still extremely low, the percentage of college students who were women grew very quickly. In 1870 about 20 percent of all college students were women; by 1900, when only 5 percent of all college-age citizens attended college, nearly half of them were women. By then, many places were available to women students because most college-age men began to view higher education as an unnecessary detour, preferring to go directly into the real world of business. The opportunity presented itself, however, and women were ready to act upon it. Many of these elite women's schools, including the so-called "Seven Sisters," trained their graduates for careers as educators, and a fair number of those graduates joined the faculties of these single-sex institutions, remaining there for life.

Women's colleges were often criticized by male educators for promoting an ethos detrimental to the health and well-being of women—that is, one of intellectual stimulation—but they nevertheless remained steadfast in their educational mission, and their students came away with far more than anyone bargained for: identity, purpose, enormous confidence, and a sense of community. Even so, the overwhelming majority of female college graduates did not go on to careers in the professions. Most returned to their homes, and the majority of them eventually married. Critics were most concerned at the low marriage rate for female college graduates. In the 1890s, 90 percent of the female population married. But a lower percentage of college graduates married, and the marriage rate for Seven Sisters graduates was even lower.

College-educated women were still an exception in the general population. Unlike male college graduates, who could immediately enter professions or careers where their education proved to be a valuable asset, women had no such ready avenue to employment. Nor was it easy for women graduates to put aside their intellectual pursuits in favor of a traditional marriage once they left college. So the gap between the marriage rates of college-educated and non-college-educated females remained wide in the early years of female education and would not begin to close until more women attended colleges and female graduates became less of an exception.

Women still had difficulty in entering so-called "male" professions. With few notable exceptions, including **Antoinette Brown Blackwell, Olympia Brown, Anna Howard Shaw**, and the formidable Mary Baker Eddy, the ministry was still closed to women. The only organized religious body to routinely accept women preachers and ministers was that of the Quakers, but they were a minor religion in terms of numbers. The law was also notoriously difficult for women to penetrate. Those women who did enter the profession usually prepared by studying with a relative, since law schools did not accept women students until the 1890s—and even then only a handful did so. If a woman did manage to get licensed to practice law, she was usually prohibited from appearing in court on behalf of a client. Although **Belva Lockwood** persuaded Congress to pass legislation allowing women lawyers to argue before the U.S. Supreme Court in 1879, most state courts refused to allow women to appear before the bar until well into the twentieth century.

The medical profession proved more accessible for women. Beginning with **Elizabeth Blackwell**'s acceptance into medical school in 1853, the number of women doctors began to grow. Institutions such as the **Philadelphia Women's Medical College** and Blackwell's New York Infirmary for Women, although both were short-lived, proved a useful avenue for women aspiring to become doctors. Ironically, the success of both women's medical schools and women's hospitals also ensured their demise. As soon as these institutions gained a solid foothold, they were taken over and incorporated into existing hospitals and medical schools.

Unlike women lawyers, who had trouble in establishing their own practices, women doctors, especially those who specialized in services for women and children, found it much easier to establish a practice. The medical profession had its limits regarding the number of women physicians it would accommodate. By the first decade of the twentieth century, the percentage of women physicians reached a peak of 6 percent, a figure that declined for several decades thereafter.

Women in nonmedical science fields were in much shorter supply. Until colleges and universities allowed women students to study sciences, women with a desire or a talent for pursuing science were either self-taught or learned from a relative or friend. **Maria Mitchell**, the first woman inducted into the

American Academy of Arts and Sciences (AAAS), studied under her father, an astronomer, and in 1848 discovered the comet that bears her name and won her acceptance into the AAAS. When Vassar College opened in 1865, Mitchell was invited to become a member of its first faculty and was able to encourage women's pursuit of studies in math and sciences. Many of her students went on to science careers in academe.

Many more women went into professions considered "women's work," including teaching, library work, nursing, and, toward the end of the nineteenth century, social work. By the late nineteenth century teaching had become considered women's work, particularly on the grammar and secondary school levels. Increasingly, as more women graduated from college, they also pursued academic careers, often returning to their alma mater as faculty members. Teaching on all levels was becoming more professional, however, increasingly requiring proper credentials.

Both the medical establishment's and the public's attitudes toward nursing as a profession were ambivalent at best throughout the century. Equated on the one hand with domestics, nurses nevertheless needed professional training in order to get employment. Hospitals exemplified the general attitude toward nursing, routinely hiring student nurses to work for low wages but refusing to hire graduate nurses. Graduate nurses had to compete with domestic workers for home nursing jobs. The combination of poor pay and the association of nursing with domestic work precluded the possibility of nursing ever becoming a male occupation.

Library work was also poorly paid and deemed "appropriate" for women. Libraries, like public schools, had sprung up in communities throughout the country, supported mostly by taxes. Closely aligned with academics and teaching, libraries, as repositories of the nation's culture among other things, fell naturally into women's sphere.

The one truly new professional opportunity that developed in the nineteenth century appeared with the growth of social work as a profession. Social work grew generally out of the settlement house movement and particularly out of the establishment of **Jane Addams's Hull House**.

HULL HOUSE

When Jane Addams graduated from Rockford Seminary in 1882, she entered into a society not yet ready to usefully absorb female college graduates. The death of her father, with whom she had had a close relationship, several months after her graduation left her feeling further alienated from the traditional expectations of marriage and domestic life. Addams was seeking something, as yet unknown, that would give her life meaning and direction. A chance visit to London's Toynbee Hall opened a door that transformed both Addams and American social reform. For Addams, Toynbee Hall was something of an epiphany, crystallizing in her mind the sense of responsibility she believed went hand-in-hand with her privileged life. She and her college roommate and traveling companion, **Ellen Gates Starr**, returned to Chicago and founded a settlement house on that city's West Side in 1889.

While Hull House was not the first settlement house in America, it was the one that became the model for all those that followed. Addams and Starr had two goals: to provide a place where poor people could find the assistance they needed to cope with a whole range of problems from economic to personal, and to provide a place for immigrants to receive help in assimilating into American life and culture.

Hull House quickly became a haven for Chicago's neediest and often most desperate residents, offering them assistance and programs that addressed their immediate concerns, as well as providing them with cultural enrichment. Natives and immigrants alike could avail themselves of medical services, child care, legal aid, day nurseries, English classes, sewing classes, vocational instruction, citizenship classes, a variety of clubs and activities for children and adults, and meeting places for community groups including labor unions. Hull House offered lodging for single working women, and it sponsored plays, musicals, concerts, and lectures. Immigrants learned what they needed to obtain jobs, to become citizens, and to attend city schools where English was the only language. Hull House was the safety net that cities like Chicago lacked but sorely needed. By the 1890s an average of 2,000 Chicagoans attended one or more Hull House functions and services every week. By any measure, Hull House met and exceeded the goals of its founders. If it had achieved nothing else, it still would have been counted among the successes of nineteenth-century America.

But Hull House was also the genesis of a new profession—social work—that attracted some of the brightest and most innovative minds of the time. Hull House became a leader in pressing for social legislation to institutionalize some of the projects Addams and others had started on an experimental basis. The list of women and men who lived and worked at Hull House at various times reads like an index of Progressive era leaders, and includes: Edith Abbott, dean of the University of Chicago's School of Social Work, who helped to professionalize social work and who established the first national association of schools of social work; Grace Abbott, an advocate for women and children who succeeded Lathrop as director of the Children's Bureau; Sophonisba Breckinridge, the first woman in the world to earn a Ph.D. in political science and whose students became the innovators of the New Deal; historian Charles Beard; philosopher and educator John Dewey; Alice Hamilton, who conducted studies of lead poisoning in the modern factory system and became the first female faculty member at Harvard's Medical School, in addition to being the leading expert on medical toxicology; Florence Kelley, founder of the Consumers League; and Julia Lathrop, the first director of the United States Children's Bureau.

These activists and others worked for reforms in child labor, sanitation, housing, and work conditions and were instrumental in securing legislation mandating factory inspections, a juvenile court system, required schooling for children, recognition of labor unions, and protection for immigrants against exploitation. Legislatures across the country adopted statutes protecting their citizens and changing expectations for social responsibility. Other activists followed the Hull House example, including Lillian Wald, who founded the Henry Street Settlement on New York City's Lower East Side. By century's end, social work was a full-fledged profession, dominated by women who came out of the nation's colleges and universities seeking to establish meaningful public lives. Social work professionals in turn helped to fuel a movement—the Progressive Movement—that ushered in a generation of change that affected how cities were organized, how services were delivered to residents, how politics was conducted, and how people lived and worked.

CHAPTER EIGHT

Sexuality, Reproduction, and Gender Roles

The lives of nineteenth-century women were transformed by great shifts in population growth, by the lengthening of life spans, and by changes in marital rates, childbirth rates, and other important demographic factors.

The average age of marriage went up and the average number of children went down during the century. Health care improved, as did women's ability to control factors that influenced this personal side of their lives. Women sought to determine their choice in marital partners and increasingly hoped to limit their fertility. During the antebellum era, state laws responded to these efforts by criminalizing abortion in the 1840s, while women's rights activists launched campaigns in the middle of the century to promote "voluntary motherhood."

With the death of 600,000 men during the American Civil War, heterosexual marriage was unavailable to many women. Some, especially professional women, cultivated female friendships that, in some cases, replaced more conventional marriages. Poor and immigrant women were often forced into prostitution, which grew exponentially from the 1860s onward. Social reformers campaigned to clean up vice in the cities.

Changes in attitude toward female sexuality and women's choices led to new reproductive strategies, new attitudes toward marriage and divorce, and a greater recognition of women's crucial contributions to the family and the larger society over the course of the nineteenth century.

SEXUAL PURITY

In colonial America, it was acknowledged that women's sex drive was equal to men's, or perhaps even greater. Pre-Revolutionary church records, court documents, folktales, and other evidence suggest lust and adultery were not unknown to American women. Pregnant brides were quite common in the eighteenth century. But by the early nineteenth century, ideals about refined and purified femininity were sweeping the country. One southern husband testified: "The only security a husband has is found in the purity of his wife's character before her marriage."[1]

In 1808 an American author advised young men to test the virtue of a prospective bride by making sexual advances; if she failed to register "abhorrence," he should be warned that she was not a suitable mate. Women who failed to repress or disguise sexual urges were subjected to severe reprisals within American society by the opening decades of the century. Indeed, within a quarter century, "passionlessness" was a coveted ideal for proper young ladies.

This deification of Victorian ideals was supposedly about enhancing women's status, but it also conformed to male prerogatives about women's sexuality. Historians have suggested that many antebellum middle-class white women's and—later in the century—most African American women's embrace of the ideals of sexual purity was a means to an end—that females would struggle to shape male dictates to their own ends. This struggle to project images of piety, chastity, and purity was not natural to women; rather, it reflected a social ideal imposed on American women by moral arbiters.

Changing views about sexuality shifted the blame for moral transgression even more heavily onto American women's undeserving shoulders. As society began to tax women more heavily for any perceived moral failings, women attempted to seize the initiative and increasingly struggled to gain control over their bodies. Following the American Revolution, many women insisted that marriage should no longer be a mere transaction between two families but, rather, a mutual decision made by two individuals—that single women rather than their families should be able to agree to a union. With this campaign to create "companionate marriages," American women struck a blow against wives' status as merely the property of their husbands.

At the same time as women advocated for a more egalitarian role in the choice of a marital partner, some struggled for more of a voice within the marriage, including attempts to regulate sex and pregnancy. This was a revolutionary development for American women, one that had an effect on women of all classes and all races by the end of the century.

The birth rate at the turn of the nineteenth century was an average of seven children per white female. By 1900 this had dropped to four, nearly cut in half, even with only limited access to and means of contraception. Although African American women had a higher birth rate than white women (but not a higher number of surviving children) at the beginning of the century, they too had declining birth rates by century's end. Foreign-born Americans usually had a birth rate slightly above that of native-born whites, but immigrants' daughters usually shaped their childbearing patterns within a generation to conform to American norms.

After the Civil War sexual purity crusaders launched an attack on the age of consent for marriage in most states, which remained shockingly low until closer to the twentieth century. As late as 1880 Maine had an age of consent of ten for females, and in Arkansas it was twelve. Many states raised the age of consent to eighteen, and in 1910 reformers pushed through the Mann Act, which prohibited the transportation of girls across interstate lines for immoral purposes. This law was aimed at both seduction and prostitution.

DRESS REFORM

Dress reform, regardless of the health rationale of its advocates, was one of the most ridiculed movements in the first half of the nineteenth century. Temperance activist Amelia Bloomer championed dress reform in her journal, *The Lily*, as early as 1849. Because of her suggestion that women abandon wearing skirts for the more practical pantaloons—at first called "Turkish trousers"—this costume was nicknamed "bloomers." Their namesake was roundly lambasted. Cartoons and editorials, caricatures and critics fixated on the topic. An earlier generation of political writers employed biting humor to attack women who entered the public arena, deriding them as she-devils promoting a "petticoat government." The advocates of bloomers found that their suggestions raised even more ire. The scathing undertone of all this rhetoric was, "How dare women try to wear the pants in society?" Clothing was intended to reflect status and propriety, but above all, clothes were intended to conceal and reveal—they would conceal sex and reveal gender. From the earliest colonial days cross-dressing was a transgression that received swift and severe response. Dress reform was considered an outlandish attack, a thinly veiled threat to the entire network of gender maintenance.

Feminists tried to undermine women's "sexualization" by adapting fashions to suit changing times and values. **Elizabeth Cady Stanton** responded with alacrity when she saw her cousin, **Amelia Bloomer**, wearing bloomers for the first time; Stanton later recalled that "to see my cousin, with lamp in one hand and a baby in the other, walk upstairs with ease and grace while, with flowing robes, I pulled myself up with difficulty, lamp and baby out of the question" was enough to alter her own manner of dress.[2]

Women's rights advocates in the antebellum era attacked the tight lacing and whalebone corsets that kept women imprisoned, as well as their billowing skirts and bustles. This campaign would last throughout the century and only become successful at the beginning of the twentieth century, when medical experts would allow that fresh air and exercise might eliminate women's frailty. At the end of the nineteenth century swimming, cycling, croquet, archery, and other fitness trends came into vogue for women, with greater public approval.

Women's rights' advocates did not want their campaigns derailed when rabid critics suggested women were advocating "loose" attire to promote "loose" womanhood. Even though women preached dress reform as a "health" issue, men's attacks cast the debate as a moral one—and drove the reform under-ground.

VOLUNTARY MOTHERHOOD

Stanton, although a strong advocate of dress reform, concentrated her energies on other pressing campaigns for the rights of women, most notably suffrage. She was also a forerunner, a member of her generation of nineteenth-century women who was willing to publicly advocate "voluntary motherhood." This program of educational, moral, and health reform was an important outgrowth of women's concerns about the quality of their lives in the private realm, even as feminists like Stanton campaigned for the vote in the public realm.

Evidence abounds that from the beginning of the nation's history women tried to regulate pregnancies: tansy, cottonrool, penny royal, black or blue cohosh—all abortifacients (materials ingested in order to terminate a preg-nancy)—appeared in recipe books. These botanical remedies were far from foolproof. By the 1840s advertisements in urban magazines and papers offered "medicines for ladies" through the mail, evidence that literate, middle-class women did have access to and interest in family limitation. This trend of advertising abortifacients offered safe, cheap means of disposing of unwanted pregnancies. Women might seek remedy via mail order. These kinds of cures were remedial methods of dealing with unwanted pregnancy.

Beginning with midwives in the colonial era, American women passed down information on how to *prevent* pregnancies. Douches, spermicides, vaginal sponges, and other means were employed to prevent conception. By the 1850s rubber condoms were advertised and sold in eastern cities. The diaphragm had been invented but was not widely distributed until the early twentieth century. Edward B. Foote's book, *Medical Common Sense* (1864), referred to a "womb veil," demonstrating that cervical caps were medically prescribed as well.

The problems associated with unwanted conceptions drove some Ameri-cans into utopian experiments advocating alternate sexual practices, such as the community known as Modern Times, founded in New York City in the 1840s, and the Oneida community in upstate New York, founded by John Humphrey Noyes in 1847. His followers did not advocate celibacy, like the fol-lowers of Mother Ann Lee, the Shakers, who established communities of men and women, practicing abstinence (unless "angel visits" produced children) who were scattered throughout New England.

Oneida residents followed the plans outlined by Noyes (whose own wife had given birth to five children—four stillborn—in six years) in his "Male

Continence and Complex Marriage": "We are opposed to random procreation which is unavoidable in the marriage system . . . women shall bear children only when they choose."[3] Men and women at Oneida were encouraged to practice *coitus reservatus* or male withdrawal. Noyes also attacked monogamy, and discouraged pair bonding. By 1879 the advanced philosophy and unconventional behavior of the members of Oneida forced the community to disband, following outside attacks. Many such groups were branded as advocates of "free love" and became popular targets of moralists and clerics.

Some antebellum purity crusaders targeted seduction and prostitution as one of their several campaigns. An offshoot of this campaign was the church and state's desire to reduce illegitimacy. Before the Civil War the only women to reproduce in large numbers without the legal status of marriage were slaves, although apparently most slave mothers were involved in monogamous relations with the fathers of their children. Evidence from the slave community indicates that prohibitions in that community against premarital sexual relations may have produced as strong a barrier to pregnancy before establishing a household as the preoccupation with premarital virginity for brides among slaveowners.

White American females in both the North and the South had very low rates of illegitimate birth in the first half of the nineteenth century. After the Civil War, poor white working-class women began to have higher illegitimacy rates. Society responded with a series of solutions, most notably the Crittenden Homes for unwed mothers in 1882. The first Salvation Army Home was established in 1887, and rescue homes appeared in urban communities throughout the country.

Such a stigma was attached to these mothers of illegitimate children that the poor, unmarried women who gave birth in "lying-in" or charity hospitals were turned away—denied the chance to give birth in a public almshouse if they had previously given birth to an illegitimate child.

Some urban reformers conflated the issues of purity and voluntary motherhood, joining together to campaign against "sexual license." Clearly, women's crusade for "voluntary motherhood" in the nineteenth century and "planned parenthood" in the twentieth century was hardly a call for sexual freedom. Rather, these programs were aimed at offering women, primarily mothers, more control over their lives.

The attacks upon voluntary motherhood after the Civil War were so vicious that many women resigned themselves to advocating abstinence instead of contraception. This was to avoid the taint of appearing to advocate "free love." A post–Civil War countermovement to the notion of voluntary motherhood was powerful and effective. Statesmen opposed "**birth control**," arguing it would weaken the country if white native-born women reduced their childbearing while African Americans and immigrant women reproduced in large numbers. Traditional church views increasingly condemned any attempts to interfere with procreation. Males believed that a crusade to limit family size would allow women more time to push against the boundaries of the domestic sphere and to find new outlets for their energies.

In 1868 contraception was banned in New York, and other states soon followed suit. In order to enforce this prohibition against free access to information and devices, in 1872 the New York Young Men's Christian Association created a special program, hiring Anthony Comstock, an investigator, "to prosecute, in all legal forms, the traffic in bad books, prints and instruments." Comstock was relentless in his pursuit, and shortly thereafter, in March 1873, the U.S. Congress passed a law providing for "the suppression of trade in and circulation of obscene literature and articles for immoral use," which became known as the **Comstock Law**. This meant that *any* information concerning birth control was declared obscene and outlawed from circulation. Physicians and educators who gave out this information were subject to prosecution.

The law became notorious after the first arrest made under its aegis, of feminist **Victoria Woodhull**, who used her New York City newspaper, *Woodhull and Claflin's Weekly*, to attack sexual hypocrisy. Woodhull's prosecution demonstrated the powerful muscle of a national crackdown, as radicals and feminists might no longer exercise the right to a free press when it clashed with the infamous moral standards put forth by Comstock's definition of "obscenity." Woodhull lost her battle as Comstock's values gained supremacy.

THE DECLINE OF THE MIDWIFE

In the eighteenth century midwives were the most likely attendees at the bedsides of women giving birth. Delivery was a women's culture, allowing many women to prevent or exert more control over child bearing during that century. By the nineteenth century middle- and upper-class women continued to give birth at home, although increasingly attended by a physician rather than a midwife.

The rise of the medicinal arts and the professionalization of medicine caused the decline of the midwife in America. The new specialty of obstetrics and women's dependence upon male physicians displaced women from a domain that had previously been theirs. The irony of this development was that it contributed to death in childbirth, a phenomenon it was intended to reduce. In the early years of the century neither midwives nor doctors had any knowledge about germs and their transmission—Louis Pasteur did not discover the existence of streptococcal bacteria until 1880. Midwifery records indicate, however, that midwives had higher survival rates—for both mother and child—than traditional heroic (rather than homeopathic) medical practitioners. Doctors, moving from illness to illness, frequently brought with them diseases that might be passed on to vulnerable women giving birth, causing a rise in the rate of maternal death from puerperal fever.

The decline in the use of midwives in the nineteenth century was engineered by physicians. Early in the century a Massachusetts doctor wrote an anonymous pamphlet proposing that female attendants were too emotional to make the rational decisions required during childbirth and that midwives were of a lower social status than the women they assisted. By 1830 no midwives in the respectable classes still maintained their practices in Boston, due to physicians' campaigns.

CRIMINALIZATION OF ABORTION

Modern scholars have estimated that one in four pregnancies in nineteenth-century America ended in **abortion**. And medical records indicate that there was one abortion for every thirty live births in antebellum America. The first state to criminalize abortion was Connecticut, which passed a state law in 1821 and was soon followed by most other northern states.

The rise in the number of physicians caused a medical revolution over the issue. Doctors argued they alone wanted to regulate this operation to protect women from dangerous substances and practices. They also wanted to remove abortion from the realm of women's control and place it at the discretion of licensed physicians. By the founding of the American Medical Association (AMA) in 1847, the criminalization of abortion was well underway. A leader in the AMA, Dr. Horatio Storer, campaigned for antiabortion statutes in every state.

Rather than simply "protecting women" from dangerous medical practices, antiabortion campaigns took on a moral tone. Increasingly, the evils of abortion were attacked by doctors, lawyers, and legislators working together. Abortion was now viewed as an "obscenity" within both the American courtroom and the larger culture. By the middle of the century contraception and even notions of female sexuality came under attack.

Women frequently terminated their pregnancies prior to what was called "quickening," when the fetus began to move in the womb in the third or fourth month. Indeed, the Catholic church earlier in the century had no prohibition against this, as it was believed that quickening also signified the period when the soul entered the unborn child. First-term abortions were therefore fairly standard within antebellum America. Some of these terminations were done in the home. But soon women were seeking outside help. Evidence suggests that even poor women could purchase the services of an abortionist. Records indicate that some female abortionists allowed women to pay the costs of the operation on the installment plan—sometimes by only pennies a week.

In New York City in 1838 Ann Lohman began advertising her services as Madam Restell, "a female physician and professor of midwifery." Business flourished, and she was reputed to have performed hundreds of abortions a year. She was put on trial in a series of sensational cases—accused of letting her patient die while performing an abortion, accused of selling a child away from its mother, and then, finally, in 1847, charged with criminal abortion. She served a year in prison on this final charge but returned to her booming business. Although medical and state authorities wanted to outlaw abortion, women were desperate to end unwanted pregnancies and sought abortions in larger and larger numbers as the century progressed, despite increasing prohibitions (the rise in illegitimate births after the Civil War might be attributed to the increasing difficulty poor women faced trying to obtain an abortion).

Medical experts continued to preach the abomination of abortion. In 1873 the *American Journal of Medical Science* reported a woman's tragedy: "She procured a piece of steel wire as long and as large as an ordinary knitting needle. . . . She had laid herself upon the bed and passing the wire up the vagina, pushed it, as she thought, very gently into the uterine canal. Suddenly it slipped and disappeared." The woman bled to death. This was not an uncommon story and was indeed a horror the medical profession wanted to avoid. Doctors were confronted with hundreds of botched abortion jobs a year, and they lobbied, not to make contraception more safe and available but to criminalize backstreet practitioners.

PROSTITUTION

The American Civil War brought about the dislocation of thousands of wives and mothers, and wiped out a generation of young men. It also stimulated the greatest boom in prostitution the country had ever witnessed. On the eve of the Civil War a New York City survey of 2,000 prostitutes found that one quarter of the women involved in the urban sex trade were married, the victims of abandonment and/or abuse. More than half listed their occupation as servant and another 25 percent listed theirs as seamstress. More than 60 percent of these women were **immigrants**. Three out of four were under 25. Half of the women were mothers, and half of the mothers bore their children out of wedlock. Fifty percent of the prostitutes surveyed were infected with venereal disease.

The advent of the war only increased the number of women involved in prostitution. Abandoned wives and destitute single mothers were often driven into the role of camp followers and once "ruined" might drift into urban centers where prostitution became a big business in the 1860s.

To take the most dramatic example, in New York before the Civil War, roughly 6,000 prostitutes worked the city streets (one per 64 adult males). By 1870 this number increased to 10,000. And 20 years later the total quadrupled to 40,000. The proportion of young, immigrant women funneled into a voracious sex trade (some right off the boats) continued to rise—peaking in the early decades of the twentieth century with campaigns to outlaw the white slave trade, the kidnapping of women for prostitution.

Throughout the nineteenth century women ventured onto the frontier. Most went as wives and mothers accompanying menfolk. But single women might also migrate westward: some as teachers, others as missionaries, and a sizable proportion as prostitutes. Frontier women who earned a living in the sex trade could, and some did, parlay their earnings into an escape from prostitution. A woman who began as a girl working in a saloon, splitting her fees with an owner and paying a fee to the bartender, might be able to marry or buy her way into the ranks of respectability within a boomtown in a decade or less.

Despite random success stories, however, the frontier sex trade, in settlements along the transcontinental railroad route, for example, could be extremely rough. Women sold themselves by the hour or by the trick, taking customers to "cribs" (crude shelter, providing bedrooms only) set up along unpaved streets. This frontier tradition was adapted in urban settings. Immigrant women were still peddling themselves to workers on their lunch hour in the slums of Chicago, using flimsy cribs crammed into alleys near factories and slaughterhouses, well into the twentieth century.

Reformers drew attention to the inequities such a trade fostered and emphasized. The plight of working-class women was highlighted by the rise in prostitution. Popular novels exploited this theme, such as Stephen Crane's *Maggie: A Girl of the Streets* (1893) and Theodore Dreiser's *Sister Carrie* (1900). Most Americans cherished the notion that prostitutes were ruined women, who could never move into respectable society but died in brothels of syphilis or old age. In fact, many women could, and did, move from an illicit sexual subculture into roles as wives and mothers, and even pillars of the community.

SEXUAL MORES

While the law and social convention might have been moving toward creating a stereotypical Victorian woman, passionless and willing to place frilly covers on piano "legs" for propriety's sake, many American women embraced other ideals in their personal lives. While medicine and law tried to prevent them having any control over their own bodies, such women sought alternatives.

There is evidence that among some educated heterosexual women, sexual beliefs and practices diverged from those prescribed by the culture. The results of a survey of forty-five married women by a female physician, Dr. Cleila Mosher, conducted between 1892 and 1920 demonstrate this divergence. Fifteen of her subjects were born before the Civil War, another third before 1870, and another third even later. Thirty-five of the women expressed a desire for sex independent of their husband's wants. Thirty-five percent of the women reported they always experienced orgasm during sex, and 40 percent responded: "Sometimes, but not always." What is striking is how straightforward women's views were in this survey, as one woman commented that sex was an appetite and, "I consider this appetite as ranking with other natural appetites and like them to be indulged legitimately and temperately."[4] Much like the push for companionate marriage at the beginning of the century, this survey suggests that by the end of the century women were increasingly seeking a more consensual sexual relationship in marriage.

However, there is also evidence that numbers of educated, middle-class women rejected traditional heterosexual relationships and sought homosocial alternatives. Female bonding was a natural outgrowth of separate spheres and the creation of a woman's culture. Increasingly, same-sex affection and romantic friendships among women flourished in the nineteenth century. Some scholars have suggested that many middle- and upper-class wives had more intimate relationships with female confidantes than they did with their own husbands. The passion of these connections is revealed in diaries, journals, and letters among nineteenth-century women.

The number of never-married women rose throughout the nineteenth century. Although in the antebellum South the proportion of white single women declined briefly at the turn of the nineteenth century, by the turn of the twentieth century, the number of southern spinsters increased, keeping pace with their northern counterparts.

Increasingly women were rejecting marriage to men as a personal choice, rather than being rejected and left for spinsterhood. Without male companionship, many women sought the company and intimacy of other women instead.

Some women developed their first intimacies with other women as school-girls. In 1897 a study published indicated that younger girls and older pupils as well as teachers and pupils often followed ritual patterns similar to those of het-erosexual courtship. Some of these relationships blossomed into love. And some of them turned into lifelong associations that excluded men.

Pairs of single women, living as a couple, were identified as "Boston mar-riages." Author **Sarah Orne Jewett** spent her life with Annie Fields, Alice James (sister of Henry James) spent many years with Katharine Loring, and actress Charlotte Cushman initiated a twenty-year liaison with sculptor Emma Stebbins. Traditional society did not frown on many of these alliances, assum-ing that these women were asexual. And because the general public also assumed there was no sexual component to the relationships, most of these women were allowed to lead their lives without public disapproval.

However, any suggestion that a female couple were sexually active attracted public outrage and condemnation. In 1892 when a young Tennessee woman, Alice Mitchell, slit the throat of her female lover, Freda Ward, the case attracted international attention. Mitchell was declared insane and locked up, and European sexologists studied her case. With the development of modern psychology and new views on female sexuality, female couples were left alone only if they were willing to condemn lesbianism and project images of "pas-sionlessness" and asexuality. The close passionate attachment of many women couples at any number of women's colleges springing up along the eastern seaboard did not generate controversy, as long as these women educators took a public stand against homosexuality, which many were forced to do, such as college president M. Carey Thomas of Bryn Mawr.

By the turn of the twentieth century women's lives had been dramatically transformed through a whole series of public campaigns: dress reform, "vol-untary motherhood," birth control, purity campaigns. All the while Ameri-can women were increasingly postponing their age of marriage, reducing their number of children, and sometimes even rejecting marriage and child-birth outright. Conversely, American society sought more control over women's bodies through the purity crusade, the criminalization of abortion, the Comstock Law, and other measures designed to keep women "morally pure" and cosseted in the domestic sphere. Although sexuality was allegedly a personal matter and confined to the private domain, women increasingly sought more open exchanges of ideas and information. Within this crucial arena, feminists dragged the issue out into the open and battled for improved female status, fighting for increasing control over their own bodies and their own destinies.

CHAPTER NINE

Suffrage and Reform Politics

Amid the demographic, urban, and industrial changes that marked the second half of the century, political changes were also felt. The Civil War itself as well as the Reconstruction governments that determined southern development until the withdrawal of federal troops from the South in 1877 caused a sea change in the status of African Americans as well as in white attitudes toward race relations.

In the South as well as much of the North, segregation became the order of the day, culturally imposed by traditional attitudes and the rise of terrorist organizations such as the Ku Klux Klan and legally upheld by the courts. New efforts to promote labor organizations resulted in a modern labor movement with the founding of new national and craft unions primarily in the cities and populist and grange movements in rural America.

This chapter highlights new and important trends in nineteenth-century women's activism, including campaigns against segregation on the part of African American women, as well as labor solidarity not only among working-class women but among reformers as well. The chapter also examines the reunified women's rights movement and the increasing focus of this group on securing women's right to vote.

FROM ABOLITION TO SUFFRAGE

Lucretia Coffin Mott was denied her seat as a designated representative to the World Anti-Slavery Convention in London in 1840. Mott had been involved in the abolitionist movement for several years by then. Befriended by William Lloyd Garrison in 1831, shortly after he founded the **New England Anti-Slavery Society**, Mott was quickly drawn to the cause and devoted years of her life to abolishing the system of slavery. Because of the strong beliefs held by most male abolitionists, however, even Garrison, who was sympathetic to women's participation, did not advocate allowing women to join the male abolitionist societies. Mott and other women abolitionists such as **Lydia Maria Child** and the **Grimké sisters** therefore began forming auxiliary antislavery societies for women in the 1820s. They did so in order to allay any objections that might be raised by those who did not condone the participation of women in public events. They did not want to divert attention away from abolitionism for any reason. In 1833 Mott organized the **Philadelphia Female Antislavery Society**. And as the abolitionist movement gathered speed, more and more women took up the cause.

Very soon after Mott organized the Philadelphia Female Anti-Slavery Society (PFASS), the **American Antislavery Society** (AASS) dropped its prohibition against women members, primarily because women were willing to and did perform most of the tedious work of gathering petitions and other similar tasks. Women now became a crucial element in the movement. Mott was active in both the national and Pennsylvania branches of the AASS, serving as an executive committee member. She also remained very involved in the PFASS and maintained her close ties with other female antislavery societies. Mott was instrumental in organizing the Anti-Slavery Convention of American Women to be held in Philadelphia in 1838.

THE WORLD ANTI-SLAVERY CONFERENCE, 1840

When the call went out in 1836 for all "friends of abolition" to convene in London at a world conference, Mott was included as a member of the American delegation. The controversy over whether women should be participants erupted even before delegates reached London, with critics asserting that the convention would be held up to ridicule if women participated. The issue stirred up deep divisions within the AASS. Garrison voiced his support of Mott, asking, "In what assembly, however select or august, is that almost peerless woman, Lucretia Mott, not qualified to take an equal part?"[1] But others, including reformer James Birney, disagreed strenuously and broke away to form the American and Foreign Antislavery Society, largely because he and most of the other male abolitionists though it an "insane innovation" to allow women to speak and serve as officers.[2]

Most organizations agreed with Birney, and the World Convention voted to exclude women delegates from being seated. The best that Garrison and other similar supporters could do was to secure seats for women delegates to watch the proceedings; they could not participate. Those voting to exclude women apparently saw no contradiction in organizing to secure freedom for slaves while at the same time denying women their rights. But the message was not lost on Lucretia Mott, nor was it lost on twenty-five-year-old **Elizabeth Cady Stanton**, who attended the convention with her delegate husband.

The World Anti-Slavery Conference turned out to be extremely important for American women—albeit unwittingly—for two reasons. It forced women to confront their own precarious place in society, and it brought together two of the Founding Mothers of the American women's rights movement. The more opportunity that Mott and Stanton had to exchange ideas over the course of the convention, the more they realized how completely in agreement they were about women's rights. Both were struck by the observation that a meeting advertised as a "world" convention would, as its first order of business, enact a ruling excluding half of the world's population. Both, as a consequence, experienced what they would thereafter refer to an a critical transformation in their thinking. Mott and Stanton concluded that they had an obligation to work on behalf of women's rights when they returned to America.

SENECA FALLS

For eight years, Stanton and Mott went their separate ways. Mott continued her work as an abolitionist, never forgetting what had happened in London but not yet sure how to proceed. Stanton returned to Massachusetts with her husband and bore seven children. The Stantons lived briefly in Boston, where Elizabeth met some of the more liberal thinkers of the day, including Garrison, John Greenleaf Whittier, Maria Weston Chapman, **Lydia Maria Child**, **Abby Kelley Foster**, and Frederick Douglass. When the Stantons moved to **Seneca Falls**, New York, in 1847, Stanton became a lobbyist on behalf of a Married Woman's Property Act then under consideration. At about the same time, she began referring to herself as Elizabeth Cady Stanton rather than as Mrs. Henry Stanton.

An invitation from a mutual friend in nearby Waterloo, New York, in the summer of 1848 reunited Stanton and Lucretia Mott. The five women in attendance—Mott, Stanton, Mary McClintock, Jane Hunt, and Martha Wright—discussed at length the issue of women's place in society. Before the day ended, they wrote out an advertisement for the *Seneca County Courier*, inviting all interested women to attend a meeting on July 19th and 20th at the Wesleyan Methodist Chapel in Seneca Falls.

All five women were experienced volunteers in abolition, temperance, and other similar voluntary associations, and they drew on that experience as they began organizing the women's rights convention. The **Declaration of Sentiments and Resolutions**, modeled on the Declaration of Independence, became the manifesto of the meeting. It included a list of eighteen grievances of women to parallel the colonists' original eighteen grievances against British rule. Beginning, "We hold these truths to be self-evident: that all men and women are created equal," the Declaration of Sentiments demanded that women have equal education, equal access to trades and professions, equality in marriage, the right to make contracts, to own property, to sue and be sued, to testify in court, to speak in public, to retain guardianship over their children, and to vote. The only grievance that elicited any disagreement among the organizers was that pertaining to the vote. Mott opposed its inclusion because she believed it was too radical for people to accept. In the end, however, she acquiesced to Stanton's arguments on behalf of the franchise. Stanton gave her first public address at the convention. She was terrified at the prospect, but it was a stunning preview of the years ahead, during which she would earn her reputation as an inspiring public speaker with an unparalleled intellect.

For two days 300 people, including about 40 men, crowded into the Wesleyan chapel, discussing, debating, and elaborating on the list of grievances. Again, **woman suffrage** was the most controversial. Many of the participants argued that efforts to secure the vote would render all the grievances frivolous in the eyes of critics. But Stanton and Frederick Douglass argued eloquently for the measure. Douglass noted that "All that distinguishes man as an intelligent and accountable being, is equally true of woman, and if that government only is just which governs by the free consent of the governed, there can be no reason in the world for denying to woman the exercise of the elective franchise." In the end, 68 women and 32 men signed the Declaration of Sentiments. All of the grievances, except for the lack of the right to vote, were passed unanimously. The suffrage grievance passed with a small majority, and the Declaration of Sentiments became the first formal statement of the women's rights movement.

Predictably, news of the convention and of the declaration was met in the press by a storm of criticism and ridicule. Even before the woman suffrage proposal was ratified at the convention, the press was expressing contempt for the entire meeting. Most editorials opposed the women, and very few did so cordially. A large part of the criticism was expressed as outrage that women would take so hallowed a document as the Declaration of Independence and dishonor it so flagrantly. Horace Greeley's *New York Tribune* was one of a mere handful of newspapers to offer support. But the vast majority characterized the convention and its attendees as malcontents, self-styled Amazons, silly, ludicrous, and worse. Moreover, criticism was not restricted to the newspapers.

Ministers throughout the country took to their pulpits to assure their congregations that the actions of the women in Seneca Falls were not just unseemly, they would diminish the nation's moral values. So severe was the reaction that many of the original 100 signers of the declaration withdrew their support. Nevertheless, within two years, women's rights conventions had been held or were planned in a number of states including Massachusetts, Pennsylvania, Indiana, and Ohio. In the rural community of Seneca Falls, New York, a women's rights movement had been born in the summer of 1848.

CAMPAIGNING FOR WOMEN'S RIGHTS

In 1851 **Susan B. Anthony** met Stanton. Until this meeting, Anthony had not thought a great deal about women's rights and had never considered changing her life for that particular cause. But Stanton so impressed her with the importance of woman suffrage that Anthony very quickly became a dedicated advocate and remained so for the rest of her life. She and Stanton created a ripple that became a stream, a river, and, finally, a relentless tide moving toward one increasingly singular focus that became the symbol of the women's movement: universal woman suffrage.

Stanton provided the intellectual ammunition for the growing movement, and Anthony carried the message from community to community, for anyone willing to listen. They consciously shed some of the unwanted baggage linked with other reforms. For one thing, they rejected the religiosity that often pervaded reform movements. Many female abolitionists had grown wary of the selective use of scripture by organized clergy as a way to justify inaction on the slavery issue—a tactic that the clergy also used to justify woman's inferior status. Stanton was convinced that the combination of the Bible and organized religion created the greatest stumbling blocks in the way of women's emancipation. And even Lucretia Mott, usually so circumspect in her public utterances, bluntly told a women's rights audience in 1854 that she believed the pulpit had been prostituted by some members of the clergy.

For another thing, the women's movement—at least in its early years—was less interested in formal organization than it was in spontaneous activities. Informal gatherings, impromptu speeches, and conventions characterized the young movement. Even so, it spread quickly throughout the Northeast, and women's rights organizations were founded as far west as Wisconsin. In 1850 the first national women's rights convention was held in Massachusetts, and for the next ten years such annual conventions dominated the movement.

Both the abolition and the women's rights movements found their respective leaders in the same pool of women activists; although this made possible some cross-support that was useful for both, it also highlighted some fundamental issues that began to emerge more clearly and that in some ways retarded the progress of the women's movement. For one thing, women were not bending their efforts toward a single goal. For another, women who did not necessarily agree with the idea of emancipation were not likely to embrace women's rights if they suspected that achieving the latter would promote the former. Similarly, abolitionists who believed that supporting women's rights might interfere with emancipation were equally reluctant to cross the line.

The stresses inherent in the mistaken assumption that one set of goals was entirely in agreement with and compatible with another set of goals was nowhere more clearly exposed than in the experience of former slave and women's rights activist **Sojourner Truth.**

SOJOURNER TRUTH

Sojourner Truth spent her early life as a slave in the Hudson Valley, in New York State. By her mid-forties, she began traveling from community to community as a public speaker. She enlisted in the abolitionist movement and spoke frequently about it. But Truth always insisted that unless the status of women was elevated, abolition would mean little to black women since they would be exchanging one set of masters for another. It was not a message that abolitionists wanted to embrace. Her words could be interpreted as a challenge to prioritize women's rights and abolition or, at the very least, to place both on an equal plane—a circumstance that many abolitionists thought would inevitably make it more difficult to secure an end to slavery. Truth's efforts to address a women's rights convention in 1851 further revealed the difficulty in reconciling the causes of abolition and women's rights, for her request to speak was initially met with resistance. She was not one of the well-dressed middle-class women who made up the vast majority of women's rights advocates. And yet, as she so eloquently pointed out, "Aren't I a woman?"[3]

Both abolitionists and women's rights activists were taken aback by Truth's challenge. After the **Civil War** African American women did support suffrage, but the woman suffrage organizations were never integrated. Instead, African American women organized their own support, forming separate societies.

Advocates of women's rights in the early years of the movement exhibited a great deal of ambivalence. Society and family reacted very differently to women's rights activists than they did to abolitionists. Stanton's husband, for example, supported his wife's abolitionist convictions but disapproved of her efforts on behalf of women's rights. Women's rights still posed more of a threat than an improvement to most women. The Seneca Falls convention made it clear that many women were willing to risk the disapproval of family and society. The reaction to the convention demonstrated that the risk was a real one. So while women's rights activists could be bold on the one hand, they also tended to be mindful of the sensibilities of the majority who viewed the situation of women as secondary to that of slaves. Thus, when the Civil War erupted it was no surprise that women's rights groups would choose to suspend their activities until such time as the slaves were liberated.

CIVIL WAR

The majority of women involved in the war effort were engaged in more traditional volunteer activities, including rolling bandages and knitting garments for the troops. Stanton, who was then living in New York City, wanted to take a more active role. She and Anthony issued a call for women to meet on May 14, 1863, to join a new organization, the National Women's Loyal League. With several hundred women responding to the call, the league adopted a resolution to collect signatures in support of the immediate emancipation of all slaves. The petition would be presented to Congress, urging members to vote accordingly. A second resolution offered moral support to the government for as long as it took to achieve its wartime goals. Finally, the league adopted a resolution committing members to secure a million signatures in support of passage of the Thirteenth Amendment, the abolition of slavery. Although the league lasted for only a little more than one year, until the war ended, it garnered more than 5,000 members. They were able to collect nearly half a million signatures, most of which came from women with no formal ties to the suffrage movement.

THE GRANGE

While most suffrage activists lived in urban communities or in small towns, the majority of women still lived in rural America and remained fairly isolated. Farm families remained intellectually, spiritually, and materially impoverished because of their isolation. On the Great Plains, especially, neighbors could be separated by miles, and towns were frequently dozens of miles away. Male farmers did travel to town on occasion, usually for supplies, and used these trips as opportunities to socialize, to exchange information and news, and to discuss politics. But since farm wives had no pressing reason to leave home and children—and indeed, had to take over in their husbands' absences—they had fewer opportunities for social exchange.

The Order of the Patrons of Husbandry, more commonly called the Grange, was founded in 1867 by farmers across America, but mainly in the South and West. The intention was to create a framework within which farm men and women could organize for informational and educational purposes as well as for social events. Intended at first as a cultural and intellectual resource, the Grange did not abandon this tradition, but it also became an important avenue to demonstrate political or economic discontent among farmers, especially when conditions made it difficult for them to maintain their livelihood. With 25,000 Grange chapters and 750,000 members, the

Grange represented a substantial force in rural America. In the 1870s the organization became a prominent voice in national politics when farmers objected to monopolistic practices employed by the railroads, practices that favored merchants over grain growers.

The Grange was one of the rare political organizations in America to promote gender equality. Women's role in the organization was institutionalized because of the structure under which local chapters had to be set up. At least four women and nine men were required for a chapter to apply for national membership, and women had equal voting rights and could hold any office within the organization. In the Midwest and in New England, women generally arranged all Grange lectures, thereby becoming very influential in determining what information the Grange membership was exposed to. Grange women were responsible for winning over male support for woman suffrage in many rural communities, and the women agrarian radicals who came out of the movement included **Mary Lease**, who ran for the U.S. Senate in Kansas in 1893, and Annie Diggs, an influential journalist who lobbied on behalf of the People's Party that was established in 1892.

WOMEN AND LABOR UNIONS

In the more populated regions, including New England and the Middle Atlantic states, women had been entering the wage labor force in significant numbers, especially in the textile and shoe industries, from the opening decades of the century. In 1834 the Factory Girls Association organized to protest wage cuts and blacklists in Lowell, Massachusetts. The association organized a walkout lasting for a day, and although their demands were not met, they thereby demonstrated a willingness to strike in order to improve their work conditions. While that particular union was short-lived, unionism surfaced again in the mid-1840s with the Female Labor Reform Association (FLRA), which allied itself with the New England Workingman's Association. Among the demands of the FLRA was a ten-hour workday. But the discontent of the women workers did not carry enough clout to shake mill owners, who were already in a position to hire a work force from among the newly arrived Irish immigrants.

The union movement continued to expand in the years immediately following the Civil War, and women continued to be active participants, especially in the industries where they were the predominant labor source. The Working Women's Union, an alliance of sewing-machine operators, was founded in 1863, and in 1866 the Troy Collar Laundry Union engaged in a strike that was supported by male workers as well. While the women launderers' strike failed to produce results, female mill workers continued to organize throughout the 1860s.

A cluster of unions came into being at the same time with the encouragement of the New England Labor Reform League and the Working Women's Club of Boston, providing women workers with some means of protesting conditions they deemed unsatisfactory. And in 1869 the Typographical Union admitted women for the first time. The first national union for women, the Daughters of St. Crispin, was also organized in 1869.

Most male unionists still considered women inappropriate candidates for union membership. It took the **Knights of Labor**, organized in 1869, to give more legitimacy to women unionists. The Knights struggled to bring together men and women, immigrants and natives, and skilled and unskilled laborers under one umbrella. The moving force behind the growth of women members in the Knights was Leonora Kearney, who for ten years organized women on behalf of the union. Kearney retired in 1890, and in the absence of a replacement, the work she had begun was abandoned. Membership in the Knights began to drop at about the same time, and without support, the union could not be sustained. The demise of the Knights had particular resonance for women, since its successor, the American Federation of Labor (AFL), discouraged women and children from industrial wage earning. The AFL painted its restrictive policies as concern for the welfare of women and children, but the underlying reason was the economic competition that the presence of women and youth posed for adult male workers.

In labor, as in other areas, women were not about to step back, however, and in the wake of the Knights, numerous unions sprang up: the Ladies Federal Labor Union (1888), the Retail Clerks International (1890), the International Boot and Shoemakers (1895). The AFL could no longer ignore women workers, and in 1892 it appointed Mary Kenney as its national organizer for women. In all of the labor activity that began in earnest after the Civil War, there was almost no place for African American women or for minorities. One lone exception was the National Labor Union/Cincinnati Colored Teachers Cooperative Association, which was organized in 1870.

WOMEN AND THE CIVIL WAR AMENDMENTS

Northern women reformers had learned a valuable lesson during the Civil War. Their unequivocal support of the Union and their suspension of efforts to secure women's rights were not rewarded as they had anticipated. But with more support forthcoming from wage-earning women and farmers, woman suffrage advocates were better positioned to pursue the vote. The formation in 1866 of the American Equal Rights Association (AERA) was intended to bring together the two divergent strands of the women's movement—abolitionists and women's rights activists—that had developed before the war. The still unresolved differences over priorities continued to separate the two movements, even with AERA leadership that included Mott, Stanton, and Anthony. While the AERA believed that women abolitionists and women's rights advocates could proceed at the same pace along a dual track, several influential male abolitionists were not as sanguine. Wendell Phillips and Frederick Douglass, in particular, were adamant that the time had arrived for freedmen to seize their rights and that any attempts to promote women's rights would muddy the waters and prove detrimental to the freedmen.

The Phillips-Douglass hardline position seemed premature when abolitionists and feminists alike supported the Thirteenth Amendment, which ensured the abolition of slavery and the slave system. But disagreements and differences over priorities suddenly took on monumental proportions, widening the chasm between abolitionists and feminists to unbridgeable length once the Fourteenth Amendment, which sought to confer upon former slaves full citizenship rights including the right to vote, was enacted in 1868. For the first time in the history of the Constitution, the wording of the amendment clearly defined whose right to vote would be assured and protected by the government—adult males who had reached the age of twenty-one and older.

Anthony, who had never been in favor of suspending efforts to secure equal rights for women even during the war, seemed now to have possessed a prescience that even Stanton lacked. Introducing sex into the Constitution would create an entirely unprecedented situation that, in the view of most feminists, would make it infinitely more difficult to secure their rights. Stanton argued that the Fourteenth Amendment was not designed simply to promote equality for former slaves, because it specifically excluded women; it was instead a simple expansion of male voting rights.

The die-hard female abolitionists declared that the Fourteenth Amendment did not pose a threat to women. They agreed with Phillips and Douglass that the hour belonged to the ex-slaves, even if that meant only the former male slaves. Women, they argued, would have to exercise patience in pursuing their own rights. Even under the circumstances women's rights advocates might have been willing to accept that argument—sensitive as they were to the freedmen issues and the necessity to strike while the iron was hot—but for the ill-timed insistence on the part of Wendell Phillips that women's rights in his opinion were not even second on the list of priorities. Phillips placed woman suffrage at the end, after black voting rights, then temperance, then the eight-hour workday movement.

This declaration, along with the refusal of abolitionists in the AERA to stand in favor of the inclusion of women in the Fourteenth Amendment, set the stage for a formal split in the women's movement. In the view of the Stanton/Anthony feminists, women had set aside their concerns in order to support abolitionism and the war. Now the abolitionists were refusing to support women's rights.

RACE AND THE SOUTH

In the South white women remained elevated at the status of icons, cherished symbols of the vanquished Confederacy. A cult of chivalry was meant to celebrate "the Lost Cause." In addition, across the defeated Confederacy white women organized memorial societies and other female voluntary movements to honor their fallen heroes and to keep the values of the Confederacy at the forefront of regional patriotism. As a result, by the turn of the century the United Daughters of the Confederacy had risen to become one of the most influential women's organizations in the South.

Southern white ladies were expected to adhere to a stereotyped image of chastity and purity, while southern black women were denied any gender privilege. Woven into this were white male projections of revenge—a revenge that, in the view of white males, might take the form of the rape of white women by black men. Vigilante groups organized to keep blacks "in their place."

The most powerful of these racist organizations was the Ku Klux Klan, a terrorist group of hooded white males who engaged in violence against blacks. The punishment of choice for real or imagined crimes was lynching. In the 1880s more than 50 lynchings a year were carried out, and by 1890 that figure had grown to just under 120 per annum. More than 160 lynchings were carried out in 1892—the worst year for such heinous acts—all but 4 of them in the South. And while the perpetrators of the lynchings insisted that they were necessary in order to protect the honor of white women, critics pointed out that only a minority of the lynching victims had even been accused of rape. Moreover, in 1892, five of the murder-by-lynching victims were women.

African American women began to fight back. A child of slavery from Holly Springs, Mississippi, Ida B. Wells became especially important to the anti-lynching campaign. She attended Rust College, a local school organized by the Freedman's Aid Bureau, and became a teacher herself at the age of sixteen. Fearlessly outspoken, Wells wrote editorials critical of facilities provided for black children. The loss of her teaching job as a consequence did not deter Wells. She became co-owner of the Memphis *Free Press* and began her writing career. Her energies were focused on the lynching issue when, in 1892, close friends were lynched. With little regard for her own well-being, Wells targeted both those who participated in the lynching and those who stood by and said nothing.

When her office was vandalized in retaliation for her articles indicting the lynch mob and the mentality that allowed it to flourish, Wells moved north. She lectured and wrote about mob violence and the lynch murders of black men. Her pamphlet, *Southern Horrors*, was a widely distributed account of the extent and acceptance of lynching in the South—a crime, Wells argued, that had nothing to do with protecting the honor of white women. She claimed that justifying the brutal, racially motivated, socially accepted public executions in the name of women's honor was mere camouflage in the most literal sense.

Wells organized antilynching committees in northern cities, engaging the already established black women's clubs. Marriage did not slow Wells-Barnett (as she called herself), and in 1895 she published yet another grisly account of lynching, *A Red Record*. When race leaders met with President William McKinley in 1898 to protest the lynching of a black postmaster in South Carolina, Wells-Barnett was a prominent member of the delegation.

Like many women, black and white, Wells-Barnett did not confine herself to a single cause. She remained active in the antilynching campaign, but she was also involved in W. E. B. DuBois's Niagara Movement—a group of intellectuals who challenged white supremacists. An avid supporter of women's rights and of the right to vote, Wells-Barnett was frequently in the parade of demonstrators marching for woman suffrage.

THE WOMEN'S RIGHTS MOVEMENT SPLITS (1869)

In May 1869 Susan B. Anthony and Elizabeth Cady Stanton organized the **National Woman Suffrage Association** (NWSA). Included among the 118 original members were Lucretia Mott, Martha Wright, and Paulina Wright Davis, all of whom were former members of the AERA. The NWSA prohibited male members and emphasized as a primary goal adding a woman suffrage amendment to the Constitution. By now, Anthony espoused a fairly radical brand of feminism that included nothing less than complete equal rights for women. She was no longer reticent about her radicalism, and the NWSA, under its first president, Stanton, reflected those views. Anthony undertook a lecture tour that carried her message to women across the country, and before long NWSA branches began appearing throughout the Northeast and the Midwest.

To counteract the NWSA, a second organization was established in November 1869. The **American Woman Suffrage Association** (AWSA) was founded by **Lucy Stone**, an abolitionist who considered herself a feminist but disagreed with the radical views espoused by Anthony and Stanton. The AWSA was eager to enlist male members as well as female members and elected Henry Ward Beecher as its first president. It also declared a willingness not only to defer woman suffrage but to seek state-by-state support rather than a federal amendment. Although it claimed to represent the views of the majority of women, the AWSA represented the views of New England abolitionists. Though the NWSA was able to attract both more supporters and more money than the AWSA, its publication, *Revolution*, was less successful and shorter-lived than the AWSA's publication, *The Woman's Journal*, which attracted a large readership and became the single most influential publication of the women's movement.

By 1870, then, lines had been clearly drawn. NWSA feminists on the one hand argued that women's rights had to be situated above or at least equal to all other current issues. Their straightforward position was that as long as the female half of the population was denied their rights, all other issues had to be secondary. The moderates of the AWSA, on the other hand, continued to believe that women's rights was only a single component of a range of desired reforms that included urban reform, **temperance**, civil rights, and other problems associated with the growth of cities.

For twenty years the two rival suffrage organizations pursued their goals. Anthony and Stanton had long held that the Constitution had no clearly stated prohibition against woman suffrage, and to test this out, NWSA members in a few locations attempted to vote in the presidential election of 1872. Anthony was arrested and tried in Rochester, New York, and although she was found guilty and fined twenty-five dollars, the fine was never paid. In St. Louis, Missouri, NWSA officer Virginia Minor brought suit against the registrar of voters in that city, Reese Happersett, alleging that he had denied her attempts to register to vote and therefore her rights as a citizen. *Minor v Happersett* went all the way to the Supreme Court, which in 1875 declared that Minor's rights had not been violated, stating that the "Constitution of the United States does not confer the right of suffrage upon anyone," and declared that suffrage was not coexistent with citizenship. This ruling was a blow to all suffragists who had hoped for a quick judicial solution to their continued exclusion from the franchise; it forced suffragists to continue their campaigns on the state or federal level, as their preferences dictated.

In 1875 Anthony authored a simple, two-sentence woman suffrage amendment: "The right of citizens of the United States to vote shall not be denied or abridged by the United States or by any State on account of sex. Congress shall have the power, by appropriate legislation, to enforce the provisions of this article." The amendment was modeled after an existing amendment, in this case the Fifteenth Amendment. The Anthony Amendment, as it eventually became known, was introduced in the U.S. Senate for the first time in 1878. Stanton and Anthony had persuaded California Senator Arlen A. Sargent to introduce the legislation. Thereafter, it would be reintroduced in each succeeding Congress until its passage in 1920.

While NWSA continued to work for a federal amendment, AWSA whittled away slowly at state constitutions. Literally hundreds of state campaigns were undertaken, with enormous resources of time and money devoted to them. But the reality was that securing woman suffrage by this method was not only costly but unacceptably slow. Anthony noted at one point that if a national amendment were secured, it would—in her view—take approximately twenty years before the requisite number of states ratified the amendment. Either way, suffragists would have to go to the states, but the advantage of a federal amendment was that it would confer the franchise on all American women even if 25 percent of the states voted against ratification.

In 1883 the legislature of Washington Territory granted women the vote. Four years later that was challenged in the territory's supreme court and reversed. When Washington sought statehood, women again waged a campaign to secure voting rights, a campaign they lost.

NATIONAL AMERICAN WOMAN SUFFRAGE ASSOCIATION (1890)

As the century approached its closing decade, American women wanted to bring together the two major suffrage organizations. In 1888 Stanton and Anthony planned a fortieth-anniversary celebration of the Seneca Falls Convention. In addition to sending invitations to women throughout the country and the world, they extended invitations to members of AWSA. To their delight, Lucy Stone accepted. In 1890 the two organizations merged into the **National American Woman Suffrage Association**.

Both Stanton and Antony were suspicious of the intentions of the moderates in AWSA, and Stanton in particular was reluctant to make any detours away from pursuit of a federal amendment. But both acknowledged that their involvement in the movement was drawing to a close, and in the end they agreed to putting their faith in the younger women entering the movement, the beneficiaries of new gains in education and social reforms. Stanton served as the first president of NAWSA, but at the age of seventy-seven she relinquished the presidency to Anthony in 1892. Anthony was not happy with the new organization, but she, too, was aging rapidly. Younger NAWSA members favored a more conservative approach, insisting that the national convention be held outside Washington, D.C., its traditional location. Anthony knew that moving the convention away from the seat of political power might diminish whatever influence suffragists had over Congress. She also knew that relocating the national convention might lead to the abandonment of a federal amendment as the primary goal. In addition, Colorado voted to grant its women the franchise in 1893, thus strengthening the position of the states' rights advocates. Although Anthony remained president of the NAWSA until 1900, she lost control over the direction in which the movement headed. For the next fifteen years, the NAWSA continued to pursue state constitutional changes as its primary goal, paying only lip service to a national suffrage amendment.

In the half-century following Seneca Falls, after spending resources of time and money in hundreds of state campaigns, only nine states had granted suffrage rights to their women citizens. All of these states were in the West and the Far West. When Susan B. Anthony died in 1906, suffragists were forced to reexamine the status of the movement. Bogged down in disagreements and still divided into two camps, the movement was in the doldrums. Even after the National Woman Suffrage Association and the American Woman Suffrage Association merged in 1890, suffrage leaders pursued the conservative approach of petitioning individual state legislatures. This was, at best, a painfully slow and plodding exercise in frustration.

While support for woman suffrage grew at the end of the nineteenth century, primarily among women but with increasing male support as well, obstacles to reform never lessened. Women had to work as hard and were subjected to as much criticism in 1900 and 1910 as they had been in 1848. In some ways, the very last years of the suffrage movement, from 1912 to 1920, required an even greater commitment, indeed a willingness to put their own freedom on the line in order to achieve their elusive goal.

CHAPTER TEN

Epilogue: The Turn of the Century

Between 1800 and 1900 the status of American women had undergone significant change. Household and family structure, work, race relations, marriage and childbirth experience, education, and political awareness all combined to give women a far different set of life choices than those they possessed at the beginning of the century. This epilogue describes the cumulative changes in women's experience and discusses their significance in the evolution of American history.

The arrival of the twentieth century brought with it as many challenges for the American nation as the post-Revolutionary generation faced on the eve of the nineteenth century. The contours of the American panorama in 1900 were almost unrecognizable from the landscape of a century earlier. The concept of Manifest Destiny had been realized as the frontier pushed inexorably west to the Pacific Ocean. While vast areas of the interior between the East and West Coasts still remained lightly settled, the nation had been geographically defined, extending from Mexico to Canada and bounded by the Atlantic on one side and the Pacific on the other. As the interior regions organized from territories into states, enormous transformations changed the lives of all Americans, none more dramatically than the lives of American Indians.

Indians had been systematically pushed off tribal lands from Georgia to Arizona. White settlers, often under the protection of the U.S. Army, had managed to force the relocation of almost every major Indian nation by the end of the nineteenth century. When Native people protested the dismantling of their homelands and the destruction of their cultures, the federal government routinely sided with migrating settlers. Indians' once boundless territories were reduced to 38 million acres, primarily in the Southwest and the West, on land that virtually no one else wanted. Indians were slowly being displaced, their pleas for justice ignored.

As white settlement extended westward, the need to develop an efficient transportation system grew more pressing. By midcentury a vast rail network connected East and West. Large numbers of people and huge quantities of goods moved with greater and greater ease and speed than had been contemplated when the century opened. While horse-drawn carriages remained the most common form of daily transportation for most Americans, they began to be replaced by streetcars in urban settings, and by 1900 more than 4,000 private cars were cruising American roadways. Industrialization partnered with technology fueled a booming economy marked by unprecedented growth, even despite a bloody **Civil War** and periodic economic downturns both before and after the combat. New York, Boston, and Philadelphia remained consummate American cities, but younger, thriving urban centers dotted the continental United States, including Atlanta, Chicago, Cincinnati, St. Louis, Kansas City, Memphis, New Orleans, Dallas, Los Angeles, and San Francisco. More than fifty thousand miles of telegraph line kept Americans linked in closer contact: technology brought the nation together even as the country expanded dramatically.

For women, this whole new world of a rapidly transforming nation was exciting and daunting, full of enormous promise but with little legal, social, or cultural support for the exploration of fresh uncharted territory. For example, women could count on women's networks to a far greater extent than had been possible a century earlier. They continued to expand these opportunities for improving their lives and relations, even as obstacles to opportunity and equality blocked their path.

For women of color, the obstacles were even more formidable. American Indian women suffered much more than any other group during the century, as they watched families shattered by cultural and economic decline. Racism and discrimination imprisoned Indian women as well as their male counterparts.

Racism and discrimination were also severe handicaps for the small number of Asian American women, who had only recently emigrated to the western regions of America by the end of the nineteenth century. Chinese and Japanese immigrants settled along the Pacific coast, with the women of these communities relegated to the lowest rungs of employment and economic opportunities. Hispanic Americans were making their minority presence felt along the southwestern borderlands, especially in Texas, New Mexico, and southern California. The Spanish-speaking women of these communities had even fewer available options than their fathers, husbands, brothers, or sons.

The climate of racial hostility continued to hobble African Americans, who had been moving in increasing numbers outside the confines of the former Confederate states. From the end of Reconstruction in 1877 onward, strategies for black self-improvement were hampered by Jim Crow legislation—segregation statutes that legalized racial discrimination. The first such law appeared on the books in Tennessee in 1881.

Black women were disproportionately represented in women's employ-ment—certainly a hangover from their days as slaves. They were also dispro-portionately confined to the worst sectors of the economy, such as farm work and domestic service—also a legacy from slavery. They made dramatic strides in education in the second half of the century, with more African American women than African American men completing a high school education and going on to higher learning. Despite these inroads in education, the turn of the twentieth century has been described as the nadir of American race relations, especially in view of the high hopes that had followed emancipation and the Reconstruction amendments.

Marriage rates for both blacks and whites continued to increase after the Civil War, while the divorce rate remained less than 1 percent of all marriages until the 1920s. However, the birth rate for all women dropped from approxi-mately 55 births per one thousand population in 1800 to 32 births per one thou-sand population in 1900. Moreover, the fertility rate during this same period was cut in half. Whereas a woman in 1800 would likely produce seven to eight children during her fertile years, the same woman in 1900 would have only three or four children. (These numbers apply only to white women, as black rates were not tabulated until the 1920s.)

The revolution in education that began in the early decades of the nine-teenth century continued unabated. At the beginning of the century only the daughters of well-to-do parents were afforded the opportunity to attend even finishing schools. With the exception of reading and writing, very little real education was provided in girls' schools in comparison to the schools attended by boys, which routinely included a more rigorous academic curriculum. By 1900 public grammar schools were available to all children. While less than 7 percent of all seventeen-year-olds graduated from high school, almost all chil-dren attended school for part of their childhood years. More important for women, their access to higher education had expanded dramatically, even if their opportunities to put their educations to work remained limited.

Females made up 60 percent of the high school graduates by 1900. More than one third of all college students were women, and women were granted almost 20 percent of all bachelor's degrees from colleges and universities. Six percent of all doctoral degrees went to women and, with the establishment of the women's colleges, 19.8 percent of all college and university faculty positions were held by women in the first decade of the twentieth century. While the numbers of young adults who graduated high school and went on to college increased as the twentieth century progressed, the percentage of women in all categories remained roughly the same. There was only a moderate increase in the number of doctorates obtained and teaching positions held by women from

1900 until well into the 1980s, as the momentum and gains by women in the late nineteenth century plateaued for the first half of the twentieth century.

For the early generations of college-educated women—including many who pioneered in a variety of professions such as academe, law, and medicine—advancement in their chosen field and prevailing social attitudes precluded their combining marriage and career, even though for many of them this would have been an ideal. At the same time, many women—particularly those involved in higher education and especially those involved in women's colleges—found satisfactory and rewarding lives within communities of women. The fears that college-educated women would remain single and childless proved, over the long run, to be largely unfounded. Attitudes toward education, wage earning, and gender underwent significant and positive transformations during the nineteenth century, so that more American women had opportunities for better education, and many more eventually pursued careers; these careers eventually did not necessarily interfere with women's roles as wives and mothers. Although cultural changes slowly began to shift gender conventions, sexism continued well into the twentieth century to determine that women who hoped to succeed within the male-dominated professional world could not easily juggle both a career and a family.

Women employed in wage labor did not have either the luxury or the handicap of this cultural stereotype; rather, their numbers were on the increase throughout the century, with no marked improvement in conditions or pay. The number of women earning wages more than doubled from 1800 to 1850, from nearly 5 percent to 10 percent. This increase was repeated in the second half of the nineteenth century so that by 1900, women in the work force rose to more than 18 percent of the total and comprised 20 percent of American women.

These statistics fail to take into account the women who worked alongside husbands on self-sustaining homesteads. Nor do they include married women who generated income from piecework, labor performed in the home.

Although by 1900 only 6 percent of American women were listed as workers, nearly 45 percent of all single women earned wages. African American women worked after marriage in larger numbers than did white women, and their representation in the wage-earning force was double that of white women.

The three largest occupational categories for women in 1900 were private household workers, or domestics (28 percent), factory workers (25 percent), and farm workers (19 percent). Immigrant women especially were heavily represented in the textile and garment industry. Their wages were well below those earned by males in similar jobs. Women in some industries, especially the garment trades, were increasingly active in labor politics, involving themselves in union movements to secure greater equity for female labor. White collar women (including sales clerks, clerical workers, managers, administrators, technical workers, and professionals) constituted just under 17 percent of all wage-earning women at the turn of the century, and women dominated nursing (93 percent) and library work (79 percent). On the eve of the twentieth century 52 percent of all social workers, 19 percent of all college professors, 6 percent of all physicians, and 1 percent of all lawyers were women.

Such changes only accelerated during the twentieth century. Women played larger and larger roles in reform, including campaigns to have greater control over their own bodies. Females wedged their way into party politics with the acquisition of the vote in 1920.

The progressive line of political activism from **Harriet Beecher Stowe** to Betty Friedan, from **Elizabeth Cady Stanton** to Rosa Parks shows that women have made great strides in the battle to participate more fully in American reform. Feminists of the nineteenth century initiated a series of debates over women's role within American society and made demands that have yet to be fully realized. They began the important process of dissent, which created protest movements in cities and towns all across the nation. They challenged bedrock assumptions about "women's place" from state houses to front parlors, within schoolrooms and board rooms, from farms to factories. Feminist discourse, from **Susan B. Anthony** to **Sojourner Truth** to **Charlotte Perkins Gilman**, provided articulate and effective rebuttals to patriarchal despotism. Women wanted no longer to be ruled, and many disdained being "taken care of." If women were given equal opportunities, then they would take care of themselves and autonomy might lead to further achievements.

Without question, the feminist foremothers of the nineteenth century paved the way for the flowering of feminist scholarship in the twentieth. As women challenged male dominance they began to question the standards that kept males at the top of the heap and confined women to an inferior status. This reevaluation led to new explorations of the past, and this revisiting of America's heritage revealed there had been women as well as men involved in the shaping of the nation.

So the late twentieth-century rediscovery of these lost heroines, as well as the efforts of women's history scholars to recapture the concrete realities of the lives of ordinary women, have done much to deepen our understanding of the nation's efforts to live up to its stated ideals of freedom, justice, and equality.

What can we learn today from these women of the nineteenth century? Perhaps that many led "invisible" lives, but that their invisibility is a historical interpretation. Women were present although not accounted for during all of the great events and movements of the nineteenth century: they were part of the booming economy; they were agitating for their rights to participate in the wider world of politics; they were invaluable contributors to the culture, even if their contributions were discounted by their contemporaries. Their invisibility may be due to their erasure from the record, not because they were insignificant apparitions. Perhaps we may best learn from these women how to ensure our own place in history by not allowing ourselves to repeat their mistakes.

American women, seeking respect and fairness in the nineteenth century, were deeply divided over the issue of equality. The formal woman suffrage movement took more than seventy years to achieve its goal of votes for women, not simply because men opposed woman suffrage but because there was a large and active group of women opposed to female suffrage and its consequences. Further, even women who campaigned for woman suffrage were divided into competing groups during much of the nineteenth-century movement. Lessons might be learned from examining closely all the obstacles that prevented American feminists from smoothly assuming what they felt was their rightful place among their fellow citizens, on equal footing before the law, on a less treacherous road toward their own liberation.

Although many women wanted improved status, they felt the sacrifices they might have to make "in the name of equality" would not be justified. A significant number of women valued what they believed was genuine difference between the sexes: some felt sex was an innate biological characteristic (or set of characteristics), and some suspected gender was a learned behavior that valued cooperation over force, sometimes translated as "feminine" over "masculine." Many women, therefore, championed women's differences from men and campaigned both to preserve (through distinctive sex roles) and even to protect (by legislation) these differences.

The pendulum has swung widely and wildly during the twentieth century. Feminist scholars are still debating the uses and abuses of affirmative action, pay equity, and other systems put in place to remedy gross inequality between the sexes. Should we look for equality of opportunity or insist upon equality of outcome? These debates are with us into the twenty-first century.

But the terms of the debates were very much shaped by the determined women who launched feminist crusades in the nineteenth century. From Abigail Adams at the beginning of the century to **Jane Addams** at the end of the century, women's voices insisted that they be heard. The intensity and scope of demands varied dramatically, but the nineteenth century witnessed a virtual cottage industry of female reform. Female entreaties and expectations created a continuous chorus of complaint. From Cherokee and Sioux women trying to preserve tribal culture and to withstand the ordeal of assimilation and enslaved women fighting the "equal exploitation" of their labor by planters to mill women comparing their plight with African American slaves and women on the overland trail dragged from their homes into a harsh, hostile, and often isolated environment—throughout the first half of the century women were finding their voices and then, after gaining them, uniting by the thousands in protest against gender discrimination. This and many other reform issues allowed women to move from their circumscribed conditions into a more active role in the larger society, forming networks and organizations that allowed them to gain skills and confidence and to eventually break onto the public platform. The actions of those women who defied social convention to become activists resulted in the flowering of American feminism.

By the time of the American Civil War, women were fighting on many fronts: for autonomy, equality, citizenship, freedom; for their own rights as well as the rights of those even more unfortunate—former slaves, children, prisoners, lunatics, and others society might abandon. However, the peace following Confederate surrender signaled a new age of feminist challenge and dissent. Women branched out into every conceivable area, breaking down barriers that would have seemed impenetrable only a short time earlier. Feminists might disagree whether women's interests were transcendent and universal or particular and equally significant. Men and women, together and apart, were struggling with the need to redefine and renegotiate gender and its consequences within American society, a priority feminists have hoped to keep in the forefront of political priorities. While race and class carried with them their own agendas, which distinctively shaped gender issues, growing numbers of women identified their interests primarily *as* women. They struggled to raise this nexus of concerns, prioritizing women's special interests and promoting them as positive for society as a whole.

By the closing decades of the nineteenth century women had fastened on every opportunity they could possibly seize and were eagerly seeking more. Barriers were still in place, resistance remained strong, but so was the resolve of most women to take advantage of their unique opportunities as Americans. Without the participation of women in nineteenth-century public life, America on the eve of the twentieth century would have look unrecognizably different.

In recognition of the important work done by these courageous and determined women, feminist scholars in the twentieth century have tried to recover a sense of those earlier generations' wonder and determination, their feeling that they could turn the world upside down. And by recapturing this moment of challenge and intrigue, by placing nineteenth-century American women within the context of both their struggles and their achievement, we are better prepared to appreciate their limitations as well as their contributions. In this way we can eliminate the former and honor the latter, as we make our way into the twenty-first century.

NOTES

1. Post-Revolutionary America

1. Alexis de Tocqueville, *Democracy in America* (New York: Knopf, 1966), 2:214.

2. Thomas Jefferson, *Writings* (New York: Library of America, 1984), p. 556.

3. Linda Kerber and Jane DeHart, *Women's America: Refocusing the Past* (New York: Oxford University Press, 1995), p. 91.

2. The Economy, Households, and Labor

1. Alice Kessler-Harris, *Out to Work: A History of Wage-Earning Women in the United States* (New York: Oxford University Press, 1982), p. 23.

2. Catherine Clinton, *The Other Civil War: American Women in the Nineteenth Century* (New York: Hill and Wang, 1984), pp. 25–26.

3. Ibid., p. 27.

4. Kessler-Harris, *Out to Work*, p. 41.

5. Sara Evans, *Born for Liberty: A History of Women in America* (New York: Free Press, 1989), p. 86.

6. John Mack Farragher, *Women and Men on the Overland Trail* (New Haven: Yale University Press, 1979), p. 74.

7. Linda Kerber and Jane DeHart, *Women's America: Refocusing the Past* (New York: Oxford University Press, 1995), p. 125.

8. Clinton, *The Other Civil War*, p. 41.

3. Education and Reform

1. John P. Cowles, "Ipswich Female Seminary." *American Journal of Education* 30:593.

4. The Church and the Law

1. Nancy Woloch, *Women and the American Experience* (New York: Knopf, 1984), p. 120.

2. Sara Evans, *Born for Liberty: A History of Women in America* (New York: Free Press, 1989), p. 73.

3. Ibid., p. 107.

4. Ibid.

5. Catherine Clinton, *The Other Civil War: American Women in the Nineteenth Century* (New York: Hill and Wang, 1984), p. 78.

6. Catherine Clinton, *The Plantation Mistress: Woman's World in the Old South* (New York: Pantheon, 1982), p. 85.

5. Natives and Immigrants

1. Theda Perdue, "Women, Men, and American Indian Policy: The Cherokee Response to `Civilization,' " in Nancy Shoemaker, ed., *Negotiators of Change: Historical Perspectives on Native American Women* (New York: Routledge, 1995), p. 93.

2. Lucy Eldersveld Murphy, "Autonomy and the Economic Roles of Indian Women of the Fox-Wisconsin Riverway Region, 1763–1832," in Shoemaker, ed., *Negotiators of Change*, p. 81.

3. Ibid., p. 77.

4. Katherine Marie Birmingham Osburn, "The Navajo at the Bosque Redondo: Cooperation, Resistance, and Initiative, 1864–1868," in Roger L. Nichols, ed., *The American Indian Past and Present* (New York: McGraw-Hill), p. 187.

5. Osburn, "Dear Friend and Ex-Husband: Marriage, Divorce, and Women's Property Rights on the Southern Ute Reservation, 1887–1930," in Shoemaker, ed., *Negotiators of Change*, p. 165.

6. Donald J. Berthrong, *The Cheyenne and Arapaho Ordeal: Reservation and Agency Life in the Indian Territory, 1785–1907* (Norman: University of Oklahoma Press, 1976), p. 224.

6. The Civil War and Reconstruction

1. John Garraty, *The Young Reader's Companion to American History* (Boston: Houghton Mifflin, 1994), p. 791.

2. Mary Livermore, *My Story of the War* (Hartford, Conn.: Worthington, 1889), p. 90.

3. Sylvia Dannett, ed. *Noble Women of the North* (New York: Thomas Yoseloff, 1959), p. 99.

4. Catherine Clinton, *Tara Revisited: Women, War, and the Plantation Legend* (New York: Abbeville Press, 1995), p. 71.

5. Ibid., p. 72.

8. Sexuality, Reproduction, and Gender Roles

1. Sara Evans, *Born for Liberty: A History of Women in America* (New York: Free Press, 1989), p. 88.

2. Kathryn Cullen-Dupont, *Elizabeth Cady Stanton and Women's Liberty* (New York: Facts on File, 1992), p. 63.

3. Catherine Clinton, *The Other Civil War: American Women in the Nineteenth Century* (New York: Hill and Wang, 1984), p. 63.

4. Ibid., p. 162.

9. Suffrage and Reform Politics

1. Frederick B. Tolles, ed., *Slavery and the "Woman Question": Lucretia Mott's Diary on Her Visit to Great Britain to Attend the World's Antislavery Convention of 1840*, Friends Historical Association no. 23 (Haverford, Penn., 1952), p. 9.

2. Kathryn Cullen-Dupont, *Elizabeth Cady Stanton and Women's Liberty* (New York: Facts on File, 1992), p. 5.

3. Elizabeth Cady Stanton, Susan B. Anthony, and Matilda Jocelyn Gage, eds., *History of Woman Suffrage*, 6 vols. (1881–1922; reprint, New York: Arno Press, 1969), 1:115–117.

PART TWO

American Women in the
Nineteenth Century A to Z

Abortion

Abortion is defined as either the involuntary—through miscarriage—or voluntary—through induction—termination of pregnancy. In the United States women have practiced voluntary abortion as a means of ending unwanted pregnancy from the very first settlement. For early American women, the question of whether or not induced abortion was a legal practice was rarely an issue. The law at best was vague. What is clear is that most women who willingly terminated pregnancy, whether or not they believed the practice was illegal, did not believe it was immoral or sinful. This concept did not take hold until the latter half of the nineteenth century. Efforts to outlaw abortion arose simultaneously with the growth of organized medicine. More and more male physicians objected to induced abortion on the grounds that it posed a danger to women's lives. While many physicians undoubtedly believed in that rationale, it is also true that physicians objected to any nonlicensed persons who practiced medicine, particularly midwives. Since midwives often assisted women in carrying out abortions, restricting abortion was a way to curtail the activities of midwives. Connecticut was the first state to outlaw abortion in 1821, and by 1860 twenty states and territories had passed similar legislation. Between 1860 and 1880 the medical profession led the move to outlaw all forms of contraception, including abortion. This, in part, led to passage of the **Comstock Law** in 1873, which made it illegal to send information regarding contraceptives, birth control, and abortion through the mails. By the end of the century, nearly all the states had either passed antiabortion laws or were on the road to doing so.

Addams, Jane (1860–1935), settlement house founder, reformer, humanitarian, peace advocate

Born in Cedarville, Illinois, Jane Addams had a particularly close relationship with her widower father. When he died shortly after her graduation from the prestigious Rockford Seminary in 1881, Addams was devastated. The loss of her father, combined with the limited options available to the first generation of American women who had graduated from college, left her rudderless for nearly a decade. After abandoning a brief attempt at medical school, she traveled to Europe with her college roommate, **Ellen Gates Starr**. There, Addams learned about the settlement house, Toynbee Hall, in London. It was her first exposure to settlement work, and it galvanized her to return home and establish an American settlement house similar to Toynbee Hall. **Hull House** opened its doors on Chicago's South Side in September 1889, and Addams worked tirelessly to attract talented women and men to the organization. Hull House proved to be an enduring and important part of Chicago and American life for two reasons: first, it provided Chicago's most needy and desperate residents—many of them immigrants—with a haven that offered immediate relief and the promise of future uplift through a variety of activities ranging from medical services, child care, English classes, legal aid, a residence for working women, vocational skills classes, sewing and cooking classes, and educational and recreational activities for children to cultural enrichment activities including plays, concerts, and lectures, as well as citizenship classes. Second, Hull House transformed the urban—and ultimately, the American—landscape, for the concept behind it proved to be the genesis of a new profession—social work—that became a driving force during the Progressive Era and the wide-reaching social changes that characterized the settlement house movement. Addams's interests, beyond Hull House, included woman suffrage, pacifism, and temperance. Well into the twentieth century, Addams continued to play a leading role in those and other causes, even when it became unpopular to hold certain views. For example, Addams refused to abandon her pacifist beliefs during World War I. As a consequence, support for both Hull House and Addams declined. But shortly before her death in 1935, Addams was awarded the Nobel Peace Prize in recognition of her exemplary work in the cause of peace.

Alcott, Louisa May (1832–88), author

Born the second of four daughters to Amos Bronson Alcott and his wife, Abigail, Louisa was brought up in a family where intellectual challenge and genteel poverty were constant companions. Louisa's father ran a school in Concord, Massachusetts, before his attempts at organizing a utopian community, Fruitlands, in nearby Harvard, Massachusetts. Her mother advocated abolitionism and was involved in several reform campaigns, including women's rights. The young Louisa was given an exceptional upbringing, at the center of her parent's coterie of literary friends, including Henry David Thoreau, Ralph Waldo Emerson, William Lloyd Garrison, and **Margaret Fuller**.

The family's chronic money problems led the young Louisa to work, following her education, as a domestic, a seamstress, a governess, and a teacher before she was able to support herself, and eventually her family, as a writer. She enlisted as a nurse in **Dorothea Dix**'s service during the Civil War, attending at a Union hospital in Washington, D.C. Unfortunately Alcott fell ill and was treated with medication containing large amounts of mercury, which rendered her semi-invalid for the rest of her life. Convalescing at home, she wrote *Hospital Sketches*, published in 1863 under her own name. Alcott had published poems, stories, and novelettes under a pseudonym from an early age.

After the war Alcott went to Europe as a ladies' companion, but upon her return secured the editorship in 1868 of a juvenile magazine, *Merry's Museum*. During this period Alcott conceived and in 1867 published the book with which her fame has been associated, *Little Women*. The book was extremely popular, selling nearly forty thousand copies its first year. When Alcott returned to Europe in 1870, she was able to afford a grand tour. For nearly twenty years Alcott published short stories and novels for children and adults, many of which were autobiographical, earning great acclaim. Although Alcott received adoration from her public and a comfortable income from her profession, she spent much of her life in restless discontent. Alcott was devoted to her family, staying at home until the death of her mother in 1877, looking after her sister May's child following May's death in 1879, and caring for her father, who suffered a crippling stroke. Alcott herself was forced to withdraw into several New England sanitariums, taking rest cures much of her adult life, under considerable duress with her many family burdens. She was visiting her dying father, when she fell ill with spinal meningitis and died on the day of her father's funeral in 1888. One of the most beloved domestic writers of the nineteenth century, a woman whose name was associated with family devotion and self-sacrifice through her many books for children and adults, Alcott died in much the way she had lived, honoring kith and kin.

American Antislavery Society (1833), voluntary association

The society, which grew to be the largest and best-known national organization fighting slavery within the United States, was founded by William Lloyd Garrison and other Boston abolitionists in 1833. The Society's Declaration of Sentiments called for the immediate emancipation of slaves and for racial equality. Garrison and his followers advocated "moral suasion," the use of argument rather than force to shift popular opinion. Garrisonians believed in petitions and prayer meetings, an appeal to conscience. Many women were intimately involved with the growth and expansion of this reform movement. **Angelina Grimké** gave antislavery lectures, and she and her sister Sarah collected twenty thousand signatures in Massachusetts in order to submit a petition to the state legislature. Maria Weston Chapman, a founding member of the Boston Female Antislavery Society in 1832, became Garrison's right hand within the powerful national campaign when it was launched the following year. Wendell Phillips, Theodore Parker, **Lydia Maria Child**, **Abbey Kelly Foster**, **Lucy Stone**, and many others advanced the agenda of this important reform crusade. The *Liberty Bell* was its annual publication; authors donated writing, and the publication netted funds for the ongoing work of the organization.

During the winter of 1840 disunion threatened the organization, as many black and white male reformers felt Garrison was leading the group astray by broadening the base of operations to embrace women's rights and Christian nonresistance. A strong wing of the organization wanted to involve the group only in activities that would directly lead to emancipation and racial equality. Several of the men of the organization were concerned about the way in which women mounted the political platform and stayed in the spotlight during the fight to end slavery. Dissent fomented rebellion, which splintered the society into warring factions.

By 1841 a breakaway group, including Lewis and Arthur Tappan and Theodore Dwight Weld, left to form their own organizations: the American and Foreign Anti-Slavery Society and the Liberty Party. Most women remained within the ranks of the American Antislavery Society, where their contributions continued to be welcomed and esteemed. Their efforts were rewarded in 1865 when Congress passed the Thirteenth Amendment, a measure to abolish slavery.

The American Female Moral Reform Society (1834), voluntary association

By the early 1830s middle-class women felt threatened and repelled by an increasingly rampant public immorality. A small group of women meeting at the Third Presbyterian Church in New York City in 1834 determined to accomplish a goal as ambitious as it was simple: eradicate prostitution and other illicit forms of what they considered male-inspired licentiousness. The moral reform movement quickly attracted support among women throughout New York State and New England. Within ten years, what began as the New York Female Moral Reform Society grew into the American Female Moral Reform Society, with more than 400 chapters throughout the region.

Prostitution remained the primary focus of the moral reformers. The nature of the problem created some ambivalence among reformers who, for the most part, believed that the fault lay with those who solicited prostitutes. At the same time many reformers viewed the prostitutes themselves as the problem. Thus there was an uneasy alliance between a middle-class scorn and condemnation of "working girls" and the desire to provide a safe haven in order to help them find the path of righteousness. Despite this conflict, reformers directed their efforts at the "bold," "reckless," and "intemperate" American male who was "drenched in sin." The *Advocate*, a society publication, routinely published the names of men who went in and out of brothels. The names were collected by women who stood watch, meticulously recording the comings and goings of the clientele.

Enthusiasm for the American Female Moral Reform Society waned during the 1850s and gradually died out altogether. While the society failed to achieve its goal of eliminating prostitution, there is some evidence that it may have contributed to a shift in mainstream morality. For example, during its years of activity, the illegitimacy rate fell markedly.

American Missionary Society (1846), voluntary missionary
teachers' association

Influenced largely by the antebellum movement among church women to sponsor, finance, and train missionary teachers, the American Missionary Society (AMS) was founded in 1846. The original intention—to provide missionary teachers for service abroad in Asia, Africa, and the Middle East—was never abandoned. But the AMS was most effective in the United States. The organization became the single most active sponsor of northern teachers in the postwar South. It helped to establish hundreds of schools and churches in the South, many of them on the very plantations where the former slaves had toiled. The AMS schools were supported in large part by northern contributors.

While most of the bureaucracy running the AMS was male, nearly 90 percent of the volunteers who made the schools work effectively were women, the majority of whom were single young women from New England. In many ways, their influence in the southern communities where schools were established mirrored the contributions made by settlement house workers in the urban North a generation later. But as the focus of the AMS shifted from elementary schools to black colleges, the number of women volunteers tapered off. By the 1890s the AMS in the South was virtually nonexistent.

American Woman Suffrage Association (1869), voluntary association

The American Woman Suffrage Association was organized specifically to provide an alternative to suffragists who were demanding immediate voting rights through passage of a woman suffrage amendment to the Constitution of the United States. Following almost on the heels of the founding of the **National Woman Suffrage Association** (NWSA) by **Elizabeth Cady Stanton** and **Susan B. Anthony** in 1869, **Lucy Stone** organized the American Woman Suffrage

Association (AWSA) in November of that year. Stone, whose abolitionist roots ran deeper than her feminist roots, disagreed with what she considered the radical stance taken by Anthony and Stanton, both of whom devoted their political energies to the cause of woman suffrage, even to the extent of allying with antiblack political elements. The AWSA, on the other hand, declared no objections to deferring woman suffrage for as long as was deemed necessary by the pro-abolitionist critics of the cause. Moreover, the AWSA prominently featured male as well as female office holders, electing as its first president Henry Ward Beecher. Hoping to build a national audience very quickly, the AWSA launched a nationwide speaking tour. In addition to its willingness to put other issues before woman suffrage, the NWSA also preferred to achieve suffrage through individual state campaigns geared to changing each state's constitution, even though it did not preclude the federal amendment supported by the AWSA.

Anthony, Susan Brownell (1820–1906), women's rights activist

Sometimes characterized as the George Washington of the American women's movement, Susan B. Anthony was born in Adams, Massachusetts, one of eight children. She began her professional career as a teacher in Rochester, New York, and thereafter considered that city her home. Although Anthony did not attend the **Seneca Falls Convention** in New York in 1848, her mother and sisters did and quickly persuaded Anthony to become involved. In addition to women's rights, Anthony also worked for abolition and temperance. But it quickly became clear to her that women, regardless of their willingness and commitment, were often unwelcome or relegated to behind-the-scenes activities in many of these reform organizations. Anthony brought to the women's movement her two most valuable assets—unflagging energy and intellectual prowess. After meeting **Elizabeth Cady Stanton**, another giant of the movement, Anthony knew she had met a soulmate with whom she could and did work tirelessly. Stanton, tied closer to home because of her five children, wrote broadside after broadside arguing for women's rights. Anthony criss-crossed the country delivering the message, recruiting other women, organizing campaigns, and, in the process, founding the **National Woman Suffrage Association** in 1869.

Although women's rights became her primary focus, Anthony continued to press for the abolition of slavery. But when the Fifteenth Amendment to the Constitution was proposed, voted on, and ratified (1870), Anthony voiced her strong objections. She wanted the amendment to guarantee voting rights for all men *and* women, not just former male slaves. Few politicians wanted to entertain the idea, and abolitionists were reluctant to support votes for women for fear of jeopardizing voting rights for freedmen. Determined to test the constitutionality of the amendment, Anthony organized women in communities across the country to demand access to the polls in the election of 1872. When Anthony tried to vote in Rochester, she was arrested and found guilty in a trial without a jury by a judge who had written his opinion before the trial started. Her hopes for a hearing in a higher court were dashed when the authorities refused to press her for payment of her fine of $100.

Anthony's objections to the Fifteenth Amendment created a split in the women's movement and the organization of a rival suffrage group, the **American Woman Suffrage Association**. In 1890 Anthony was able to bring about a reconciliation of the two groups under one banner, the **National American Woman Suffrage Association**, and from 1892 to 1900 she served as its president. By then eighty years old and having accomplished more than a half-century of work on behalf of women's rights, Anthony remained active. A leader in the International Council of Women, Anthony was still traveling widely, visiting London in 1899 and Berlin in 1904, where she was instrumental in organizing the International Woman Suffrage Association.

Throughout much of her active career, Anthony had helped Stanton publish a newspaper called *The Revolution*. It is a testament to her dedication to women's rights as well as to her power as a speaker that, when the publication accumulated debts of $10,000 and had to be sold in 1870, Anthony determined to erase the debt through speaking engagements. At $75 per speech, she had cleared the debt by 1876. Anthony and Stanton also began writing what would eventually become the monumental six-volume *History of Woman Suffrage*, the final volume of which was published in 1922. It proved to be the single most valuable source for tracking the decades-long struggle for woman suffrage.

Susan B. Anthony died at home in Rochester at the age of eighty-six. It took another fourteen years before women would finally secure the right to vote (1920). Throughout the history of the women's rights struggle, from the first meeting at Seneca Falls in 1848 to ratification of the Nineteenth Amendment in 1920, with the single exception of her longtime friend and colleague, Elizabeth Cady Stanton, no other leader came close to achieving the stature of Susan B. Anthony.

Antisuffragism (1895), movement opposed to the enfranchisement of women

The antisuffragist movement began to take shape with the establishment of antisuffrage organizations in Massachusetts (1895) and New York (1896). Eventually, more than twenty states had similar organizations. Although the antisuffragists received most of their economic support from men, the movement's membership was heavily female. The leadership tended to be white, Protestant, and middle-aged. Like suffragists, they were involved in a range of social reform and voluntary associations. They were less well-educated than suffragists, on average, and more religiously conservative. Arguments against woman suffrage were grounded in religious and theological beliefs that women were best suited to influence events not in the public sphere but in the private, family sphere. Antisuffragists rejected the idea of sex equality. The concerns expressed by the antisuffragists reflected their uncertainty about how traditional roles and values would be affected in a society where women were empowered to vote and to demand equality. The antisuffragist movement eventually went national with the founding of the National Association Opposed to Woman Suffrage (NAOWS) in 1911, led by socialite heiress Josephine Dodge. Antisuffragists continued to protest woman suffrage until the Nineteenth Amendment was ratified in 1920. Because antisuffragism remained a fairly diffuse movement despite the NAOWS, it is difficult to provide an accurate estimate of how many women embraced the movement. Despite the legitimate concerns and issues raised by the antisuffragists, they never came close to equaling the breadth and depth of the suffrage movement.

Association of Collegiate Alumnae (1882), professional organization

Founded in 1882 by **Alice Freeman Palmer**, Marion Talbot, and fifteen other recent college graduates, the Association of Collegiate Alumnae (ACA) limited membership to women graduates of selected four-year colleges and universities. Graduates of schools such as the universities of Chicago and Michigan, as well as private colleges such as Oberlin, Smith, and Wellesley, were allowed to become members of the ACA. The association sought to provide an environment where college graduates would feel less isolated by virtue of their education, unite graduates to do "practical educational work," and promote and raise standards for women's education. Because there were few opportunities for the first generations of women college graduates, many felt adrift in a society ill-prepared to utilize their knowledge, ability, and talent in any but traditional female roles. When the ACA was founded, therefore, branches quickly spring up in cities across the country. Membership continued to depend on institutional affiliation in order to differentiate ACA members from the graduates of normal schools and academies. For this reason the membership rolls remained relatively limited. During its early years the ACA initiated a variety of studies, most of which focused on women and children, including one systematically refuting the theories of the then-popular Dr. Edward Clarke, who had argued in 1893 that higher education for women was harmful to their health. In 1901 the Southern Association of Collegiate Alumnae was founded with similar goals, and in 1921 the two organizations joined together as the American Association of University Women (AAUW). With a single organization and an expansion of eligible schools, the AAUW became a much greater force than either of its parent organizations had been. By the 1980s the AAUW had chapters in every state and counted more than 150,000 members.

Bagley, Sarah (1806–47), labor activist

Little is known of Sarah Bagley's early life. She was born in Meredith, New Hampshire, received only a rudimentary education, and took a job at the Hamilton Manufacturing Company in 1836. Hamilton was part of the Lowell, Massachusetts mills system, a paternalistic operation that provided young women with both jobs and living quarters, all of which was closely supervised and regulated. Initially, Bagley was quite happy with the Lowell system. As late as 1840, an article by her in the *Lowell Offering*, the newspaper published for women workers, praised the system. But as the mill owners began to cut wages and engage in speedups (a practice whereby workers had to produce more in order to maintain the same wage), Bagley became disenchanted with working conditions. Bagley was the founder and first president of the **Lowell Female Labor Reform Association** (1845). Under Bagley's direction, the association bought out the *Voice of Industry*, a periodical previously published by the New England Workingman's Association. The *Voice of Industry* provided a counterpoint to the *Lowell Offering*, which tended to side with the mill owners on most issues. Over the course of several months in 1845 and 1846, Bagley gathered more than 2,000 signatures on a petition for a 10-hour work day. At the same time, the association increased its membership to more than 500 members. When one mill owner attempted to increase workers' responsibility from operating three looms to operating four, Bagley succeeded in making the owners abandon their efforts by getting every loom worker to refuse the increase. Bagley's position as a union leader gained her an opportunity to testify before the Massachusetts legislature in 1846, making her one of very few women to speak in the public arena, to offer testimony on behalf of anything. Union scandals unrelated to Bagley nevertheless forced her to conclude, in 1846, that the union would be better off if she resigned. Thereafter, Bagley disappears from most records, and we know little more about her activities. She did become the first woman telegraph operator in the United States when she accepted a position at the Lowell Telegraph Office in 1847. It is believed that Bagley died that same year.

Barton, Clara (1821–1912), nurse, reformer

Clarissa Harlowe Barton was the last of five children born to Stephen Barton, a farmer and sawmill owner in North Oxford, Massachusetts, and his wife, Sarah. A favorite child of her father, Clara was an apt pupil and received a good education. She taught for several years before securing a post in the U.S.

Patent Office in Washington, D.C. in 1854, a job at which she excelled. When the Democrats won the presidency in 1856, she was forced to return home to Massachusetts in 1857. But with Lincoln's election in 1860, she was recalled to Washington to resume her clerking duties. When the Civil War broke out, Barton saw a need to provide efficient collection and distribution of food and medical supplies to soldiers.

Barton set up a pipeline of private donations and solicited assistance from Senator Henry Wilson from her home state of Massachusetts to get these goods to the front. Knowing that the Sanitary Commission and **Dorothea Dix**'s nursing corps were bogged down by the machinery of government, Barton also solicited help from local ladies' societies and church groups in her home state, a totally voluntary network that was unencumbered by government bureaucracy. Barton's independence allowed her upon occasion to commandeer a mule train and get her supplies promptly and directly to the battle sites where they were most needed. Barton was present at Antietam, the Battle of Fredericksburg, at Charleston, the Battle of Fort Wagner, and at other significant encounters. Her mission of mercy caused her to be dubbed "The Angel of the Battlefield" by Union soldiers. In 1865, at Annapolis, Maryland, Barton set up an office to deal with the problem of missing soldiers and their families—an enormous postwar effort that she funded from her own pocket until the government belatedly reimbursed her. Barton lectured on her wartime experiences until 1869, when poor health forced her to take a rest cure in Europe. While in Switzerland, Barton came into contact with the International Committee of the Red Cross, founded in 1863. In 1870 Barton helped with Red Cross efforts in the Franco-Prussian War. In 1873 she returned to America and organized an American Red Cross, lobbying Congress to participate in the international peace and rescue effort. In 1882, largely due to Barton's vigorous campaign, the U.S. Senate finally ratified the Geneva Convention.

In 1881 Barton was selected the first president of the newly organized American Association of the Red Cross. Her domestic programs included flood relief at Johnston, Pennsylvania, in 1889 and hurricane relief in the Georgia Sea Islands in 1893. In 1896, at the age of seventy-seven, Barton went to Cuba during the Spanish-American War to serve and organize field hospitals and relief efforts. In 1904 she resigned from the American Red Cross, over a policy dispute. She remained active in her relief work, however, until her death at the age of ninety-one. The early strength and growth of the American Red Cross was a tribute to Barton's humanitarian vision and tireless effort.

Beecher, Catharine Esther (1800–78), writer, educator

The Reverend Lyman and Roxana Foote Beecher's eldest daughter took over family responsibilities at the age of sixteen, caring for her several younger siblings after her mother died. Her father was a leading theologian of his day and an outspoken opponent of slavery from his pulpit and as head of the Lane Theological Seminary in Cincinnati. Five of her brothers became ministers, her sister **Harriet** became the noted author of *Uncle Tom's Cabin*, and her other sister, Isabella, became a women's rights activist.

Born in East Hampton, New York, Beecher moved with her family to Litchfield, Connecticut, in 1810. After the death of her fiancé in 1823, she established a female academy in Hartford. She moved to Cincinnati, Ohio, in 1832 and founded another girls' school. As a champion of female educational reform, she initiated a "Central Committee for Promoting National Education" in 1840. Beecher organized training sessions for teachers in her Hartford Academy, then sent out disciples to found and staff schools in Ohio, Illinois, Iowa, and Wisconsin. She was responsible for the establishment and growth of many female seminaries throughout the West and provided improved education for thousands of American schoolgirls. Her *Treatise on Domestic Economy for the Use of Young Ladies at Home and at School* (1843) and *American Women's Home* (1869) (coauthored with her sister Harriet Beecher Stowe) became classics. Beecher devoted herself to her career and never married. She died at Elmira, New York, on May 12, 1878.

Birth Control

Women in America who wished to do so have employed various methods to prevent or terminate pregnancy from the earliest settlements on.

Families in early colonial society routinely had many children, partly because survival in the New World was not guaranteed, but more importantly because their religious beliefs dictated that they follow the biblical instruction to be "fruitful" and "multiply." It was not unusual for women to have multiple pregnancies despite the high mortality rates for both mothers and children.

Feminists in the nineteenth century successfully revolted against unlimited pregnancy in a campaign under the slogan of "Voluntary Motherhood." Family size decreased between 1800 and 1900; by the end of the century the average number of children per woman was nearly cut in half, despite the limited availability of contraceptive devices and limited scientific knowledge of female fertility. Contraceptive devices were rudimentary, at best, with abstinence among the most successful methods. Although toward the end of the century the rubber diaphragm came into use, reliable birth control was still decades away. Two factors militated against any real family planning throughout the nineteenth century. Congress passed the **Comstock Law** in 1873, making it illegal to disseminate information about family planning, birth control, abortion, or any other information deemed "obscene," through the U.S. mail. And the new waves of immigrants—especially those from eastern European countries—generated new fears among the largely white Anglo-Saxon population that its preeminent position would be lost if its birth rate declined too dramatically. The Comstock Law remained an effective tool for dampening any effective organized protest but could not prevent knowledge of European contraceptives from reaching women in America. By the end of the century, middle-class women were more willing to demonstrate publicly their desire for access to those contraceptives.

Blackwell, Alice Stone (1857–1950), editor, women's rights activist

Alice Stone Blackwell grew up in a family with a passionate commitment to progressive causes. Her mother, **Lucy Stone**, founded the **American Woman Suffrage Association** and was the founding editor of the *Woman's Journal*, a respected publication dedicated to women's rights and suffrage in particular. Her father, a successful businessman, became an ardent supporter of woman suffrage and a partner in his wife's activism. Her aunt, **Elizabeth Blackwell**, was the first woman to receive a medical degree in the United States, and another aunt, **Antoinette Brown Blackwell**, was the first female minister. Blackwell graduated from Boston University in 1881, one of only two women in her class, with the dual distinction of being first in her class and a Phi Beta Kappa. She immediately went to work for the *Woman's Journal*, and over the next thirty-five years would assume almost total responsibility for the publication. In the last decades of the century Blackwell became one of the two architects, along with **Harriot Stanton Blatch**, of the successful unification of the two major suffrage organizations, the **National Woman Suffrage Association** and the **American Woman Suffrage Association**, into the **National American Woman Suffrage Association**, in 1890.

Blackwell, Antoinette Brown (1825–1921), ordained minister, theologian, reformer

Antoinette Brown Blackwell was the seventh and youngest child of Joseph and Abby Brown, of Henrietta, New York. She was allowed to attend school with her older brothers and studied the same subjects. When she expressed a desire to attend Oberlin College, her parents consented. But when she stated her intention of becoming an ordained minister like her brother Joseph, Blackwell ran into opposition from everyone, including her parents. So grounded were her parents in the belief that men and women were bound by clearly defined roles that they pleaded with their daughter not to upset the natural balance. At Oberlin her professors were hard pressed to prevent her from studying religion since the school had always been defined as one in which men and women were treated equally. Moreover, Blackwell's friend and future sister-in-law, the feminist **Lucy Stone**, encouraged her fellow student to pursue her dream. Like her male counterparts, Blackwell accepted numerous invitations to preach as a student. But while the Oberlin faculty allowed her to study religion, they refused to graduate her when she completed her studies in 1850. (Oberlin finally granted her an honorary A.M. in 1878, as well as a D.D. in 1908.)

Blackwell was able to carve out a career as a public speaker, and after lengthy negotiations was ordained as a minister of the First Congregational Church in Butler, New York, in 1853. Her association with that particular church was short-lived, and Blackwell resigned in order to work in New York's slum districts with poor people. For the first twenty years of her marriage to Samuel Charles Blackwell in 1856 she raised her children and only occasionally engaged in professional work. After her husband experienced financial difficulties, Blackwell temporarily resumed public speaking, making an extensive tour in 1879 and 1880. Most of her time was spent working for social causes, including woman suffrage and activities that would encourage women to enter untraditional fields such as the ministry and science. Her husband died in 1901, and sometime after 1905 Blackwell returned to Elizabeth, New Jersey, where she founded the All Soul's Unitarian Church, serving as pastor emeritus until her death in 1921. Although well into her nineties and nearly blind, shortly before Blackwell died, she had the privilege of voting for the first time in the election of 1920.

Blackwell, Elizabeth (1821–1910), physician

Awarded her M.D. from Geneva College in 1849, Elizabeth Blackwell was the first woman to graduate from an American medical school. One of twelve children, some of whom died in infancy, Blackwell came to America with her family in 1823 from her native England. Her father died penniless in 1838, and Elizabeth and the other older siblings inherited the responsibility for providing for the younger children. After teaching for several years, she applied to medical schools but was turned down by all but one. Her excitement over her acceptance by Geneva Medical College was dampened when she learned that the Dean of Admissions had given over her application to the students and they, believing it to be a prank by a rival school, had accepted Blackwell. She was isolated and shunned not only by her fellow students but by the citizens of Geneva, who considered her something of a freak. After she graduated, she found it hard to gain credibility with hospitals—a necessity if she was going to have a career as a physician. Although Blackwell never married, she adopted a seven-year-old girl and raised her as her own. In 1852 she began to attract attention among the women at the Quaker community in New York City, where she had opened a small dispensary. Her patients' influence and loyalty helped Blackwell to expand the tiny dispensary into the New York Infirmary for Women and Children in 1857. After years of hard work, and with the assistance of her younger sister, **Emily**, who had followed her into medicine,

Blackwell opened her own medical college in 1868, where she was determined to provide women students with a curriculum and an environment as rigorous as the most prestigious men's medical colleges. The Women's Medical College of the New York Infirmary opened, with Blackwell serving as its first Chair Professor of Hygiene. The school required entrance examinations, a comprehensive course of study with clinical experience, and successful completion of examinations that were administered by an independent board of advisers composed of the leading physicians in New York.

Once the school was firmly established, Blackwell left it in the able hands of her sister Emily and returned to her native England in 1869, where she lived for the rest of her life. She built a thriving practice in London and served as Chair Professor of Gynecology at the London School of Medicine for Women. Her health, never dependable, continued to deteriorate under the stress of overwork. With her daughter, Kitty Barry, she retired to a home on the English seacoast, and for the next thirty years, until her death in 1910, lived quietly, traveling—once to the United States—and developing friendships with social reformers and activists from Herbert Spencer to Charles Kingsley to George Eliot.

Blackwell, Emily (1826–1910), physician

Although not as well-known as her famous older sister, **Elizabeth Blackwell**, Emily Blackwell was an equally talented and dedicated physician who made significant contributions to nineteenth-century medicine. Five years younger than her sister, Emily followed Elizabeth into medicine. She was rejected by eleven medical schools before she was finally accepted by the Rush Medical College in Chicago in 1852. Before her first year ended, however, Blackwell was told she could not return. Moreover, the State Medical Society censured Rush for accepting her in the first place. Fortunately, Case Western Reserve admitted her, and she graduated from there with honors in 1854. Almost immediately, she left for England where she studied with Sir James Young Simpson, a noted physician then doing groundbreaking work in the use of chloroform in childbirth. In 1856 Emily joined Elizabeth at the New York Infirmary. Because of Emily, Elizabeth was able to proceed with her plans to expand the infirmary into first the New York Infirmary for Women and Children and later the New York Infirmary Women's Medical College. By the time Elizabeth left to live permanently in England in 1869, Emily had assumed full responsibility for running both the infirmary and the medical college. The medical college required that its students finish a full, three-year training, later changed to four years—something few other medical schools required at the time. The college year was also extended to eight months, about one-third longer than other medical schools required. Women's Medical College students were also provided with unprecedented opportunity for clinical observation and hands-on training. Largely due to Emily's influence, its women students received one of the best medical educations available at the time. Before the Women's Medical College was replaced by the Cornell University Medical College in 1898, the school graduated more than 360 women physicians, many of whom went on to enjoy illustrious careers as medical pioneers. Emily Blackwell died three months after her sister Elizabeth, in 1910.

Blatch, Harriot Stanton (1856–1940), suffrage activist, reformer

Harriot Stanton Blatch was the youngest daughter and sixth child of **Elizabeth Cady Stanton** and Henry B. Stanton. Born in Seneca Falls, New York, the site of the **Seneca Falls Convention**, Blatch was educated at a series of private schools and graduated from Vassar College in 1878. Her degree only supplemented the education she had long before absorbed in her parents' home, hearing and discussing on a daily basis the philosophy and the politics of abolition and women's rights. After graduating from Vassar, Blatch began helping her mother and **Susan B. Anthony** gather and edit the vast amounts of information that comprised the six-volume *History of Woman Suffrage*. It was she who pointed out to Stanton and Anthony in 1880 that the *History* thus far contained everything relevant to the **National Woman Suffrage Association** (NWSA) activities, but nothing about the **American Woman Suffrage Association** (AWSA). Blatch spent the next year writing a one-hundred-page account of the AWSA that was included as a final chapter in the second volume of the *History*. Blatch left the United States in 1881 and did not return, except for visits, until 1902. But the connections she made while writing her piece on the AWSA made it possible for her to work with **Alice Stone Blackwell** in persuading the NWSA and the AWSA to unite in 1890.

Bloomer, Amelia Jenks (1818–94), reformer, editor

Born in upstate New York to a garment maker, the young Amelia received a very rudimentary formal education but learned enough to become a schoolteacher and governess. While working in a household in Waterloo, New York, she met and married Dexter Bloomer, a lawyer and antislavery activist. Her husband was the coeditor of a newspaper, the *Seneca County Courier*, for which Amelia began to write after their wedding in 1840. In 1848 she established and headed a women's temperance group, and the next year founded a publication for the society, called *The Lily*. Bloomer began to print articles on women's rights, many contributed by **Elizabeth Cady Stanton**, as well as on temperance. As early as 1849 she advocated abandoning skirts in favor of the "Turkish trousers" that had been made famous by actress **Fanny Kemble**, a dress reform with which Amelia Bloomer's name became primarily identified. Ladies' trousers were nicknamed "bloomers" by friends and detractors, and Bloomer remarked that she was amazed by the furor she had unwittingly caused. Bloomer's friendship with Stanton blossomed; she introduced Stanton to women's rights advocate **Susan B. Anthony**, and the two became a formidable reform team.

In 1853 the Bloomers moved to Ohio where *The Lily* flourished, but when the couple ventured farther westward to Iowa in 1855, Bloomer ran into difficulties putting out her paper and sold the enterprise. She spent the rest of her life in Iowa, organizing soldier's aid societies during the Civil War and supporting woman suffrage. Bloomer was an Iowa delegate to the Equal Rights Association convention in New York City in 1869. She died of a heart attack in 1894, and her husband published the *Life and Writings of Amelia Bloomer* as a memorial to her in 1895.

Bly, Nellie (1865–1922), journalist

Born Elizabeth Cochrane, Nellie Bly chose her *nom de plume* while working as a reporter for the *Pittsburgh Dispatch* while she was still a teenager. Bly earned her job when she wrote a letter to the editor criticizing his antisuffrage views. Always willing to take risks, Bly became an exposé writer, usually working undercover in order to get a first-hand account of her subject. She traveled to Mexico in 1886, interested in the vast disparity between rich and poor in that country. The articles she sent back were widely reprinted and brought her national recognition. They also got her expelled from Mexico by a government less than pleased with the unfavorable publicity. The following year Bly wrote *Six Months in Mexico* (1887), again recounting her experiences. Shortly thereafter she left Pittsburgh for New York City, where Joseph Pulitzer, the publisher of the *New York World*, impressed by Bly's reporting, gave her free rein to write for his newspaper. Bly continued to write compelling stories. Feigning insanity, she had herself committed to an asylum for ten days in order to see how the mentally ill were treated. Her book, *Ten Days in a Madhouse*, resulted in an official investigation into conditions and ultimately in an increase in funding for mental hospitals, which helped to improve conditions for the patients. Bly's best-known exploit by far was a re-creation of the around-the-world journey that Jules Verne attributed to Phineas Fogg in the novel, *Around the World in Eighty Days*. Bly completed the trek in seventy-two days, sending back stories that the public relished. In 1895 Bly married millionaire M. Robert Seaman. After his death in 1904, she tried to run his business but was unsuccessful. The business failed, and Bly returned to reporting in 1919, this time at the *New York Journal*. She died three years later.

Brown, Olympia (1835–1926), minister, feminist, suffragist

Born in rural Michigan, Olympia Brown attended **Mount Holyoke Seminary** after being refused admission to the University of Michigan. She soon transferred to Antioch College, graduating in 1860. While at Antioch, Brown was responsible for inviting **Antoinette Brown Blackwell**, the first ordained woman minister of a recognized denomination in the United States, to speak. Inspired by Antoinette, Olympia decided to follow her into the ministry. She entered St. Lawrence University's theological school in Canton, New York and in 1863 became the first woman ordained with the full blessing of an entire denomination. Although Antoinette Brown Blackwell had preceded Olympia into the ministry a few years earlier, Blackwell had only had the support of her congregation, not the entire denomination. As a minister of the Universalist Church, Brown went first to Weymouth, Massachusetts, before accepting a pastorate in Bridgeport, Connecticut, where she met and married John H. Wills in 1873. In 1878, after the birth of her second child, Brown took her family to a church in Racine, Wisconsin. Long a believer in women's rights (she chose to retain her own name even after her marriage), Brown helped to organize the Wisconsin woman suffrage association, and served as its president for twenty-eight years. She was also elected vice president of the **National Woman Suffrage Association**. In 1886 Brown met **Elizabeth Cady Stanton** and **Susan B. Anthony**. Possessed of a talent nurtured by public speaking lessons, Brown was immediately drafted to speak on a lecture tour throughout Kansas in support of woman suffrage. The following year Brown resigned from her church pastorate in order to devote more time to women's rights and to her children, thus ending a twenty-one-year career as a full-time minister. Brown continued her activism throughout her life. Her autobiography, *Acquaintances Old and New, Among Reformers* (1911), was an inspiring self-portrait. Already in her eighties, Brown joined the women suffragists who picketed the White House in 1917 and 1918, braving not only a hostile government that arrested and imprisoned the protesters but also a hostile public outraged that the women had not stopped their activities after the United States entered World War I. Brown was the only original suffragist to live long enough to witness the ratification of the Nineteenth Amendment. She died in 1926 at the age of ninety-one.

Cary, Mary Ann Shadd (1823–93), abolitionist, author, lawyer

The eldest of thirteen children born to free blacks in Wilmington, Delaware, the young Mary Ann learned about abolitionism from her father, a conductor on the Underground Railroad, which helped southern slaves escape to the North. When Shadd's family moved to Pennsylvania, she attended Quaker schools. Shadd eventually opened her own school for African American children in her birthplace of Wilmington. After 1850 she moved to Canada to continue her career as an educator, working with the fugitive slaves who had settled there. She promoted self-reliance in a pamphlet she authored in 1849, and in 1852 she published a tract encouraging free blacks in America, subjected to injustice and discrimination, to emigrate to Canada.

Shadd became the editor of an antislavery journal, the *Provincial Freeman*, struggling to advance her race. In 1856 she married Thomas Cary of Toronto, but she was widowed in 1860 and left with two young children. In 1863 she returned to the United States and devoted her energies to recruiting black men for the Union army in the middle of the Civil War. After the war ended, she opened a school for black children where she had settled, in Washington, D.C.

Shadd also earned a degree from Howard University Law School in 1870 and became the first black woman lawyer in the United States. She immediately used her law degree to break down the barriers to equality for women and challenged laws denying women the vote. She was an active member of the Colored Women's Progressive Franchise Association from her founding of the organization in 1880 until her death in 1893.

Cassatt, Mary (1844–1926), impressionist painter, artist

Mary Cassatt, one of seven children of Robert and Katherine Cassatt, was born in Allegheny City, Pennsylvania, remaining there for four years until the family moved to Pittsburgh. When she announced at age eighteen that she intended to become an artist, her banker father told her that he would rather she were dead. The determined Cassatt persuaded her family to let her study in Paris, and in 1866, living with family friends, she began a four-year sojourn there, studying art and painting on her own. She then spent two years traveling in Italy, Spain, and Holland, as well as in France. By 1874 Cassatt had begun to develop the style that would influence her greatest works. She also met and was invited by Edgar Degas to join a a new group of independent French painters who referred to themselves as impressionists.

Over the next four years Cassatt produced a series of paintings that began to attract more and more critical attention. In 1879 Cassatt accepted the invitation of American painter J. Alden Weir to show her works at the newly organized Society of American Artists. That exhibition marked the introduction of impressionism to American audiences. Cassatt also began to introduce her American friends to impressionism. Most notably, she guided American sugar heiress Louisine Havemeyer in the latter's art acquisitions. As a result, when Havemeyer died in 1928, she bequeathed her unparalleled collection to the Metropolitan Museum of Art in New York. Through this acquisition of dozens of works by Cassatt, Monet, Manet, Degas, Cezanne, and Courbet, the museum became a leader in the field of impressionist art.

Cassatt's reputation as an artist grew, and she began to focus her work on the themes of women and children. In 1891 Mrs. Potter Palmer, a Chicago social leader and early collector of impressionist art, invited Cassatt to paint the mural for the Women's Building at the **World's Columbian Exposition**, scheduled for 1893. While the two-year effort was not Cassatt's best work, the commission was nevertheless a fitting tribute to her talent and reputation.

Cassatt spent most of the remainder of her life creating works of art. Ironically, adult-onset diabetes gradually impaired her eyesight until she was virtually blind. Although she underwent surgery in 1921, it failed to restore her sight. She died in 1926.

Chesnut, Mary Boykin (1823–86), Confederate diarist

The eldest daughter of a prominent South Carolina upcountry planter family, Mary Chesnut was steeped in politics from an early age. Her father, Stephen Decatur Miller, was governor of South Carolina and then a U.S. Senator during her childhood. She attended Madame Talvande's academy in Charleston, South Carolina, before her marriage in 1840 at the age of seventeen to James Chesnut, Jr., the only surviving child of a wealthy South Carolina slaveholder. The Chesnuts lived on a plantation near Camden, South Carolina, until they moved to Washington when Chesnut joined the U.S. Senate in 1859.

When South Carolina seceded in December 1860, Mary Chesnut began to keep a detailed record of events and life in wartime Richmond, filled with vivid descriptions and tart observations of Confederate struggles. She was at the very center of the social set who frequented Varina Davis's Confederate White House. Chesnut was equally at ease describing the intricate details of secessionist politics as she was lamenting women's role within the slaveholder's republic. Her poignant accounts of sacrifice and her wrenching details of Confederate decline provide dramatic reading.

Following Confederate defeat, the Chesnuts returned to South Carolina, where Mary Chesnut began revising her wartime diary for publication, a task she left unfinished at her death in 1886. She entrusted her manuscript to a young woman friend, who collaborated with another woman editor to publish Chesnut's diary in 1903.

Child, Lydia Maria Francis (1802–80), writer, reformer

Born Lydia Maria Francis in Medford, Massachusetts, Child was educated in Massachusetts schools until her mother died in 1814. Maria, as she was called, went to live with a sister and complete her education before teaching school.

She moved in with another sibling in Watertown, Massachusetts, in 1820 and made her mark as a writer by publishing her first novel, *Hobomok*, in 1824. She was welcomed into Boston's literary circles, befriending the young **Margaret Fuller**, among others. In 1828, over her family's objections, she married David Child, a lawyer and reformer. The couple became increasingly dependent on Maria Child's writing for income. Child's *The Frugal Housewife* (1829) became a great success. Maria Child also became more involved in reform, most especially abolitionism, and the couple were prominent in literary and antislavery circles.

David Child bought an experimental beet farm in 1837 (an economic alternative to growing sugar cane with slave labor), and the fact that the farm lost money contributed to a marital separation. In 1841 Maria Child left the hardship of her isolated farm to edit an abolitionist weekly, *The Antislavery Standard*, in New York City. In 1849 Maria left New York to reunite with her husband.

Antislavery friends bought the impoverished couple another farm in Massachusetts, where the couple tried to eke out a living. They eventually moved in with Maria's ailing father in Wayland, where she nursed him until his death in 1856. She was a tireless champion of reform, writing *An Appeal in Favor of the Class of Americans Called Africans* (1833), *The History of the Condition of Women* (1835), and *An Appeal for the Indians* (1868). She was an outspoken advocate of emancipation from the early days of the antislavery movement. Child called for expanding women's roles outside of the home and put her ideas into practice with her own career. Further, she believed that American Indians should not be treated like second-class citizens and spoke out against federal policy during the Indian Removal of 1838–39. Her political writings alienated the audience she had acquired as a popular "domestic writer." She wrote syndicated weekly columns, "Letters from New York" (in 1843 and 1845), in an attempt to recapture her readership, but never regained the adulation accorded her initial literary efforts. Her strong stand for African American rights lost her both income and reputation. Following David Child's death in 1874, Lydia Maria Child spent the rest of her years alone, embracing spiritualism and writing her final work, *Aspirations of the World* (1878). She died on October 20, 1880.

Chinese Exclusion Act (1882), the first law to significantly restrict immigration into the United States

After the end of the Civil War, declining wages along the Pacific Coast and economic woes created a prejudice against foreign workers, especially the Chinese. Asian immigrants, mainly Chinese men, had been imported to complete work on the railroad. This hardworking minority was willing to take jobs for less money than native-born laborers, and maintained their own language and customs despite their many years in America. Only a handful of Chinese women had been allowed into the country as well, which was a handicap to Chinese Americans in their quest to establish families and stable communities. This small population of Asians (less than .01 percent of the national total) nevertheless became the focus of a controversial debate in West Coast politics, pressuring Congressional leaders to bow to racist rhetoric and discriminatory attitudes. The 1882 law suspended immigration from China for ten years, and was renewed in 1892. This ban was made permanent with new legislation in 1902 and prevented Chinese Americans from being granted fair treatment and equal rights, declared "undesirable" by restrictive immigration laws. It was not until 1943 that the Chinese were given the opportunity to apply for U.S. citizenship. Only decades later, with the passage of the Immigration Act of 1965, were substantial numbers of Asians allowed to immigrate to America.

Chopin, Kate (1851–1904), author, feminist

Born into a French Creole and Irish family in St. Louis, Missouri, Kate O'Flaherty married Oscar Chopin in 1870. She and her husband lived in New Orleans for a time, but Oscar's business failed and they moved to the Chopin family property where they took up residence. Eventually, the Chopins located in Natchitoches Parish, Louisiana, the setting for much of Chopin's fiction. In 1882 Oscar Chopin died, leaving his young wife with six children to raise. Two years later, Chopin moved her family to New Orleans and began writing. Most of her early work consisted of short stories, and her early themes remained central to her work—women's independence or lack thereof, the effect it had on a woman's life, the sexuality of women, and biology as a determinant in the lives of men and women. Her best-known novel, *The Awakening* (1899), explored all of these themes and the conflicts that they brought to women's lives. Chopin's sympathetic treatment of her heroine, Edna Pontellier, and Edna's subsequent suicide as the only relief from social, religious, and biological conflicts, provoked adverse criticism. But the novel's fame also brought attention to Chopin's earlier works, which had, until then, met with little success or attention. Chopin continued to write until her death in 1904. *The Awakening* fell into oblivion shortly after it was published but was rediscovered in the 1960s and has remained in print in several editions ever since.

Civil War, Women in the (1861–65)

When the Civil War broke out, women rallied to the cause in both the North and the South. In theory, women's role as caretakers of their families well prepared them for nursing. In reality, it was considered improper for women to have intimate contact with strangers, and hospitals, far from bastions of cleanliness and hygiene, were little more than places to die. However, some female nurses served on "floating hospitals," ships pressed into service to take in the dying and wounded. And pioneers such as "Mother" Mary Bickerdyke endeared themselves by braving danger and going to the front to nurse the fallen soldiers. **Dorothea Dix** was so severe with her corps of nurses that she was nicknamed "Dragon Dix."

Females also mobilized to provide necessary support to soldiers headed for the front and prepared to help their men who went off to battle. "Keeping the home fires burning" and maintaining a strong economic momentum on the home front was an important mission for women within both the Union and the Confederacy.

The two largest voluntary organizations in the North were the Christian Commission and the Sanitary Commission. The Christian Commission focused on spiritual welfare and coordinated sending supplies to soldiers. Fresh fruits and sweets were handed out in camps and prayer meetings were organized. More than two thousand "delegates" were enlisted in the campaign, and many women were involved in the distribution of more than half a million Bibles and more than 4 million religious pamphlets to tuck into soldiers' knapsacks. Women spearheaded fundraising campaigns, and the Christian Commission collected more than $6 million during the war.

The Sanitary Commission was a formidable institution that drew strength from its diversity, enlisting hundreds of ladies' aid societies across the North. Feeding the soldiers became a challenge, and Annie Wittenmyer trained more than 200 hospital diet kitchen managers. Her manual became the standard guide for cooks in Union mess halls and tents. Hundreds of dedicated women solicited, donated, sorted, and distributed millions of hospital supplies. **Clara Barton** evaded government red tape and drove her loaded oxcarts to Antietam Creek, Maryland. Over time, women volunteers shifted from genteel taskmistresses into "women warriors."

White southern women were equally devoted to their cause, but failed to coordinate voluntary organizations on the scale achieved by Union women. Southern matrons in Montgomery formed the Ladies Hospital Association in 1862, but like so many similar groups, their efforts were localized rather than regional or military in scope. Perhaps the most effective hospital volunteer in the South was Confederate Sally Tompkins, who left her family plantation in Virginia to run the Robertson Hospital, a volunteer facility in Richmond. For her dedicated service, President Jefferson Davis awarded her the rank of captain in the Confederate army, an honor she accepted, although she returned her salary "for the cause."

Women on both home fronts found themselves equally challenged at war's outset. Yankee women pledged themselves to volunteerism as a secular faith—and found a ready outlet for their energies from St. Louis to Boston. Confederate women were equally committed, but as the war took its toll, their spirits were dampened by the appalling sacrifices being borne by Confederates. Southern plantations, which had been showcases of conspicuous consumption before the war, were now expected to switch gears and feed the army and the civilians—and by 1863 they were failing badly on both counts. The search for necessities preoccupied most southern women, trapped within the Union blockade. Many were forced to resort to the woods, which one woman called "our drug stores."

In southern cities, conditions became critical. Even the Confederate capital of Richmond fell on hard times. When several hundred women took to the streets the first week of April in 1863, in the "Bread Riot," the mayor called out troops, but even the appearance of President Jefferson Davis failed to quell protests. Finally, the distribution of sacks of rice caused the crowd of women to disperse.

African American labor was deserting the plantations, as the Union army lured slaves to freedom when they invaded the South. Long before Lincoln's Emancipation Proclamation in January 1863, black men and women had fled slavery for freedom, entering Union lines first as "contrabands." They quickly proved invaluable to the northern troops as teamsters and cooks, laundresses and nurses.

Black women of the South, like their white counterparts, suffered when men went off to war. Some sent letters to the War Department, even to President Lincoln, protesting and asking that men be sent back to their families. Since only 11 percent of American blacks were free at war's beginning, however, slaves knew that military service was the quickest path to freedom. Most black women trapped within the Confederacy therefore supported men's efforts to fight for the Union and end slavery permanently.

Lee's surrender on April 9, 1865, ended the Confederate dream, and the ensuing struggle to reunite the country would involve women's efforts as well as men's. While the Freedman's Bureau, established during wartime, tried to move into the shambles of the postwar South to set up schools, protect black voting rights, and initiate economic self-sufficiency among African American families, white Confederate women resisted this invasion as mightily as they had Union occupation. The economic devastation in the South was enormous, and the human consequences were dire: the 1870 census revealed 36,000 more women than men in Georgia and 25,000 more women than men in North Carolina. Some desperate Confederate families fled to Canada or sailed for Brazil. But most simply remained to try to build a new society.

Once the war was over, thousands of families faced the harsh reality that many men would never be coming home. Clara Barton launched a campaign to try to trace the many thousands of men missing during wartime and received more than 63,000 letters in her small office in Annapolis, Maryland. She eventually provided over 22,000 families with information on missing soldiers.

The Comstock Law (1873), anti-obscenity legislation

Nineteenth-century moral reformers, ever alert for practices and habits that promoted social evil, began focusing on birth control following the Civil War. The perception had been growing since the 1820s that abortion was an immoral if not illegal act. Opposition to both abortion and birth control, issues often supported in tandem, stemmed from several sources. Middle-class fears about perceived promiscuity abounded, along with the fear that perhaps abortion contributed to this promiscuity. Reformers preached against "race suicide" and fed into the growing desire to limit information about contraception.

Anthony Comstock, a moral reformer who headed the New York Society for the Suppression of Vice, waged an increasingly successful campaign aimed at outlawing the dissemination of literature that he characterized as pornographic. In 1873 the U.S. Congress passed the Act for the Suppression of Trade in, and Circulation of, Obscene Literature and Articles of Immoral Use. Popularly known as the Comstock Law, it prohibited disseminating so-called obscene literature through the mail. Included in the list of outlawed materials was anything having to do with birth control and contraceptives. The penalties for violators of the Comstock Law included imprisonment with hard labor for anywhere from six months to five years for *each* violation, as well as fines ranging from $100 to $2,000 dollars. Comstock himself became one of the chief enforcers of the law after he was appointed a "special" postal agent. He routinely resorted to entrapment schemes by posing as an author of banned materials and soliciting advertisers to market his publication using the mail. Comstock also pursued high-profile cases that generated enough press to let the whole country know that no one was immune to prosecution. Noted New York writer Edward Bliss Foote, and his son and daughter-in-law, both physicians, were accused by Comstock of violating the obscenity laws. It was not until 1936 that the U.S. Supreme Court ruled that the Comstock Law's definition of obscenity had to be reevaluated and could not, in any event, include the subject of birth control (*United States v One Package*).

Cooper, Anna Julia Haywood (1858–1964), feminist, educator

Born the daughter of a slave concubine and her North Carolina master, Anna was sent to the St. Augustine Normal School in Raleigh, North Carolina, at the age of nine. There she met and fell in love with a teacher of Greek, the Reverend George A. C. Cooper, fourteen years her senior. They married in 1877, but Cooper, who had encouraged his wife to pursue her ambitions, died less than two years later. The young widow went on to earn a B.A. in 1884 and a M.A. in 1887 from Oberlin College in Ohio. She joined the faculty at the prestigious M Street High School in Washington, D.C., and in 1902 become its principal.

During the 1890s Cooper earned a national reputation as a leader of her race, publishing her influential *A Voice From the South by a Black Woman of the South* (1892). In 1893 she was a featured speaker at a special meeting of the Women's Congress in Chicago, during the World's Columbian Exposition. Cooper was the only woman elected to the American Negro Academy, founded in 1897. She traveled to London in 1900 to address the first Pan-African Conference, organized by W. E. B. DuBois.

Throughout this period Cooper was also a staunch supporter of women's rights, a voice raised against lynching, and an advocate of improved educational opportunities for male and female African Americans. During a curriculum controversy in 1906, Cooper was forced to resign from her post at the M Street School. She took the opportunity to devote her energies to raising several young relatives, including her grand-niece and namesake, Anna Julia Cooper Haywood Beckwith, whom she adopted in 1915 when the child was only six months old. She also decided to pursue her educational interests.

After attending summer classes at Columbia University (1915–17), Cooper applied to the Sorbonne, where in 1924, at the age of sixty-six, she earned her Ph.D., one of a handful of black American women to achieve such distinction. In 1930 she assumed the presidency of Frelinghuysen University, a black school in Washington, D.C. When the college lost its charter in 1937, Cooper's role became limited and ceremonial, although she did not retire until the age of eighty-four. She died in her home in Washington, D.C., at the age of 105.

Crandall, Prudence (1803–30), abolitionist, educator

Born into a Rhode Island Quaker family, Prudence attended boarding school in Providence before she opened her own school in Plainfield, Connecticut, to educate young ladies in the surrounding countryside. Her Canterbury Female Boarding School came under fire in 1831 because Crandall wanted to admit the daughter of a local black farmer. White parents withdrew their support when Crandall insisted upon admitting her. When opposition to Crandall's attempts at integration forced her school to close, she decided to reopen it as a teacher-training school for black girls only.

Outraged local citizens then persuaded the legislature to pass a law forbidding schools for African Americans. When she defied the law, Crandall was arrested and held in jail. William Lloyd Garrison and other New England abolitionists drummed up support for her, but despite antislavery sentiment, Crandall was convicted. The decision was reversed by a higher court, but when she attempted to return to her school, mob violence made life unbearable for both her and her pupils, and she was finally forced to close the school in 1834. Crandall resumed her career in education following her marriage to the Reverend Calvin Philleo, a fellow abolitionist. She conducted a home school in 1842 after she and her husband moved out to the Illinois frontier. She was involved in reform and women's suffrage for the rest of her life. The state of Connecticut voted Crandall a pension in 1886, four years before her death.

Dall, Caroline Wells Healey (1822–1912), author, feminist

Caroline Wells Healey, the daughter of a wealthy businessman and descended from several generations of New England ministers, turned her back on the comfortable materialistic aspirations her parents held for her. Instead, she devoted herself to religious duty, charity, and reform. She established a nursery school in Boston's North End, where she worked from 1837–42. In 1844 she married Unitarian minister Charles Dall. The union produced several children, after which the Reverend Dall decided to leave the United States—and his family—in order to pursue missionary work in India. Faced with the prospect of raising her children alone, Dall quickly developed an empathy for the plight of other working women in her position who lacked the family resources she could command. Dall became active in the women's rights movement and with Paulina Davis organized a feminist convention in Boston in 1855. In 1859 she spearheaded the campaign for the New England Woman's Rights Convention, also in Boston. Her addresses at these events were reportedly electrifying. They earned her a reputation as an eloquent and forceful advocate of equality for women and resulted in her career as a public lecturer. In 1865 she became a founder of the American Social Science Association, a group in which she continued active until 1905. Dall wrote several books examining the educational barriers and employment constraints facing American women. Her best-known book on the subject, *The College, the Market, and the Court; or, Women's Relation to Education, Politics, and the Law,* was published in 1867. In it she argued the necessity of more and better economic options for women. Despite her pioneering early career as a writer and lecturer, she spent much of her later life absorbed in her Sunday school work and in writing tributes to friends, among them a biography of pioneering woman physician, Dr. Marie Zakrewska.

Declaration of the Rights of Women (1876), feminist doctrine

On July 4, 1876, the country prepared to celebrate its centennial. Women of the National Woman Suffrage Association made their own preparations to include in the official record of the day a Declaration of the Rights of Women. The declaration, written by **Matilda Joselyn Gage** and **Elizabeth Cady Stanton**, demanded total equality for women. Falling short of that, the declaration stated that women were prepared to "foment rebellion," as Abigail Adams had advised her husband, John Adams, when he left to join the other Founding Fathers in creating a Constitution for the new nation one hundred years earlier. "Do not forget the ladies," Adams had implored. Feminists in 1876 believed that women were still being denied both their rights as citizens and the protection of the Constitution. Official ceremonies at the Capitol on the July 4th celebration included a reading of the Declaration of Independence. Gage, **Susan B. Anthony**, Sara Andrews Spencer, Lillie Devereaux Blake, and Phoebe Couzins devised a plan to quickly deliver to the president pro tempore of the Senate a copy of their own declaration upon completion of the reading of the Declaration of Independence. Aware that they could be stopped at any moment, the women hurried to the front of the gathering, unwittingly aided by startled onlookers who moved aside to let them pass. Gage handed their declaration to Anthony, who in turn handed it to presiding officer Thomas Ferry. Ferry, too, was startled at the event and accepted the scroll without protest. Thus, through the efforts of courageous feminists, the Declaration of the Rights of Women became an official part of the proceedings of the centennial celebration.

Declaration of Sentiments and Resolutions (1848), feminist protest document

The first women's rights convention in the United States, held at Seneca Falls, New York in 1848, produced a germinal document, the Declaration of Sentiments and Resolutions, which became the Bible for the women's rights movement. Convention organizers **Elizabeth Cady Stanton** and **Lucretia Mott** intentionally modeled their declaration on the Declaration of Independence, stating, "We hold these truths to be self-evident, that all men and women are created equal." The declaration went on to list a series of eighteen areas in which women were treated as second-class citizens and that the collective members of the convention believed had to be addressed immediately. It was a demand for full economic, legal, social, and political equality for women. The eighteen demands listed in the declaration included the right to equal education, equal access to trades and professions, equality in marriage, the right to make contracts, to own property, to sue and be sued, to testify in court, to speak in public, to retain guardianship over their children, and to vote. More important, it was the first document that outlined the intentions and goals of the women's rights movement. It is interesting to note that the grievance most troublesome to those who attended the convention was the issue of suffrage. A significant minority of those in attendance believed that asking for the vote for women was simply too radical a demand and would jeopardize their entire program. It was the one issue over which heated debate took place before its inclusion was assured by a majority vote. In retrospect, the suffrage issue turned out to be far less radical than some of the declaration's other demands, including the demands for economic and social equality. Within two decades of the Declaration of Sentiments, suffrage would become the focus of the women's movement. Women's rights advocates, both main-streamers and radicals, accepted the necessity of securing the vote as a first step to achieving more fundamental equality for women.

Dickinson, Emily (1830–86), poet

Emily Dickinson was born in Amherst, a small town in western Massachusetts, and lived her entire life in her father's house there. She traveled infrequently, except for periods of time spent in Washington (in 1854 when her father served a term in Congress) and Boston (briefly in the 1840s, and for several months in 1864 and 1865 when she was being treated for eye problems). She graduated from Amherst Academy in 1847 and enrolled at the Mount Holyoke Seminary, remaining there for only one year. During that year Dickinson became a target for Mary Lyons in Lyons's quest to convert all her students to Christianity. It was a measure of Dickinson's individuality and inner strength that she resisted where others gave in, but she tired of the constant entreaties and chose not to return to Mount Holyoke. Dickinson had her share of friends and even engaged in rela-tionships that went deeper than friendship, although perhaps never beyond the platonic stage. A young law clerk in her father's firm, Benjamin F. Newton, became Emily's first mentor from 1847 to 1849. He encouraged her in her choice of reading, what authors she should know, and to recognize the fullness of nature, including "faith in things unseen." Later, she engaged in long correspondences with Reverend Charles Wadsworth of Philadelphia and with Samuel Bowles, a family friend who was the editor of the *Springfield Daily Republican*. But as she got older, Dickinson became more and more reclusive, often remaining secluded upstairs in her bedroom when visitors came to call. She did, in later years, fall deeply in love with Judge Otis P. Lord, a friend of her father's. The rela-tionship lasted from 1877 until Lord's death in 1884. After Lord's death, Emily suf-fered a physical breakdown from which she was never able to recover.

During her lifetime, Emily Dickinson wrote some eighteen hundred poems. Seven were published before her death, and she often confided in her brother Daniel and her sister Lavinia, seeking their advice on her writing abil-ity. A contemporary of the poets of the American Renaissance (1830s to 1850s) and the transcendentalists (**Margaret Fuller** and Ralph Waldo Emerson), Dickinson was unknown to any of them, although Emerson was one of her favorite poets. Much of her poetry remained undiscovered until after her death. As the depth and breadth of her profound talent became clear to critics and the world at large, her life as a near recluse became more and more an enigma. What was clear, however, is that the more circumscribed that Dickinson's physical world became, the more expansive her mind became. Her poetry transcended the boundaries of time and place, making Emily Dickinson a preeminent American poet of the nineteenth century.

Dix, Dorothea (1802–87), medical reformer

At the age of twelve, Dix left her unhappy childhood home in Maine, where her father was often absent and her mother was constantly ill. She went to live with a grandmother in Boston where, at the age of fourteen, her interest in education led her to open her own school for younger children. Struck down by illness in 1828, she began to write. When she was asked to teach Sunday school to women in the East Cambridge jail in March 1841, the horrible conditions there—foul, unheated cells crowded with women—led her to become an activist. Dix discovered that mentally ill women were mixed in with criminals. From then on, she campaigned for the proper treatment of the mentally ill, to have them properly sheltered and fed and to prevent such inhuman treatment.

Her survey of Massachusetts penal institutions, completed in 1843, was a model of social welfare research and prompted the state legislature to earmark funds to improve conditions in a state asylum in Worcester. Dix expanded her crusade across state borders and launched several state campaigns for better conditions for the mentally ill. Once her attempts at national legislative reform failed, she carried her crusade to England and Scotland, where she toured in 1856.

With the outbreak of the Civil War, Dix was appointed superintendent of army nurses; she was a strong leader who required her nurses to be older women, "plain" in appearance, presumably to prevent bedside romances. Her severe administrative style caused her to be dubbed "Dragon Dix" by her detractors. Her loyal service to the Union cause kept the nursing corps efficient and effective until her resignation in 1866.

Following the war, Dix turned her energies toward the South, visiting hospitals, asylums, and orphans' homes, continuing to work for reform. But the aging Dix slowed her efforts during the 1870s. Ill and infirm, she retired to a state hospital in Trenton in 1881, where she lived until her death at the age of eighty-three.

Duniway, Abigail Scott (1834–1915), reformer, women's rights advocate

When Abigail Scott Duniway was seventeen in 1852, her father moved the family from Illinois over the Oregon Trail to the Northwest Territory. During the grueling trek, Duniway's mother died from cholera, leaving behind nine children, of whom Abigail was the second. After teaching for a year, Abigail married Benjamin Duniway in 1853 and began a life of childbearing and farming. After six children and fifteen years of hard work, the farm that seemed about to pay off was confiscated by the bank. Abigail's husband had cosigned notes for a friend who was unable to pay his debt. Although Abigail had opposed the actions of her husband, the laws allowed him full control of the family assets. Her husband later became fully supportive of her determination to work to change the law so that women would not be held hostage to a system over which they had no control.

Duniway moved her family to Portland in 1871 and, with the help of her children, started a newspaper, the *New Northwest*, promoting the cause of women's rights. She also organized a speaking tour in the Northwest for **Susan B. Anthony** and discovered, in the process, that she also had a talent for public speaking. Thereafter, Duniway lectured often on women's rights. In 1873 she helped to found the Oregon Equal Suffrage Association. She attended legislative sessions regularly and sometimes even testified on behalf of woman suffrage. She played a large role in winning suffrage for women in Washington (1883) and Idaho (1896). Duniway resigned from the **National American Woman Suffrage Association** (NAWSA) after Anthony's retirement in 1896, because she disagreed with the direction taken by the new NAWSA leadership, women who were increasingly insistent upon linking woman suffrage and temperance. She continued to work for suffrage, however. Although Duniway did not live to see the federal suffrage amendment passed and ratified, she was instrumental in helping Oregon women win the vote in 1912, even though by then she was confined to a wheelchair.

Forten, Charlotte (1837–1914), author, educator

Born into one of the most prominent free black families in antebellum Philadelphia, Charlotte Forten lost her mother when she was only three years old. She received a classical education in Philadelphia and later in Salem, Massachusetts, where she was sent as a young girl to complete her education. Forten became involved with abolitionism early in life, following in her grandfather's footsteps, as James Forten remained an outspoken opponent of slavery and a leading black abolitionist all his life. After she graduated from the State Normal School in Salem, she was hired in 1856 by the Epes Grammar School and became the first black teacher to instruct white children in Salem. In 1858 ill health forced her to resign her teaching position. She remained at home to teach her young cousins and began to write and publish essays and poems.

With the advent of the Civil War, many free educated blacks wanted to contribute to the Union cause. Forten went to the Sea Islands in South Carolina to work as a teacher among the "contrabands," escaped slaves housed within Union camps. She was one of the first black teachers to join the campaign that W. E. B. DuBois later dubbed the "Tenth Crusade." At her outpost on St. Helena Island, she began to keep a journal, which was published in *The Atlantic Monthly* in 1864 as "Life on the Sea Island." Upon the death of her father, Forten returned to the North, but went South again in 1871 to teach in Charleston, South Carolina, for a year before moving to Washington, D.C., where she was offered a post at the prestigious, all-black Dunbar High School. In the nation's capital, she met her future husband the Reverend Francis Grimké, nephew of the white abolitionist sisters Angelina and Sarah Grimké. Forten and Grimké were married in 1878 and had one child, who died in infancy. Forten continued her career as a writer and reformer until her death in Washington in 1914.

Foster, Abby Kelley (1811–87), abolitionist, feminist

A native of Massachusetts, Abby Kelley Foster's Quaker background imbued her with a strong belief in both pacifism and equality of the sexes. She converted to abolitionism by reading William Lloyd Garrison's *Liberator* and became secretary of the Lynn Female Anti-Slavery Society in Massachusetts from 1835 to 1837. In 1838 she joined with Garrison in founding the New England Non-Resistant Society, advocating nonresistance as a doctrine to oppose slavery, among other evils. In 1839 she launched a speaking career, and, in the face of heckling and virulent attacks, preached the doctrine "No Union With Slaveholders" throughout the country, from the Indiana frontier to upstate New York.

In 1841 Kelley met Stephen Foster, a likeminded radical activist who had abandoned his plans for the ministry. The death of her mother in 1842 left her free from family responsibility, and Kelley became single-minded in her pursuit of radical reform, traveling and lecturing almost constantly. After four years of courtship, Kelley and Foster were married in 1845. Foster respected his wife's feminist position and encouraged her to continue her political activism, even after the birth of their daughter, Alla. Leaving her child in the care of relatives or her husband, Foster continued to lecture in public. Far ahead of her contemporaries on many issues, Foster insisted that women could both raise a family and enjoy a vibrant intellectual and activist life. Unlike most women reformers and nearly all men, Foster insisted that women must speak their minds in public and disregarded the name-calling, branded as "Jezebel" when she stood before a "promiscuous" audience, one with both men and women. Despite her feminist philosophy, however, Foster was adamant on the issue of separating abolitionism and women's rights. She was steadfast in support of securing freedom for slaves and ensuring voting rights for former male slaves before attempting to secure voting rights for women. After ratification of the

Thirteenth Amendment (1865) and the Fifteenth Amendment (1870), Foster devoted her support to women's suffrage.

Fuller, Margaret   (1810–50), writer, feminist, philosopher

One of the nineteenth century's most remarkable and talented women, Margaret Fuller was born in Cambridgeport, Massachusetts. Her father, a Harvard professor, believed in exposing his daughter to an intellectual environment usually reserved for males. As a consequence, most of Fuller's early years were spent in her father's library, soaking up its contents and mastering Latin, Greek, French, Italian, and German. Although she did attend a local female academy, she received much of her education at home. By her early teens Fuller took responsibility for educating her younger siblings. In 1836 she took a position at the experimental Temple School in Boston, and later she taught at the Greene Street School in Providence, Rhode Island. But teaching did not fulfill her intellectual needs, and Fuller returned to Boston in 1839. Already acquainted with Ralph Waldo Emerson and Henry David Thoreau, Fuller became an integral part of the New England transcendentalist movement. By then she had already begun to work on her own writing as well as a translation of the work of philosopher Immanuel Kant. To support herself, Fuller began to hold a series of "conversations" in the parlor of her Boston home. Discussions were wide-ranging and so stimulating that Boston matrons were soon subscribing to the once-weekly lectures and conversations. The conversations continued from 1839 to 1844 and were exclusively for women, except for a brief period in 1841 when men were allowed to participate. In 1840 Emerson, Thoreau, and Fuller founded the *Dial*, America's first literary journal. At the urging of Emerson and Thoreau, Fuller became its editor for two years.

In 1845 Fuller accepted an offer from Horace Greeley to become the first literary critic in America, at the *New York Tribune*. During this period Fuller expanded an early essay entitled "The Great Lawsuit: Man Versus Men. Woman Versus Women" into her signature volume, *Woman in the Nineteenth Century*. Published in 1845, the book quickly became a classic of American feminist thought. Its influence can be clearly discerned in the manifesto of women's rights that came out of the **Seneca Falls Convention** held in 1848, when Fuller had already been abroad in Europe for more than a year. Once again, Greeley offered Fuller an opportunity that she could not pass up: foreign correspondent for the *Tribune*. Traveling in England, France, and Italy, Fuller's prodigious reputation and her correspondent's position brought her into contact with many of Europe's most important writers and philosophers. In Italy in 1847, the revolution to unify that country was underway. There, Fuller met Giovanni Angelo, Marchesi d'Ossoli, with whom she fell in love.

As a writer, Fuller contributed to the revolution in Italy, working alongside Ossoli in Rome. In May 1848 the couple had a son, Angelo Eugene. When the revolution began to go badly, they were forced to flee to Florence. In 1850, despite an unsettling foreboding of disaster, Fuller and Ossoli decided to sail for America. Within sight of Fire Island, New York, their ship went down in a storm. There were no survivors. Margaret Fuller was dead at the age of forty.

Gage, Matilda Joslyn (1826–98), women's rights activist, suffragist

Matilda Joslyn Gage, the only child of Dr. Hezekiah and Helen Joslyn, was born in Cicero, New York. Dr. Joslyn opened his home to abolitionists, women's rights activists, and temperance advocates. He also directed his daughter's education, teaching her Greek, math, and physiology and always encouraging her to think for herself. Matilda married Henry Gage in 1845, and for the next several years her life was occupied with raising four of her five children, the fifth having died in infancy. Although she had been exposed all her life to the issues surrounding women's rights, Gage only became active in the movement in 1852 when she attended a women's rights convention in Syracuse. For the next decade she worked for the cause when time permitted. But in 1869, with her children grown, Gage felt free to get more involved. She joined the **National Woman Suffrage Association** (NWSA) and became vice president and secretary of the New York State Woman Suffrage Association. She corresponded voluminously with people not only in America but abroad as well, promoting women's rights. From 1878 to 1881, Gage edited NWSA's monthly newspaper, *National Citizen and Ballot Box*. From 1881 to 1886, Gage worked closely with **Elizabeth Cady Stanton** and **Susan B. Anthony**, producing the first three volumes of *The History of Woman Suffrage*.

By 1886 Gage had begun to despair that woman suffrage would ever be achieved, and she began to turn her attention to religious organizations, convinced that the teachings of the churches trained men to believe in the inferiority of women. In 1890 she organized the Woman's National Liberal Union, dedicated to exposing organized religion as the major cause of women's continued status as second-class citizens. She considered it her life crusade to free women from the "bondage" of organized religion. In *Woman, Church, and State* (1893), Gage stated unequivocally that the church was the "chief means of enslaving woman's conscience and reason." *Women, Church, and State*, which stands alongside the **Declaration of Sentiments and Resolutions** as one of the most significant documents to come out of the nineteenth-century women's movement, was Gage's most important theoretical treatise. Gage was disappointed when the National and the American woman suffrage associations united in 1890, for she believed that the conciliatory attitude of the American suffragists would slow down the quest for woman suffrage and equal rights. After 1890 most of her efforts were directed toward exposing organized religion as sexist and oppressive to women.

General Federation of Women's Clubs (1890), voluntary organization

Throughout the latter part of the nineteenth century, middle-class women looking for a nonpolitical outlet to channel their desire to expand the boundaries of homemaking and child rearing joined a variety of local clubs. Most of these fell into two categories: local civic organizations and literary discussion groups. When journalist June Cunningham Croly invited a number of organizations to help her celebrate the twenty-fifth anniversary of Sorosis in 1889, a club she had organized as a literary discussion group, the idea for a federation of clubs was established. Within a year, the General Federation of Women's Clubs (GFWC) was born. Croly believed that a federation of clubs could wield power in accomplishing changes in local communities. Although most of the women who belonged to the organization were not women's rights activists, all were concerned about bettering their communities. Many participated in public health campaigns, in campaigns to establish kindergartens, and in beautification movements. Most crucial, the GFWC worked to establish local libraries — funding projects, soliciting donations, getting buildings erected and filled with books. The Federation could claim responsibility for founding more libraries than any other single organization by the turn of the century, and was credited with providing dramatic improvement of public educational facilities. While the GFWC remained fairly apolitical for its first quarter century, it did nevertheless represent the mindset of many middle-class women and eventually, as Croly had predicted, endorsed political goals such as woman suffrage.

Gilman, Charlotte Perkins (1860–1935), economist, author, feminist

Charlotte Perkins Gilman's troubled and impoverished childhood led her to develop a strong mistrust of socially accepted norms and conventions. Initially attracted to art, Gilman attended the Rhode Island School of Design where she met and married artist Walter Stetson. Nine months later Gilman and Stetson had a baby daughter. A severe case of postpartum depression led eventually to a nervous breakdown. This threw Gilman into an even deeper depression. In 1892 she described her ordeal in dramatic detail in a short story entitled "The Yellow Wallpaper." She and Stetson were divorced four years after their marriage, and Gilman courageously left her daughter behind when she went to live in California.

The cumulative effects of her life experiences propelled Gilman into a long if informal study of women's status in society. She began lecturing and writing both fiction and nonfiction. In 1898 Gilman published her most important work, *Women and Economics*, in which she proposed a series of family living arrangement changes that she believed would benefit not only women but society as a whole. These included communal kitchens and nurseries so that women could share housekeeping and child rearing, thus reserving time to pursue their own interests and achieve economic independence, something she considered far more radical than being able to vote.

In 1900 Gilman married a distant cousin, a member of the Beecher family, as was her father. She took his name (Gilman) and dropped the name Stetson. For the remainder of her life, Gilman continued to write and lecture. She wrote numerous articles for *The Independent* as well as for other periodicals. In addition, she continued working on a manuscript that she believed would be her most important publication. When *Human Work* was published in 1904, it was not well received, however. Arguing that work was an end in itself, the book lacked the passion of *Women and Economics*. From 1909 to 1916 Gilman wrote, edited, and published her own monthly magazine, *The Forerunner*. Its pages were filled with fiction and nonfiction, essays and poetry, all commenting on the status of women and the necessity for social change. Although the magazine never achieved financial stability, Gilman did keep it going for seven years before she was finally forced to give it up. She also continued to publish books, including *Man-Made World* (1911) and *His Religion and Hers* (1923). In January 1915 Gilman, along with **Jane Addams** and others, founded the Woman's Peace Party, an organization dedicated to keeping the United States out of the hostilities in Europe. After the war and after the passage of the Nineteenth Amendment, Gilman wrote and lectured, generally on the themes already familiar in her past writings. When, in 1935, she was diagnosed with cancer, Gilman chose to take her own life rather than to suffer a prolonged illness.

Godey's Lady's Book, the single most influential magazine for women in the nineteenth century

Founded in 1828 as the *Ladies Magazine*, its editor, **Sarah Josepha Buell Hale**, defined the model for all subsequent women's periodicals. The magazine offered a combination of fashion, helpful tips to homemakers, fiction, poetry, recipes, and noncontroversial articles on social issues. It helped to establish a national standard of social form and grace, etiquette and taste. In addition, the magazine opened the door for many American writers, including women, who previously had few venues for their talents. When Louis Godey bought the magazine in 1837, he changed the name to *Godey's Lady's Book*, and it quickly became known by the reading public as *Godey's*. Sarah Hale remained its editor until her retirement in 1879. Hale and Godey concurred in keeping controversy out of the pages of the magazine, particularly anything of a political nature. Even so, the tenor of many of the editorials helped to advance women's rights in ways that perhaps Hale did not intend. A firm believer in "the woman's sphere," the traditionally accepted role of women as wives and mothers, Hale very much supported higher education for women because she was persuaded that an educated woman could only strengthen the social hierarchy within the family. Her editorials applauded the founding of women's colleges. She also supported women in medicine and other occupations that she believed were extensions of woman's sphere. By the 1870s *Godey's* reached a subscription level of more than 150,000, and it managed to sustain its readership even after Hale retired and Godey was no longer associated with the magazine. Subscriptions declined slowly but steadily for the next 20 years. By the end of the century a new generation of magazines such as *Vogue* and the *Ladies Home Journal* had begun to win over readers ready for more progressive views and *Godey's* disappeared.

Greenhow, Rose O'Neal (1815–64), Confederate spy, author

Born the daughter of a wealthy Maryland planter, Rose Greenhow was introduced into Washington society when her sister married Dolly Madison's nephew. She met and married Virginia lawyer Robert Greenhow, who worked for the Department of State.

A popular Washington couple, the Greenhows had four daughters over the next few years. Following her husband's death in 1854, Greenhow remained in Washington and had a close relationship with President James Buchanan. Greenhow's parlor was a well-known gathering spot for politicians from both sides of the aisle.

When the Civil War broke out in 1861, Greenhow was deeply involved in the gathering of intelligence for the Confederate government, reputedly extracting state secrets from Senator Henry Wilson of Massachusetts, with whom she was reported to have been intimate. She sent key information to Richmond before the First Battle of Bull Run and was put under house arrest in Washington in August 1861. The houseful of female prisoners became known as "Fort Greenhow." Finally, Greenhow and her eight-year-old daughter were confined to the Old Capitol Prison, charged with espionage. Greenhow was eventually released in June 1862 and sent to Richmond, where she was showered with praise and reward by President Jefferson Davis.

In 1863 she sailed to Europe as a special envoy of the Confederate government. She published a propaganda volume, *My Imprisonment and the First Year of Abolition Rule at Washington* (1863), which turned her into a celebrity. She was presented at court in England and met with Napoleon III in France. She was sailing home in September 1863 on the *Condor*, with important documents and gold sewn into her gown, when Union gunboats threatened her blockade-running ship. Greenhow and two companions tried to escape, but their lifeboat capsized, and Greenhow was drowned. Her body washed ashore near Wilmington, North Carolina, and she was buried with full military honors, as a martyr to the Confederate cause.

Grimké (Weld), Angelina (1805–79), abolitionist, feminist author

The youngest of fourteen children born to prominent South Carolina planter John Grimké, Angelina was more influenced by her older sister **Sarah** than any other sibling or her parents. When her father died in 1819, she rejected slavery by emancipating those slaves she inherited. Angelina was so passionately opposed to slavery that she followed her sister Sarah into exile in the North in 1829 and never returned to her birthplace.

In 1835 Angelina decided to take up her pen in defense of her deep antislavery sentiments and published *An Appeal to the Christian Women of the South* (1836). William Lloyd Garrison, editor of the *Liberator*, helped her to secure an appointment with the **American Anti-Slavery Society**. Her stirring abolitionist tract, written from the point of view of the daughter of a prominent slaveholding family, and her willingness to speak in public stirred controversy up and down the eastern seaboard, where she toured. Charleston banned her from returning, and southern ministers preached against her and called her "Devilina."

In 1837 Angelina published *An Appeal to the Women of the Nominally Free States*, an attempt to stir northern females to take up the abolitionist cause. She also testified in front of the Massachusetts legislature in support of antislavery petitions, the first female ever to address a body of state representatives in the United States. Shortly thereafter, a pastoral letter condemned her and her sister Sarah's "unwomanly behavior." But both sisters vigorously defended female participation in the public sphere, advocating strong words and political action. The controversy only attracted more of an audience to Angelina's lectures.

After a brief courtship, Angelina married abolitionist activist and author Theodore Weld on May 14, 1838. The newlywed Angelina addressed a Philadelphia antislavery convention the day before a protest mob burned the hall to the ground. Following this violent protest, the Welds decided to abandon Philadelphia and moved to Fort Lee, New Jersey, where her sister Sarah made her home with the couple.

Angelina had bouts of ill health following the births of each of her three children. Financial difficulties forced the couple to open a school in 1851. In 1863 Theodore Weld attempted to revive his speaking career, but following his failure, the family moved to Hyde Park, Massachusetts, near Boston. Angelina, her husband, and her sister Sarah all taught at a ladies' academy in Lexington.

In 1868 the Grimké sisters discovered that two students at the all-black institution of Lincoln University in Philadelphia went by the name of Grimké and were sons of their brother Henry by a slave woman. They adopted these black nephews and supported them as family. In 1873 Angelina Grimké Weld suffered a debilitating stroke that kept her partially paralyzed until her death six years later at the age of seventy-four.

Grimké, Sarah Moore (1792–1873), abolitionist, feminist author

Sarah Grimké, the sixth of fourteen children, was the daughter of John Grimké, a prominent legal scholar and wealthy Hugenot planter in South Carolina. Young Sarah was shy and introverted, and felt deprived of the education and considerable benefits her brothers enjoyed. She frequently traveled to the North with her ailing father, serving as his nurse as he journeyed to Pennsylvania and New Jersey seeking relief. Following his death in 1819, she abandoned her Episcopal upbringing and converted to the Society of Friends (Quakers). Sarah moved to Philadelphia at the age of twenty-eight. Her sister **Angelina**, the youngest in the family, followed in Sarah's Quaker footsteps, and the two women turned their backs on planter privilege and slaveholding. Both freed the slaves they inherited upon their father's death.

During this period, Sarah turned down a marriage proposal from a Quaker merchant and seemed content to pursue a celibate life. Sarah was unable to speak in public like her accomplished sister Angelina, but was no less passionate about antislavery; her *Epistle to the Clergy of the Southern States* (1836) contained a detailed theological refutation of religious arguments that were being used to defend slavery.

In 1837 a pastoral letter condemned both sisters' "unwomanly behavior," and Sarah and Angelina were drawn into feminist debates within the antislavery movement. Several abolitionist colleagues counseled them to concentrate on antislavery, although most women abolitionists and a few prominent male abolitionists such as William Lloyd Garrison also championed women's rights. Nevertheless, both sisters became staunch defenders of their sex and advocated female participation in the public sphere. In 1838 Sarah Grimké completed *Letters on the Equality of the Sexes and the Condition of Women*, which argued forcefully that women had a moral duty to advocate on behalf of equal rights and that increasing their role in the public sphere would improve the larger society and fulfill God's purpose.

The two sisters became acquainted with antislavery activist Theodore Weld, who courted and married Angelina. Sarah made her home with the couple. The sisters effectively retired from public life, but both circulated antislavery petitions and compiled and published a collection based largely on reports from southern journals: *American Slavery As It Is: Testimony of a Thousand Witnesses* (1839). This documentary remains one of the most vivid and compelling first-hand portrayals of the brutal treatment of African Americans in the antebellum South; surprisingly, these accounts were often taken from southern newspapers.

Sarah helped her sister to take care of her three children, including her niece and namesake, Sarah Weld, born in 1844. Financial difficulties forced the Welds to open a school in 1851. In 1863 Theodore Weld attempted to revive his speaking career, but following his failure, the household transplanted to Massachusetts, where Sarah taught in a female academy in Lexington to help support the family.

Hale, Sarah Josepha Buell (1788–1879), editor

Sarah Hale, a self-educated New Hampshire native, became one of the nineteenth century's most influential women as editor first of the *Ladies Magazine*, and later of *Godey's Lady's Book*. Hale was widowed at the age of thirty-five and left with five young children to support. Faced with sole responsibility for the family's welfare, she began by writing poetry, which she sold under a pseudonym before publishing her first collection under her own name. Shortly after that, in 1827, she published her first novel. Her literary efforts were noticed by the publisher of the fledgling *Ladies Magazine*, Reverend John Lauris Blake, and he offered her a job as editor. Because the magazine industry was still in its infancy, Hale was able to establish the model for women's magazines and exercise enormous influence, first over the makeup of the magazine and later over the hearts and minds of her readers. With regular features that included fashion, recipes, health and beauty tips, homemaking advice, and a combination of fiction, nonfiction, and poetry, the *Ladies Magazine* quickly built a broad base of readers. In 1837 Louis Godey bought the magazine, convinced Hale to remain as editor, and rechristened the magazine *Godey's Lady's Book*. In her ten years as editor of *Ladies Magazine*, Hale had progressed from writing virtually every article, fiction and nonfiction, every editorial, and every review article, to building a publication that attracted the talented writers her readers came to expect. But more than that, Hale was exclusively responsible for the tone and direction the magazine, and later, *Godey's*, adopted. She became the arbiter of what was socially fashionable and culturally acceptable. Women swore by what they read in the pages of *Godey's* and revered Mrs. Hale, as she was known.

Hale was able to exercise influence over the progress made by women in specific areas. Because she had had to earn a living for herself and five children, Hale believed deeply in the right of women to be educated and was a great proponent of women teachers. Thus she supported the establishment of normal schools throughout the country. She also supported the founding of women's colleges as well as the entrance of women into fields previously closed to them, particularly medicine. She was also supportive of women entering into the foreign missions field and charity organization societies. Hale also came to support the Married Women's Property Act, on the grounds that the right to earn a living to support a family was simply an extension of woman's domestic sphere. On the other hand, Hale steadfastly refused to support purely political goals, including suffrage, because she deemed politics to be an unacceptable pursuit for women.

Hale retired as editor of *Godey's* in 1878 but continued to write on her own. Her multivolume series on American women, *Women's Record, or Sketches of Women*, an ambitious biographical dictionary containing 2,500 entries and published between 1853 and 1876, remains a valuable source for the history of women during this period. Hale died in 1879, while *Godey's* was still a mainstay for women readers. By the century's end, however, other publications, including the *Ladies Home Journal*, had pushed *Godey's* aside. But for thousands of women during the nineteenth century Mrs. Hale was the voice to whom they turned for advice and gentle guidance.

Harper, Frances Ellen Watkins (1825–1911), author, reformer

Harper was a popular and prolific author—one of the few bestselling African American writers published during her lifetime. Born to free blacks in Maryland, Harper was orphaned at a young age. She attended her uncle's Academy for Negro Youth in Baltimore before moving to Ohio in 1850, where she became the first female teacher at what later became Wilberforce University. She moved to Philadelphia in 1853 and devoted her energies to the cause of antislavery reform.

Her first known book of poems, *Forest Leaves* (1854), has not survived, but her second, *Poems on Miscellaneous Subjects* (1854), sold 10,000 copies in its first printing and went into an astounding 20 editions during her lifetime. In it, she combined her literary aspirations and political interests to produce "protest poetry." These protest poems, such as "The Slave Mother" and "Slave Auction," were widely embraced by a white northern audience, who welcomed her lyrical testimonials against slavery. When John Brown led his historic raid on Harper's Ferry, Virginia, in October 1859, Harper pledged solidarity with Brown's cause and moved in with Brown's wife in order to help her with the ordeal of her husband's trial and subsequent execution. Harper wrote a letter to one of the African American men who had participated in the raid and, like Brown, was condemned to death, enclosing her "Bury Me in A Free Land," one of the most widely anthologized antislavery poems.

Harper continued to publish, never cutting back on her literary output after she married in 1860. Her husband died in 1864. Harper made extensive speaking tours of the South following the Civil War, encouraging blacks to demand fairness during Reconstruction and advocating the vote for women, black and white. In 1896 she was one of the founding members of the **National Association of Colored Women**. She was lauded at her death for both her distinguished literary reputation and her role as a civic activist.

Howe, Julia Ward (1819–1910), author, poet, activist

Julia Ward Howe, a New York City native, was by all accounts a brilliant child whose lack of formal education did not prevent her from acquiring the foundation necessary to achieve critical and social fame as an author, lecturer, and social activist. A well-known poet and writer during her lifetime, Ward is best remembered today as the author of the "Battle Hymn of the Republic." During the Civil War the poem was set to music and became the anthem of the republic. She taught herself Latin and Greek, and while she was still very young her writings and poetry began appearing in literary journals. In 1842 she married Samuel Gridley Howe, an abolitionist who later became famous as an innovative educator. The marriage, which produced six children, was not a happy one, although the couple never formally separated. Howe resented his wife's intellectual ability, her fame, the inheritance she received from the family estate, and not the least, her lack of any real interest in homemaking. Active in the **American Woman Suffrage Association**, serving as its first president, Howe's personal fame helped to attract huge audiences when she began lecturing in public. She helped to found the *Woman's Journal* in 1870, one of the most influential women's publications for several decades thereafter.

Despite being identified as a member of the conservative branch of suffragists, Howe consistently advocated a wider role for women in society. In 1873, with **Frances Willard**, she cofounded the Association for the Advancement of Women, which encouraged women to enter the professional ranks as scientists, educators, and lawyers, among other things. Howe also supported and was active in the women's club movement, serving as president of the New England Women's Club in 1871 and as the first president of the Massachusetts Federation of Women's Clubs in 1893. By then, the rift between the two suffrage branches, the **American Woman Suffrage Association** and the **National Woman Suffrage Association**, had ended. Howe and **Susan B. Anthony**—who had been a critic of Howe's conservatism—became allies in their old age. Both were honored in 1906 at the annual woman suffrage convention. In 1906 Howe became the first woman elected to the American Academy of Arts and Letters in recognition of her literary career, which included publication of *Sex and Education* (1874), *Modern Society* (1881), a biography of Margaret Fuller (1883), and her own autobiography, *Reminiscences* (1899), as well as her poetry including, of course, the "Battle Hymn of the Republic." She died at her cottage in Newport, Rhode Island at the age of ninety-one. Her memorial service at Boston's Symphony Hall featured a choir of four thousand voices singing the stirring words that had so moved Abraham Lincoln the first time he heard them fifty years earlier.

Hull House (1889), settlement house

Hull House, the Chicago settlement house founded by **Jane Addams** and **Ellen Gates Starr**, opened its doors in September 1889. Hull House was designed as an experiment that would bring educated middle-class people into a poor, immigrant, and working-class environment in order to provide a variety of services from instruction in English to job training to health care and child care. Hull House offered residents of Chicago's South Side a place to learn a trade or develop a skill, a place for unmarried working women to live, and a place for mothers to leave their children or to enroll them in nursery and kindergarten programs. Very quickly, Hull House became a vital, integral part of South Side Chicago. It offered the poor free access to an array of instructional classes designed both to acculturate the largely immigrant residents and to provide practical skills and services. It also sponsored lectures and art shows, taught English and citizenship classes, and offered day nursery care and medical care. The settlement house also became a residence for working women, and a meeting place for clubs and labor unions. By 1893 as many as two thousand Chicagoans took advantage each week of one or more Hull House programs. Hull House's mission attracted a broad spectrum of individuals who significantly contributed to progressive reform. Out of this movement was born the social work profession. Among those who lived in Hull House for various periods of time were Grace and Edith Abbott, Charles Beard, Sophonisba Breckenridge, John Dewey, and Florence Kelley. These and other Hull House residents became advocates and activists working for a variety of social reforms, including child labor, sanitation, housing conditions, working conditions, education, industrial safety, and immigrants' rights. Hull House became the prototype for similar undertakings around the country, including the Henry Street Settlement House in New York City.

Immigration

The first large nineteenth-century waves of immigration began with the Irish. Driven away from home by the potato famine in the 1840s, Irish immigrants tended to settle mostly in and around urban areas. However, because of rules governing inheritance in Ireland, more single women left home than did single men or married women. Irish women tended to go into domestic service, and as late as 1925, 43 percent of all domestic servants were Irish immigrants or first-generation Irish Americans. Moreover, because many women were supporting families back home, a large proportion of Irish women who immigrated alone remained unmarried.

Political unrest in Europe in 1848 prompted significant German immigration, along with the first large-scale wave of Scandinavian immigrants. Most women in these ethnic groups traveled with families, usually as either wives or daughters, and tended to settle in the Midwest and on farms. By the time the Civil War ended, the country's overall rate of immigration had begun to expand and continued to do so until after the turn of the century. Immigrants from southern and eastern Europe began arriving in large numbers, including Jews from Poland, Germany, and Russia, as well as Italians and Slavs. Large numbers of Jewish and Irish single women tended to settle in large urban areas, in ghettos where Jewish or Irish families gathered. Jewish women were a significant factor in the garment industry, and Irish women often went into domestic service. Italians and Slavs tended to travel in family units, and most gravitated toward urban areas, especially along the eastern seaboard. Italian women were perhaps the most restricted by family and culture. Single Italian women who sought employment usually did so in industries that employed few males, such as hat making or artificial flower production. More Slavic women were drawn to heavy industry than any other female immigrant group.

There were very few Asian women immigrants in the nineteenth century. Most Asian immigrants in general settled on the West Coast, their point of entry into the United States. But early Asian immigrants tended to be male, many of whom worked on building the continental railroads. Later in the century restrictive legislation such as the **Chinese Exclusion Act of 1882** prohibited Asian immigration or significantly limited the numbers allowed to enter. Throughout the nineteenth century Asian immigration totaled less than a million people. During the 1890s, European immigration often exceeded a million immigrants per year.

Most single immigrant women, and some married women as well, worked for wages, thus helping to provide the labor force necessary to fuel the growing industrial economy. Low wages and long hours in unskilled jobs characterized the working life of most urban immigrant women. Women on the frontiers and on farms usually worked as long and as hard within the family unit but generally were not considered part of the work force.

Until Congress enacted immigration restriction laws in 1924, which created a formula for future immigration and severely limited the numbers of immigrants allowed to enter the country in any given year, approximately 35 million immigrants from western Europe, eastern Europe, Scandinavia, Asia, and other countries had come to the United States. Of this number, approximately one third were women.

Incidents in the Life of a Slave Girl, Written by Herself (1862), slave narrative

Published by Harriet Jacobs under the pseudonym of Linda Brent, this work is acknowledged by historians as the most important memoir written about slavery by an African American woman. Jacobs was born in North Carolina in 1812, the daughter of a slave, but the granddaughter of a free woman of color. *Incidents* tells the gripping story of a young woman's defiance and triumph, struggling against a white master who wants to conquer her, body and soul. Jacobs writes of resisting her owner's overtures by taking a white lover, by whom she had two children, and hoping her children might be bought by their father and set free. When this did not happen, Jacobs's master plotted to send her children away. Jacobs ran away in 1835, but instead of fleeing North Carolina, she hid herself in a crawlspace in a house nearby, so she could remain near her children. In 1842 Jacobs escaped to New York City, and soon after her children were spirited North to be reunited with her. She worked as a domestic, but lived in fear of recapture. In 1852 her freedom was finally secured and her children's safety protected.

Encouraged by abolitionist Amy Post in Rochester, New York, Jacobs worked on her memoir and tried to sell the manuscript, without success until abolitionist Lydia Maria Child wrote an introduction. When *Incidents* appeared in 1862, it was a minor sensation, especially among Union readers. This moving testimonial, replete with the language of Victorian morality, which Jacobs employed skillfully to advance her cause, was a stinging indictment of the sexual exploitation of slavery. Jacobs painted a vivid portrait of the evils the system fostered within both black and white families. *Incidents* remains an important document for understanding American slavery.

Jewett, Sarah Orne (1849–1909), author

The daughter of a prosperous shipbuilder, Jewett spent most of her life in South Berwick, Maine, her birthplace. Jewett graduated from the Berwick Academy in 1865. She published her first story in 1868 and her first volume of short stories, *Deephaven*, in 1877. Many of her published writings revolve around the history and characters of the Down East seacoast. Her fame rested on her popularity as one of a group of writers known as "local colorists."

Her father's death in 1878 devastated Jewett. She leaned even more heavily on her intimate friendship with Annie Adams Fields, wife of the Boston publisher. When James Fields died in 1881, his widow traveled and lived with Jewett. Jewett's work blossomed as she continued to experiment with the short story, publishing several collections: *A Marsh Island* (1885), *A White Heron and Other Stories* (1886), and *A Native of Winby* (1893). Her novels include *A Country Doctor* (1884) and *The Tory Lover* (1901). Her most accomplished piece of fiction is *The Country of the Pointed Firs* (1896). As an esteemed New England author, Jewett maintained a small circle of literary friends, including the young Willa Cather. Between trips to Europe and seasons in her beloved Maine, Jewett spent part of the year in Boston with Annie Fields. She died in the same house in which she was born. A volume of her poetry, *Verses*, was published posthumously in 1916.

Kemble (Butler), Frances Anne (1809–93), actress, author

Born in London in 1809 into the first family of the British stage, Fanny Kemble followed in the footsteps of her famous aunt, Sarah Siddons, the most acclaimed actress of her generation. When money troubles threatened foreclosure of the family's London theater, Covent Garden, Charles and Maria Kemble decided to put their nineteen-year-old daughter on stage. Her debut in 1829 catapulted her to international stardom, but Kemble was more interested in her budding career as a writer than in continuing as an actress. In 1832 she went on tour to America, where she met and married Pierce Butler of Philadelphia in 1834. Kemble retired from the stage but still wanted to write. Soon, she and her husband clashed over her literary pursuits, as she published a controversial journal of her tour of America. The couple's disagreements became even more vehement, especially over Kemble's interest in antislavery. In 1836 Butler inherited one of the largest slaveowning estates in Georgia from his mother's family. The couple had two daughters who accompanied them on an ill-fated journey to the Butler plantations on the Georgia sea islands in the winter of 1838–39. Kemble kept a journal of her experiences, which her husband refused to allow her to publish.

After several more years of discord, the couple separated. In 1849 they finally divorced and Butler was awarded custody of their daughters until they reached the age of twenty-one. Kemble was crushed by this blow but continued her acting career and achieved international success by offering public readings of Shakespeare's plays.

During the American Civil War, Kemble feared that England might support the Confederacy. Despite her younger daughter's objections that making public such a personal document would cause her pain, in 1863 Kemble published her *Journal of Residence on a Georgian Plantation*, a work that condemned both slavery and her ex-husband's role as slaveowner. This eyewitness account caused a sensation on both sides of the Atlantic and may have shifted British public opinion against the South. Kemble continued her career as a diarist, eventually publishing eleven volumes of memoirs, in addition to several plays, volumes of poetry, and, at the age of eighty, her first novel. She provided guidance and inspiration for her grandson, Owen Wister, a popular American novelist, author of *The Virginian*. Kemble died in England.

Knights of Labor   (1869), national labor union

The Knights of Labor was the first national labor union to accept women as members. Organized by Uriah S. Stephens in 1869, the Knights operated under the principle that all wage laborers had a common interest that transcended individual crafts or industries and therefore would be better served by belonging to "one big union." Stephens opened membership to anyone who "toiled," with a few notable exceptions including lawyers, bankers, gamblers, and liquor dealers. The question of accepting women into the union was discussed from the beginning. Because the Knights began as a secret society, women, considered incapable of maintaining secrecy, were excluded from membership in the early years. At the same time, the official constitution drawn up at the first national convention in 1878 made clear that the primary goal of the organization was to secure equal pay for equal work "for both sexes." The turning point for women came in 1881, when a Philadelphia shoemakers' strike led to the drafting of women workers to fill in for the strikers. One of the substitutes, Mary Strikling, agitated for and persuaded the scab women workers to join in the walkout in support of the unionized shoemakers. The Philadelphia Knights promptly inducted the women strikers into the organization, opening the door to other women workers. Within five years there were more than one hundred women's assemblies in the Knights of Labor, including domestic workers in Washington, D.C., Wilmington, North Carolina, Philadelphia, Pennsylvania, and Norfolk, Virginia. More important, the Knights became the first American labor organization to establish a Department of Women's Work, which focused specifically on issues affecting women workers.

The 1890s witnessed the decline of the Knights of Labor, from which it never recovered. But within its lifetime, the Knights, by accepting women into the union, improved women's status in the union movement.

Larcom, Lucy   (1824–93), mill worker, author, editor

Born the daughter of a sea captain in Beverly, Massachusetts, Larcom moved to Lowell, Massachusetts, when her widowed mother went to work in the textile mills there. After a few years of rudimentary schooling, Larcom joined her older sisters in the mills. She spent nearly ten years working as a factory girl and wrote for the factory journal, *The Lowell Offering*. She left Lowell to attend a seminary in Illinois from 1849–52. In 1854 she returned to her hometown of Beverly, offering classes in writing. In 1854 she won a poetry prize sponsored by the Emigrant Aid Society (a group that sponsored abolitionist settlers in Kansas) and shortly thereafter was offered a teaching position at Wheaton Seminary, in Wheaton, Illinois. Exhausted by the demands of teaching, she resigned her position in 1862, to devote herself to her literary career. In 1865 she was editor of a children's magazine, *Our Young Folks*. Larcom never married and spent much of her later career publishing for young adult readers. During the 1870s she produced several anthologies of children's poetry, and in 1889 she published her autobiographical *A New England Girlhood*, which described her youth and years as a mill girl. She died in Boston at the age of sixty-nine and was buried in her birthplace of Beverly.

Lease, Mary Elizabeth (1850–1933), union activist, reformer

One of the first women to run for a major political office, Mary Elizabeth Clyens Lease campaigned for a U.S. Senate seat from the state of Kansas in 1893. A popular and talented orator who spoke on a number of issues ranging from populism and the plight of the farmer to women's rights, temperance, suffrage, and the Irish Rebellion, Lease was one of the Populist party's most influential leaders in the 1890s. She herself had to endure most of the difficult times that beset farmers in the Midwest. Several of her efforts at farming failed. For her, political activism seemed the only way to resolve the severe hardships imposed by a combination of forces that included weather, economic depression, and unfair practices that limited farmers' earning capacity. Lease, usually called Mary Ellen, had a reputation as a straight-talking and outspoken critic of big business and was often referred to as "Mary Yellen" by her opponents. Urging her fellow farmers to "raise less corn and more hell," Lease also edited and wrote for political newspapers. A "master workman" in the **Knights of Labor**, Lease's oratorical skills earned her an invitation to second the nomination of James Weaver, the Populist Party presidential candidate, at the party's national convention in 1892. When the 1893 **World's Columbian Exposition** held its Kansas Day, Lease was chosen to deliver the main address. Although she lost her bid for the Senate seat in Kansas, Lease continued to speak out on issues. Her book, *The Problem of Civilization Solved*, published in 1895, was a collection of Lease's solutions to economic and social problems; it ranged from advocating an industrial Napoleon who would maximize production and minimize worker exploitation to the nationalization of railroads and banks. Her ability to turn a phrase caught the attention of the publisher of the *New York World*, and she was invited to become a political writer. She spent her remaining years in New York City, writing and campaigning in various elections, including Theodore Roosevelt's run for the presidency as the Progressive Party candidate in 1912. Lease worked tirelessly for causes she advocated, including woman suffrage and birth control.

Lee, Jarena (1783–?), evangelist, author

Born a free black in Cape May, New Jersey, the young Jarena proclaimed that she had been "moved by the holy spirit" to take up religious work. In 1809 she petitioned the Bethel African Methodist (AME) Church in Philadelphia, requesting permission to preach—a request that was denied because of her sex. In 1811 she married an AME pastor, the Reverend Joseph Lee, and settled in Snow Hill, New Jersey. Widowed in 1817 and left with two children, Lee again petitioned to hold prayer meetings in her own hired house, as a means of spiritual comfort and financial necessity. This time AME Bishop Richard Allen granted her request. Lee not only preached in Philadelphia but also became an itinerant evangelical speaker, traveling throughout New England.

In 1836 she published *Life and Religious Experience of Jarena Lee, A Colored Lady, Giving an Account of Her Call to Preach.* As an early advocate of equality for women in the church, as an outspoken black woman in a society dominated by white males, Jarena Lee's ministry was pathbreaking. Her exemplary career paved the way for other African American women to seek a larger role in the growing AME church, a role that would continue to expand as increasing numbers of women were "called to testify" later in the century.

Lockwood, Belva (1830–1917), lawyer, feminist

Belva Lockwood holds the distinction of being the first woman to plead a case before the U.S. Supreme Court. Born in Royalton, New York, she became a teacher. When her husband was killed, leaving her with a young child to support, Lockwood managed to earn a degree from Genesee College in 1857, while continuing to teach. She met another New York teacher, **Susan B. Anthony**, just as Anthony was launching her own full-time career as a women's rights advocate. Lockwood remained in education in upstate New York throughout the Civil War, but later decided to move to Washington, D.C., where she opened her own coeducational school. She also got involved in politics, helping to select a representative to Congress from the District. When Lockwood remarried in 1871, she had the freedom to pursue other interests and decided to become a lawyer. Overcoming many obstacles, she was finally admitted to the recently opened National University Law School in Washington. Throughout her law student days and the years establishing a practice, Lockwood maintained an active interest in woman suffrage. She volunteered her services and was a member of the National Woman Suffrage Association, and lectured in public. Lockwood had to battle mightily in order to be able to argue cases in the federal courts, and in 1879 helped to open the doors of the U.S. Supreme Court to women litigators when she argued a case before the Court in 1879. When Lockwood became the presidential candidate for the National Equal Rights Party in 1884 and again in 1888, she did not have the support of most suffragists because they believed her efforts were premature and would detract from the seriousness of the cause. Lockwood continued to campaign for suffrage, but she also began looking outward, beyond national boundaries. Much of her later career was concerned with the world peace movement, particularly as an advocate of arbitration to resolve international disputes.

Lowell Female Labor Reform Association (1844), labor organization

The Lowell Mills in Lowell, Massachusetts, established during the second decade of the century, had long been considered an ideal working environment for young, single women from Massachusetts and surrounding New England states. A recognized model for industry, the mill owners had designed Lowell as not only a physical workplace but also a self-contained living arrangement, with dormitories, shops, and recreational facilities for the female workers. The patriarchal nature of the mills was an important element in the successful recruitment of young rural women who sought wage labor and whose families needed the assurance of propriety where their daughters were concerned. Each Lowell employee had to agree to abide by the rules and regulations that governed activities on a twenty-four-hour daily basis, including Sundays. The complex of mills that made up Lowell routinely required twelve-hour workdays. When, in 1836, the Hamilton Manufacturing Company attempted to impose wage cuts that would decrease even further the already meager hourly rates, factory worker **Sarah Bagley** helped organize a job walk-out, demanding a ten-hour workday and higher wages. Pitted against the power of the mill owners, the strike failed in its immediate goals. It succeeded, however, in persuading workers that they needed their own organization to do battle with the mill owners in the future. Despite the attempted strike, conditions did not deteriorate until the early 1840s. But the loosely organized 1836 action led to the formation in 1844 of the large and vigorous Lowell Female Labor Reform Association. With several hundred members, the association gathered more than 2,000 signatures in support of a 10-hour day. Sarah Bagley, one of the organizers, became one of only a handful of women to ever address a state legislature when she testified before the Massachusetts legislature on behalf of a 10-hour day. These early efforts ultimately failed to achieve their goals, but they alerted mill owners to women's growing militance.

McCord, Louisa Susannah Cheves (1810–79), author, political theorist

The daughter of a leading South Carolina politician, Louisa McCord was exposed to political discourse from an early age. She married widower David McCord at the age of twenty-nine and was encouraged by her husband to pursue her intellectual interests, an unusual phenomenon among the antebellum southern elite. Despite the births of three children, her career as a writer flourished. McCord published her first literary efforts under the initials "L. S. M."

Her polemical essays and literary reviews gained her a national reputation. She prepared a searing attack on Harriet Beecher Stowe's *Uncle Tom's Cabin*, in which she methodically provided theological and political defenses of slavery while caustically chipping away at what she believed was the hypocrisy of New England abolitionists who condemned slavery only after their ancestors had reaped the financial windfall of the slave trade.

With the death of her husband in 1855 and her father in 1857, McCord sank into a depression. She took two of her children to Europe for a rest cure, returning just as secession and conflict led the country into war. During the Civil War, McCord was an ardent Confederate, donating time, money, and her only son, whose death was a terrible loss. After the war she threw herself into commemorative activities and was a leading activist within the ladies' memorial movement, which evolved into the United Daughters of the Confederacy. In 1870 she abandoned South Carolina for Canada, distraught by what she contemptuously referred to as "Negro rule." McCord finally returned to Charleston in 1876, when she felt the political tide was turning against Republican reform. She spent the rest of her life writing a biography of her father, which was still incomplete at her death.

Minor v Happersett (1875)

In 1872 Virginia Minor brought suit against the Registrar of Voters in St. Louis, Missouri, on the grounds that as a citizen of the United States, Minor was entitled to vote. Minor was not the only woman who tried to vote in the election of 1872. In that first election following ratification of the Fifteenth Amendment, women in communities across the country attempted to cast their ballots. The Fifteenth Amendment, since its inception, had been a source of discontent for feminists since it guaranteed voting rights only to former male slaves. Women had lobbied, unsuccessfully, for the inclusion of votes for all women, regardless of color or status, but politicians had little interest in women voting. Advocates for the freedmen, fearful of jeopardizing gains for African American males, chose not to support feminists' efforts. Influenced by the National Woman Suffrage Association, women engaged in massive and impassioned acts of civil disobedience by attempting to vote. The efforts resulted in many court cases, including the trial of **Susan B. Anthony**, who had led a small group of women to the Rochester polls and was arrested. Anthony was convicted at a trial held without a jury, by a judge who had written his opinion before the trial even started.

The decision in *Minor v Happersett* dashed hopes for a judicial solution to women's quest for the vote. Thereafter, suffragists turned their full attention to a series of state and federal campaigns to change both state constitutions and, ultimately, the U.S. Constitution, in order to achieve voting rights for women.

Maria Mitchell (1818–89), astronomer, educator

Born into a Quaker family of ten children on the island of Nantucket, Massachusetts, Mitchell worked as a librarian at the Nantucket Athenaeum. She also helped her father, a self-taught astronomer, gather data for a coastal survey for the U.S. Coast Guard. Her father's example led Maria to pursue her own self-education. When the library was closed, she spent hours reading scientific and astronomy books and teaching herself German and French in order to read scientific treatises in those languages. Mitchell also attended lectures sponsored by the Athenaeum, including talks given by William Ellery Channing, Ralph Waldo Emerson, Lucy Stone, and Theodore Parker.

On October 1, 1847, while assisting her father, Mitchell discovered a new comet, which was subsequently named after her. Harvard anthropologist Louis Agassiz nominated her for membership in the American Association for the Advancement of Science, making her that organization's first woman member and the only one until 1943. She was awarded a gold medal by the King of Denmark.

In 1861 Matthew Vassar, founder of Vassar College, invited Mitchell to become a member of the college's original faculty. Vassar's pledge to build her an observatory with a twelve-inch telescope helped Mitchell to overcome her initial reluctance to accept the offer. For the next twenty years Mitchell worked with some of the country's brightest minds, training the first generation of women astronomers who went on to staff universities, colleges, and observatories throughout the country. They carried with them Mitchell's philosophy: accept nothing as given beyond the first mathematical formulae, question everything, and learn from observation. In 1869 Mitchell became the first woman accepted into the American Philosophical Society. As president of the American Association of University Women in 1875, Mitchell used her platform to encourage young women to enter the sciences. Maria Mitchell once described herself as possessing "average ability but extraordinary persistence." Her impact on science and in particular on the first generations of women scientists suggests, in retrospect, that Mitchell underestimated her own talents.

Mott, Lucretia Coffin (1793–1880), abolitionist, suffragist

Lucretia Mott is widely recognized as having done more to promote women's rights and establish a women's rights movement in nineteenth-century America than anyone else, with the exception of **Elizabeth Cady Stanton** and **Susan B. Anthony**. Born in Nantucket, Massachusetts, Mott attended schools in Boston and Poughkeepsie, New York. Prior to her marriage to fellow-Quaker and minister, James Mott, she was a teacher. Both she and her husband were ardent abolitionists. Mott helped to organize the Female Antislavery Society in Philadelphia in 1833, and she organized the first national abolition meeting for women only in 1837. Her exclusion from taking a delegate's seat at the World Abolition Conference in England in 1840 brought her into contact with Elizabeth Cady Stanton, with whom she would work closely for the remainder of her life. Because of events in England, both Mott and Stanton became committed to the cause of women's rights. Their resolve to do something about it was not realized for another eight years. But in 1848 the **Seneca Falls Convention** heralded the beginning of the women's rights movement in the United States. Mott and Stanton were largely responsible for the **Declaration of Sentiments** and the drafting of the resolutions that came out of the convention. By this time Mott was a widely recognized lecturer around the country. Her staid, conservative appearance helped to disarm audiences who otherwise might not have been so receptive to her radical message of equality for women and freedom for slaves. In 1850 Mott wrote her *Discourse on Women*, arguing for political and legal equality for females. During the Civil War she and her husband opened their home to slaves escaping bondage via the Underground Railroad. Mott continued to lobby for equality for women and freedom and equality for African Americans until her death.

Mount Holyoke Seminary (1837), first women's college in the United States

In the summer of 1833 educator **Mary Lyon** traveled throughout the Northeast and as far west as Detroit, visiting schools and academies for young girls. She also touched base with other notable educators, including her mentor, **Emma Willard**, the founder of the Troy, New York, Female Seminary and a long-time advocate for equal education for girls. When she returned to Ipswich Academy where she taught, in the fall of 1833, Lyon was convinced that the time was right to establish an institution for the higher education of young women. By that time many communities had begun to accept female education as a positive enhancement to the ideals of republican motherhood forged during the Revolutionary War. If women were the guardians of strong and moral families and responsible for raising good republican sons, then they should have some formal grounding in those things that would promote such virtue. When Mary Lyon began raising money for her new school, she found several communities willing to invest in the future. South Hadley, Massachusetts, offered Lyon an $8,000 grant to begin construction of the school, and the offer was accepted.

Lyon insisted on a rigorous curriculum that mirrored the course of study at New England's oldest colleges for men, Harvard and Yale. Hers would not be a finishing school, as were many of the female academies founded in the 1820s and 1830s. Mount Holyoke students were expected to take courses ranging from

Greek and Latin to human anatomy. Moreover, the school would be a four-year institution, again modeled on the older male schools. In order to defray expenses and to provide practical training, Lyon also insisted that each student would be responsible for daily chores of housekeeping throughout the school.

Beginning in 1837, with a single four-story, red-brick Georgian building that doubled as both academic and dormitory facility, and a handful of full-time instructors, Mary Lyon opened the doors of Mount Holyoke Seminary, so named because South Hadley lay nestled within sight of Mt. Holyoke. To provide adequately for the eight students, the full-time staff was supplemented by professors from nearby schools, such as Amherst, who agreed to lecture on academic subjects. Characterized as a "seminary" in its early years, Mount Holyoke achieved the status of a college in 1888. It was the first of several women's colleges, counterparts to the elite male "Ivies," that eventually became known as the **Seven Sisters**: Mount Holyoke, Smith, Barnard, Bryn Mawr, Radcliffe, Wellesley, and Vassar.

National Association of Colored Women (1896), voluntary organization

This group emerged from several strands of black women's activism at the end of the nineteenth century. Black women after the Civil War were disproportionately involved in education and charity. Many important local institutions were founded and supported through women's charitable and reform efforts, such as the Colored Woman's League, founded in Washington, D.C., in 1892 and the Woman's Era Club of Boston, founded in 1893. The national organization evolved as a protest against white clubs, which banned black membership. First, the Board of Lady Managers organizing for the **World's Columbian Exposition** in Chicago rejected the inclusion of black women. Next, a national conference was called in support of black women who had been shunned. Josephine St. Pierre Ruffin of Boston, Helen Cook of Washington, and Margaret Murry Washington (representing Tuskegee women's clubs) convened delegates from across the country to promote a national organization. This group, representing fifty-four clubs from across the country, created the National Federation of Afro-American Women. The group then organized a delegation to participate in the Cotton States Exposition in Atlanta in 1895, defying white discrimination.

Unfortunately northern and southern black women came into conflict over several issues, most notably the regional responses to segregation, racial violence, and the southern practice of public lynching. Finally, black women's organizations recognized that only through unity could black women advance within American society. They set their differences aside and in July 1896 formed the National Association of Colored Women (NACW), dedicated to "self-protection" for black women and "self-advancement." **Mary Church Ter-**

rell, the nationally known educator, became the first president of the group. Black women within the movement rallied to other causes as well: temperance, purity, suffrage. However, the women of the NACW came together to promote racial unity. During its 1897 Nashville convention the group claimed 5,000 members.

During the early days of the NACW, the membership was mainly drawn from northern urban women, although more than 90 percent of black Americans lived in the South. But over the years the NACW expanded and soon boasted a healthy, strong southern membership, many of whom rose through the ranks to become leaders. Black women of the NACW raised funds to care for the aged, to set up industrial schools for girls, to form hospital auxiliaries, and to create children's homes and social clubs for girls. Literary societies and suffrage campaigns were also funded from NACW coffers. Many of the local branches threw themselves into fund-raising and institution building to help black migrants pouring into northern cities from the South. Between 1910 and 1920 black populations in Detroit, Cleveland, New York, and Chicago exploded. The NACW provided community centers to help the migrant families find food, shelter, work, and education in these strange city streets where they sought new lives.

National Woman Suffrage Association (1869), suffrage organization

Following the World Anti-Slavery Conference in London in 1840, when women delegates had been refused seating, the infant women's movement developed along two increasingly divergent paths. The **Seneca Falls Convention** in 1848 addressed the issues involving priorities and grievances. It was not until 1866, however, that women leaders took formal steps in an effort to halt the growing fissure between abolitionists and women's rights advocates. The American Equal Rights Association, led by **Lucretia Mott**, **Susan B. Anthony**, and **Elizabeth Cady Stanton**, intended to ensure that women could remain involved in both women's and antislavery activities. Die-hard male abolitionists immediately raised objections, declaring that women were willing to jeopardize abolition at a critical juncture in order to achieve their own selfish ends. Like abolitionist and former slave Frederick Douglass, who was a strong advocate of woman suffrage, many abolitionists believed that it was "the Negro's hour." Feminists countered that they had deferred their suffrage quest long enough; virtually all women's rights activity had been suspended for the duration of the Civil War. Abolitionist Wendell Phillips, looking for what he believed to be a reasonable solution, announced that the reform agenda had to be first Negro suffrage, then temperance, then labor reform. Finally, when everything else had been accomplished, woman suffrage. Feminists were less than thrilled with Phillips's pronouncement, but it was not until the Fifteenth Amendment specifically excluded women by establishing voting rights only for former male slaves that they were prompted to take more direct action. In May 1869, at the New York Women's Bureau, Anthony and Stanton organized the National Woman Suffrage Association (NWSA), with 118 initial members. Because of their recent experience with male abolitionists, the NWSA excluded men from leadership positions and elected offices. The organization also determined that its goal would be to secure an amendment to the Constitution that would guarantee to all women their right to vote.

National American Woman Suffrage Association   (1890), suffrage organization

The merger of the **National Woman Suffrage Association** and the **American Woman Suffrage Association** (AWSA) into the National American Woman Suffrage Association (NAWSA) in 1890 focused on efforts to unite the women's movement and thus strengthen its influence. **Harriot Stanton Blatch**, the daughter of **Elizabeth Cady Stanton**, one of the founders of the National Woman Suffrage Association, and **Alice Stone Blackwell**, the daughter of **Lucy Stone**, the founder of the American Woman Suffrage Association, were the architects of unification. Blatch and Blackwell noted that significant changes in the status of women since the Civil War made the time a propitious one to combine efforts. By 1890 there were more women than men in high schools, one third of all college students were women, the women's club movement had united under the banner of the **General Federation of Women's Clubs**, and the **Women's Christian Temperance Union** was moving into its most powerful phase. Suffrage was no longer an isolated vehicle for change — it was now part of a larger women's movement with a younger, better-educated, more active constituency. To placate those feminists who still insisted on a federal suffrage movement, including **Susan B. Anthony** and Stanton, the new NAWSA still advocated pursuit of federal suffrage. In reality, a few hard-won victories in the hundreds of state campaigns that the AWSA had engaged in since 1869, especially a victory in Colorado in 1893, persuaded the majority of NAWSA members to pursue state suffrage as the primary focus.

Although Stanton and Anthony were elected the first and second presidents of the NAWSA, their influence was on the wane. Anthony, in particular, found the NAWSA's new direction to be a bitter pill to swallow. Although she remained president from 1892 to 1900, when she finally retired from active work, Anthony was especially appalled when, in 1893, she was unable to prevent other NAWSA leaders from moving the headquarters from Washington, D.C., to Ohio. To Anthony, that action spoke volumes regarding the intent to abandon the focus on federal suffragism. While the women's movement united for the sake of efficiency, conflicts remained between those who wanted women's rights to remain their only priority and those moderates who viewed women's rights as conditional and dependent on whatever other issues existed at a given time. As the nineteenth century wound down, the moderates had succeeded in dominating the organized suffrage movement. For the next two decades the NAWSA would wage hundreds of state campaigns aimed at winning over enough legislators in each state to change the state's constitution. This strategy was replaced by twentieth-century activists, who eventually triumphed with the Nineteenth Amendment in 1920, which granted women the vote.

Oakley, Annie (1860–1926), sharpshooter, performer

Born in Darke County, Ohio, one of eight children, the death of Oakley's father in 1864 permanently disrupted her childhood. Oakley was sent to the county poor farm, from which she eventually ran away at the age of twelve. She was reunited with her family and became so proficient with a gun that she supported the family not only by the game she was able to kill but also by winning local shooting contests.

Visiting her sister in Cincinnati at the age of fifteen, Oakley met Frank Butler, a professional sharpshooter, whom she married in 1876. The couple toured vaudeville theaters and eventually joined the Buffalo Bill Exhibition in New Orleans in 1885. During her sixteen years with the Wild West show, Annie Oakley became not only the most famous trick shot in the country but also the highest paid wage-earning woman in America. Nicknamed "Little Sure Shot," by fellow performer Sitting Bull, Oakley could shoot down a dozen balls tossed in the air, then ride a horse into the ring, snatch a pistol from the ground, and hit her target while still moving. She would also shoot a hole through playing cards tossed into the air, and these treasured mementos became known as "Annie Oakleys."

Her fame spread internationally when Bill Cody took his show to London in 1887, and she spent four years abroad before her triumphant run during the **World's Columbian Exposition** in Chicago in 1893. Annie Oakley's Wild West career ended following injuries sustained in a train wreck while on tour in 1901. She was able to return to the stage to play western heroines, but she never returned to the ring. Oakley and her husband continued to perform at shooting resort hotels throughout the country. Oakley eventually retired to Florida, but returned to her native Ohio in 1926 where she died a few months later. Oakley became a legendary icon, impressing her audience by ranking top in the "man's world" of the Wild West but maintaining a ladylike demeanor, which was her trademark. This quirky combination made her a household name and an international star.

Palmer, Alice Freeman (1855–1902), educator

A precocious child born in Seneca Falls, New York, Alice Freeman Palmer learned to read by the age of three. By the time she was a teenager, her parents agreed to send her to college if she would remain single. Fully intending to abide by the agreement, Palmer graduated from the University of Michigan. She accepted a faculty position at Wellesley College in the Department of History in 1879, and in 1881 she became the second president of the college, at the age of 27. Palmer proved to be an innovative advocate for the college. She established a series of Wellesley prep schools, designed to prepare women for the rigorous curriculum they would undertake as college students. By the time she retired, there were fifteen of these female prep schools located throughout the country. Five years after accepting the presidency of Wellesley, Palmer married Herbert Palmer, requiring her to resign as president since married women were not allowed to remain on Wellesley's faculty.

Fortunately, the University of Chicago was less concerned with marital status and invited Palmer to accept a deanship that would require only a twelve-week-per-year commitment. Palmer quickly made it her primary task at Chicago to create an atmosphere more receptive and more attractive to women students, establishing within the university what she referred to as a "western Wellesley." After three years with the University of Chicago, Palmer resigned. She served as a board member for the Massachusetts State Board of Education. She also lectured on behalf of suffrage and temperance. Palmer died at the age of forty-seven, from complications following relatively minor surgery.

Rollin, Frances Anne (1845–1901), author

Born into a family of free blacks in Charleston, South Carolina, Frances was the oldest of five sisters. Educated at a Quaker school in Philadelphia during the Civil War, Rollin returned home to Charleston to find her father's business in ruins; he had been a supporter of the Confederacy, while Frances and her sisters were staunch supporters of the Union cause. Rollin became a teacher with the Freedman's Bureau in the South Carolina sea islands. She once sued a ferry captain who denied her a first-class accommodation. Her winning lawsuit put her in contact with Captain Martin Delaney, the only black officer commissioned by the Union during the Civil War, who was attached to the Freedman's Bureau after the war. When Rollin confided her hopes of becoming a writer to Delaney, he offered her financial support if she would write his biography. Rollin moved north to Boston to work on Delaney's life story in the winter of 1867–68. She enjoyed the intellectual tempo of the city, but missed her home and worried about her future when she was unable to find a publisher for her manuscript and was forced to support herself by sewing.

Rollin finally secured a publisher for her life of Delaney but decided to return home anyway when an offer of a clerkship materialized. She arrived in Columbia, South Carolina, in August 1868 to take a job with William Whipper, a state senator from Beaufort, a widower with two sons. Shortly thereafter they married.

Rollin helped her husband fight the battle for black rights in the state legislature, and her two sisters Lottie and Louisa organized a political salon in the state capital of Columbia to promote African American equality. Her book, *The Life and Times of Martin R. Delaney*, appeared in the fall of 1868, with the author listed as "Frank A. Rollin." This volume remains not only a powerful biography of Delaney but also a stirring portrait of an era: Rollin used Delaney's career to celebrate the role of African Americans during the Civil War. Rollin indicted the government for failing to honor the key role played by African American soldiers in the battle against the Confederacy. She charged that racism had prevented black soldiers from being recognized for their heroism and was responsible for the failure of the Union government to shower black veterans with the medals and laurels they deserved. She argued that the Civil War was only the beginning of the revolution whereby African Americans would seize their rightful place as citizens and equal participants on the national stage. Delaney, Rollin asserted, would be one of the many in this pioneering vanguard of black leadership.

Once married, Rollin raised Whipper's two sons, and the couple had three surviving children of their own. She taught at the Avery Institute in Charleston, South Carolina, and wrote for local black papers. During her troubled marriage, Rollin moved to Washington without her husband, where she supported the family. One son became a famous stage actor, one daughter attended medical school, and another daughter became a Washington, D.C., teacher (see also **Civil War, Women in the**).

Sacajawea (1786–1812), guide and interpreter

Born into the Shoshone nation, also known as the Snake Indians, who lived in central Idaho at the end of the eighteenth century, Sacajawea was kidnapped and sold while still a teenager. She became the property of Toussaint Charbonneau, a Canadian guide and trapper. In 1804 Charbonneau was hired by the Lewis and Clark expedition, a pioneering mission funded by President Jefferson to chart the path westward to the Pacific Coast. He took along Sacajawea and their two-month-old son, Jean-Baptiste, on the trail west from North Dakota.

The presence of the Indian woman and her child indicated to the natives they encountered that Lewis and Clark were not leading a war party, which played an important role in the expedition's success. Crossing the Continental Divide was eased by Sacajawea's discovery that the chieftain of the Shoshone, where the Divide was located, was her brother. During the expedition's return journey, Sacajawea showed the group the Bozeman Pass. Following Lewis and Clark's triumphant return, Charbonneau and Sacajawea settled in St. Louis in 1810. But Sacajawea became ill in 1811, and the couple pulled up stakes and moved to the Dakotas. She reportedly died of a fever in 1812.

Seneca Falls Convention   (1848), first women's rights convention

When **Lucretia Mott**, one of the moving forces in the American abolitionist movement, and **Elizabeth Cady Stanton** found themselves denied access to the floor of the World Abolitionist Convention in London, England, in 1840, the irony of their position could not be ignored. Mott and Stanton determined to do something to make women's rights as visible as antislavery had become. Eight years later, Mott, Stanton, Martha Wright, Jane Hunt, and Mary McClintock issued a call to women to meet at the Seneca Falls, New York, Wesleyan Methodist Church on July 19th, 1848. Two hundred forty women attended the first session of the convention, chaired by James Mott, the husband of Lucretia, and a similar number were present at the second session two weeks later at the Rochester Community Church. After lively discussions and debates, the convention issued its revolutionary **Declaration of Sentiments**, modeled after the Declaration of Independence. "We hold these truths to be self-evident, that all men and women are created equal," the Declaration of Sentiments proclaimed. It then listed eighteen legal constraints imposed on women including their inability, under law, to keep their own children, their own wages, and even their own person. Women were limited in their educational and economic opportunities, and they had to endure a moral double standard. In addition, women could not vote. A series of twelve resolutions were put forth, each of which addressed one or more of the legal constraints that branded women as second-class citizens. The convention voted on the twelve amendments, with the first eleven receiving unanimous endorsement from the participants. The twelfth resolution, that which demanded equal voting rights for women, was considered too radical a demand. This proposal divided conventioneers, including Mott and Stanton, who stood on opposite sides of the issue. In the end, a majority of conventioneers did vote to include a suffrage resolution in the Declaration of Sentiments.

The women who attended the Seneca Falls Convention and the convention itself were ridiculed by public and press alike. The major exception, Horace Greeley's *New York Tribune*, treated the convention issues as a serious set of propositions put forth by women, deserving respect and consideration.

Seneca Falls marked the beginning of the women's rights movement in America, but it would take many years before a majority of American women supported its goals and even longer before most people in general took it seriously, regardless of their stand on the matter. The resolutions put forth in the Declaration of Sentiments became the agenda for the women's rights movement thereafter. Ironically, equal suffrage, which had caused such a division among the women of Seneca Falls, ultimately became the political focus of the women's rights movement. But it would take more than seventy years for equal suffrage to become a reality.

Seven Sisters Colleges, elite educational institutions for women

Between 1826 and 1893 a series of women's colleges were established, beginning with Mount Holyoke Seminary, founded by **Mary Lyon**. In addition to Mount Holyoke, the schools included Vassar (1861), Wellesley (1875), Smith (1871), Radcliffe (1874), Bryn Mawr (1880), and Barnard (1889). Most of the school founders believed in the necessity of providing young women an education commensurate with that of the men they would eventually marry. Such an education, founders promoted, would enable the women to run homes and raise children, creating a benefit to society. The one exception to this formula was Bryn Mawr. Under M. Carey Thomas, its president from 1894 to 1922, Bryn Mawr advanced the principle that women should be educated so that they might pursue careers. The Seven Sisters eventually came to be associated with the all-male elite Ivy League schools, although only Barnard and Radcliffe were actually begun as sister schools of Columbia and Harvard, respectively. Barnard had its own faculty, however, while Radcliffe students took courses from Harvard professors. The association with the Ivies created homogeneous student bodies drawn largely from middle- and upper-class all-white families with the means to afford private school tuitions. These exclusive women's colleges earned the nickname the "Seven Sisters" after they combined to form a Seven College Conference in 1926.

Sex in Education; or, A Fair Chance for the Girls (1873), publication on women and education

In 1873 Edward H. Clarke, a physician and former professor of medicine at Harvard University, published a pseudoscientific book purporting to prove scientifically that women were not physically capable of engaging in intellectual pursuits. Clarke, who made no effort to disguise his opposition to women seeking entrance to Harvard Medical School, claimed that young women who studied regularly risked, among other things, atrophy of the uterus, sterility, insanity, and even premature death. He said that American women had become unhealthy and incapable of reproducing because their "vital force" had been diverted to the brain. Clarke insisted that women should engage in no more than four hours of study a day and that they needed to remain at complete rest during menstruation—a prescription that precluded any possibility of pursuing any form of higher education or work that took them outside the home. To substantiate his claims, Clarke relied on quotes from unidentified experts, as well as on seven case histories from his own practice. Clarke's book was criticized in numerous articles, reviews, and other books by teachers, college professors, physicians, and public figures, who jointly pointed out that his evidence was flawed at best and that his motives were highly suspect. Because credentials, science, and expertise were highly regarded, Clarke's thesis was given enough credence so that it influenced higher education for women well into the twentieth century. Many schools cited Clarke's work as a reason to refuse to admit women altogether, while others that did admit women insisted that their course of study had to be tailored in order to protect female students from potential physical and intellectual damage.

Shaw, Anna Howard (1847–1919), suffragist, minister, physician

Born in Newcastle, England, Anna Howard Shaw came to the United States at the age of four. Her family settled first in Massachusetts before moving to the Michigan frontier shortly before the Civil War. After the war Shaw left home to attend high school, where she met the Reverend Marianna Thompson. Inspired by Thompson, Shaw determined to become a minister in the Methodist Church. She attended Albion College for two years, before moving on to study at Boston University. After she graduated in 1878, Shaw spent several years as a pastor in East Dennis on Cape Cod, Massachusetts. In 1880 she was ordained a church elder in the Methodist Protestant Church. By 1883 Shaw returned to school to get a medical degree. She did not leave the ministry at that time, and in 1886 she became the first American woman to hold both a divinity and a medical degree.

A suffrage advocate, Shaw began lecturing on behalf of women's rights under the aegis of the **Women's Christian Temperance Union** in 1887. By that time she had resigned her ministry. In 1888 **Susan B. Anthony** heard Shaw lecture. She persuaded Shaw that it was more important to devote her life fully to the suffrage cause and to leave temperance to others. From 1888 on, Shaw and Anthony became close allies and friends. The contrast between the angular Anthony and the more rotund Shaw prompted people to begin referring to them as the "ruler and the ball." Anthony groomed Shaw to become a moderate suffrage advocate—a role she was well suited to—in order to allay public fears that suffragists were all radicals. Shaw served as the first vice president of the **National American Woman Suffrage Association**, and in 1904, at Anthony's request, she took over the reins as president. Shaw remained in the post until 1915, when she was replaced by Carrie Chapman Catt. Hewing the moderate line, Shaw was asked personally by President

Woodrow Wilson in 1917 to serve on the Woman's Committee of the Council of National Defense. Wilson rewarded Shaw two years later for her service to the country by presenting her with the Distinguished Service Medal. Shaw died in 1919, just a few months before ratification of the Nineteenth Amendment granting women the vote.

Slavery, chattel and bondage system

Of the two million African Americans in 1820, less than 15 percent were free people of color. The rest were enslaved. When the Civil War broke out forty years later, the number of free people of color had shrunk to a little over 10 percent. The overwhelming majority of African Americans in antebellum America were subjected to the dehumanizing confines of slavery, and the overwhelming majority of slaves resided in the American South. Slavery took its toll on both men and women.

But it was a system that deprived people not only of their labor but also of their kin. Within bondage, the child of a slave mother became the property of her owner. The exploitation of American female slaves was doubly harsh, as women's labor was expropriated by owners and at the same time women were expected to reproduce. Slave children provided planters with more workers and more property. With the closing of the international slave trade in 1808, slave women were the only means of increasing American slavery.

The work of slave women was an essential part of the plantation economy. Masters sought profit and expansion of their system, and women were an integral part of the plan. Slave owners extracted as much labor as they could from their female workers. Further, slave females were not exempt from household duties in slave cabins. After spending a day in the master's fields, women returned home to their families, with the burden of household chores still before them. Recent mothers were expected to nurse their infants in the fields. Older and pregnant women might be given less exhausting tasks, but no females were exempt from the work force, and most had to labor side by side with men. Women were integrated into almost all aspects of plantation production, although they were excluded from supervisory roles, such as drivers.

Skilled women—nurses or midwives, weavers or seamstresses, cooks, maids, laundresses, and personal servants—might be assigned roles outside agricultural labor. But during harvest all workers, men and women, might be called into the fields. Slave children were put to work at a very young age, roughly six years old. Some were required to perform repetitive mindless tasks, such as fanning flies, to instill in them a sense of duty and submissiveness. Adolescent slaves were placed under the supervision of whites, which could and did lead to psychological and physical abuses. Slave women recalled whimsical and cruel treatment at the hands of harsh masters and mistresses. Further, postpubescent slave women could be preyed upon by white men and subjected to unwanted sexual advances. Sexual coercion and rape were constant threats to enslaved females. Although a prime field hand might sell in the antebellum South for $800, in city slave markets, a young female octoroon (a mixed-race person only "one eighth black") might be priced at more than $1,000, signaling the price of licentiousness and the taste for sexual exploitation among the slaveowners.

Miscegenation caused anxiety, ambivalence, and frustration for men and women, but slave mothers found this burden particularly painful. Many of the children produced by illicit liaisons across the color line received less than welcome treatment by either parent. Some slave mothers treated their mulatto infant as a badge of shame, while others hoped their child's lighter skin might result in more favorable treatment. This theory could and did backfire when vengeful white mistresses took out their frustrations on their husbands' illegitimate, mixed-race offspring. Slave mothers nevertheless struggled to teach their children how to survive within the confines of slave society. Many women passed on maternal names, family history, tribal customs, and other important vestiges of African ancestry to their children. These African survivals were an integral part of slave culture. Kin and community values were often exalted over individual desires within the slave community. Women tried to instill in their offspring a sense of humanity and pride, while the larger society appended labels of "property" and "degraded" to those born into slavery. They created a counterculture of values, cherishing the bonds of womanhood among their slave sisters. Most slave women, when given the opportunity, displayed devotion to evangelical Christianity. Despite the odds against them, slave women were part of a culture of resistance that created a slave community that offered its members dignity and identity.

The federal government declared slavery abolished in the Confederate States with the Emancipation Proclamation in 1863 (although the system was not truly dismantled until after the defeat of the Confederacy) and outlawed throughout the nation with the Thirteenth Amendment in 1865.

Society of Friends, religious organization

The Society of Friends, or Quakers, is a religious organization founded in the mid-seventeenth century in England. Its founders, from the start, included women as equal participants in church affairs: both men and women could serve as lay ministers, serve congregations as church elders, and address their constituents publicly. Quaker William Penn founded Pennsylvania in the seventeenth century as a Quaker colony, even though the secular government was organized along lines that conformed to the other colonies. As part of the church, however, women could and did hold women's meetings, an important element of the church. Church business was conducted in women's meetings and included interviewing couples who wanted to marry and helping to resolve family problems when they arose. Women lay ministers, such as **Lucretia Mott**, traveled and preached once their own children reached an age of greater self-sufficiency. Quaker women were frequently involved in social causes and were particularly active in both the abolitionist movement and women's rights. Lucretia Mott founded the Philadelphia Female Antislavery Society, and all four women involved with organizing the women's rights convention at Seneca Falls, New York, were Quakers. The opportunity to assume leadership roles within the church, as well as their experience—however limited—with public speaking in the women's meetings and as lay preachers, made them better suited, when the time came, to perform similarly in non-church-related groups and organizations.

Stanton, Elizabeth Cady (1815–1902), suffragist, women's rights advocate, writer, lecturer

A native of Johnstown, New York, Elizabeth Cady Stanton benefited from a father who encouraged her to pursue intellectual interests. His library, accumulated over the course of a career as a lawyer and jurist, remained open to his daughter. Although she attended **Emma Willard**'s Troy Female Seminary, Stanton was largely self-taught. From an early age she championed women's rights. When she married abolitionist Henry B. Stanton in 1840, he, too, encouraged her to continue her intellectual pursuits. She accompanied her husband to England for the World Abolition Conference in 1840. While there, Stanton sought out delegate **Lucretia Mott**, who had been denied a seat because of her gender. Together they vowed to do something about the inequitable conditions affecting women and to make women's rights as visible an issue as abolition.

Stanton's marriage produced seven children, leaving her little time to participate in activities. She and her husband moved to Seneca Falls, New York, in the mid-1840s. Feeling more and more isolated in the rural atmosphere, Stanton began to despair of making contributions outside of her domestic sphere. In the summer of 1848 Stanton and Lucretia Mott were ready to call a convention to discuss women's rights. The **Seneca Falls Convention** attracted hundreds of women who discussed in depth issues ranging from economics to religion. The **Declaration of Sentiments** issued by the convention enumerated eighteen conditions that the participants believed had to be changed, including women's right to their own wages, access to professions, educational and marital equality, the right to sit on juries, the right to make a will and to sue and be sued in a court of law, and the right to vote.

Stanton worked with **Susan B. Anthony** for the first time in 1851, collaborating with Anthony on a proposed lecture tour. From then on the two worked tirelessly on behalf of women's rights. Stanton's brilliant writing, combined with Anthony's ability to convey the spirit and essence of Stanton's message to women throughout the country, made them a formidable team. With Anthony, Stanton founded the **National Woman Suffrage Association** (NWSA) and served as its first president. The division between those who believed in securing black male suffrage first and those who believed that women's rights ought not be sublimated for any reason intensified after the Civil War. But after passage of the Fourteenth and Fifteenth Amendments, there was less reason for two suffrage organizations. In 1890 the NWSA and the **American Woman Suffrage Association** joined forces as the **National American Woman Suffrage Association**, with Stanton as the first president. By then, Stanton was seventy-five, and age had begun to take its toll. Moreover, she was never comfortable with the direction that the new suffrage association was taking, with its efforts to pull back from pursuit of a federal woman suffrage amendment.

Stanton, along with Anthony and **Matilda Joselyn Gage**, was also responsible for the first three volumes of the monumental six-volume *History of Woman Suffrage*, the single best account of the decades-long campaign. Stanton also wrote *The Woman's Bible*, published in 1895 and 1898. Long distrustful of organized religion, Stanton took religion to task in this book. She declared that organized religions were not only obstacles to progress for women but a threat to republican government as well. Stanton died at the age of eighty-seven.

Starr, Belle (1848–89), outlaw

Myra Belle Shirley Starr, the legendary "Bandit Queen" of the Southwest, was born near Carthage, Missouri, the youngest of three children. The oldest son, Edward, rode briefly with Quantrill's Raiders, the Confederate irregulars and bandits led by William Quantrill. Edward was shot by Federal troops in 1863, and in that same year, the Shirleys moved to Texas. By 1865 the remains of Quantrill's Raiders had moved into the Southwest, sometimes taking refuge at the Shirley farm. A notorious group, the gang included the Younger brothers and their cousins, Jesse and Frank James.

By 1868 Belle was living intermittently with Cole Younger. She had a daughter, Pearl Younger, in 1869. Belle resisted involvement in any of the acts of banditry committed by the Younger and the James brothers, becoming instead a fixture at local dancehalls, casinos, and saloons. Entreaties from her father to return to the farm fell on deaf ears, and Belle eloped with outlaw Jim Reed, whom she had known since childhood. She and Reed fled to Los Angeles in 1870 after he killed a man, and there her second and last child, Edward Reed, was born. The Reeds returned to Texas in 1874, and in April, Jim Reed engineered a spectacular hold-up of the Austin–San Antonio stage. Both Reeds were indicted for the robbery, but Reed was killed shortly thereafter, and the prosecution could not make a credible case against Belle. She operated a stable for a time, dealing in stolen horses. In 1880 she left her children with relatives and moved to Oklahoma. There she married for the third time, this time to Cherokee Indian Sam Starr, who rode with the James and Younger brothers. The Starrs settled near Fort Smith, Arkansas, at Younger's Bend, which became a hideaway for bandits and outlaws. Belle was convicted of only one crime in her life—that of robbery—and was sent to prison in 1883 for nine months. In 1885 Belle ran off with outlaw John Middleton, but he was drowned crossing a stream. She returned to Younger's Bend and remained there with Sam Starr until he was shot in 1887. Another Cherokee, Jim July, moved in with Belle. In February 1889, while July was making a court appearance, Belle Starr was shot in the back and killed. No one was indicted for her murder but it was widely suspected that Edward Reed, Belle's younger child, fired the fatal shot.

Starr, Ellen Gates (1859–1940), social reformer

Born on a farm in Laona, Illinois, Ellen Gates Starr, a cofounder of Hull House, met **Jane Addams** when both were students at Rockford Seminary in 1877. While traveling together in Europe, where they visited London's Toynbee Hall, they began to think in concrete terms about establishing an American institution with similar objectives. The two women pooled their resources to open Hull House on Chicago's West Side in 1889. Starr was crucial to the early survival of Hull House, thanks to both her unflagging support and her extensive list of contacts. Starr chose to make her primary concerns art and labor. She introduced many of the Hull House constituents to the world of art, insisting that such awareness was as important to survival as a roof over one's head. Starr also crusaded for higher wages and shorter hours. She believed the labor movement had failed to grasp that modern industry by its nature devalued the worth and dignity of labor. Starr advocated the adoption of handicrafts as a means to reinvest labor with the dignity she felt it deserved. To that end, she apprenticed herself to a London bookbinder for two years, learning the craft of book production. She returned to Hull House with her new skill. By the 1920s Starr had wearied of the task and abandoned the hope that others might emulate her reliance on craftsmanship as an alternative to industrial labor. The forces militating against her views of labor were simply too overwhelming. Starr retired from active participation, choosing to live quietly until her death.

Stone, Lucy (1818–93), suffragist, editor

Lucy Stone was born in Coy's Hill, Massachusetts, the eighth of nine children. Determined to receive an education, she saved money from an early teaching job and enrolled first at **Mount Holyoke** in 1839 and then at Oberlin College in 1843. Working part-time to pay her own way, Stone graduated from Oberlin, making her the first Massachusetts woman to graduate from a degree-granting college. Stone accepted an offer from William Lloyd Garrison to work for the American Abolition Society in 1847. Speaking on weekends at abolitionist gatherings, Stone volunteered in the cause of women's rights the rest of the time. Stone organized the first national women's rights convention, held in Worcester, Massachusetts, in 1850. In 1855 Stone married Henry Blackwell, the brother of **Elizabeth Blackwell** and **Emily Blackwell**, and the brother-in-law of Stone's college classmate and friend, **Antoinette Brown Blackwell**. She insisted on retaining her own last name when she married, preferring to be known as Lucy Stone. For a while, women who retained their own names after marriage were called "Stoners." While Stone was one of the nineteenth century's most ardent feminists, she disagreed with **Susan B. Anthony** and Elizabeth Cady Stanton over several issues. While Anthony and Stanton placed women's rights before all other issues, Stone believed that progressive women should work first to secure freedom and citizenship for slaves. After the Civil War she founded the **American Woman Suffrage Association** in 1869. This organization was a deliberate alternative to the **National Woman Suffrage Association**. Stone's greatest contribution to the women's movement arose out of her more than three decades of editorship of the *Woman's Journal*, a publication that provided an ongoing and invaluable account of the women's rights movement for more than forty-seven uninterrupted years. More than any other woman's publication, the *Woman's Journal* was the "voice of the woman's movement." Under Stone's editorship, the newspaper gained a reputation for journalistic excellence and writing. On issues other than women's rights, Stone's views were more conservative and in line with the views of the Republican party. Maintaining the publication was always burdensome, and Stone once characterized it as very much like a "big baby which never grew up and always had to be fed." When Stone retired, her daughter, **Alice Stone Blackwell**, took over the reins. Advancing age caused Stone's voice to weaken, and after 1887 she spoke only to small groups, though she did not stop making public appearances. She died in Dorchester, Massachusetts.

Stowe, Harriet Beecher (1811–96), author, reformer

Born into a family of prominent reformers, Harriet was the seventh child of nine born to Lyman and Roxana Beecher. Educated at her sister **Catharine**

Beecher's Hartford Female Seminary, she eventually became a teacher herself. Religious and political debates enlivened the dinner table in the Beecher household, and as a young girl, Harriet took a great interest in the Calvinism preached by her father, a leading antislavery theologian. In 1832 Harriet relocated with her family to Cincinnati, Ohio, when Lyman Beecher went to head the Lane Theological Seminary. A sensitive young woman, Harriet Beecher was horrified by the stories recounted about slavery—barbaric and inhuman practices only a few miles away in the slave state of Kentucky.

She married a professor at her father's school, Calvin Ellis Stowe, in 1836. The couple had several children in quick succession. When her sixth child, a particular favorite, died of cholera in 1849, Harriet Stowe sank into a deep depression. Stowe confessed that at her son's graveside, she identified with slave mothers who were unwillingly parted from their offspring. In response to her spiritual crisis, she threw herself passionately into the antislavery cause.

When Calvin joined the faculty of Bowdoin College, the family moved to Brunswick, Maine, in 1850. The country was engulfed in the political debates surrounding passage of the Fugitive Slave Act. Influenced by the debates, Harriet began to write her most famous work, the American classic, *Uncle Tom's Cabin*. Her manuscript was first published serially in the Washington *National Era*, an antislavery paper, before appearing in book form in 1852.

Stowe's moving tale featured a loyal slave named Tom, an angelic young girl named Little Eva, and a wicked overseer named Simon Legree and included the melodramatic tale of the slave mother Eliza clutching her baby as she crossed an icy river, with dogs and slave catchers hot on her trail, literally leaping for her freedom. Stowe argued that her fictional story was culled from real stories she had learned from fugitives making their way to freedom along the Underground Railroad. This authenticity as well as its sentimental tone made Stowe's novel a bestseller, with sales of over a quarter million copies in less than a year. *Uncle Tom's Cabin* depicted slavery's most brutal aspects for thousands of readers innocent of the cruelties slavery might impose. The accessibility and alleged "eyewitness" quality the book projected fueled grassroots support for the flagging abolitionist movement during the 1850s. Abraham Lincoln, when he met Stowe many years later, credited her with "starting the war." Certainly the white South harbored special venom for Stowe, banning her book and charging her with "crimes against the South."

This work catapulted Stowe into literary celebrity, and she subsequently published *A Key to Uncle Tom's Cabin* (1853) and another antislavery novel, *Dred: A Tale of the Great Dismal Swamp* (1856). But subsequent work did not focus exclusively on race, as she became an advocate for other causes. Most controversially, with her *Lady Byron Vindicated* (1870), Stowe charged Lord

Byron with incest, causing an international scandal. She published several volumes about life in New England, including *The Minister's Wooing* (1859), *The Pearl of Orr's Island* (1861), and *Oldtown Folks* (1869). None of these later works ever reached the popular audience of her first novel. Once dismissed as a sentimental novel of domestic fiction, contemporary critics universally agree that *Uncle Tom's Cabin*, despite defects, remains an enduring and powerful literary creation, a symbol of its age.

Taylor, Susie Baker King (1848–1912), teacher, Civil War nurse, author

The first child of a slave mother in Liberty County, Georgia, Susie left the plantation when she was young. The Baker children moved to Savannah to live with their grandmother, where she was able to send them to clandestine schools for African American children. When the **Civil War** erupted, Taylor was forced to return to the plantation. But when Union troops moved into the area, Taylor fled to the sea islands, where the army drafted her to teach runaway slaves who had sought protection behind Union lines. She joined with the first South Carolina Volunteers, first as a laundress and then as a nurse, working side by side with **Clara Barton** in 1863, attending the wounded after the battle of Fort Wagner. Taylor married Sargeant Edward King, a carpenter from Savannah, and they remained with the regiment until it was disbanded in 1865. The couple settled in Savannah, where King found work as a longshoreman, and Taylor ran a school for black children.

Her husband's death in 1866 left her alone, pregnant, and facing uncertainty. Taylor gave birth to a son and moved to Liberty County to start a rural school. Mother and child returned to Savannah, where Taylor ran another school until 1872. She invested her husband's wartime pension in the Freedman's Bank, which subsequently failed, and she was forced to leave her child with her mother and go into domestic service. Taylor was able to secure a job working for a family in Massachusetts. Within a few years she married Russell Taylor and devoted herself to Union veterans' affairs and relief activities. In 1898 her son's illness forced her to return to the South to nurse him in Louisiana. While in the South, Taylor was deeply shaken by the discrimination she encountered and the horrors she witnessed, including a lynching in Mississippi. This experience convinced her to write a memoir: *Reminiscences of My Life in Camp with the U.S.C.T. Colored Troops, Late First South Carolina Volunteers* (1902), the only black woman's Civil War memoir published to date. Besides chronicling her own adventures during wartime and those of the black soldiers with whom she served, Taylor wanted her readers to recollect that the war had not been won by whites only. She hoped the generation that reaped the benefits wrought from the sacrifice of Civil War veterans, living and dead, would acknowledge the heroic role played by black men and "noble women as well." Her stirring indictment challenged the politics of racial amnesia that prevailed at the turn of the century. Taylor's demands for racial justice were echoed by other black women contemporaries, such as **Mary McLeod Bethune** and **Anna Julia Cooper**, among others, but Taylor was the only black woman who spoke from the vantage point of her service to Union troops during the Civil War.

Temperance Movements   anti-liquor campaigns

In 1810 the adult per capita consumption of alcohol in the United States had reached approximately seven gallons a year. By 1820 per capita consumption had increased nearly 50 percent to ten gallons annually. Alcohol had always been an important factor in both the economic and cultural components of American life. From the extensive rum trade dating back to the seventeenth century to the routine consumption of ale on a daily basis by both adults and children throughout the colonies and, later, the states, alcohol maintained its significant presence in society. But this rapid increase in consumption alarmed reformers, who attributed to alcohol a diverse array of evils, particularly problems that beset family life. In 1826 the American Society for the Promotion of Temperance was founded. Among its earliest and most persistent supporters were women who often witnessed first hand the destructive consequences of excessive alcohol consumption and who, along with their children, most often bore the brunt of alcohol abuse. For this reason primarily, hundreds—and then thousands—of women joined the temperance movement. In addition, middle-class reformers, again largely women, joined the fray. Thus women became and remained the major force for change and reform related to alcohol.

The first national conference on alcohol was held in Philadelphia in 1833. Representatives from all over the country attended and helped to establish the objective that would remain paramount throughout the nineteenth century and into the twentieth century: the prohibition of alcohol. The extent to which temperance advocates were gaining legitimacy was highlighted in 1851 when the Maine legislature voted to prohibit alcohol consumption in that state, the first in the Union to do so. The largest and most influential temperance organization, the **Women's Christian Temperance Union** (WCTU), founded in 1874, brought together large numbers of women who were concerned with a variety of issues including temperance. Over the course of the nineteenth century temperance and women's role in its leadership grew dramatically. Temperance advocates never lost sight of the ultimate goal—national prohibition—and their efforts were rewarded with the ratification of the Eighteenth Amendment in 1919.

Terrell, Mary Church (1863–1954), clubwoman, educator

Born in Memphis, Tennessee, Mary Church was the child of former slaves, Robert and Louisa Church, who tried to shield her from the racism raging in the postwar South. They sent her north to school in Yellow Springs, Ohio, one of Antioch College's "model schools," which had integrated classrooms. Terrell graduated from Oberlin College in 1884 and taught at Wilberforce University in Ohio before moving to Washington, D.C., to teach at the High School for Colored Youth. It was during this period that she met her future husband, Robert H. Terrell.

After touring Europe for two years and polishing her foreign language skills, young Mary Church was offered the position of registrar of Oberlin College in 1891, the first black woman to be offered such a high-status job at a primarily white institution. She declined this offer and chose instead to marry Terrell, who later became judge of the Municipal Court of the District of Columbia. In the nation's capital, the Terrells raised two children, a daughter named after poet Phillis Wheatley and an adopted daughter, Mary. Despite her domestic obligations, Terrell continued as a pathbreaker, becoming the first black woman to serve on the Washington school board. Terrell also spearheaded a campaign to involve black women in the woman suffrage movement. She was a founder of the District's Colored Woman's League and in 1896 organized the **National Association of Colored Women** (NACW), an organization that sponsored mother's clubs, kindergartens, and day nurseries. She became the first president of the NACW. Terrell was a delegate to the International Congress of Women in Berlin in 1904 and addressed the International League for Peace in Zurich in 1919.

Terrell spent her entire life engaged in the fight against racial injustice, continuing her activism well into the twentieth century. She was a founding member of the National Association for the Advancement of Colored People in 1910. She fought segregation in its various guises, from hiring policies to separate dressing rooms in Washington, D.C., department stores. She wrote her autobiography, *A Colored Woman in a White World*, which was published in 1940. Terrell led a protest to desegregate a Washington restaurant in 1950, which led to a lawsuit, *District of Columbia v John Thompson*. This case was a triumph for Terrell, when in 1953 the court ruled that segregated eating facilities in the District were unconstitutional. Mary Church Terrell died in Annapolis, Maryland, in 1954.

Transcendentalism (1830–50), reform movement

The group of New England writers and thinkers whose reform efforts caused them to be identified as a group during the antebellum era took their name from the German philosopher Immanuel Kant. The trancendentalists believed that people could transcend, or rise above, both experience and reason to arrive at a better understanding of the universe and their place in it. Transcendentalism encouraged personal growth and self-realization.

This democratization of Christian doctrine attracted women reformers and romantic writers, who rejected the cold conservatism of their Puritan forbears. The converts included Margaret Fuller, Ralph Waldo Emerson, Henry David Thoreau, and Amos Bronson Alcott, among others. They formed a Transcendentalist Club, which met to discuss literary and economic theory. Members of the transcendentalist group also launched experiments in communal living, including Brook Farm (1840–47) and Fruitlands. These short-lived experiments failed to attract a wide following. Nathaniel Hawthorne wrote a thinly veiled portrait of Fuller in the character Zenobia, in his novel *The Blithedale Romance*, published shortly after Fuller's death by shipwreck as she was returning to America from Europe.

Truth, Sojourner (1799?–1883), evangelical, reformer

Born Isabella, a slave in Ulster County, New York, Truth inherited a deep sense of mysticism from her mother. Sold at a young age, she had several Dutch and Yankee masters before securing her freedom in 1827. While living in New Paltz, New York, from 1810 to 1827, Truth gave birth to five children. She fled from her master in 1826 and successfully sued for the return of a son who had been illegally sold as a slave and shipped to Alabama. When Truth converted to Methodism, she became an ardent evangelist.

Truth moved to New York City in 1827 and began her preaching and missionary work. She was a devoted follower of a prophet named Matthias (Robert Matthews). Between 1832 and 1835 she joined Matthias's cult and lived with the group near Ossining, New York. When this religious sect collapsed in 1835, Truth was forced to return to domestic service. Following another religious conversion, she adopted the name Sojourner Truth and left New York City in 1843. She claimed a heavenly voice directed her to go forth and speak the truth. Illiterate, hampered by a thick Dutch accent, yet a towering presence at six feet tall, Truth held her audience through the force of her extraordinary personality. On the platform she began her performance by singing. She could entrance listeners with spiritual stories, mesmerizing them with her deep and powerful voice. After several years she joined the Northampton Association, a utopian commune in rural Massachusetts that advocated both women's rights and the abolition of slavery. In the mid-1850s Truth migrated to Battle Creek, Michigan, which became her home for the rest of her life.

She was a well-known speaker at women's rights conventions and was reported to have delivered a memorable speech in Akron, Ohio, in 1851 where she allegedly demolished a male critic who argued women were too delicate for equality by arguing "Aren't I a Woman?" From her first woman's rights meeting in Worcester, Massachusetts, in 1850 until the end of her life, she was a staunch defender of woman suffrage.

During the Civil War, Truth labored tirelessly for black soldiers, even meeting with Abraham Lincoln on behalf of these former slaves. She started a job placement service for African Americans, working out of her Michigan home. During Reconstruction, Truth sold copies of her autobiography and photographs to support herself. She continued her petition and stump speech efforts on behalf of black improvement and reform and remained active until old age crippled her.

Tubman, Harriet (1821?–1913), Underground Railroad conductor, Civil War scout and spy, humanitarian

Born on a plantation in Dorchester County, Maryland, one of eleven children of slave parents, Tubman was given the name of Araminta, which she later changed to Harriet, after her mother. She worked in the fields from a very early age. When she was only a teenager, a white overseer, annoyed by her rebellious streak, struck her on the head with a two-pound weight. This injury caused headaches and a dizziness that periodically plagued her throughout the rest of her life. In 1844 she married John Tubman, a free black man, who sought freedom for his wife but did not share her fears that she would be sold south. When Harriet decided to flee Maryland, following her master's death in 1849, she fled alone. She walked to Pennsylvania and settled in Philadelphia, where the only work she could find was living as a domestic servant.

Saving her earnings, she was able to fund a journey south, where she rescued her sister and her sister's two children. When Tubman returned to her Maryland home, she discovered her husband had taken another wife. She returned north and began to work with the loose network of secret activists known as the Underground Railroad. This group broke the law, braved danger, and helped escaping slaves to safety. After the Fugitive Slave Law was passed (with a bounty of $10 for each returned slave and the entire federal government behind the work of slave catchers), Tubman moved her base of operations from the United States in 1851 northward to Saint Catharine's in Ontario, across the Canadian border. Over the next decade she returned south almost 20 times, helping more than 300 runaways to freedom, including both of her parents in 1857.

Tubman was well known for her resourcefulness: appearing in various disguises, dosing infants with medicine to stop them crying, threatening any in her party who might want to bail out (in the face of danger along the road north) with the pistol she always carried. Tubman was such an effective abolitionist agent that southern planters placed a bounty of $40,000 on her head. Tubman persisted, making her last raid in 1860. She was known as the Moses of her people.

Tubman spoke at abolitionist meetings and supplied material to the *National Anti-Slavery Standard*. She was a great admirer of John Brown and supported his many abolitionist schemes. With the coming of the Civil War, Tubman attached herself to the Union Army in South Carolina, serving as cook and scout for raiding parties and, more important, spying behind Confederate lines. She led numerous expeditions in the South Carolina low country, assisting Union Colonel James Montgomery during his raids on Combahee River plantations during the summer of 1863, when nearly 800 slaves fled plantations to join the Union army. Tubman was present at the assault on Fort Wagner, where so many black soldiers, many from the Massachusetts 54th Regiment, fell in battle. Tubman tirelessly worked with the freedpeople during wartime. She helped to establish schools, although she herself remained illiterate.

After the war Tubman settled in Auburn, New York, where she had resettled her parents. She married a Civil War veteran, Nelson Davis, in 1869, but outlived her husband. She continued her work on behalf of fellow African Americans. It took Tubman until 1897 to force the government to pay her the pension of $20 a month she had earned by her Union service. (Several of her commanding officers supported her repeated appeals.) She used this money to fund her Home for Indigent and Aged Negroes, which she ran for many years and which continued its work after her death. Tubman attended woman suffrage conventions and was at the first meeting of the **National Association of Colored Women** in 1896. She was given full military honors at her burial. In 1974 the Department of the Interior declared her home a National Historic Landmark.

Ward, Nancy (1738?–1822), leader, trader

The daughter of a Cherokee mother of the Wolf clan and a Delaware father, Ward was given the Cherokee name of Nanye'hi following her birth in a Cherokee settlement along the Little Tennessee River. She married a Cherokee, Kingfisher, and they had two children—a son named Fivekiller and a daughter named Catherine. During war with the Creeks (ca. 1791–92), Kingfisher fell in battle, and his wife took his place, earning her the title and privileges of "War Woman." She married a white trader named Bryant Ward, took the name Nancy Ward, and gave birth to another daughter, named Elizabeth. She and her husband settled in South Carolina where Ward is credited with saving a white settlement in 1776 by warning the settlers of an impending Cherokee attack.

In 1781 Ward addressed a treaty conference between the Cherokee and the United States. She offered her political advice to Cherokee chieftains, negotiating with American authorities in 1817. The gradual assimilation of the Cherokee into white society diminished the role of Ward and other Indian war women. She was running an inn along the Ocee River in eastern Tennessee when she died.

Wells-Barnett, Ida Bell (1862–1931), author, reformer

Born to slave parents in Mississippi in the middle of the Civil War, Ida Bell Wells did well in the freedman's school she attended in Holly Springs, Mississippi, which later became Rust College. Ida became a teacher herself at the age of sixteen. After both her parents died in a yellow fever epidemic, she moved to Memphis to live with relatives. Wells became militant about racial segregationist policies that were hampering black progress. In 1884 she brought a lawsuit challenging Jim Crow segregation on railway cars. Wells won her case and was awarded $500 in damages. This set her on a path of protest and agitation. She began to write for local papers and soon edited her own journal, campaigning for racial justice. In 1892 the savage and unprovoked lynching of respectable local black businessmen deeply affected Wells, whose outspoken protest of their murders led to her exile from the South. She lectured against racial murders in the North and made two successful tours of England, launching a lifelong antilynching campaign.

After marrying Chicago lawyer Ferdinand Barnett in 1895 and having several children, Ida Wells-Barnett curtailed her lecture tours but not her involvement in political crusades. In 1895 she published *A Red Record*, a detailed account of the violent crimes committed against blacks in the South, and at the same time joined with other black reformers to launch the Niagara Movement, an antidiscriminatory campaign spearheaded by W. E. B. DuBois. Wells-Barnett was a founding member of the National Association for the Advancement of Colored People, but left the group when she found their tactics not radical enough. In Chicago Wells-Barnett was involved in women's rights, supporting suffrage and encouraging club women to organize and agitate. Her roles as a journalist and civic leader kept her at the center of reform during the Progressive era until her death.

Willard, Emma Hart (1787–1870), educator

Born in Berlin, Connecticut, Emma Hart Willard was the sixteenth of seventeen children. Blessed with a father who encouraged her intellectual development, Willard attended a local female academy and, like many women in her era, opened her own dame school in the family home in 1805. In 1807 she accepted a position as preceptress of girls at a school in Middlebury, Vermont, but when she married widower Dr. John Willard in 1809, she gave up her work. For the next few years, Willard taught her husband's four children and their one child at home. When John Willard's nephew lived with them while attending Middlebury College, Emma Willard had her first opportunity to examine at first hand textbooks traditionally excluded from female schools. She quickly set about teaching herself subjects previously denied her, including mathematics.

When Dr. Willard's fortunes began to ebb, Willard returned to teaching. With her new knowledge, she was determined to provide girls with educations usually reserved for male students. Between 1814 and 1821 Willard had to move her school three times, primarily for economic reasons. During that time it became clear to Willard that the lack of public funding for women's education was as detrimental as the limitation on curriculum. In 1818, in New York City, Willard wrote "An Address to the Public Particularly to the Members of the Legislature, Proposing a Plan for Improving Female Education," in which she proposed using taxes to support female education. The legislature turned down her proposal but Willard was not without supporters, including Thomas Jefferson. Ultimately, the city of Troy, New York, offered Willard a subsidy of $4,000 to move her school there. In 1821 the Troy Female Seminary opened its doors and within 10 years became a profitable institution with more than 300 enrolled students. Willard students were accepted from across the country, selected according to ability and tending to be from affluent families. Her graduates formed a nucleus of future teachers and school founders, including **Mary Lyon**, the founder of **Mount Holyoke College**, who believed in and spread the Willard philosophy. Willard also wrote a number of textbooks that became standards of the time and provided her a generous personal income. Widowed in 1825, she remarried in 1838 and turned her school over to her daughter. Willard obtained a divorce in 1843 and returned to Troy, where she remained until her death.

Willard, Frances (1839–98), temperance advocate, social reformer

Frances Willard's parents had both been students at Oberlin College. They wanted their daughter Frances, born in Churchville, New York, to grow up with a strong belief in the value of women's contributions to society. The Willards moved to Wisconsin when Frances was just an infant. She grew up there and attended Milwaukee Female College before graduating from Northwestern Female College in 1859. During the Civil War Willard taught in Methodist schools in Illinois and Pennsylvania. A trip to Europe from 1868 to 1870 broadened both her intellectual horizons and her personal sensibilities. In 1871 Willard accepted a position as president of the Evanston College for Ladies. When Evanston College combined with Northwestern, Willard became the dean of women, the first woman to hold such a high administrative position in an American university. The post brought her national fame. In 1873, with **Julia Ward Howe**, she cofounded the Association for the Advancement of Women and served as its first president. At the same time, Willard was developing her interest in temperance and the temperance movement. When she left Northwestern in 1874, she went to work full time for the **Women's Christian Temperance Union** (WCTU). Serving first as president of the Chicago WCTU from 1874 to 1877, Willard was also the first corresponding secretary for the national organization. Willard used her WCTU platform to lecture on other social issues, including **woman suffrage**, and laid down a network of strong ties with feminist leaders of the suffrage movement, ties that would sustain over time and prove valuable for the temperance cause. In 1879 Willard was elected national president of the WCTU, a position she held until her death. During her tenure Willard helped to transform temperance. Her leadership broadened the base of support, and over time temperance was endorsed by millions.

Woman Suffrage, voluntary crusade

While there had always been calls for voting rights for women in the United States from the earliest days of the Republic, they were voices in the wilderness until the beginning of an organized women's rights movement in the mid-nineteenth century. Always a controversial issue, woman suffrage was no less so at the **Seneca Falls** women's rights convention in 1848. When **Elizabeth Cady Stanton** wanted to include woman suffrage in a list of grievances, other notable feminists, including **Lucretia Mott**, were opposed. Mott argued that woman suffrage was so radical an idea that all of their legitimate grievances would be undermined if they had to defend it. Stanton prevailed. By the end of the Civil War woman suffrage was embroiled in a controversy that split the women's movement. The moderates, led by women like **Lucy Stone**, believed that demanding woman suffrage at that crucial time in history would jeopardize efforts to secure the vote for black males. Their opponents, led by Stanton and **Susan B. Anthony**, argued that correcting one inequity should not mean that half the population had to endure less than full citizenship. In 1869 two suffrage organizations were founded, each reflecting their founders' views. Stone's **American Woman Suffrage Association** (AWSA) continued to counsel moderation. Stanton and Anthony's **National Woman Suffrage Association** (NWSA) demanded a federal woman suffrage amendment. For the next two decades, each organization went its own way. The AWSA developed a strategy of conducting state campaigns with the intention of amending state constitutions allowing women to vote. The NWSA continued to seek federal suffragism. During these years Stanton,

Anthony, and **Matilda Joselyn Gage** worked on what would eventually become a six-volume *History of Woman Suffrage*. The project began in 1876, and over the next 14 years the first three volumes, totaling nearly 3,000 pages, were published. When Gage died, Ida Husted Harper took on the task of completing the project, devoting nearly 30 years to the job. The result is still generally regarded as the single best source of information on the woman suffrage movement in America.

By 1890, with the Civil War and the Fourteenth Amendment well behind them, both sides in the suffrage movement decided it was time to reconcile in order to pursue their goal with a united front. In the 1870s and 1880s the movement's greatest triumph had been simply to survive the repeated rejections of politicians at all levels of government, from local to federal. Thus the **National American Woman Suffrage Association** (NAWSA) was founded in 1890, in an effort to speed up the process. Stanton served as the first president of the NAWSA, followed by Anthony. But it was clear that neither of these women could prevent the organization from going in a direction not of their choosing. The moderates won the day. Rather than pursuing a national suffrage amendment to the Constitution, which by one action would grant all women the right to vote, the moderates insisted on changing individual state constitutions. With fewer than ten woman suffrage statutes on the books by 1900, it was clear that pursuing the state constitution method was going to take many more decades.

In 1912 the NAWSA, at the urging of some younger members led by Alice Paul, formed a committee called the Congressional Union, charged with pursuing the federal amendment. Frustration over the lack of real commitment to federal suffragism caused a second split in the suffrage movement when Alice Paul organized the National Woman's Party (NWP). Dedicated to the single goal of securing a federal suffrage amendment to the Constitution, the NWP seemed much more the intellectual heir of the Stanton-Anthony philosophy. The final years of the suffrage campaign were filled with conflict, confrontation, and civil disobedience. In 1915 the new NAWSA president, Carrie Chapman Catt, committed that organization to federal suffragism. Once again suffragists were pursuing their goal with a more or less united front. The Nineteenth Amendment was passed by Congress in 1919 and ratified by the states in 1920 in time for women to vote in the presidential election.

Woman's Medical College of Pennsylvania, pioneering female educational institution

Founded in 1850 by a group of Philadelphia Quakers, the Female Medical College of Pennsylvania became the first women's medical school in the nation. With an entering class of eight women, including three who had already had extensive training in medicine (apprenticing privately to male physicians), the school faced early opposition from the male medical establishment despite its founding charter from the Pennsylvania legislature. The first graduation was held in 1851 for the students whose previous training had accelerated their studies at the college. Dr. Ann Preston returned two years later to teach at the school and became influential in its growth. Both external opposition and internal conflict among faculty members caused the school to shut down briefly in 1860. In 1862 it reopened as the Woman's Medical College of Pennsylvania. The faculty, in addition to male physicians, also included four women who had graduated from the college. In 1863 a nursing school became part of the college. Three years later Preston was named dean of the college, a position she held until her death in 1872. Her successor, Emeline Horton Cleveland, established the surgical standards for the hospital. The college remained a women's school until 1969 when the first male students were admitted. Thereafter its name was shortened to the Medical College of Pennsylvania.

Woodhull, Victoria Claflin (1838-1927), feminist reformer and entrepreneur

The seventh of ten children, Woodhull was born into an unconventional Ohio family that ran a traveling medicine show. At the age of fifteen, she married a physician, bore him two children, and continued her life on the road, dabbling in theater. Her husband's drinking led to their separation in the late 1850s. Woodhull and her younger sister, Tennessee Claflin, joined forces and became involved in spiritualism, often performing together. Along the way, Woodhull acquired a new male companion, a clairvoyant named Colonel James Blood, whom she claimed to have married in 1866. Arriving in New York City in 1868, Woodhull secured an introduction to Cornelius Vanderbilt, a wealthy financier, who helped the sisters to establish a brokerage firm. Their establishment, the only women's firm on Wall Street, became successful under Vanderbilt's sponsorship, and Woodhull turned her attention to reform politics.

In 1870 she and her sister founded *Woodhull & Claflin's Weekly*, a flamboyant paper that printed everything from woman suffrage editorials to an English translation of the *Communist Manifesto*. Woodhull sought a leading role in the **National Woman Suffrage Association** and, before scandal derailed her public career, testified before the U.S. Congress on feminists' behalf. In 1871 Woodhull's first husband, the alcoholic physician, appeared at her home in New York, while she was still living with Colonel Blood—whom she had been claiming as her second husband. The local press charged she was guilty of bigamy. But Woodhull accused her critics of hypocrisy and revealed that a powerful Brooklyn minister, Henry Ward Beecher, was involved with the wife of one of his parishioners, Elizabeth Tilton. The Beecher-Tilton scandal rocked New York and led to a notorious trial.

Woodhull's weekly was one of the first publications charged under the infamous **Comstock Law**—named after crusader Anthony Comstock who had campaigned against the circulation of information concerning birth control and other sexual materials. Charged with "obscenity," as it was broadly applied under this federal statute, Woodhull was acquitted after seven months of legal battle. Even though the scandal permanently damaged her reputation, she ran for president under the banner of the Equal Rights Party in 1876 (with Frederick Douglass as her vice-presidential candidate). This same year Woodhull divorced Colonel Blood.

With the death of her patron, Cornelius Vanderbilt, in 1877, Woodhull and her sister departed for England and a lecturing career abroad. Woodhull became involved with eugenics, and she and her daughter published a journal, *Humanitarian*, between 1892 and 1901 to promote her radical views. The sisters frequently returned to the United States over the years but never recaptured their following. Woodhull died quietly at her home in England, a forgotten figure after years of notoriety among American reformers.

World's Columbian Exposition (1893), international fair

Organized to celebrate the four-hundredth anniversary of Columbus's arrival in the New World, the World's Columbian Exposition had particular significance for American women. It marked the first time that women took sole responsibility for planning, funding, building, and managing a project, the Women's Exhibit, to highlight female contributions. The Women's Exhibit consisted of three separate buildings: the Woman's Building, the Children's Building, and the Woman's Dormitory. Women architects working with the Ladies Board of Governors designed the buildings to accommodate what they perceived as the sensibilities of the modern woman. Planners for the exhibit, moreover, were not restricted to one particular socioeconomic group, but included a broad spectrum from working women to upper-class women. The planners tried to project a progressive ideal in some areas. Although the exhibit's planners were all white, the "color line" was not enforced in the Children's Building. Exhibitors represented women and cultures from around the world, and women from around the world, primarily Americans, were invited to donate their talent and expertise to help make the Women's Exhibit a memorable one. Mary Cassatt painted one of the murals in the Woman's Building. The success of the Women's Exhibit at the exposition provided ample proof that women could participate in areas once deemed appropriate only to men.

Wright, Frances (1795–1852), feminist, utopian reformer

Born in Scotland, the young Frances Wright became caught up in the ideas of the American Revolution, as her father was an ardent admirer of Thomas Paine. Orphaned at an early age, Wright and her sister Camilla were sent to live in England, but both set sail for the United States in 1818. Wright returned to England and published her popular memoir, *Views of Society and Manners in America* (1821). She went to France and became romantically involved with the Marquis de Lafayette, who accompanied her on a tour of the United States in 1824.

Wright decided to settle in America. She was an advocate of the principles of British utopian thinker Robert Dale Owen and decided to use her inheritance to create a new community in 1825, dedicated to antislavery and equality on the southern frontier. She was a frequent visitor at New Harmony, Indiana, where Owen supervised his experimental community. Her own settlement at Nashoba, Tennessee, was in ruins by 1828, but Wright remained committed to racial and sexual equality.

Wright accompanied Robert Owen to New York City in 1829, where they became coeditors of the *Free Enquirer* and helped with the creation of the Workingmen's Party. She left the United States for Haiti and then France, where she married French physician and fellow utopian, Guillaume D'Arusmont, in 1831. While in France, Wright gave birth to two daughters. In 1835 she returned to the United States with her husband and only surviving child and reentered the political arena. When she failed to draw an audience, she returned to France in 1839. Wright spent the rest of her life criss-crossing the Atlantic, divorcing her husband, plotting radical schemes—a generous, striving, and restless spirit. Wright died in Cincinnati, virtually forgotten at the age of fifty-seven, an unsung heroine of women's rights and utopian activism.

Young Women's Christian Association, religious organization

Both the Young Men's Christian Association (YMCA) and the Young Women's Christian Association (YWCA) had their origins in mid-nineteenth-century London. The YMCA was organized in the United States in 1851, but the women's organization did not materialize until the onset of the Civil War, when several organizations, including the Ladies Christian Association of New York, united to provide temporary living quarters for young women traveling on their own during the war years. Before first the war, then employment drew women away from their traditional home settings, lone women living in cities were often perceived as morally little better than prostitutes. The war and the necessity for women laborers created an urgent need to alter that image. The YWCA was formally organized in Boston in 1866. During the latter part of the nineteenth century the YWCA continued to provide accommodations in a Christian environment for young women on their own for various reasons. Young working women in particular, it was believed, needed an inexpensive and respectable living situation since the wages they earned were too little for them to find suitable quarters on their own. In addition to room and board, the YWCAs provided religious guidance and a variety of inexpensive recreational and educational programs that appealed to young women.

PART THREE

Concise Chronology

1783 New Jersey grants property-holding women and African Americans of both sexes the right to vote.

1790 On the grounds that it would instill a healthy degree of self-respect, Judith Sargent Murray argues for equal education for women, in an article published in *Gentlemen and Ladies Town and Country Magazine.*

1791 Samuel Slater opens the first textile mills in New England, in Pawtucket, Rhode Island.

1792 Mary Wollstonecraft's *A Vindication of the Rights of Woman* published in the United States.

1805 Mercy Otis Warren publishes her three-volume history of the Revolutionary War, entitled *History of the Rise, Progress, and Termination of the American Revolution, Interspersed with Biographical and Moral Observations.*

Indian guide Sacajawea, carrying her two-year-old son, leads explorers Meriwether Lewis and William Clark to the Pacific Coast.

1807 Women and African Americans denied the right to vote in New Jersey. Perceptions within the state that women vote in their own best interest alarm authorities, and the legislature once again changes the statutes.

1820s Second Great Awakening

1820 Maria Becraft, a fifteen-year-old African American, founds a school in Georgetown, D.C., for young black women.

1821 Emma Willard's Seminary opens in Troy, New York.

1822   Sara Josepha Hale begins tenure as editor of *Godey's Lady's Book*.

1825   Frances Wright founds Nashoba, a utopian community in Tennessee.

1826   American Society for the Promotion of Temperance founded.

1829   St. Francis Academy for Colored Girls founded by The Oblate Sisters of Providence, a Catholic order of black women, in Baltimore, Maryland.

1830   Robert Owen publishes first book advocating birth control in the United States. *Moral Physiology* argues not only that women would fare better with fewer children and more education but also that women ought to be free to decide if and when they wish to bear children.
      Godey's Lady's Book editor, Sara Josepha Hale, writes popular children's nursery rhyme, "Mary Had a Little Lamb."

1832   Boston Female Anti-Slavery Society founded.

1833   Prudence Crandall establishes Canterbury School for African American women in Canterbury, Connecticut. Local opposition forces the school to close its doors the following year.
      Lydia Maria Child publishes *Appeal in Favor of that Class of Americans Called Africans*.
      Lucretia Mott organizes the Female Anti-Slavery Society of Philadelphia.
      Oberlin College founded in Oberlin, Ohio.
      First National Temperance Convention held in Philadelphia, Pennsylvania.

1834   First Lowell Mills girls' strike, protesting lower wages.
      Sarah Purvis, a free black woman in Philadelphia, becomes the first African American female to be issued a United States passport.
      American Female Moral Reform Society founded in New York City.

1836   Angelina Grimké publishes *Appeal to the Christian Women of the South*.

1837   Mount Holyoke College, the first women's college, founded by educator Mary Lyon in South Hadley, Massachusetts.
      Sarah and Angelina Grimké censured by Massachusetts clergy for offering lectures to mixed audiences of men and women.

1839   Mississippi passes Married Women's Property Act.
      First normal school (teachers college) established in Massachusetts.

Margaret Fuller initiates "Conversations" in Boston.

1840 Lucretia Mott attends World Anti-Slavery Conference in London and is denied a seat at the Conference because of her gender.

Abolitionist movement divides over issue of women's rights.

Georgia Female College founded; first southern school to grant full bachelor's degree to women.

Esther Howland produces first printed valentine in America.

1843 Oliver Wendell Holmes Sr. publishes *The Contagiousness of Puerperal Fever*, documenting the danger of the common and often fatal childbirth disease of puerperal fever and its spread through unsanitary practices in hospitals and by physicians.

Dorothea Dix testifies before the Massachusetts Legislature in January, exposing the horrendous treatment accorded patients in mental hospitals throughout the state.

Sojourner Truth begins her career as a preacher and reformer.

1844 Lowell Female Labor Reform Association founded in December by activist Sarah Bagley, in order to combat deteriorating work conditions in the Lowell Mills.

1845 Margaret Fuller publishes *Woman in the Nineteenth Century*.

1848 First women's rights convention organized by Elizabeth Cady Stanton and Lucretia Mott in Seneca Falls, New York.

Maria Mitchell, a self-taught astronomer, elected to the American Academy of Arts and Sciences.

1849 Elizabeth Blackwell graduates from Geneva Medical College.

1850 Harriet Tubman makes her first Underground Railroad rescue.

Female Medical College of Pennsylvania founded by Elizabeth Blackwell and a group of Philadelphia Quaker women. It is the first female medical school and is later renamed the Woman's Medical College of Pennsylvania.

Amelia Bloomer introduces divided skirts for women, gathered at the ankles and known as "bloomers."

1851 Sojourner Truth delivers "Aren't I a Woman" speech.

1852 Harriet Beecher Stowe publishes *Uncle Tom's Cabin*.

Emily Dickinson's first poem, "The Valentine," published without the reclusive poet's consent or knowledge.

1853   Mary Ann Shadd Cary becomes the first black woman editor of *The Provincial Freeman*.

Antoinette Blackwell becomes the first woman to be ordained as a Protestant minister.

Government hires first female employees. Despite objections, the U.S. Commissioner of Patents hires women to work as clerks in his department. Clara Barton is one of the first women thus employed.

1854   Postmaster profession first to establish pay equity for male and female employees.

1855   St. Luke's Hospital, New York City, founded. The first hospital to treat women's diseases, it gains reputation for developing gynecology as a specialty.

1856   Infanticide in Ohio. When Margaret Garner, a Kentucky slave attempting to escape to freedom with her children, is tracked down by slave catchers in Ohio, she kills one of her children when threatened with recapture and a return to slavery.

1857   New York Infirmary for Women and Children opens.

1859   American Medical Association opposes abortion. Its stand is critical in redefining the legal status of abortion in America.

Harriet Hosmer completes her sculpture, "Zenobia in Chains."

Harriet Wilson publishes *Our Nig*, first novel published by an African American woman.

1861   Dorothea Dix appointed Superintendent of Nursing for Union army.

Frances Spinner becomes the first woman to head the U.S. Department of the Treasury, supervising more than 100 women clerks.

Emily Edson Briggs becomes the first woman White House correspondent.

1862   Laura Towne establishes Penn School on St. Helena Island, South Carolina.

Julia Ward Howe writes "The Battle Hymn of the Republic," which is adopted as Union army anthem.

Mary Patterson earns a master's degree from Oberlin College, the first African American woman to do so.

1863 National Women's Loyal League endorses emancipation. Organized by Elizabeth Cady Stanton and Susan B. Anthony, hundreds of women eager to express their support of the Union convene in New York City to petition Congress to vote for the immediate emancipation of all slaves in the Union.

Working Women's Union organized by sewing machine operators in New York City. Ellen Patterson, a union organizer, is elected its first president.

Americans celebrate first Thanksgiving Day, after Sara Josepha Hale successfully lobbies President Lincoln to declare it a national holiday.

1864 Troy (New York) Collar Union founded.

1865 Clara Barton opens agency to locate missing Civil War soldiers.

1866 Equal Rights Association founded by, among others, Susan B. Anthony, Frederick Douglass, Lucretia Mott, and Elizabeth Cady Stanton.

Young Women's Christian Association organized in United States.

Dr. Mary Walker nominated for Congressional Medal of Honor for her work during the Civil War.

Lucy Hobbs Taylor becomes the first woman in America to earn a degree in dentistry.

1867 The Grange admits women on equal basis with men.

1868 Elizabeth Cady Stanton and Susan B. Anthony launch feminist publication, *The Revolution*.

New England Women's Club founded by Julia Ward Howe and Caroline Severance.

Sorosis network founded by newswoman Jane Croly and other journalists and professional women in New York City.

Drs. Elizabeth and Emily Blackwell establish the Women's Medical College of New York Infirmary.

1869 First woman suffrage law in the United States passed in Wyoming.
Knights of Labor founded.
Daughters of St. Crispin founded; first national union for women.

Typographical Union admits women for the first time. The first woman to hold national office in the union is Augusta Lewis, the corresponding secretary.

Arabella Mansfield becomes first woman admitted to the bar. Despite an Iowa state constitution that provides a legal basis for rejecting her application, Judge Francis Springer notes Mansfield's outstanding qualifications and admits her to the Iowa bar.

National Woman Suffrage Association organized.

American Woman Suffrage Association founded.

Leonora Barkaloo becomes first woman admitted to an American law school (Washington University).

1870s   Esther McQuigg Morris becomes first woman judge in the United States. As Justice of the Peace in Wyoming, Morris holds court in a log cabin, serving many of the mining towns in the area.

1870   The *Woodhull & Claflin's Weekly* begins publication. Published by Victoria Woodhull to promote a variety of women's rights issues including suffrage, sexual freedom, and dress reform, as well as her presidential candidacy.

Utah grants full suffrage to women.

Inventor Margaret Knight patents the square-bottom, brown-paper grocery bag.

1871   Vinnie Ream statue of President Lincoln unveiled in the Capitol Rotunda, Washington, D.C. Ream is the first woman to be awarded a federal commission. In 1881 her statue of Admiral Farragut is also unveiled in Washington, D.C.

Frances Willard becomes first woman college president (Evanston College for Ladies, Evanston, Illinois).

1872   Susan B. Anthony arrested in Rochester, New York for attempting to exercise her constitutional right to vote as a citizen.

Victoria Woodhull and Frederick Douglass run for president and vice president on the People's Party ticket.

Charlotte E. Roy, a Howard Law School graduate, becomes first African American woman admitted to the bar (in Washington, D.C.). Her race and lack of business connections force her to abandon the practice of law within a short time.

Belva Lockwood, lawyer, drafts landmark legislation providing equal pay for equal work for government employees.

1873   Congress passes Comstock Law.

Remington Typewriter manufactured. Within ten years the machine has revolutionized office procedure and opened up a new avenue for employment for women.

Ladies Social Science Association founded.

Ellen Swallow Richards becomes first woman graduate of MIT. Founds sciences of ecology and home economics.

The Women's Uprising, a temperance campaign, begins in Hillsboro, Ohio, and the Women's Christian Temperance Union is founded.

1874   Dr. Annie Angel appointed to previously all-male staff of Mount Sinai Hospital in New York City.

Mary Ewing Outerbridge introduces tennis to America.

Massachusetts legislature passes the first ten-hour limit on workday for women and minors.

1875   Susan B. Anthony drafts a national suffrage amendment for the U.S. Constitution. Thereafter, the amendment is referred to as the Anthony Amendment.

Minor v Happersett. The U.S. Supreme Court rules that the Constitution does not guarantee the right of suffrage for anyone, because suffrage is a state privilege and not to be confused with citizenship.

Lydia Pinkham begins marketing "Lydia E. Pinkham's Vegetable Compound," the most advertised product in the United States.

Smith College founded and endowed by Sophia Smith.

1876   Congress revokes Utah female suffrage at the same time as making polygamy illegal in Utah.

Sarah Hackett Stevenson becomes first woman member of the American Medical Association.

Edmonia Lewis exhibits her work at the Philadelphia Centennial Exposition. Lewis, of mixed African American and Chippewa ancestry, is the first minority woman to have her art exhibited in public. Among her famous pieces are *The Death of Cleopatra*, *The Marriage of Hiawatha*, and *Forever Free*.

1878   First woman suffrage amendment submitted to Congress.

Emma M. Nutt becomes first female telephone operator in the United States, in Boston.

1879   Frances Willard elected president of Women's Christian Temperance Union.

Mary Mattoney becomes the first African American woman to earn a nursing degree from the New England Hospital for Women and Children.

Radcliffe College founded.

The First Church of Christ Scientist is founded by Mary Baker Eddy in Massachusetts four years after the publication of *Science and Health with Key to the Scriptures* (1874), in which she explained the central idea of Christian Science: the power of mind over matter.

Congress passes bill enabling women to practice before the Supreme Court. Belva Lockwood becomes first woman admitted to appear there.

1881   Clara Barton founds the American Red Cross.

Association of Collegiate Alumnae founded.

University of Mississippi admits women, first southern university to do so.

Women's National Press Association organized; Emily Edson Briggs, the first woman White House correspondent, elected president.

Eliza Ann Otis becomes first woman reporter for the *Los Angeles Times*.

1883   *Ladies Home Journal* begins publication. When publisher Cyrus Curtis's farm journal begins including a women's section, it quickly becomes the most popular part of the magazine. Curtis drops the farm journal, expands the new *Ladies Home Journal*, and appoints his wife, Louisa Knapp Curtis, editor.

Lillian D. Wald founds Henry Street Settlement House in New York City.

Emma Lazarus writes poem inscribed on base of Statue of Liberty. The poem opens with the lines: "Give me your tired, your poor, your downtrodden . . . your huddled masses yearning to be free."

1885   Widespread trafficking in young girls exposed. British journalists publish articles exposing the practice of white slavery, revealing to a shocked American public not only its prevalence but the fact that in some states the age of consent for girls is as low as ten years old. Moral reformers begin lobbying states to raise the legal age of consent.

Annie Oakley joins Wild West Show and becomes the highest-paid woman in America.

1886   Sophia Gregoria Hayden becomes first woman architecture student admitted to MIT.

Persis F. Eames Albee becomes first Avon lady, in Winchester, New Hampshire.

1887   Anthony Amendment voted on by Senate and rejected by thirty-four to sixteen members, with twenty-five members absent. This is the only time in the nineteenth century that the amendment is brought to a vote.

H. Sophie Newcombe Memorial College for Women founded and funded in New Orleans by Josephine Newcombe.

1888   National Council of Women founded. Frances Willard elected first president.

1889   Hull House, a settlement house, founded by Jane Addams and Ellen Gates Starr in Chicago.

Investigative reporter Nellie Bly goes around the world in seventy-two days.

Barnard College in New York City founded by Annie Nathan Meyer after she learns that women taking exams at Columbia University have to answer questions about information provided in lectures from which they were barred.

Gift from philanthropist Mary Elizabeth Garrett opens Johns Hopkins Medical School to women.

1890   Alice Freeman Palmer becomes dean of women at the University of Chicago.

Two rival suffrage groups combine to form the National American Woman Suffrage Association. Elizabeth Cady Stanton serves as first president.

General Federation of Women's Clubs organized by Jane Croly, the founder of the Sorosis network.

Rose Knox cofounds the Knox Gelatin Company. After the death of her husband, Knox institutes a style of leadership she calls a "woman's way," which includes a five-day work week, two-week vacations, and sick leave.

Susie Elizabeth Frazier becomes first African American woman to be offered a teaching position in New York City public schools.

1891   National Women's Alliance founded as an outgrowth of the populist movement.

MIT architecture graduate Sophia Hayden wins first place in a competition for the design of the Woman's Building at the Chicago Exposition.

1892   Sissieretta Jones, "The black Patti," invited to sing at the White House, the first black female entertainer to be so honored.

1893   Florence Bascom earns a Ph.D. in geology from Johns Hopkins University.

National Council of Jewish Women founded in Chicago by Hannah Greenbaum Solomon, who becomes its first president.

Woman's Building of the World's Columbian Exposition opens to record-breaking crowds; building features wide array of exhibits by and about women.

Colorado women granted suffrage.

First golf course for women opens: Shinnecock Hills Golf Club, Southampton, New York.

1894   University of California awards first engineering degree to a woman graduate.

1895   M. Carey Thomas becomes president of Bryn Mawr.

Ida Wells Barnett publishes *A Red Record*, a scathing indictment of lynching.

1896   Charlotte Perkins Gilman publishes *Women and Economics*, a groundbreaking analysis of women's economic status.

Utah granted statehood. Utah women are once again granted the full suffrage rights revoked by Congress in 1876.

Idaho women granted suffrage.

Fannie Farmer publishes first cookbook.

National Association of Colored Women founded; Dr. Mary Church Terrell elected first president.

1897   Parent-Teacher Association (PTA) founded by Alice McLellan Birney, who serves as its first president.

1900   Sister Julia (Susan McGroarty) founds Trinity College in Washington, D.C.; first college offering higher education for Catholic girls.

Barnard College president Emily Smith Putnam is forced to step down by the board of directors when she reveals that she is pregnant.

1903   St. Luke Penny Saving Bank of Richmond, Virginia, appoints Maggie L. Walker, who is African American, as the first woman bank president in the United States.

1920   Women's suffrage amendment ratified as Nineteenth Amendment.

PART FOUR

Resources

INTRODUCTION

There was a time and not so long ago when a good bibliography and resource guide to women's history could be contained in twenty pages, more or less. Those early guides did what they were intended to do—to lead students and researchers to material that would, in turn, help them uncover new material, expanding the contours of our collective past and providing both new answers and exciting new challenges. The good news is that a bibliographic and resource guide can no longer be contained in twenty pages or even in fifty pages. The better news is that the explosion of scholarship that has yielded such a wealth of information promises to continue.

It would be impossible to list every single citation that is presently on record somewhere in one bibliography. It would be futile and indeed meaningless to make the attempt even if we were afforded unlimited space to do so—and a motorized vehicle to cart the thing around. Our goal here is to provide enough references and of such a depth and breadth that anyone seeking information on any aspect of the lives and history of American women in the nineteenth century will find a means of tracking down that information.

This section is divided into eight parts, each of which contains two or more subsets. In all, there are more than one hundred different headings for which information is provided. The first part is the introduction, intended to provide the reader with an overview of the bibliography in order to make its use more efficient.

Section I, "Topics," is subdivided into twenty discrete headings, fifteen of which have from two to nine subheadings. The headings cover all of the subjects discussed in the narrative overview, from demography to labor to race and ethnicity to sexuality to suffrage. Not all of the topic headings and subheadings contain equal numbers of citations; obviously some topics have a much richer literature than others. We have included a minimum of two citations under every topic heading and subheading. The result is a balanced and inclusive bibliography that reflects the current state of scholarship for each topic and that will easily lead the reader to additional sources.

Section II contains bibliographic and reference works.

Section III contains general historical works and overviews including pioneering works, surveys, and anthologies.

Section IV presents biographies (including group biographies), autobiographies and memoirs, letters and diaries, and documentary collections.

Section V is a listing of journals and periodicals (primary and secondary), historical projects of importance currently in progress, and archival resources. While we have listed major archival resources and some of their holdings in order to give the reader an idea of the depth of information available in archival collections, we could by no means list every resource. For that reason, we have included section VI, which is a listing of CD-ROMs and websites. The website listings are of particular value because they will take the reader into countless available archival resources around the world. For individuals unfamiliar with websites or online research, the amount of information available is simply staggering. Tapping into one good website can take the user anywhere she or he wishes to go. With several websites and good search engines, there is very little that is currently housed in an archive or a library anywhere in the world that will be overlooked. You may not be able to gain online access to each archive, but you will know where the resources are located. Moreover, an amazing amount of information is actually retrievable online to help you in your search.

The final section of this guide, section VII, is a sample listing of the novels and films available about women in America in the nineteenth century. Because of the space limitations already mentioned, only a sample could be provided. As in other categories, however, the references within this section will lead the interested reader to volumes of information about both novels and films.

Finally, a word about annotations. In order to be able to include more citations, we have chosen not to annotate each and every bibliographic entry. Many reference works and articles, for example, are self-explanatory, and annotating would mean excluding other citations altogether. But the majority of references do include a brief comment constructed in such a way as to convey to the reader the place we believe that the specific source holds in the context of women's history, especially within the past three decades.

SECTION I. TOPICS

A. Demography

Taeuber, Conrad and Irene Taeuber. *The Changing Population of the United States.* New York: Wiley, 1958.

U.S. Department of Commerce. *Historical Statistics of the United States, Colonial Times to 1970*, part 1, bicentennial ed. Washington, D.C.: Bureau of the Census, 1975.

Wells, Robert. *Revolutions in American Lives: A Demographic Perspective on Americans, Their Families, and Society.* Westport, Conn.: Greenwood, 1982.

A compelling and powerful overview. The classic work, brimming with important data and insight.

1. Fertility

Coale, Ansley J. and Melvin Zelnick. *New Estimates of Fertility and Population in the United States.* Princeton: Princeton University Press, 1963.

Wells, Robert. "Family Size and Fertility Control in Eighteenth-Century America." *Population Studies* 25 (1971).

Wells shows the way in which Quakers may have pioneered family limitation in early America.

2. Marital Rates

Department of Commerce and Labor. *Marriage and Divorce, 1887–1906*, Bulletin 96. Washington, D.C.: Bureau of the Census, 1908.

U.S. Department of Commerce. *Historical Statistics of the United States, Colonial Times to 1970*, part 1, bicentennial ed. Washington, D.C.: Bureau of the Census, 1975.

3. Mortality Rates

U.S. Department of Commerce. *Historical Statistics of the United States, Colonial Times to 1970*, part 1, bicentennial ed. Washington, D.C.: Bureau of the Census, 1975.

B. Revolutionary America

Kerber, Linda. *Women of the Republic: Intellect and Ideology in Revolutionary America.* Chapel Hill: University of North Carolina Press, 1980.

Important analysis of women's role in the American Revolution and the intellectual origins of American feminism during the early national era.

Norton, Mary Beth. *Liberty's Daughters: The Revolutionary Experience of American Women, 1750–1800.* Boston: Little, Brown, 1980.

A classic work on women's role in wartime and the impact of the American Revolution on white and black women, northern and southern.

Salmon, Marylynn. " 'Life, Liberty, and Dower': The Legal Status of Women After the American Revolution." In Carol Berkin and Clara Lovett, eds., *Women, War, and Revolution*. New York: Holmes and Meier, 1980.

An excellent survey.

Wilson, Joan Hoff. "The Illusion of Change: Women and the American Revolution." In Alfred Young, ed., *The American Revolution: Explorations in the History of American Radicalism*. DeKalb: Northern Illinois University Press, 1976.

An imaginative look at the political ramifications of women's role in the American Revolution.

C. Domesticity and Women's Culture

Bloch, Ruth. "American Feminine Ideals in Transition: The Rise of the Moral Mother, 1785–1815." *Feminist Studies* 4 (1978).

Bloch analyzes intellectual trends outlining issues of "republican motherhood."

Boydston, Jeanne. *Home and Work: Housework, Wages, and the Ideology of Labor in the Early Republic*. New York: Oxford University Press, 1990.

An in-depth look at the politics of separate spheres and its consequences for northern women in the early national era.

Cott, Nancy. *The Bonds of Womanhood: "Women's Sphere" in New England, 1780–1835*. New Haven: Yale University Press, 1977.

A pioneering and important look at the rise of the middle class in the North during the early national era and the role of women within this development. Cott explores literacy, voluntary organizations, and the development of a women's culture in the North.

Douglas, Ann. *The Feminization of American Culture*. New York: Knopf, 1977.

A tour-de-force look at the role of northern women in religion and literature, and their ability to transform the culture over the course of the nineteenth century.

Green, Harvey. *The Light of the Home: An Intimate View of the Lives of Women in Victorian America*. New York: Pantheon, 1983.

An excellent overview of Victorian households, with stunning visual material.

Sklar, Kathryn. *Catharine Beecher: A Study in American Domesticity*. New Haven: Yale University Press, 1973.

Sklar's biography of Beecher is really a portrait of an era, a germinal cultural study of nineteenth-century women's lives.

1. Family Life

Greven, Philip. *The Protestant Temperament: Patterns of Religious Experience, Childrearing, and Self in Early America*. New York: Knopf, 1977.

An interesting analysis of patterns of cultural changes in child rearing and family life. Theoretical issues may hold for the antebellum era.

Smith, David Blake. *Inside the Great House: Planter Family Life in Eighteenth Century Chesapeake Society*. Ithaca, N.Y.: Cornell University Press, 1980.

Excellent background for the domestic politics of plantation households and family life among the southern elite during the Revolutionary era.

2. Literacy, Reading, and Writing

Baym, Nina. *Woman's Fiction: A Guide to Novels by and About Women in America, 1820–1870*. Ithaca, N.Y.: Cornell University Press, 1978.

A heroic and valuable guide to women's literature in the nineteenth century by a leading literary scholar in the field. Accessible and perceptive.

Conrad, Susan. *Perish the Thought: Intellectual Women in Romantic America, 1830–1860*. New York: Oxford University Press, 1976.

A thorough but not very engaging study of the topic.

Fryer, Judith. *The Three Faces of Eve: Women in the Nineteenth-Century American Novel*. New York: Oxford University Press, 1976.

An interesting cultural interpretation, by examining women characters in major nineteenth-century fiction.

Kelley, Mary. *Private Woman, Public Stage: Literary Domesticity in Nineteenth-Century America*. New York: Oxford University Press, 1983.

A vivid and engaging look at the lives of women writers and their relationship with their audience. Excellent use of source material, and terrific stories.

D. Antebellum South

Bynum, Victoria. *Unruly Women: The Politics of Social and Sexual Control in the Old South, 1840–1865*. Chapel Hill: University of North Carolina Press, 1992.

An important look at women from other than the planter class, with special attention paid to court records and other interesting sources.

Censer, Jane Turner. *North Carolina Planters and Their Children, 1800–1860*. Baton Rouge: Louisiana State University Press, 1984.

An absorbing account of the lives of wealthy planter families; especially good on roles of women as wives and mothers.

Clinton, Catherine. *The Plantation Mistress: Woman's World in the Old South*. New York: Pantheon, 1982.

A survey of the lives of elite white women with emphasis on slavery (shaping all women's lives, black and white), on sexuality and race, and on interlocking systems of gender and racial oppression within white southern ideology.

Clinton, Catherine and Michele Gillespie, eds. *The Devil's Lane: Sex and Race in the Early South*. New York: Oxford University Press, 1997.

Several important articles on the Gulf South, with articles on adultery, interracial sex, castration, cross-dressing, religion, and other topics.

Fox-Genovese, Elizabeth. *Within the Plantation Household: Black and White Women of the Old South*. Chapel Hill: University of North Carolina Press, 1988.

An important analysis of the role of gender and slavery within the Old South. Fox-Genovese posits that white women were strong defenders of slavery and played a key role in the maintenance of mastery.

Lebsock, Suzanne. *The Free Women of Petersburg: Status and Culture in a Southern Town, 1784–1860*. New York: Norton, 1983.

An engaging look at the role of gender among free black and white women in one southern town. Lebsock's was one of the first studies to examine the role of women's culture within a southern context. Intriguing look at women's legal status, the role of property, and female literacy.

Lewis, Jan. *The Pursuit of Happiness: Family and Values in Jefferson's Virginia*. New York: Cambridge University Press, 1983.

A model family history. A sophisticated look at the role of family, child rearing, and dynasty in early national Virginia.

Scott, Anne Firor. *The Southern Lady: From Pedestal to Politics, 1830–1930*. Chicago: University of Chicago Press, 1970.

A pioneering book by a foremother of modern southern women's history. This survey looks at the changing role for southern white women from their antebellum ladyhood, through the crisis of the Civil War, on to the strong bonds of womanhood forged through voluntary organizations during the Progressive era and onward.

Wyatt-Brown, Bertram. *Southern Honor: Ethics and Behavior in the Old South.* New York: Oxford University Press, 1982.

One of the first books by a distinguished male scholar of southern history to integrate gender issues and the role of women fully into an analytical framework. A work that continues to engage.

1. Slavery

Davis, Angela. "Reflections on Black Women's Role in the Community of Slaves." *Black Scholar* 3 (December 1971).

A pioneering theoretical work on race, class, and gender within the antebellum South. A classic.

Gutman, Herbert. *The Black Family in Slavery and Freedom, 1750–1925.* New York: Pantheon, 1976.

A pioneering and important look at the role of black men and women struggling within the slaveholding South. Excellent insight into the role of the Civil War and Emancipation, but the bulk of the book concentrates on the antebellum era.

Hine, Darlene Clark. "Female Slave Resistance: The Economics of Sex." *Western Journal of Black Studies* 3 (Summer 1979).

An important introduction into the thinking of a leading and prolific scholar of African American women's history.

Morton, Patricia, ed. *Discovering the Women in Slavery: Emancipating Perspectives on the American Past.* Athens: University of Georgia Press, 1996.

An important collection of original articles tracing the lives of black and white women within the slaveholding South. Especially sensitive to the issue of regionalism.

White, Deborah. *Aren't I a Woman: Female Slaves in the Antebellum South.* New York: Norton, 1985.

A pioneering study of the lives of African American women on antebellum plantations. Emphasis on female bonding within the slave community, family, and work roles.

E. Antebellum North

Halttunen, Karen. *Confidence Men and Painted Women: A Study of Middle-Class Culture in America, 1830–1870.* New Haven: Yale University Press, 1983.

A compelling portrait of gender in the North at midcentury.

Ryan, Mary. *Cradle of the Middle Class*. New York: Cambridge University Press, 1981.

A classic study of northern women and urban reform in the first half of the nineteenth century.

Smith-Rosenberg, Carroll. "Beauty, the Beast, and the Militant Woman: A Case Study in Sex Roles and Social Stress in Jacksonian America." *American Quarterly* 23 (October 1971).

Important pioneering work on gender roles in antebellum America.

1. Rise of the Mills

Dublin, Thomas. *Women at Work: The Transformation of Work and Community in Lowell, Massachusetts, 1826–1860*. New York: Columbia University Press, 1979.

A pioneering work by a leading labor historian. Excellent statistics and fine interpretive study.

Eisler, Benita, ed. *The Lowell Offering: Writings by New England Mill Women, 1840–1845*. Philadelphia: Lippincott, 1977.

A well-edited selection, especially useful for labor and political views.

Foner, Philip. *The Factory Girls: A Collection of Writings on Life and Struggles in the New England Factories of the 1840s*. Urbana: University of Illinois Press, 1977.

An excellent collection.

Larcom, Lucy. *A New England Girlhood*. 1890; reprint, New York: Corinth, 1961.

An important memoir by one of the Lowell mill girls.

Ware, Caroline. *Early New England Cotton Manufacture*. Boston: Houghton Mifflin, 1931.

A pioneering study by a leading labor scholar.

2. Urbanization

Addams, Jane. *Twenty Years at Hull House*. New York: Macmillan, 1910.

Contemporary account of life in late nineteenth-century Chicago for immigrants and working poor.

Chambers, Clarke A. *A Seedtime of Reform*. Minneapolis: University of Minnesota Press, 1963.

A dated but nevertheless useful discussion of the problems of the cities and the urban poor.

Chudacoff, Howard. *The Evolution of American Urban Society*. Englewood Cliffs, N.J.: Prentice-Hall, 1975.

Stansell, Christine. *City of Women: Sex and Class in New York, 1789–1860*. New York: Knopf, 1986.

Excellent study of working women in New York shaping new lives in sweat shops, tenements, and streets; innovative scholarship.

F. Labor

Kessler-Harris, Alice. *Out to Work: A History of Wage-Earning Women in America*. New York: Oxford University Press, 1982.

A classic study. The most comprehensive and impressive analysis of women involved in labor and wage earning. More work has been done on the role of African American women, but this study remains an important first look.

Schwartz, Ruth Cowan. *More Work for Mother*. New York: Basic, 1983.

A brilliant look at the role of technological developments that increased rather than decreased work within the home for women.

Strasser, Susan. *Never Done: A History of American Housework*. New York: Pantheon, 1982.

An engaging and accessible look at the household labor of average American women from the colonial era to the present. Anecdotal and entertaining.

1. Working Women

Abbott, Edith. *Women in Industry: A Study in American Economic History*. New York: Appleton, 1919.

A ground-breaking study by one of the pioneers in social science.

Baxandall, Rosalyn, Linda Gordon, and Susan Reverby, eds. *America's Working Women: 1600 to the Present*. 1976; reprint, New York: Norton, 1995.

A chock-a-block, overflowing compendium of documents on wage-earning women. This latest edition has doubled the number of sections and the coverage of women of color found in the first edition.

Dublin, Thomas. *Transforming Women's Work: New England Lives in the Industrial Revolution*. Ithaca, N.Y.: Cornell University Press, 1995.

Dublin begins with women in the cottage industry of weaving, then examines the rise of textile mills and shoe factories in industrializing Massachusetts, then looks at women teachers in New Hampshire.

Dudden, Faye. *Serving Women: Household Service in Nineteenth-Century America*. Middletown, Conn.: Wesleyan University Press, 1983.

A very accessible and informative survey of white household labor.

Josephson, Hannah. *The Golden Threads: New England's Mill Girls and Magnates*. New York: Duell, Sloan and Pearce, 1949.

A classic study of the paternalistic Lowell System.

Kennedy, Susan Estabrook. *If All We Did Was Weep at Home: A History of White Working-Class Women in America*. Bloomington: Indiana University Press, 1979.

A useful early look at working-class lives, the role of work and family for the female wage-earning minority in nineteenth-century America.

Neil, Charles P. *Wage-Earning Women in Stores and Factories*, vol. 5. *Report on Condition of Woman and Child Wage Earners in the United States*. Washington, D.C.: Government Printing Office, 1910.

Contains valuable information about work conditions, demography, wages, etc.

Wertheimer, Barbara. *We Were There: The Story of Working Women in America*. New York: Pantheon, 1977.

A pioneering example of 1970s scholarship. Outdated.

2. Labor Organization

Blewett, Mary. *Men, Women, and Work: Class, Gender, and Protest in the New England Shoe Industry*. Urbana: University of Illinois Press, 1988.

This is a very good monograph on women and the labor movement.

Foner, Philip S. *Women and the American Labor Movement: From Colonial Times to the Eve of World War One*. New York: Free Press, 1979.

Early study of women in the labor movement; still valuable.

Jeffrey, Julie Roy. "Women in the Southern Farmers' Alliance." *Feminist Studies* 3 (Fall 1975).

Excellent study of women in one of the first mixed-sex organizations that gave rural women an opportunity to hold office.

Levine, Susan. *Labor's True Woman*. Philadelphia: Temple University Press, 1984.

Levine demonstrates that women wage earners were pro-union and very supportive.

G. Education

Farnham, Christine. *The Education of the Southern Belle*. New York: New York University Press, 1994.

An important study of antebellum white women.

Frankfort, Roberta. *Collegiate Women: Domesticity and Career in Turn-of-the-Century America*. New York, 1978 (out of print).

Graham, Patricia A. "Expansion and Exclusion: A History of Women in American Higher Education." *Signs: Journal of Women in Culture and Society* 3 (Summer 1978).

A fine analytical framework for thinking about gender discrimination in higher education—and its consequences.

Horowitz, Helen Lefkowitz. *Alma Mater: Design and Experience in the Women's Colleges from Their Nineteenth-Century Beginnings to the 1930s*. New York: Knopf, 1984.

A look at the mission statements, curricula, and evolution of women's colleges.

Lutz, Alma. *Emma Willard: Daughter of Democracy*. Boston: Houghton Mifflin, 1929.

Recounts Willard's monumental contribution to the development of women's education.

Newcomer, Mabel. *A Century of Higher Education for Women*. Washington, D.C.: Zenger, 1959.

Informationally valuable; good survey of development of private and coeducational institutions.

Solomon, Barbara Miller. *In the Company of Educated Women: A History of Women and Higher Education*. New Haven: Yale University Press, 1985.

Solid study with attention to the Seven Sisters colleges.

Woody, Thomas. *A History of Women's Education in the United States*. 2 vols. New York: Science Press, 1929.

An important pioneering classic. No other comprehensive work has surpassed it yet.

Vinovskis, Maris and Richard Bernard. "Beyond Catharine Beecher: Female Education in the Antebellum Period." *Signs: Journal of Women in Culture and Society* 3 (Summer 1978).

A thoughtful look at the role of education in transforming northern women's lives.

1. Schools and Academies

Gordon, Sarah. "Smith College Students: The First Ten Classes, 1879–1888." *History of Education Quarterly* 14 (Spring 1974).

An informative survey of elite college women.

Green, Elizabeth Alden. *Mary Lyon and Mount Holyoke: Opening the Gates*. Hanover, N.H.: University Press of New England, 1979.

A study of the first women's college, which set the standard for academic rigor. Mary Lyon's philosophy of education is abundantly explored.

Hogeland, Ronald. "Coeducation of the Sexes at Oberlin College: A Study of Social Ideas in Mid-Nineteenth Century America." *Journal of Social History* 6 (Winter 1972–73).

A fine case study of the debates over gender equality in nineteenth-century higher education.

McGuigan, Dorothy. *A Dangerous Experiment: One Hundred Years of Women at the University of Michigan*. Ann Arbor: University of Michigan Press, 1970.

An adequate case study.

Palmieri, Patricia. *In Adamless Eden: The Community of Women Faculty at Wellesley*. New Haven: Yale University Press, 1995.

An important case study of the community of women at a pioneering single-sex college.

Scott, Anne Firor. "The Ever-Widening Circle: The Diffusion of Feminist Values from the Troy Female Seminary." *History of Education Quarterly* 19 (Spring 1979).

Scott traces Emma Willard's overwhelming impact on women's education—in the North and the South—during the nineteenth century, through the training of several generations of teachers.

Walsh, Mary and Francis Walsh. "Integrating Men's Colleges at the Turn of the Century." *Historical Journal of Massachusetts* 10 (June 1982).

A crucial look at the coeducation movement at the end of the nineteenth century.

2. Teaching

Hoffman, Nancy, ed. *Woman's "True" Profession: Voices from the History of Teaching*. Old Westbury, N.Y.: Feminist Press, 1981.

Jones, Jacqueline. *Soldiers of Light and Love: Northern Teachers and Georgia Blacks, 1865–1873*. Chapel Hill: University of North Carolina Press, 1980.

A fascinating and authoritative look at the roles of race, gender, and education during Reconstruction.

Strober, Myra H. and Audrey Gordon Lanford. "The Feminization of Public School Teaching: Cross Sectional Analysis, 1850–1880." *Signs: Journal of Women in Culture and Society* 11 (Winter 1986).

How and why teaching became a woman's "occupation" in the mid-nineteenth century. Well constructed.

H. Moral Reform

Berg, Barbara. *The Remembered Gate: Origins of American Feminism*. New York: Oxford University Press, 1978.

Women in urban reform during the first half of the nineteenth century. How voluntary movements led to gender consciousness.

Ginzberg, Lori D. *Women and the Work of Benevolence: Morality, Politics, and Class in the Nineteenth Century*. New Haven: Yale University Press, 1992.

An important look at the intersections of class and gender values within mid-nineteenth-century culture.

1. Purity

Pivar, Dale. *Purity Crusade: Sexual Morality and Social Control, 1868–1900*. Westport, Conn.: Greenwood, 1973.

An important examination of the ways in which women's evangelicalism led to the purity crusade and the way in which reform became gendered in nineteenth-century public discourse.

Rothman, Sheila M. *Woman's Proper Place: A History of Changing Ideas and Practices, 1870 to the Present*. New York: Basic, 1978.

2. Dress Reform

Lauer, Jeanette and Robert Lauer. "The Battle of the Sexes: Fashion in Nineteenth-Century America." *Journal of Popular Culture* 13 (June 1980).
An interesting introduction to the vocabulary of nineteenth-century dress reform.

Leach, William. *True Love and Perfect Union: The Feminist Reform of Sex and Society*. New York: Basic, 1980.
An engaging and important study covering a wide range of topics; see especially his analysis of feminist Anna Dickinson on the issue of dress reform.

3. Utopian Communities

Foster, Lawrence. *Women, Family, and Utopia: Communal Experiments of the Shakers, the Oneida Community, and the Mormons*. Syracuse, N.Y.: Syracuse University Press, 1991.
Especially illuminating on the Oneida experiment, good on issues of sexuality.

Francis, Richard. *Transcendental Utopias: Individual and Community at Brook Farm, Fruitlands, and Walden*. Ithaca, N.Y.: Cornell University Press, 1997.
A revisionist interpretation of gender and work issues within utopian communities.

Hayden, Dolores. *Seven American Utopias: The Architecture of Communitarian Socialism, 1790–1975*. Cambridge: MIT Press, 1976.
Much more architectural than cultural analysis, but a fine study.

Kolmerton, Carol. *Women in Utopia: The Ideology of Gender in the American Owenite Communities*. Bloomington: Indiana University Press, 1990.
A solid case study.

4. Abolition

Hersch, Blanche. *The Slavery of Sex: Feminist-Abolitionists in Nineteenth-Century America*. Urbana: University of Illinois Press, 1978
Dated, but still contains some excellent biographical data.

Lerner, Gerda. *The Grimké Sisters of South Carolina: Pioneers for Women's Rights and Abolition*. Boston: Houghton Mifflin, 1967.
A very fine analysis of these two remarkable reformers.

Lutz, Alma. *Crusade for Freedom: Women of the Antislavery Movement*. Boston: Beacon, 1968.
A dated study of pioneering abolitionist women.

Melder, Keith. *Beginnings of Sisterhood: The American Woman's Rights Movement, 1800–1850.* New York: Schocken, 1977.
An excellent survey of women abolitionists, but dated.

Yee, Shirley. *Black Women Abolitionists: A Study in Activism, 1828–1860.* Knoxville: University of Tennessee Press, 1992.
A splendid analysis of the role of black women in the abolitionist crusade and black women's communities.

Yellin, Jean and John Van Horne, eds. *The Abolitionist Sisterhood: Women's Political Culture in Antebellum America.* Ithaca, N.Y.: Cornell University Press, 1994.
An important and illuminating anthology on abolitionist women.

I. The Early Women's Rights Movement (to 1879)

DuBois, Ellen. *Feminism and Suffrage: The Emergence of an Independent Women's Movement in America, 1848–1869.* Ithaca, N.Y.: Cornell University Press, 1978.
The authoritative study of Stanton and Anthony's early movement and their campaigns during Reconstruction to achieve votes for women.

Flexner, Eleanor. *Century of Struggle: The Women's Rights Movement in the United States*, with new introduction by Ellen Fitzpatrick. 1959; reprint, Cambridge: Harvard University Press, 1995.
Path-breaking account of the suffrage movement; focus is primarily on the mainstream suffragists. Important new biographical information on Flexner by Fitzpatrick.

Grimes, Alan P. *The Puritan Ethic and Woman Suffrage.* Westport, Conn.: Greenwood, 1967.
Discusses early acceptance of suffrage in western states. The contributions made by women to survival and success in settling the frontier invested them with more influence in securing political rights.

Turner, Edward. "Women's Suffrage in New Jersey." *Smith College Studies in History* 1 (1916).
Pioneering piece on early voting in New Jersey, 1787–1808.

J. Civil War and Reconstruction

Clinton, Catherine. *Tara Revisited: Women, War, and the Plantation Legend.* New York: Abbeville, 1995.

More than 150 illustrations accompany this analysis of the reality and "legendary" roles of women on plantations during wartime. Emphasis on the role of "remembrance of things imagined" by neo-Confederates after defeat.

Clinton, Catherine and Nina Silber, eds. *Divided Houses: Gender and the Civil War*. New York: Oxford University Press, 1992.

Full of important articles on the home front, gender issues, women and war work— black and white women in wartime.

Faust, Drew Gilpin. *Mothers of Invention: Women of the Slaveholding South in the American Civil War*. Chapel Hill: University of North Carolina, 1996.

An important synthesis of the role of slaveholding Confederate women, suggesting they were strongly involved in the maintenance of the slaveholding system, but felt betrayed by the costs of war and turned against the "glorious Cause," thus contributing to the defeat of the Confederacy.

Leonard, Elizabeth. *Yankee Women: Gender Battles in the Civil War*. New York: Norton, 1994.

A bright, engaging study of exemplary northern women during wartime.

Massey, Mary Elizabeth. *Bonnet Brigades*. New York: Knopf, 1966.

An excellent pioneering survey, looking at the North as well as the South.

Rable, George. *Civil Wars: Women and the Crisis of Southern Nationalism*. Urbana: University of Illinois Press, 1989.

A solid and revisionist survey of white women's role in the slaveholding South. Rable argues that white women lost interest in the Confederate cause during wartime.

Whites, LeeAnn. *The Civil War as a Crisis in Gender: Augusta, Georgia, 1860–1900*. Athens: University of Georgia Press, 1995.

An important analysis, by looking at one Georgia community, of the way in which war "gendered" all social relations.

1. Women Soldiers and Spies

Burgess, Lauren, ed. *An Uncommon Soldier: The Civil War Letters of Sarah Rosetta Wakeman, alias Private Lyons Wakeman, 153rd New York State Volunteers*. New York: Oxford University Press, 1995.

An extraordinary collection of documents revealing the role of this woman soldier in combat.

Hall, Richard. *Patriots in Disguise: Women Warriors of the Civil War*. New York: Paragon House, 1993.

A superficial study of the topic.

2. Home Front

Jones, Katherine. *When Sherman Came: Southern Women and the "Great War."* Indianapolis: Bobbs Merrill, 1964.
A pioneering and well-researched monograph by a leading scholar of women's Civil War history.

Paludan, Philip. *"A People's Contest": The Union and the Civil War, 1861–1865.* New York: Harper and Row, 1988.
Excellent insights into northern women's roles on the home front.

Woodward, C. Vann. *Mary Chesnut's Civil War.* New Haven: Yale University Press, 1981.
A prize-winning edition of this classic wartime memoir.

3. Emancipation

Edwards, Laura. *Gendered Strife and Confusion: The Political Culture of Reconstruction.* Urbana: University of Illinois Press, 1997.
Excellent look at the racial and gender issues in conflict in the South during Reconstruction; focus on North Carolina.

Jacoway, Elizabeth. *Yankee Missionaries: The Penn School Experiment.* Baton Rouge: Louisiana State University Press, 1979.
Study of Laura Towne's South Carolina venture and her lifelong devotion to black education.

Painter, Nell. *Exodusters: Black Migration to Kansas After Reconstruction.* New York: Knopf, 1977.
The engaging story of the freedpeople who left the South following "Redemption" and settled black towns in Oklahoma and Kansas.

Rose, Willie Lee. *Rehearsal for Reconstruction.* New York: Oxford University Press, 1964.
A pioneering and important study of the role of race, gender, and region. Rose's look at the South Carolina sea islands during Union occupation is an exemplary case study.

Schwalm, Leslie. *A Hard Fight for We: Women's Transition from Slavery to Freedom in South Carolina.* Urbana: University of Illinois Press, 1997.
An important study of African American women's lives, in struggle during Reconstruction.

K. Religion

Epstein, Barbara Leslie. *The Politics of Domesticity: Women, Evangelism, and Temperance in Nineteenth-Century America*. Middletown, Conn.: Wesleyan University Press, 1981.

A nice survey of the connections between women in religious movements and subsequent reform campaigns.

Heyrman, Christine. *Southern Cross: The Origins of the Bible Belt*. New York: Knopf, 1997.

An erudite and important analysis of southern evangelicalism in the early republic, with an important chapter on women's roles.

Juster, Susan. *Disorderly Women: Sexual Politics and Evangelicalism in Revolutionary New England*. Ithaca, N.Y.: Cornell University Press, 1994.

An important look at gender and religious revivalism in New England from the Revolution to the turn of the nineteenth century.

Lindley, Susan Hall. *"You Have Stept Out of Your Place": A History of Women and Religion in America*. Louisville, Ky.: Westminster John Knox, 1996.

Nearly half of this survey text covers the nineteenth century. Chapters include the distinctive experiences of American Indian, African American, Roman Catholic, and Jewish women.

1. Protestantism

Boyd, Lois A. and R. Douglas Brackenridge. *Presbyterian Women in America: Two Centuries of a Quest for Status*. Westport, Conn.: Greenwood, 1983.

Reuther, Rosemary R. and Rosemary S. Keller, eds. *Women and Religion in America*. 2 vols. San Francisco: Harper and Row, 1981.

Comprehensive survey of women in various religious denominations.

a. Quakers

Bacon, Margaret Hope. *Valiant Friend*. New York: Walker, 1980.

Biography of Lucretia Mott with ample attention to her Quaker beliefs.

Cadbury, Henry J. "George Fox and Women's Liberation." *The Friends Quarterly* 19 (October 1974).

Calvo, Janis. "Quaker Women Ministers in Nineteenth-Century America." *Quaker History* 63 (1974).

Dunn, Mary Maples. "Women of Light." In Carol Ruth Berkin and Mary Beth Norton, eds., *Women in America: A History*. Boston: Houghton Mifflin, 1979.

Green, Dana. "Quaker Feminism: The Case of Lucretia Mott." *Pennsylvania History* 48 (1981).

b. Shakers

Brewer, Priscilla. *Shaker Communities, Shaker Lives*. Hanover, N.H.: University Press of New England, 1986.

Campbell, D'Ann. "Women's Life in Utopia: The Shaker Experiment in Equality Reappraised." *New England Quarterly* 51 (March 1978).

Campion, Nardi Reed. *Ann the Word: The Life of Mother Ann Lee*. Boston: Little Brown, 1976.

Biography of Shaker founder, Ann Lee.

Foster, Lawrence. *Religion and Sexuality: The Shakers, the Mormons, and the Oneida Community*. Urbana: University of Illinois Press, 1984.

Good presentation of the relationship between religion and utopian communities.

c. Christian Science

Peel, Robert. *Mary Baker Eddy: The Years of Authority*. New York: Holt, Rinehart & Winston, 1977.

———. *Mary Baker Eddy: The Years of Discovery*. New York: Holt, Rinehart & Winston, 1966.

———. *Mary Baker Eddy: The Years of Trial*. New York: Holt, Rinehart & Winston, 1971.

d. Mormons

Beecher, Maureen Ursenbach and Lavinia Fielding Anderson, eds. *Sisters in Spirit: Mormon Women in Historical and Cultural Perspective*. Urbana: University of Illinois Press, 1987.

Discusses Mormon philosophy, women in the Mormon church, and Mormon marriages in the context of American culture.

Foster, Lawrence. *Religion and Sexuality: The Shakers, the Mormons, and the Oneida Community*. Urbana: University of Illinois Press, 1984.

Whittaker, David J. and Carol C. Madsen. "History's Sequel: A Source Essay on Women in Mormon History." *Journal of Mormon History* 6 (1979).

2. Catholicism

Ewens, Mary. *The Role of the Nun in Nineteenth-Century America*. New York: Arno, 1978.

Monastic and religious life of women in the American Catholic tradition.

Kennelly, Maureen, ed. *American Catholic Women: An Historical Exploration*. New York: Macmillan, 1989.

Excellent source for Catholic women, immigrants, religious mores, set in historical context.

McCaffrey, Lawrence J. *The Irish Catholic Diaspora in America*, rev. ed. Washington, D.C.: Catholic University of America Press, 1998.

Contains a wealth of information on Catholics in America and Irish Catholics in particular; focuses on, among other topics, sources of nativist attacks and the significance of religion as the core of Irish identity.

3. Judaism

Glenn, Susan A. *Daughters of the Shtetl: Life and Labor in the Immigrant Generation*. Ithaca, N.Y.: Cornell University Press, 1994.

Focuses on immigrant culture in urban ghettos, work and family, transition to American life.

Kantrowitz, Melanie Kaye and Irena Klepfisz, eds. *The Tribe of Dina: A Jewish Women's Anthology*. Montpelier, Vt.: Sinister Wisdom, 1986.

Documentary history and contemporary status of Jewish women throughout the world; presented in series of biographical sketches.

4. Spiritualism

Braude, Ann. *Radical Spirits: Spiritualism and Women's Rights in Nineteenth-Century America*. Boston: Beacon, 1989.

Braude does an excellent job of explaining spiritualism and fitting it into the context of women's rights and American culture.

Meade, Marian. *Free Woman: The Life and Times of Victoria Woodhull*. New York: Knopf, 1976.

Discusses Woodhull's attraction to spiritualism.

5. Missionary Movements

Hunt, Alma. *Woman's Missionary Union*. Birmingham, Ala.: Woman's Missionary Union, 1964.

Origins of the WMU, a Southern Baptist Church organization consisting of smaller individual missionary societies.

Keller, Rosemary Skinner. "Lay Women in the Protestant Tradition." In Rosemary Radford Reuther and Rosemary Skinner Keller, eds., *Women and Religion in America*. San Francisco: Harper and Row, 1981.

Comprehensive survey of women in various religious denominations; discusses the foreign mission "mandate" of some of the Protestant churches.

Mather, Juliette. "Woman's Missionary Union." In Norman W. Coxe, ed., *Encyclopedia of Southern Baptists*. Nashville, Tenn.: Broadman, 1958.

L. Women's Legal Status

Basch, Norma. *In the Eyes of the Law: Women, Marriage, and Property in Nineteenth-Century New York*. Ithaca, N.Y.: Cornell University Press, 1982.

An important case study that outlines the reforms pushed by feminists in the nineteenth century and legal responses.

Gunderson, Joan and Gwen Campbell. "Married Women's Legal Status in Eighteenth-Century New York and Virginia." *William and Mary Quarterly* 39 (January 1982).

Good comparative analysis and background of women's property rights and marital laws into the early national era.

Hoff, Joan. *Unequal Before the Law: A Legal History of U.S. Women*. New York: New York University Press, 1991.

A sweeping, critical analysis of the legal status of women in the United States since the American Revolution. Hoff's thesis: the United States has never granted women full citizenship under the law.

Jenson, Carol Elizabeth. "The Equity Jurisdiction and Married Women's Property in Ante-Bellum America: A Revisionist View." *International Journal of Women's Studies* 2 (1978).

Legal and technical analysis of changing attitudes toward women's role.

Kerber, Linda. *No Constitutional Right to Be Ladies: Women and the Obligations of Citizenship*. New York: Hill and Wang, 1998.

An impressive survey providing numerous nineteenth-century case studies.

1. Family Law

Bardaglio, Peter. *Reconstructing the Household: Family, Sex, and the Law in the Nineteenth-Century South*. Chapel Hill: University of North Carolina Press, 1995.

A pioneering and important view of southern laws, with invaluable insights into the role of women and children, and the use of the law for social and sexual control.

Grossberg, Michael. *Governing the Hearth: Law and Family in Nineteenth-Century America*. Chapel Hill: University of North Carolina Press, 1985.

A comprehensive and informed account of transformations within the law and its effects upon women.

2. Divorce and Custody

Cott, Nancy. "Divorce and the Changing Status of Women in Eighteenth-Century Massachusetts." *William and Mary Quarterly* 39 (January 1982).

Good background on marriage and divorce in colonial and Revolutionary America.

Griswold, Robert L. *Adultery and Divorce in Victorian America, 1800–1900*. Legal History Program Working Papers. Madison: University of Wisconsin, Madison, Law School, 1986.

A broad overview.

M. Race and Ethnicity

Davis, Angela. *Women, Race, and Class*. New York: Random House, 1982.

An important pioneering look at the role of race and gender with dynamic analysis of the relationship between whites and African Americans.

1. American Indians

Green, Rayna. *Native American Women: A Contextual Bibliography*. Bloomington: Indiana University Press, 1983.

This survey is a dated but useful guide to work on American Indian women by one of the leading scholars in the field.

———. "The Pocahantas Perplex: The Image of Indian Women in American Culture." *The Massachusetts Review* 16 (Autumn 1975).

A pioneering interpretation of the sexism and racism surrounding images of Native women in cultural and historical literature.

Hill, Sarah H. *Weaving New Worlds: Southeastern Cherokee Women and their Basketry*. Chapel Hill: University of North Carolina Press, 1997.

Important use of material culture to interpret Indian women's lives.

Perdue, Theda. *Cherokee Women*. Lincoln: University of Nebraska Press, 1998.

A sensitive and stellar look at gender within this important southern Indian nation from the colonial era through the Removal era.

2. African Americans

Jones, Jacqueline. *Labor of Love, Labor of Sorrow: Black Women, Work, and the Family from Slavery to the Present*. New York: Basic, 1985.

A magisterial and pioneering synthesis of the lives of African American women over the past 150 years.

a. Revolutionary and Early National Eras

Cody, Cheryll. "Naming, Kinship, and Estate Dispersal: Notes on Slave Family Life on a South Carolina Plantation, 1786–1833." *William and Mary Quarterly* 39 (January 1982).

Gregory, Chester. "Black Women in Pre-Federal America." In Mabel Deutrich and Virginia Purdy, eds., *Clio Was a Woman: Studies in the History of American Women*. Washington, D.C.: Howard University Press, 1980.

Kulikoff, Alan. "The Beginnings of the Afro-American Family in Maryland." In A. D. Land, L. G. Carr, and E. C. Papenfuse, eds., *Law, Society, and Politics in Early Maryland*. Baltimore: Johns Hopkins University Press, 1977.

Mills, Gary. "Coincoin: An Eighteenth-Century 'Liberated' Woman." *Journal of Southern History* 42 (May 1976).

Newman, Debra. "Black Women in the Era of the American Revolution in Pennsylvania." *Journal of Negro History* 66 (1976).

b. Antebellum Era

Bogin, Ruth. "Sarah Parker Remond: Black Abolitionist from Salem." *Essex Institute Historical Collections* 110 (April 1974).

A sketch of an early and important black female antislavery activist.

Davis, Angela. "Reflections on the Black Woman's Role in the Community of Slaves." *Black Scholar* 3 (December 1971).

A pioneering theoretical work on race, class, and gender within the antebellum South. A classic.

Gutman, Herbert. *The Black Family in Slavery and Freedom, 1750–1925*. New York: Pantheon, 1976.

A pioneering and important look at the role of black men and women struggling within the slaveholding South. Excellent insight into the role of the Civil War and Emancipation, but the bulk of the book concentrates on the antebellum era.

Hancock, Harold B. "Mary Ann Shadd: Negro Editor, Educator, and Lawyer." *Delaware History* 15 (1973).

A cursory survey of the highlights of Shadd's career.

Stevenson, Brenda. *Life in Black and White: Family and Community in the Slave South*. New York: Oxford University Press, 1996.

A splendid and pioneering study featuring women in a Virginia county from the colonial era until the Civil War.

White, Deborah. *Aren't I a Woman: Female Slaves in the Antebellum South*. New York: Norton, 1985.

A pioneering study of the lives of African American women on antebellum plantations. Emphasis on female bonding within the slave community, family and work roles.

c. Civil War and Reconstruction. See Section J, 3.

d. Postbellum Era

Hunter, Tera. *To 'joy My Freedom: Southern Black Women's Lives and Labors after the Civil War*. Cambridge: Harvard University Press, 1997.

Terrific analysis of black women in the New South, especially their role as workers.

3. Immigrant Minorities

Neidle, Cecyle. *American Immigrant Women*. Boston: Twayne, 1975.

Pioneering early work, but outdated.

a. French and Dutch

Hall, Gwendolyn Midlo. *Africans in Colonial Louisiana: The Development of Afro-Creole Culture in the Eighteenth Century*. Baton Rouge: Louisiana State University Press, 1993.

A pathbreaking look at the mixture of African and Creole peoples in Louisiana. Important analysis of the roles of women in this evolving culture.

Zee, Henri A. van der. *A Sweet and Alien Land: The Story of Dutch New York*. New York: Viking, 1978.

A useful look at the early Dutch settlements with some insight into the lives of Dutch immigrant women and their slaves.

b. Irish

Diner, Hasia R. *Erin's Daughters in America: Irish Immigrant Women in the Nineteenth Century.* Baltimore: Johns Hopkins University Press, 1983.

This important study offers a vision of Irish immigrant women with their own economic aspirations for financial security; questions some perceptions of nineteenth-century women.

Groneman, Carol. "Working-Class Immigrant Women in Mid-Nineteenth Century New York: The Irish Woman's Experience." *Journal of Urban History* 4 (May 1978).

Examines female wage earners' contributions to family organization.

c. Germans

Esslinger, Dean R. *Immigrants and the City: Ethnicity and Mobility in a Nineteenth-Century Midwestern Community.* Port Washington, N.Y.: Kennikat, 1975.

Focuses in part on German immigrants and their settlements in the Midwest.

Ragsdale, Crystal Sasse. *The Golden Free Land: The Reminiscences and Letters of Women on an American Frontier.* Austin, Tex: Landmark, 1976.

Smith, Clifford Neal. *Immigrants to America (Mainly Wisconsin) From the Former Recklinghausen District (Nordrhein-Westfalen, Germany) Around the Middle of the Nineteenth Century.* McNeel, Ariz: Westland, 1983.

Case study of immigrants from a particular region and their transition to life in a midwestern community.

d. Scandinavians

Forbes, Kathryn. *Mama's Bank Account.* New York: Harcourt Brace, 1943.

Wonderful memoir written by the daughter of Norwegian immigrants in San Francisco at the turn of the century.

Wargelim-Brown, Mayanne and Carl Ross. *Women Who Dared: The History of Finnish-American Women.* St. Paul: Immigration History Research Center, University of Minnesota, 1981.

Valuable contribution to immigration history of an often overlooked minority.

e. Italians

McLaughlin, Virginia Yans. *Family and Community: Italian Immigrants in Buffalo, 1880–1930*. Ithaca, N.Y.: Cornell University Press, 1977.

A valuable study of an important ethnic immigrant group.

Smith, Judith E. "Our Own Kind: Family and Community Networks in Providence." *Radical History Review* 17 (Spring 1978).

Smith focuses on both Italian and Jewish women and their family networks.

f. Eastern European Jews

Glenn, Susan A. *Daughters of the Shtetl: Life and Labor in the Immigrant Generation*. Ithaca, N.Y.; Cornell University Press, 1994.

Study focuses on immigrant culture in urban ghettos, work and family, transition to American life.

Smith, Judith E. "Our Own Kind: Family and Community Networks in Providence." *Radical History Review* 17 (Spring 1978).

Smith focuses on both Italian and Jewish women and their family networks.

g. Hispanic Americans

Deutsch, Sarah. *No Separate Refuge: Culture, Class, and Gender on an Anglo-Hispanic Frontier in the American Southwest, 1880–1940*. New York: Oxford University Press, 1987.

An intriguing and useful study, including information on women in the Southwest at the turn of the century.

Gonzales, Deena J. *Refusing Favor: The Spanish-Mexican Women of Santa Fe, 1820–1880*. New York: Oxford University Press, 1999.

Scadron, Arlene, ed. *On Their Own: Widows and Widowhood in the American Southwest, 1848–1939*. Urbana: University of Illinois Press, 1988.

Using case studies of Spanish-speaking and Anglo populations as well as American Indians, the author delivers a fascinating portrait of the impact of diverse cultural traditions on the lives of widows.

h. Asian Americans

Herata, Lucie Cheng. "Free, Indentured, Enslaved: Chinese Prostitutes in Nineteenth-Century America." *Signs: Journal of Women in Culture and Society* 5 (August 1979).

A splendid survey of the role of ethnicity and sexuality in nineteenth-century America.

Ichioka, Yuji. "Ameyuki-san: Japanese Prostitutes in Nineteenth-Century America." *Amerasia Journal* 4 (1977).

A pioneering piece on a neglected topic.

Takaki, Ronald. *Strangers from a Distant Shore: A History of Asian-Americans*. Boston: Little, Brown, 1989.

Yung, Judy. *Chinese Women of America: A Pictorial*. Seattle: University of Washington Press, 1986.

Full of rich photography and interesting visual materials.

———. *Unbound Feet: A Social History of Chinese Women in San Francisco*. Berkeley: University of California Press, 1995.

An important pioneering study of Chinese immigrants in California and their settlement in San Francisco.

N. Westward Migration

1. Southern

Cashin, Joan. *A Family Venture: Men and Women on the Southern Frontier*. New York: Oxford University Press, 1991.

2. Overland Trail and Frontier

Faragher, John. *Women and Men on the Overland Trail*. New Haven: Yale University Press, 1981.

A well-researched and impressive study of the role of gender and the life on the trail westward.

Holmes, Kenneth L., ed. *Covered Wagon Women: Diaries and Letters from the Western Trails*. Lincoln: University of Nebraska Press, 1996.

Fascinating compendium, with absorbing accounts.

Jeffrey, Julie Roy. *Frontier Women: "Civilizing" the West?, 1840–1880*. New York: Hill and Wang, 1998.

A pioneering and important study of women's role in the westward migration. A fresh, engaging read.

Luchetti, Cathy *"I do!": Courtship, Love, and Marriage on the American Frontier, 1715–1915*. New York: Crown, 1996.

An engaging volume, full of images and primary material.

Patterson-Black, Sheryll. "Women Homesteaders on the Great Plains Frontiers." *Frontiers* 1 (Spring 1976).

Engaging stories of women on the plains.

Riley, Glenda. *Frontierswomen: The Iowa Experience*. Ames: Iowa State University Press, 1981.

An excellent case study; informative and illuminating.

Stratton, Joanna. *Pioneer Mothers: Voices from the Kansas Frontier*. New York: Simon and Schuster, 1981.

A compelling and refreshing look at the lives of women on the Kansas frontier through their own words; jargon-free annotation.

3. Far West

Barnhart, Karen. "Working Women: Prostitution in San Francisco from the Gold Rush to 1900." Ph.D. diss., University of California, Santa Cruz, 1978.
Larson, T. A. "Dolls, Vassals, and Drudges: Pioneer Women in the West." *Western Historical Quarterly* 3 (1972).

An early look at the stereotypes and the realities of life on the frontier for women.

Laury, Jean Ray. *Ho for California: Pioneer Women and Their Quilts*. New York: Dutton, 1990.

A good use of visual material.

Pascoe, Peggy. *Relations of Rescue: The Search for Female Moral Authority in the American West, 1874–1939*. New York: Oxford University Press, 1993.

An impressive theoretical and interpretive analysis of ethnicity and gender within western postbellum culture.

Swagerty, William. "Marriage and Settlement Patterns of Rocky Mountain Trappers and Traders." *Western Historical Quarterly* (April 1980).

Interesting look at gender issues on in the Far West, among random households rather than white settlements.

O. *Women and the Professions*

Brumberg, Joan J. and Nancy Tomes. "Women and the Professions: A Research Agenda for American Historians." *Reviews in American History* 10 (June 1982).
Harris, Barbara. *Beyond Her Sphere: Women and the Professions in American History*. Westport, Conn.: Greenwood, 1978.

A survey of women's movement into the professions.

Meyer, Annie Nathan. *Woman's Work in America*. 1891; reprint, New York: Arno, 1972.

A really stunning early survey of women's accomplishments. Dated, but historiographically valuable.

1. Educators

Hoffman, Nancy, ed. *Woman's "True" Profession: Voices from the History of Teaching*. Old Westbury, N.Y.: Feminist Press, 1981.

A nice collection of memoirs and personal recollections from women teachers in both urban and rural settings.

Scanlon, Jennifer and Shaaron Cosner. *American Women Historians, 1700–1900s: A Biographical Dictionary*. Westport, Conn.: Greenwood, 1996.

Catalogs the contributions made by women historians along with biographical descriptions of the two hundred women included.

Vinovskis, Maris and Richard Bernard. "The Female School Teacher in Antebellum Massachusetts." *Journal of Social History* 10 (March 1977).

An interesting case study of the role of teaching and teacher's lives.

2. Writers, Artists, and Performers

Ammer, Christine. *Unsung: A History of Women in American Music*. Westport, Conn.: Greenwood, 1980.

Dewhurst, C. Kurt et al., eds. *Artist in Aprons: Folk Art of American Women*. New York: Dutton, 1979.

An important alternative view of women's contributions to the arts; richly illustrated volume.

Dudden, Faye. *Women in the American Theater: Actresses and Audiences, 1790–1870*. New Haven: Yale University Press, 1994.

Combining splendid biographical sketches, feminist analysis, and cultural history. Dudden illuminates women's crucial role in the development of the American entertainment industry.

Ebel, Otto. *Women Composers: A Biographical Handbook of Woman's Work in Music*, 3d. ed. Brooklyn, N.Y.: Chandler-Ebel Music Co., 1913.

Elbert, Sarah. *A Hunger for Home: Louisa May Alcott and Little Women*. Philadelphia: Temple University Press, 1983.

An engaging study of Alcott and her world.

Gerdts, William H. *Women Artists of America, 1707–1964*. Newark, N.J.: The Newark Museum, 1965.

Gordon, Jean. "Early American Women Artists and the Social Context in Which They Worked." *American Quarterly* 30 (Spring 1978).

Useful and pioneering piece.

Greer, Germaine. *The Fortunes of Women: Painters and Their Work*. London: Farrar, Straus and Giroux, 1979.

Harris, Ann Sutherland and Linda Nochlin. *Women Artists, 1550–1950*. New York: Knopf, 1976.

Kelley, Mary. *Private Woman, Public Stage: Literary Domesticity in Nineteenth-Century America*. New York: Oxford University Press, 1984.

Good study of the way in which novelists viewed women's roles.

Paine, Judith. "The Women's Pavilion of 1876." *The Feminist Art Journal* (Winter 1975–76).

A nice analysis of the way in which women's clubs integrated their concerns into a centennial celebration in 1876.

Rubenstein, Charlotte Streifer. *American Women Artists from Early Indian Times to the Present*. Boston: G. K. Hall, 1982.

Shockley, Ann Allen. *Afro-American Women Writers, 1746–1933: An Anthology and Critical Guide*. Boston: G. K. Hall, 1988.

The first two sections cover women writers from the colonial period to 1900; contains historical, social, political, economic, and racial climate overview for each section; a wealth of information.

Tuchman, Gaye with Nina E. Forrin. *Edging Women Out: Victorian Novelists, Publishers, and Social Change*. New Haven: Yale University Press, 1989.

Fascinating study argues that novel writing became a male white-collar occupation, where once it had been practiced primarily by women, when it became clear that novel writing was prestigious and economically profitable.

Tufts, Eleanor. *American Women Artists, 1830–1930*. Washington, D.C.: National Museum of Women in the Arts, 1987.

3. Medicine

Chafe, Sandra, Ruth Haimbach, Carol Fenichel, and Nina Woods, eds. *Women in Medicine: A Bibliography of the Literature on Women Physicians*. Metuchen, N.J.: Scarecrow, 1977.

A useful reference.

Drachman, Virginia G. *Hospital with a Heart: Women Doctors and the Paradox of Separatism at the New England Hospital*. Ithaca, N.Y.: Cornell University Press, 1984.

Good study of how the success of the New England Women's Hospital marked its downfall as a separate institution.

Moldow, Gloria. *Women Doctors in Gilded-Age Washington: Race, Gender, and Professionalism*. Urbana: University of Illinois Press, 1987.

Examines the careers of more than two hundred women doctors and medical students from 1880–1900.

Morantz-Sanchez, Regina Markell. *Sympathy and Science: Women Physicians in American Medicine*. New York: Oxford University Press, 1987.

A broad, sweeping, yet penetrating look at women's role in American medicine in the nineteenth and into the twentieth centuries.

Reverby, Susan. "The Search for the Hospital Yardstick: Nursing and the Rationalization of Hospital Work." In Reverby and David Rosner, eds., *Health Care in America: Essays in Social History*. Philadelphia: Temple University Press, 1979.

Stage, Sarah. *Female Complaints: Lydia Pinkham and the Business of Women's Medicine*. New York: Norton, 1979.

An excellent biographical study of Pinkham, weaving in the culture of women's pharmacology in the nineteenth century.

Walsh, Mary. *"Doctors Wanted, No Women Need Apply": Sexual Barriers in the Medical Profession, 1835–1975*. New Haven: Yale University Press, 1977.

A compelling and engaging analysis of women's challenges at integrating into the medical profession. Interesting data on how the growth of testing, standards, and regulated institutions offered women more opportunity in the profession.

4. Law

Drachman, Virginia G. *Women Lawyers and the Origins of Professional Identity in America: The Letters of the Equity Club, 1887 to 1890*. Ann Arbor: University of Michigan Press, 1993.

Lazourou, Kathleen. " 'Fettered Portias': Obstacles Facing Nineteenth-Century Women Lawyers." *Women Lawyers Journal* 64 (Winter 1978).

A competent chronicle of discrimination against women lawyers in nineteenth-century America.

Wallach, Anita. "Arabella Bobbs Mansfield, 1846–1911." *Women's Rights Law Reporter* 2 (April 1974).

A piece on a pioneering midwestern woman lawyer.

Weisberg, D. Kelley. "Barred from the Bar: Women and Legal Education in the United States, 1870–1890." *Journal of Legal Education* 38 (1977).

5. Other

Abir-Am, Pnina and Dorinda Outram, eds. *Uneasy Careers and Intimate Lives: Women in Science, 1789–1979.* New Brunswick, N.J.: Rutgers University Press, 1988.

Pays particular attention to the mutual impact of both the family life and the scientific careers of women over a period of two centuries.

Benson, Susan Porter. *Counter Cultures: Saleswomen, Managers, and Customers in American Department Stores, 1890–1940.*

Examines the culture of department store sales clerks, one of the chief white-collar occupations of women in the late nineteenth century.

Garrison, Dee. *The Apostles of Cultures: The Public Libraries and American Society, 1876–1920.* New York: Macmillan, 1979.

The feminization of library work is the subject of this study of an important topic.

Kohlstedt, Sally. "In from the Periphery: American Women in Science, 1830–1880." *Signs: Journal of Women in Culture and Society* 4 (Autumn 1978).

Lubove, Roy. *The Professional Altruist: The Emergence of Social Work as a Career, 1880–1930.* Cambridge: Harvard University Press, 1965.

Rosenberg, Rosalind. *Beyond Separate Spheres: Intellectual Roots of Modern Feminism.* New Haven: Yale University Press, 1982.

A pioneering and important look at how the first generation of feminist social scientists attempted to reshape the academy, as well as their worlds.

Rossiter, Margaret. *Women Scientists in America: Struggles and Strategies to 1940.* Baltimore, Md.: Johns Hopkins University Press, 1981.

An amazing, absorbing, and authoritative study of the role of women scientists, including nineteenth-century women. The classic work on the topic.

Warner, Deborah Jean. "Women in Science in Nineteenth-Century America." *Journal of American Medical Women's Association* 34 (February 1970).

A good introductory analysis.

P. Marriage and Reproduction

1. Courtship and Marriage

Bleser, Carol, ed. *In Joy & in Sorrow: Women, the Family, and Marriage in the Victorian South, 1830–1900.* New York: Oxford University Press, 1992.
Important essays on marriage and the roles of both black and white women in the nineteenth-century South.

Gordon, Linda. *Heroes of Their Own Lives: The Politics and History of Family Violence, Boston, 1880–1960.* New York: Viking, 1988.
Luchetti, Cathy *"I do!": Courtship, Love, and Marriage on the American Frontier, 1715–1915.* New York: Crown, 1996.
An engaging volume, full of images and primary material.

Lystra, Karen. *Searching the Heart: Women, Men, and Romantic Love in Nineteenth-Century America.* New York: Oxford University Press, 1989.
Convincing, persuasive, and absorbing—an excellent study on a neglected topic.

Rothman, Ellen. *Hands and Hearts: A History of Courtship in America.* New York: Basic, 1984.
A sensitive and solid study, gathering important data from private papers.

2. Pregnancy and Childbirth

Leavitt, Judith Walzer. *Brought to Bed: Childbearing in America, 1750–1950.* New York: Oxford University Press, 1985.
A sweeping and important study.

Scholten, Catherine. *Childbearing in American Society, 1650–1850.* New York: New York University Press, 1985.
An excellent study of shift from female midwives to male physicians.

Smith, Daniel Scott and Michael Hindu. "Premarital Pregnancy in America, 1640–1971: An Overview and Interpretation." *Journal of Interdisciplinary History* 5 (1975).
A sketchy survey of rates and attitudes.

Wertz, Richard and Dorothy Wertz. *Lying In: A History of Childbirth in America*. New York: Free Press, 1977.

Within the body of this extensive survey, the authors trace the history of midwifery and the rise of the physician in early nineteenth-century America.

3. Never-Married and Widowhood

Chambers-Schiller, Lee Virginia. *Liberty, a Better Husband, Single Women in America: The Generations of 1780–1840*. New Haven: Yale University Press, 1984.

A wonderful look at never-married women in the antebellum North.

Scadron, Arlene, ed. *On Their Own: Widows and Widowhood in the American Southwest, 1848–1939*. Urbana: University of Illinois Press, 1988.

Using case studies of Spanish-speaking and Anglo populations as well as American Indians, the author delivers a fascinating portrait of the impact of diverse cultural traditions on the lives of widows.

Wilson, Lisa. *Life After Death: Widows in Pennsylvania, 1750–1850*. Philadelphia: Temple University Press, 1992.

A valuable case study.

4. Birth Control

Brodie, Janet Farrell. *Contraception and Abortion in Nineteenth-Century America*. Ithaca: Cornell University Press, 1994.

A modest but solid study of the topic.

Brown, P. S. "Female Pills and the Reputation of Iron as an Abortifacient." *Medical History* 21 (July 1977).

Women's use of medicinal remedies to limit families in the nineteenth century.

Fee, Elizabeth and Michael Wallace. "The History and Politics of Birth Control: A Review Essay." *Feminist Studies* 5 (Spring 1979).

A useful roundup of 1970s scholarship.

Gordon, Linda. *Woman's Body, Woman's Right: A Social History of Birth Control in America*. New York: Vintage, 1976.

A classic study, and still useful in courses and for research. A well-argued, well-written, thoroughly engaging and enlightening volume.

Reed, James. *From Private Vice to Public Virtue: The Birth Control Movement and American Society Since 1830*. New York: Basic, 1978.

A solid and comprehensive study of voluntary motherhood and its evolution.

5. Abortion

Brodie, Janet Farrell. *Contraception and Abortion in Nineteenth-Century America*. Ithaca, N.Y.: Cornell University Press, 1994.

Reveals the depth and breadth of information available to men and women and the criminalization of that information primarily because of the Comstock Law.

Hayler, Barbara. "Abortion." *Signs: Journal of Women in Culture and Society* 5 (Winter 1979).

A wonderful review essay on 1970s scholarship.

Mohr, James. *Abortion in America: The Origins and Evolution of National Policy, 1800–1900*. New York: Oxford University Press, 1978.

An important and pioneering survey of the rise of male physicians and the criminalization of abortion in the nineteenth century.

Reagan, Leslie J. *When Abortion Was a Crime: Women, Medicine, and Law in the United States, 1867–1973*. Berkeley: University of California Press, 1997.

A first-rate scholarly survey of postbellum developments, with riveting detail.

Q. Sexuality

Banner, Lois. *American Beauty*. New York: Knopf, 1983.

A cosmetic look at standards of female beauty within America.

Barker-Benfield, G. J. *Horrors of the Half-Known Life: Male Attitudes Toward Women and Sexuality in Nineteenth-Century America*. 1976; reprint, New York: Routledge, 1999.

A pioneering and important study of sexual mores and attitudes in Victorian America. This volume contains important insights into women and the medical profession, women and nervous disorders, and especially women and hysteria in nineteenth-century America.

Haller, John S. Jr. and Robin Haller. *The Physician and Sexuality in Victorian America*. Urbana: University of Illinois Press, 1974.

A pioneering survey. Full of good information, even if volume is outdated.

Smith-Rosenberg, Carroll. "The Hysterical Woman: Sex Roles and Role Conflict in Nineteenth-Century America." *Social Research* (Winter 1972).

A pioneering view of the cultural definitions of women's illnesses in nineteenth-century America—the way in which femininity and madness are linked by male medical discourse.

Walters, Ronald, ed. *Primers for Prudery: Sexual Advice to Victorian America*. Englewood Cliffs, N.J.: Prentice-Hall, 1974.

An out-of-print but not out-of-date collection.

1. Heterosexuality

Hodes, Martha. *White Women, Black Men: Illicit Sex in the Nineteenth-Century South*. New Haven: Yale University Press, 1998.

An interesting interpretation of case studies and legal materials, with important implications for larger issues of attitudes toward interracial sex in the nineteenth century.

Upton, Dell, ed. *Madaline: Love and Sin in Antebellum New Orleans*. Athens: University of Georgia Press, 1996.

The remarkable story of a kept woman in New Orleans, told through her diary.

2. Prostitution

Barnhart, Karen. "Working Women: Prostitution in San Francisco from the Gold Rush to 1900." Ph.D. diss., University of California, Santa Cruz, 1978.

Bullough, Vern L. *The History of Prostitution*. New Hyde Park, N.Y.: University, 1964.

An encyclopedic volume, not hindered or helped by any theoretical framework or ideological analysis.

Herata, Lucie Cheng. "Free, Indentured, Enslaved: Chinese Prostitutes in Nineteenth-Century America." *Signs: Journal of Women in Culture and Society* 5 (August 1979).

A splendid survey of the role of ethnicity and sexuality in nineteenth-century America.

Hill, Marilynn Wood. *Their Sisters' Keepers: Prostitution in New York City, 1830–1870*. Berkeley: University of California Press, 1993.

Ichioka, Yuji. "Ameyuki-San: Japanese Prostitutes in Nineteenth-Century America." *Amerasia Journal* 4 (1977).

A pioneering piece on a neglected topic.

Rosen, Ruth. *The Lost Sisterhood: Prostitution in America, 1900–1918*. Baltimore: Johns Hopkins University Press, 1983.

A pioneering work that looks at the layers of influence and conflict at the heart of the sex trade during the early twentieth century. Rosen is especially adept at illuminating the lives of prostitutes, utilizing evidence creatively.

Rosen, Ruth and Sue Davidson, eds. *The Maimie Papers.* Old Westbury, N.Y.: Feminist Press, 1977.

A fascinating look at a correspondence between a prostitute and a middle-class reformer at the turn of the century.

Washburn, Josie. *The Underworld Sewer: A Prostitute Reflects on a Life in the Trade, 1871–1909.* Lincoln: University of Nebraska Press, 1997.

A western prostitute's memoir.

3. Lesbianism and Homosexuality

Cook, Blanche Wiesen. " 'Women Alone Stir My Imagination': Lesbianism and the Cultural Tradition." *Signs: Journal of Women in Culture and Society* 4 (1979).

A pioneering article by a leading theoretician in the field.

D'Emlio, John and Estelle Freedman. *Intimate Matters: A History of Sexuality in America,* 2d ed. Chicago: University of Chicago Press, 1997.

An important and sweeping survey, even more invaluable in its second edition.

Faderman, Lillian. *Surpassing the Love of Men: Romantic Friendship and Love Between Women from the Renaissance to the Present.* New York: William Morrow, 1981.

A pioneering and comprehensive study, looking at same-sex friendship and romance, as well as attitudes toward homosocial and homosexual relations.

Katz, Jonathan, ed. *Gay American History: Lesbian and Gay Men in the U.S.A.: A Documentary.* New York: Thomas Cromwell, 1976.

A wonderful, pioneering work.

Smith-Rosenberg, Carroll. "The Female World of Love and Ritual: Relations Between Women in Nineteenth-Century America." *Signs: Journal of Women in Culture and Society* 1 (Autumn 1975).

A pioneering article by a leading scholar in the field who posited in this early work that female attachments to one another even superseded their marital bonds. She suggests that many women's friendship may have had a romantic or erotic component.

Taylor, William R. and Christopher Lasch. "Two 'Kindred Spirits': Sorority and Family in New England, 1839–1846." *New England Quarterly* 36 (March 1963).

This important article on female friendship laid the groundwork for the theoretical and analytical work that followed.

R. *Postbellum Reform*

Brenzel, Barbara. *Daughters of the State: A Social Portrait of the First Reform School for Girls in North America, 1856–1905*. Cambridge: MIT Press, 1983.

The treatment of female juvenile offenders and the development of the reform school in Massachusetts.

Hayden, Dolores. *The Grand Domestic Revolution: A History of Feminist Designs for American Homes, Neighborhoods, and Cities*. Cambridge: MIT Press, 1981.

A pioneering and important study of the ways in which women attempted to restructure the household to reflect their changing role within society, and how this domestic "revolution" led to social movements.

Freedman, Estelle. *Their Sisters' Keepers*. Ann Arbor: University of Michigan Press, 1981.

A pioneering and classic look at prison reform and the treatment of women prisoners in nineteenth-century America.

Leach, William. *True Love and Perfect Union: The Feminist Reform of Sex and Society*. New York: Basic, 1980.

An engaging and very imaginative analysis of women reformers, with especially important analysis of the links between consumer culture and the expansion of women's roles into the public domain.

Rosenberg, Rosalind. *Beyond Separate Spheres: Intellectual Roots of Modern Feminism*. New Haven: Yale University Press, 1982.

A pioneering and important look at how the first generation of feminist social scientists attempted to reshape the academy, as well as their worlds.

1. Social Work and Settlement Houses

Davis, Allen F. *Spearheads for Reform: The Social Settlements and the Progressive Movement, 1890–1914*. New York: Oxford University Press, 1967.

An early and pioneering work on the settlement house movement. Outdated.

Kraus, Harry P. *The Settlement House Movement in New York City, 1886–1914*. New York: Arno, 1980.

A useful look at one city's progressive reform.

Lasch, Christopher. "Jane Addams: The College Woman and the Family Claim." *The New Radicalism in America, 1889–1963: The Intellectual as a Social Type*. New York: Knopf, 1965.

2. Temperance

Bordin, Ruth. *Women and Temperance: The Quest for Power and Liberty, 1873–1900*. Philadelphia: Temple University Press, 1981.

Bordin's work includes fresh insight into connections between feminism and the battle to control alcoholism.

Epstein, Barbara Leslie. *The Politics of Domesticity: Women, Evangelism, and Temperance in Nineteenth-Century America*. Middletown, Conn.: Wesleyan University Press, 1981.

A nice survey of the connections between women in religious movements and subsequent reform campaigns.

3. Populism

Jeffrey, Julie Roy. "Women in the Southern Farmers' Alliance: A Reconsideration of the Role and Status of Women in the Late Nineteenth-Century South." *Feminist Studies* 3 (Fall 1975).

An excellent introduction into women's roles in the populist movement in the South.

Juster, Norton. *So Sweet to Labor: Rural Women in America, 1865–1895*. New York: Viking, 1979.

A compelling and careful survey of the lives of the majority of American women, the forgotten farmwives who predominated numerically until the turn of the century.

Marti, Donald. "Woman's Work in the Grange: Mary Ann Mayo of Michigan, 1882–1903." *Agricultural History* (Winter 1982).

An illuminating look at a strong woman leader in the Grange, a forerunner of the populist movement.

4. Socialism and Radicalism

Buhle, Mary Jo. *Women and American Socialism, 1870–1920*. Urbana: University of Illinois Press, 1982.

A pioneering study that includes important analysis of Frances Willard and her role as a radical feminist.

Marsh, Margaret. *Anarchist Women, 1870–1920*. Philadelphia: Temple University Press, 1980.
A survey of movements and leaders.

5. Progressivism

Diner, Steven J. *A Very Different Age: Americans of the Progressive Era*. New York: Hill and Wang, 1998.
Fitzpatrick, Ellen. *Endless Crusade: Women Social Scientists and Progressive Reform*. New York: Oxford University Press, 1990.
An illuminating study of several pioneering women of the Progressive era, with especially good portrait of Sophinisba Breckenridge.

Schneider, Carl J. and Dorothy Schneider. *American Women in the Progressive Era, 1900–1920*. New York: Facts on File, 1993.

6. Club Women

Blair, Karen. *The Clubwoman as Feminist: True Womanhood Redefined, 1868–1914*. New York: Holmes and Meier, 1980.
Blair provides an impressive framework and a lot of data to demonstrate her thesis that the end of the nineteenth century marked the rise of club women and the politicization of women's networks by the turn of the century.

Croly, Jennie C. *The History of the Women's Club Movement in America*. New York: H. G. Allen, 1898.
Classic history of the club movement.

Ginzberg, Lori D. *Women and the Work of Benevolence: Morality, Politics, and Class in the Nineteenth-Century United States*. New Haven: Yale University Press, 1990.
Studies a broad spectrum of benevolent work by women, including club women, from the 1820s to 1885; provides an interesting interpretation of political contexts and meaning.

Martin, Theodora Penny. *The Sound of Our Own Voices, Women's Study Clubs, 1860–1910*. Cambridge, Mass.: Beacon, 1987.
A revealing look at the club women who met in small groups to study art, literature, politics, philosophy, math, etc., and their influence on women's college enrollments.

Neverdon-Morton, Cynthia. *Afro-American Women of the South and the Advancement of the Race, 1895–1925*. Knoxville: University of Tennessee Press, 1989.

A detailed look at the club movement in Maryland, Georgia, Tennessee, Virginia, and Alabama; discusses origins of female networks and the intellectual and social commitment of southern black women.

Weimann, Jeanne. *The Fair Women*. Chicago: Academy Press, 1981.
A beautiful and engaging book that recaptures the excitement of women's challenges and struggles to participate fully in the World's Columbian Exposition in 1893.

Wells, Mary White. *Unity in Diversity: The History of the General Federation of Women's Clubs*. Washington, D.C., 1958.
Wesley, Charles H. *The History of the National Association of Colored Women's Clubs: A Legacy of Service*. Washington, D.C.: National Association of Colored Women's Clubs, 1984.
Provides a wealth of information about the NACW state by state, along with a historical overview.

Woods, Mary I. *The History of the General Federation of Women's Clubs*. New York, 1912.

S. The New South

Bernhard, Virginia, Elizabeth Turner, Theda Perdue, and Martha Swain, eds. *Hidden Histories of Women in the New South*. Columbia: University of Missouri Press, 1994.
Important articles on a wide range of subjects from birth control to antisuffrage to prison life and racial issues.

Massey, Mary Elizabeth. "The Making of a Feminist." *The Journal of Southern History* 39 (February 1973).
The story of one woman's evolution in the wake of Confederate defeat: Ella Gertrude Clanton Thomas of Augusta, Georgia.

Janiewski, Dolores. *Sisterhood Denied: Race, Gender, and Class in a New South Community*. 1985; reprint, Philadelphia: Temple University Press, 1992.
An absorbing and compelling analysis of the lives of women in Durham, North Carolina. Important implications for the role of race, gender, and wage earning.

Jones, Ann Goodwyn. *Tomorrow is Another Day: The Woman Writer in the South, 1859–1936*. Baton Rouge: Louisiana University Press, 1981.
A splendid cultural history looking at leading white southern women writers' lives and their work.

Silber, Nina. *The Romance of Reunion: Northerners and the South, 1865–1900*. Chapel Hill: University of North Carolina Press, 1993.

A creative and compelling look at the role of the South in the northern imagination. Solid cultural history.

Wheeler, Marjorie Spruill. *New Women of the New South: The Leaders of the Women's Suffrage Movement*. New York: Oxford University Press, 1993.

A pioneering look at southern suffrage that looks at questions of race and class and provides important analysis of southern strategies to obtain votes for women.

T. The Suffrage Movement, 1880–1919

Banner, Lois. *Elizabeth Cady Stanton: A Radical for Women's Rights*. Boston: Little, Brown, 1980.

Blackwell, Alice Stone. *Lucy Stone, Pioneer of Women's Rights*. Boston: Little, Brown, 1930.

Blatch, Harriot Stanton and Alma Lutz. *Challenging Years: The Memoirs of Harriot Stanton Blatch*. New York: Putnam, 1940.

Elizabeth Cady Stanton's daughter's account of her years in England and the later years of the American suffrage movement.

Camhi, Jane Jerome. *Women Against Women: American Antisuffragism, 1880–1920*. Brooklyn, N.Y.: Carlson, 1994.

A neglected and vital subject. An excellent study of the antisuffrage campaign.

Catt, Carrie Chapman and Nettie Rogers Shulman. *Woman Suffrage and Politics: The Inner Story of the Suffrage Movement*. New York: Charles Scribner's, 1926.

The suffrage movement from the perspective of the last president of the National American Woman Suffrage Association.

Cullen-Dupont, Kathryn. *Elizabeth Cady Stanton and Women's Liberty*. New York: Facts on File, 1992.

Straightforward biography, aimed at general readership.

Dorr, Rheta Child. *A Woman of Fifty: The Equal Suffrage Movement in the Pacific Coast States*. 1914; reprint, New York: Funk and Wagnalls, 1924.

Duniway, Abigail Scott. *An Autobiographical History of the Equal Suffrage Movement in Pacific Coast States, with Sidelights on Protection*. Portland, Ore: James, Kearns, and Abbott, 1914.

Good account of West Coast suffrage politics and related issues.

Evans, Richard J. *The Feminists: Women's Emancipation Movements in Europe, America, and Australia, 1840–1920*. New York: Barnes and Noble, 1977.
Overview of comparative suffrage movements.

Gluck, Sheila, ed. *From Parlor to Prison: Five American Suffragists Talk About Their Lives*. New York: Vintage, 1976.
Gordon, Ann D. and Patricia G. Holland, eds. *The Papers of Elizabeth Cady Stanton and Susan B. Anthony* [microfilm]. Wilmington, Del: Scholarly Resources, 1992.
Griffith, Elisabeth. *In Her Own Right: The Life of Elizabeth Cady Stanton*. New York: Oxford University Press, 1984.
The best of the biographies; well-researched, insightful.

Irwin, Inez Haynes. *The Story of the Woman's Party*. New York: Harcourt Brace, 1921.
———. *Up Hill with Banners Flying*. Penobscot, Maine: Traversity, 1964.
Good contemporary accounts of the Woman's Party, Alice Paul, and the disagreements with the National American Woman Suffrage Association.

Jablonsky, Thomas James. *The Home, Heaven, and Mother Party: Female Anti-Suffragists in the United States, 1868–1920*. Brooklyn, N.Y.: Carlson, 1994.
Kenneally, James J. "The Opposition to Woman Suffrage in Massachusetts, 1868–1920." Ph.D. diss., Boston College, 1963.
Kraditor, Aileen. *The Ideas of the Woman Suffrage Movement, 1890–1920*. New York: Columbia University Press, 1965.
A classic political theorist's interpretation of mainstream feminism.

———. *Up from the Pedestal*. Chicago: Quadrangle Books, 1968.
Lunardini, Christine A. *From Equal Suffrage to Equal Rights: Alice Paul and the National Woman's Party, 1910–1928*. New York: New York University Press, 1986
A pioneering look at the unique contributions of Alice Paul to the American woman suffrage movement.

Lutz, Alma. *Created Equal: A Biography of Elizabeth Cady Stanton, 1815–1902*. New York: Day, 1940.
Early biography by a prolific writer on women and women's rights. Still worth looking at.

Morgan, David. *Suffragists and Democrats*. East Lansing: Michigan State University Press, 1972.

Morgan discusses the relationship between the Democratic party and the major suffrage groups, particularly the National Women's Party and the National American Woman Suffrage Association.

Moynihan, Ruth Barnes. *Rebel for Rights: Abigail Scott Duniway*. New Haven: Yale University Press, 1983.

An excellent cultural biography of the Oregon feminist who led the western women's suffrage strategy and brought votes to western women.

National American Woman Suffrage Association. *Victory! How Women Won It: A Centennial Symposium, 1840–1940*. New York: H. H. Wilson, 1940.

Neu, Charles. "Olympia Brown and the Woman Suffrage Movement." *Wisconsin Magazine of History* 43 (1959/60).

Peck, Mary Grey. *Carrie Chapman Catt: A Biography*. New York: Octagon, 1975.

Standard biographical treatment of last National American Woman Suffrage Association president.

Rothman, Sheila M. *Woman's Proper Place: A History of Changing Ideas and Practices, 1870 to the Present*. New York: Basic, 1978.

Scott, Anne Firor and Andrew Scott, eds. *One Half the People: The Fight for Woman Suffrage*. Philadelphia: Lippincott, 1975.

A collection of documents with narrative placing them in historical context of the women's movement.

Stanton, Elizabeth Cady. *Eighty Years and More: Reminiscences, 1815–1897*. 1898; reprint, New York: Schocken, 1971.

In her own words; a memoir by intellectually gifted leader of the women's rights movement.

Stanton, Elizabeth Cady et al. *The Women's Bible*, parts 1 and 2. 1895–98; reprint, New York: Schocken, 1971.

Stanton's argument against organized religion. Thought-provoking even today.

Stanton, Elizabeth Cady, Susan B. Anthony, and Matilda Gage, eds. *History of Woman Suffrage*. 6 vols. New York: Fowler and Wells, 1881–1922.

The classic compendium of woman suffrage material, compiled by the movement's leaders.

Stevens, Doris. *Jailed for Freedom*. New York: Boni and Liveright, 1920.

Focuses on her prison ordeal for picketing the White House. Interesting, more gossipy than the works by Inez Haynes Irwin cited earlier.

Terborg-Penn, Rosalyn. *African American Women in the Struggle for the Vote, 1850–1920*. Bloomington: Indiana University Press, 1998.

The valuable study of this important topic.

Trecker, Janice Law. "The Suffrage Prisoners." *The American Scholar* 21 (Summer 1972).

Wheeler, Marjorie Spruill. *New Women of the New South: The Leaders of the Women's Suffrage Movement*. New York: Oxford University Press, 1993.

A pioneering look at southern suffrage that looks at questions of race and class and provides important analysis of southern strategies to obtain votes for women.

Zimmerman, Loretta Ellen. "Alice Paul and the National Woman's Party, 1912–1920." Ph.D. diss., Tulane University, 1964.

Interprets the NWP as more of a well-meaning hindrance than a positive force in the suffrage movement.

SECTION II. BIBLIOGRAPHIES AND REFERENCE WORKS

Bass, Dorothy C. *American Women in Church and Society, 1607–1920: A Bibliography*. New York: Union Theological Seminary, 1973.

Blair, Karen J. *An Annotated Bibliography of Sources on the History of Oregon and Washington Women*. Seattle: University of Washington Press, 1997.

Chafe, Sandra, Ruth Haimbach, Carol Fenichel, and Nina Woods, eds. *Women in Medicine: A Bibliography of the Literature on Women Physicians*. Metuchen, N.J.: Scarecrow, 1977.

A useful reference.

Fischer, Gayle V. *Journal of Women's History Guide to Periodical Literature*. Bloomington: Indiana University Press, 1992.

An important reference work in women's history.

Goodfriend, Joyce D. *Diaries and Letters of American Women: An Annotated Bibliography*. New York: Macmillan, 1987.

Guide to a treasure trove of primary sources.

Green, Carol and Barbara Sicherman, eds. *Notable American Women: The Modern Period*. Cambridge, Mass.: Belknap, 1981.

A sequel to the original volumes, which is much more modern in its prose and conceptual frameworks, presenting women's lives in a more cultural context. Vivid and lively reading, as well as a thorough reference guide.

Green, Rayna. *Native American Women: A Contextual Bibliography*. Bloomington: Indiana University Press, 1983.

A dated but useful survey of work on Native women by one of the leading scholars in the field.

Haber, Barbara. *Women in America: A Guide to Books*. Urbana: University of Illinois Press, 1981.

This useful guide to texts in American history and literature was prepared by the Schlesinger Library bibliographer and includes those classic and important early works that fueled the flowering of women's history in the 1960s.

Hinding, Andrea et al., eds. *Women's History Sources: A Guide to Archive and Manuscript Collections in the United States*. 2 vols. New York: R. R. Bowker, 1979.

Comprehensive; locates hundreds of collections containing diaries, journals, and other accounts of women housed in major research collections, college and university archives, professional associations, and small county and municipal agencies.

Hine, Darlene Clark et al., eds. *Black Women in America. An Historical Encyclopedia*. 2 vols. Brooklyn, N.Y.: Carlson, 1993.

Outstanding collection of biographies of African American women. Contributors include scholars, field experts, colleagues.

James, Edward T., Janet James, and Paul Boyer, eds. *Notable American Women: A Biographical Dictionary*. 3 vols. Cambridge, Mass.: Belknap, 1970.

The pioneering reference of American women's history—a biographical dictionary sponsored by Radcliffe College. Although the volume is weak on racial and ethnic issues, the articles are well-researched, thorough, and polished. Excellent starting point for biographical research.

Lerner, Gerda *Women Are History: A Bibliography of the History of American Women*. 4th ed. Madison, Wisc.: Graduate Program in Women's History, 1986.

A work supervised by the godmother of American women's history.

Mehaffey, Karen Rae. *Victorian American Women, 1840–1880: An Annotated Bibliography*. New York: Garland, 1992.

Soltow, Martha Jane. *Women in American Labor History, 1825–1935: An Annotated Bibliography*. East Lansing: School of Labor and Industrial Relations, Michigan State University, 1972.

Pioneering; very technically and economically oriented.

Stanton, Elizabeth Cady, Susan B. Anthony, and Matilda Gage, eds. *The History of Woman Suffrage*. 6 vols. New York: Foster and Wells, 1881–1922.

Monumental. Remains one of the best collections of primary source documents annotated and narrated by the women who led the women's rights movement from its
inception, including Elizabeth Cady Stanton, Lucretia Mott, and Susan B. Anthony.

Stevenson, Louise, ed. *Women's History: Selected Reading Lists and Course
Outlines from American Colleges and Universities*, vol. 9, 3d ed. Bridgeport,
Conn.: Markus Wiener, 1992.

Now in its third incarnation, this is an excellent way to get at specific new reading lists for
courses in African American women's history, in Latina history, on special topics such as
lesbian women's history and women and religion, as well as general courses in the field.

Weatherford, Doris. *American Women's History: An A to Z of People, Organizations, Issues, and Events*. New York: Prentice Hall General Reference,
1994.

Self-explanatory. Some issues are treated in depth while others have only scant
information.

Zophy, Angela Howard with Frances M. Kavenik, eds. *Handbook of American
Women's History*. Garland Reference Library of the Humanities. New York:
Garland, 1990.

Useful compendium of people and events.

SECTION III. GENERAL HISTORICAL WORKS
AND OVERVIEWS

A. Pioneering Works

Beard, Mary Ritter. *Woman as a Force in History*. 1946; reprint, New York: Col-
lier, 1962.

Originally published in 1946, a classic that was among the first to present women as
active voices in history.

Benson, Mary Summers. *Women in Eighteenth-Century America: A Study of
Opinion and Social Usage*. New York: Columbia University Press, 1935.

A pioneering classic. Useful for background on women in the early national era.

Flexner, Eleanor. *Century of Struggle: The Women's Rights Movement in the
United States*. 1959; reprint, with new introduction by Ellen Fitzpatrick,
Cambridge: Harvard University Press, 1995.

Pathbreaking account of the suffrage movement; focus is primarily on the mainstream
suffragists. Fitzpatrick provides important new biographical information on Flexner.

Jones, Jacqueline. *Labor of Love, Labor of Sorrow: Black Women, Work, and the Family from Slavery to the Present.* New York: Basic, 1985.

A magisterial and pioneering synthesis of African American women over the past 150 years.

Lerner, Gerda. *The Majority Finds Its Past: Placing Women in History.* New York: Oxford University Press, 1978.

Sweeping and thematic analysis by a leading women's history expert.

Meyer, Annie Nathan. *Woman's Work in America.* 1891; reprint, New York: Arno, 1972.

A vibrant and invaluable collection of essays on pioneering nineteenth-century women.

B. Surveys

Clinton, Catherine. *The Other Civil War: American Women in the Nineteenth Century.* 1984; reprint, New York: Hill and Wang, 1999.

An accessible introduction to the issues of women's history presented in the first wave of 1970s scholarship. New bibliography in reprint edition.

Degler, Carl. *At Odds: Woman and the Family in America from the Revolution to the Present.* New York: Oxford University Press, 1980.

A valuable survey, with special emphasis on women's roles within the family by a pioneering and distinguished historian. Especially good on topics of sexuality and birth control.

Evans, Sara M. *Born for Liberty: A History of Women in America.* New York: Free Press, 1989.

Lunardini, Christine A. *Women's Rights.* Foreword by Betty Friedan. Phoenix, Ariz.: Oryx, 1996.

Covers first settlements to contemporary America. The section on the nineteenth century discusses abolition, education, reform, women's rights. Each chapter is followed by a biographical vignette of a woman, appropriate to the topic.

Ryan, Mary. *Womanhood in America from Colonial Times to the Present.* 3d ed. New York: New Viewpoints, 1982.

Although Ryan is episodic in her narrative, her prose nevertheless powerfully chronicles women's struggles, especially in terms of the labor movement and sexual conventions. A fine historiographic read.

Welter, Barbara. *Dimity Convictions: The American Woman in the Nineteenth Century.* Athens: Ohio University Press, 1976.

Welter was one of the first scholars to pioneer the concept of the "cult of domesticity," included in an article within this volume. Interesting material on the role of women missionaries is also included.

Wolfe, Margaret Ripley. *Daughters of Canaan: A Saga of Southern Women.* Lexington: University of Kentucky Press, 1995.

The first comprehensive survey of southern women, looking at women from the colonial era to the present with particular attention paid to wage earning and regionalism.

Woloch, Nancy. *Women: The American Experience,* 2d ed. New York: Knopf, 1993.

This book is a very compelling read to appreciate the first half of the nineteenth century—the period from 1865–1900 is not very accessible in its current format. However, vignettes at the front of each chapter pull the reader into the issues.

C. Anthologies

Berkin, Carol and Mary Beth Norton, eds. *Women in America: A History.* Boston: Houghton Mifflin, 1979.

A pioneering anthology by two distinguished eighteen 1-century historians. Good pieces on women in education, and good coverage of ethnicity.

Cantor, Milton and Bruce Laurie, eds. *Class, Sex, and the Woman Worker.* Westport, Conn.: Greenwood, 1977.

An important early work on the role of gender in the wage-earning force and the way in which women workers shaped labor issues.

Clinton, Catherine and Michele Gillespie, eds. *The Devil's Lane: Sex and Race in the Early South.* New York: Oxford University Press, 1997.

Several important articles on the Gulf South, with pieces on adultery, interracial sex, castration, cross-dressing, and religion in the colonial and early national era.

Cott, Nancy and Elizabeth Pleck, eds. *A Heritage of Her Own: Towards a New Social History of American Women.* New York: Simon and Schuster, 1979.

A valuable compendium of useful articles on women's role from the colonial period until the modern era. Especially good pieces on colonial women, some coverage of race and ethnicity in the nineteenth century.

DuBois, Ellen and Vicki Ruiz, eds. *Unequal Sisters: A Multicultural Reader in U.S. Women's History.* 2d ed. New York: Routledge, 1994.

An excellent survey of ethnic, racial, and class differences among American women. A lively and eclectic book for teaching, with excellent bibliographies for further research.

Farnham, Christie, ed. *Women of the American South: A Multicultural Reader.* New York: New York University Press, 1997.

A fine collection of essays looking at American Indian southern women, the African American experience, lesbianism, and other insights into southern diversity from the colonial era to the present.

Friedman, Jean and William Shade, eds. *Our American Sisters: Women in American Life and Thought.* 3d ed. Lexington, Mass.: D. C. Heath, 1982.

An outdated but solid collection.

Harley, Sharon and Rosalyn Terborg-Penn, eds. *The Afro-American Woman: Struggles and Images.* Port Washington, N.Y.: Kennikat, 1978.

An outdated but still useful collection of pioneering articles.

Kerber, Linda and Jane Matthews, eds. *Women's America.* 1982. 3d ed., New York: Oxford University Press, 1994.

A collection of excellent articles (especially in revised edition), integrated with introductory sections and primary sources.

Morton, Patricia, ed. *Discovering the Women in Slavery: Emancipating Perspectives on the American Past.* Athens: University of Georgia Press, 1996.

An important collection of original articles tracing the lives of black and white women within the slaveholding South. Especially sensitive to the issue of regionalism.

SECTION IV. BIOGRAPHIES, AUTOBIOGRAPHIES, AND PRIMARY SOURCES

A. Group Biographies

Buhle, Mary Jo, Paul Buhle, and Harvey J. Kaye. *The American Radical.* New York: Routledge, 1994.

Engaging study of important radicals, including Frances Wright and Sojourner Truth.

Foner, Philip Sheldon. *Three Who Dared: Prudence Crandall, Margaret Douglass, Myrtilla Miner—Champions of Antebellum Black Education.* Westport, Conn.: Greenwood, 1984.

A pioneering look at these neglected women, especially the little-known Margaret Douglass, by distinguished scholar Philip Foner, whose documentary and analytical work has been pathbreaking.

Fitzpatrick, Ellen. *Endless Crusade: Women Social Scientists and Progressive Reform*. New York: Oxford University Press, 1990.

An illuminating study of several pioneering women of the Progressive era, with especially good portrait of Sophinisba Breckenridge.

Lerner, Gerda. *The Grimké Sisters of South Carolina: Pioneers for Women's Rights and Abolition*. Boston: Houghton Mifflin, 1967.

A very fine analysis of these two remarkable reformers.

B. Individual Biographies

Amanda America Dickson

Leslie, Kent A. *Woman of Color, Daughter of Privilege: Amanda America Dickson, 1849–1893*. Athens: University of Georgia Press, 1995.

Gripping portrait of the daughter of a slave woman and a wealthy planter; Dickson's legacy and inheritance as a mixed-race woman in the nineteenth-century South provide fascinating reading.

Jane Addams

Davis, Allen F. *American Heroine: The Life and Legend of Jane Addams*. New York: 1973.
Lasch, Christopher. "Jane Addams: The College Woman and the Family Claim." *The New Radicalism in America, 1889–1963: The Intellectual as a Social Type*. New York: Knopf, 1965.

Susan Brownell Anthony

Barry, Kathleen. *Susan B. Anthony: A Biography of a Singular Feminist*. New York: New York University Press, 1988.

An interesting interpretation of America's leading suffragist.

Harper, Ida Husted. *The Life and Work of Susan B. Anthony*. 3 vols. 1891; reprint, Salem, N.H.: Ayer, 1983.

Harper, one of the editors of *History of Woman Suffrage*, applied the same detail for inclusion in this tribute to Anthony. Dated but still worth looking at.

Sherr, Lynn. *Failure Is Impossible: Susan B. Anthony in Her Own Words*. New York: Times, 1995.

An accessible assessment of Anthony by a journalist.

Clara Barton

Oates, Stephen B. *A Woman of Valor: Clara Barton and the Civil War.* New York: Free Press, 1994.

A riveting portrait of Barton's wartime experience, evoking this woman's passionate launch as a reformer.

Pryor, Elizabeth Brown. *Clara Barton: Professional Angel.* Philadelphia: University of Pennsylvania Press, 1987.

Despite its title, this is a balanced, judicious assessment of Barton's shortcomings and accomplishments.

Catharine Beecher

Sklar, Kathryn. *Catharine Beecher: A Study in American Domesticity.* New Haven: Yale University Press, 1973.

Sklar's biography of Beecher is really a portrait of an era, a germinal cultural study of nineteenth-century women's lives.

Antoinette Brown Blackwell

Cazden, Elizabeth. *Antoinette Brown Blackwell.* Old Westbury, N.Y.: Feminist Press, 1983.

Useful study of this pioneering feminist, the first to earn a divinity degree (from Oberlin) and to be ordained.

Harriot Stanton Blatch

DuBois, Ellen. *Harriot Stanton Blatch and the Winning of Women Suffrage.* New Haven: Yale University Press, 1998.

Definitive interpretation of the daughter of Elizabeth Cady Stanton, who played a vital role in the passage of the Nineteenth Amendment.

Myra Bradwell

Friedman, Jane. *America's First Woman Lawyer: The Biography of Myra Bradwell.* Buffalo, N.Y.: Prometheus, 1993.

A solid biography of this pioneering woman lawyer.

Mary Cassatt

Mathews, Nancy M. *Mary Cassatt: A Life*. New York: Villard, 1994.

A sumptuous biography of this nineteenth-century American painter who spent much of her career abroad in France.

Carrie Chapman Catt

Peck, Mary Grey. *Carrie Chapman Catt, A Biography*. New York: Octagon, 1975.

Standard biographical treatment of last president of the National Woman Suffrage Association.

Van Voris, Jacqueline. *Carrie Chapman Catt: A Public Life*. Old Westbury, N.Y.: Feminist Press, 1996.

First modern biography; focuses on Catt's superior organizational skills as key to suffrage success. Highly recommended.

Kate Chopin

Seyerstud, Per. *Kate Chopin: A Critical Biography*. New York: Octagon, 1980.

The definitive study of this late nineteenth-century Louisiana writer.

Mary Boykin Chesnut

De Credico, Mary. *Mary Boykin Chesnut: Confederate Woman's Life*. Madison, Wisc.: Madison House, 1996.

A traditional and solid study of this Civil War diarist.

Muhlenfeld, Elisabeth. *Mary Boykin Chesnut: A Biography*. Baton Rouge: Louisiana State University Press, 1981.

A pioneering biography, which sets Chesnut within her literary context as a nineteenth-century woman writer.

Prudence Crandall

Strane, Susan. *A Whole-Souled Woman: Prudence Crandall and the Education of Black Women*. New York: Norton, 1990.

A modest but accessible portrait of Crandall, a pioneering antebellum white educator who fought to educate African Americans in her home state of Connecticut.

Dorothea Dix

Brown, Thomas J. *Dorothea Dix: New England Reformer*. Cambridge: Harvard University Press, 1998.
Excellent cultural biography.

Gollaher, David. *Voice for the Mad: The Life of Dorothea Dix*. New York: Free Press, 1995. ·
Standard biographical fare, the life of a pioneering reformer who defended the rights of asylum inmates and worked for improved, more humane conditions.

Abigail Scott Duniway

Moynihan, Ruth Barnes. *Rebel for Rights: Abigail Scott Duniway*. New Haven: Yale University Press, 1983.
An excellent cultural biography of the Oregon feminist who led the western woman suffrage strategy and brought votes to western women.

Margaret Fuller

Capper, Charles. *Margaret Fuller: An American Romantic Life*. Vol. 1. New York: Oxford University Press, 1992– .
An ambitious, multivolumed study of this significant nineteenth-century feminist thinker.

Chevigny, Bell, ed. *The Woman and the Myth: Margaret Fuller's Life and Writings*. 2d. ed. Old Westbury, N.Y.: Feminist Press, 1987.
A marvelous biographical sourcebook.

Charlotte Perkins Gilman

Berkin, Carol. "Private Woman, Public Woman: The Contradictions of Charlotte Perkins Gilman." In G. J. Barker-Benfield and Catherine Clinton, eds., *Portraits of American Women*. New York: Oxford University Press, 1998.
Hill, Mary A. *Charlotte Perkins Gilman: The Making of a Radical Feminist, 1860–1896*. Philadelphia: Temple University Press, 1980.
An interesting portrait of this key nineteenth-century feminist author, lecturer, and economist.

Lane, Ann J. *To Herland and Beyond: The Life and Work of Charlotte Perkins Gilman*. Madison, Wisc.: University of Wisconsin Press, 1991.
An important feminist reading of this critical feminist author.

Harriet Hosmer

Sherwood, Dolly. *Harriet Hosmer, American Sculptor, 1830–1908*. Columbia: University of Missouri Press, 1991.

A pioneering study of this neglected American artist.

Sarah Orne Jewett

Sherman, Sarah Way. *Sarah Orne Jewett: An American Persephone*. Hanover, N.H.: University Press of New England, 1989.

An accessible literary and cultural biography of this New England author known as a "local colorist."

Fanny Kemble

Clinton, Catherine. *Fanny Kemble's Civil Wars*. New York: Simon & Schuster, 2000.

Grace King

Bush, Robert. *Grace King: A Southern Destiny*. Baton Rouge: Louisiana State University Press, 1983.

A good, serviceable study of this important southern writer.

Mary Todd Lincoln

Baker, Jean. *Mary Todd Lincoln: A Biography*. New York: Norton, 1987.

The definitive study of this complex, misunderstood nineteenth-century figure, the wife of Abraham Lincoln.

Lucretia Mott

Bacon, Margaret Hope. *Valiant Friend: The Life of Lucretia Mott*. New York: Walker, 1980.

And important look at this Quaker feminist and abolitionist.

Annie Oakley

Riley, Glenda. *The Life and Legacy of Annie Oakley*. Norman: University of Oklahoma Press, 1994.

A standard scholarly treatment of this legendary performer in Buffalo Bill's Wild West Show.

Lydia Pinkham

Stage, Sarah. *Female Complaints: Lydia Pinkham and the Business of Women's Medicine*. New York: Norton, 1979.

An excellent biographical study of Pinkham, weaving in the culture of women's pharmacology in the nineteenth century.

Sarah Parker Remond

Bogin, Ruth. "Sarah Parker Remond: Black Abolitionist from Salem." *Essex Institute Historical Collections* 110 (April 1974).

A sketch of an early and important black female antislavery activist.

Sacajawea

Kessler, Donna J. *The Making of Sacajawea: A Euro-American Legend*. Tuscaloosa: University of Alabama Press, 1996.

Demystification and biographical insight into this legendary American Indian guide.

Anna Howard Shaw

McGovern, James P. "Anna Howard Shaw: New Approaches to Feminism." *Journal of Social History* 3 (1970).

A controversial interpretation of Shaw and feminism.

Elizabeth Cady Stanton

Banner, Lois. *Elizabeth Cady Stanton: A Radical for Women's Rights*. Boston: Little, Brown, 1980.

A useful survey of Stanton's major achievements.

Cullen-Dupont, Kathryn. *Elizabeth Cady Stanton and Women's Liberty*. New York: Facts on File, 1992.

Straightforward biography, aimed at general readership.

Griffith, Elisabeth. *In Her Own Right: The Life of Elizabeth Cady Stanton*. New York: Oxford University Press, 1984.

The best of the biographies; well researched, insightful.

Rose Pastor Stokes

Zipser, Arthur. *Fire and Grace: The Life of Rose Pastor Stokes*. Athens: University of Georgia Press, 1989.

Absorbing account of this legendary labor activist, dubbed "the Cinderella of the sweatshops" because of her marriage to a millionaire philanthropist.

Lucy Stone

Kerr, Andrea Moore. *Lucy Stone: Speaking Out for Equality*. New Brunswick, N.J.: Rutgers University Press, 1992.

An excellent introduction to this legendary abolitionist feminist, who was one of the first feminists "to keep her name" following her marriage.

Harriet Beecher Stowe

Hedrick, Joan D. *Harriet Beecher Stowe: A Life*. New York: Oxford University Press, 1994.

A scholarly tour de force: absorbing, enlightening, and a pleasure to read.

Sojourner Truth

Painter, Nell Irvin. *Sojourner Truth: A Life, a Symbol*. New York: Norton, 1996.

Painter's provocative and brave reinterpretation of Truth's life—and her controversial assessment of the layers of meaning attached to her legend.

Ida Bell Wells-Barnett

McMurry, Linda O. *To Keep the Waters Troubled: The Life of Ida B. Wells*. New York: Oxford University Press, 1998.

Sarah Winnemucca

Canfield, Gae Whitney. *Sarah Winnemucca of the Northern Paiutes*. Norman: University of Oklahoma Press, 1983.

Excellent introduction to the life of this legendary American Indian woman.

Victoria Woodhull

Goldsmith, Barbara. *Other Powers: The Age of Suffrage, Spiritualism, and the Scandalous Victoria Woodhull*. New York: Knopf, 1998.

A fascinating view of Woodhull, which places her within her cultural era; a broad, sweeping, study.

Underhill, Lois Beachy. *The Woman Who Ran for President: The Many Lives of Victoria Woodhull.* New York: Penguin, 1996.

An excellent contextual biography evaluating Woodhull's role as a political leader.

Frances Wright

Morris, Celia Morris. *Fanny Wright: Rebel in America.* Cambridge: Harvard University Press, 1984.

An accessible, entertaining account of this iconoclastic American reformer.

C. Autobiographies and Memoirs

Addams, Jane. *Twenty Years at Hull House.* New York: Macmillan, 1910.

Addams's own account of the Hull House years that spawned the social work profession; also informative about her involvement with other issues, especially the peace movement but including suffrage.

——. *The Second Twenty Years at Hull House.* New York: Macmillan, 1930.

Andrews, William L., ed. *Sisters of the Spirit: Three Black Women's Autobiographies of the Nineteenth Century.* Bloomington: Indiana University Press, 1986.

Illuminating writings of Jarena Lee (b. 1783), Zilpha Elaw (b. ca. 1790), and Julia A. J. Foote (1823–1900), with an excellent introduction by Andrews, a distinguished scholar of African American literature.

Blatch, Harriot Stanton and Alma Lutz. *Challenging Years: The Memoirs of Harriot Stanton Blatch.* New York: Putnam, 1940.

Elizabeth Cady Stanton's daughter's account of her years in England and the later years of the American suffrage movement.

Catt, Carrie Chapman and Nettie Rogers Shulman. *Woman Suffrage and Politics: The Inner Story of the Suffrage Movement.* New York: Charles Scribner's, 1926.

The suffrage movement from the perspective of the last president of the National Association for American Woman Suffrage.

Dorr, Rheta Child. *A Woman of Fifty: The Equal Suffrage Movement in the Pacific Coast States*. New York: Funk and Wagnalls, 1924.

Duniway, Abigail Scott. *An Autobiographical History of the Equal Suffrage Movement in Pacific Coast States, with Sidelights on Protection*. Portland, Ore: James, Kearns, and Abbott, 1914.

Good account of West Coast suffrage politics and related issues.

Duster, Alfreda, ed. *Crusade for Justice: The Autobiography of Ida B. Wells*. Reprint, Chicago: University of Chicago Press, 1991.

Excellent posthumously published memoir of Wells-Barnett's career.

Edmonds, Emma. *Nurse and Spy in the Union Army*. Hartford: W. S. Williams, 1865.

An important memoir of Edmonds's wartime service, when she disguised herself as a man.

Gilman, Charlotte Perkins. *The Living of Charlotte Perkins Gilman: An Autobiography*. New York: D. Appleton-Century, 1935.

Gilman's autobiography sheds light on both her own life and the social and intellectual ferment of the time.

Irwin, Inez Haynes. *The Story of the Woman's Party*. New York: Harcourt Brace, 1921.

——. *Up Hill With Banners Flying*. Penobscot, Me: Traversity, 1964.

Good contemporary accounts of the Woman's Party, Alice Paul, and the disagreements with the National American Woman Suffrage Association.

Jacobs, Harriet. *Incidents in the Life of a Slave Girl*, ed. Jean F. Yellin. Cambridge: Harvard University Press, 1987.

The definitive edition of the riveting memoir of Harriet Jacobs; the pioneering and powerful first American slave narrative by a woman.

Kearney, Belle. *A Slaveholder's Daughter*. 1900; reprint, Westport, Conn.: Greenwood, 1981.

A revealing memoir by this outstanding white southern woman activist and club woman.

Larcom, Lucy. *A New England Girlhood*. 1890; reprint, New York: Corinth, 1961.

An important memoir by one of the Lowell mill girls.

Livermore, Mary A. *My Story of the War: A Woman's Narrative of Four Years Personal Experience*. Hartford: A. D. Worthington, 1890.

A memoir by a Union woman who worked for the Sanitary Commission during wartime.

Stanton, Elizabeth Cady. *Eighty Years and More: Reminiscences, 1815–1897.* 1898; reprint, New York: Schocken, 1971.

In her own words, a memoir by intellectually gifted leader of the women's rights movement.

Stevens, Doris. *Jailed for Freedom.* New York: Boni and Liveright, 1920.

Focuses on her prison ordeal for picketing the White House. Interesting, more gossipy than the works by Inez Haynes Irwin cited earlier.

Taylor, Susie King. *A Black Woman's Civil War Memoir: Reminiscences of My Life in Camp with the 33d U.S. Colored Troops, Late 1st South Carolina Volunteers.* 1903; reprint, New York: M. Wiener, 1988.

The only memoir by a black woman who served with the army during the Civil War. Taylor was a nurse, laundress, and teacher in Georgia and South Carolina during wartime, before moving to Boston and becoming active in the Grand Army of the Republic Women's Auxiliary.

Wilson, Edith Bolling. *My Memoir.* Indianapolis: Bobbs-Merrill, 1939.

Woodrow Wilson's second wife; provides interesting comment on Wilson and suffrage.

D. Letters and Diaries

Bleser, Carol, ed. *The Hammonds of Redcliffe.* New York: Oxford University Press, 1981.

A riveting and important collection tracing the fortunes of the family of South Carolina Senator James Henry Hammond, through the Civil War and into the modern era through family letters. A model of scholarship.

Burr, Virginia, ed. *The Secret Eye: The Journal of Ella Gertrude Clanton Thomas.* Chapel Hill: University of North Carolina Press, 1990.

An excellent portrait of a planter wife who endured wartime hardship.

East, Charles, ed. *The Civil War Diary of Sarah Morgan.* Athens: University of Georgia Press, 1991.

An excellent edition of the wartime diary of a Louisiana girl.

Mohr, James C., ed. *The Cormany Diaries: A Northern Family in the Civil War.* Pittsburgh: University of Pittsburgh Press, 1982.

An interesting Yankee saga.

Myers, Robert Manson, ed. *Children of Pride: A True Story of Georgia and the Civil War*. New Haven: Yale University Press, 1972.

A spectacular family saga, full of the letters of a Liberty County, Georgia, slaveholding family. The Jones family women are articulate and engaging.

Robertson, Mary D., ed. *Lucy Breckenridge of Grove Hill: The Journal of a Virginia Girl, 1862–1864*. Kent, Ohio: Kent State University Press, 1979.

A compelling diary by a Confederate girl in Virginia during wartime.

Rosen, Ruth and Sue Davidson, eds. *The Maimie Papers*. Old Westbury, N.Y.: Feminist Press, 1977.

A fascinating look at a correspondence between a prostitute and a middle-class reformer at the turn of the century.

Stevenson, Brenda, ed. *The Journal of Charlotte Forten Grimké*. New York: Oxford University Press, 1988.

A wonderful edition of this important diary of a black northern woman who went South to teach freedpeople in South Carolina during the Civil War.

Stratton, Joanna. *Pioneer Mothers: Voices from the Kansas Frontier*. New York: Simon and Schuster, 1981.

A compelling and refreshing look at the lives of women on the Kansas frontier through their own words. Jargon-free annotation.

Swisshelm, Jane Grey. *Crusader and Feminist: Letters of Jane Grey Swisshelm, 1858–1865*. Westport, Conn.: Hyperion, 1976.

A nice collection of material on this northern woman activist.

Upton, Dell, ed. *Madaline: Love and Sin in Antebellum New Orleans*. Athens: University of Georgia Press, 1996.

The remarkable story of a kept woman in New Orleans in the early nineteenth century, told through her diary.

Woodward, C. Vann. *Mary Chesnut's Civil War*. New Haven: Yale University Press, 1981.

A prize-winning edition of this classic wartime memoir.

E. Documentary Collections

Axtell, James, ed. *The Indian Peoples of Eastern America: A Documentary History of the Sexes*. New York: Oxford University Press, 1981.

Baxandall, Rosalyn, Linda Gordon, and Susan Reverby, eds. *America's Working Women: 1600 to the Present*. 2d. ed. New York: Norton, 1995.
A chock-a-block overflowing compendium of documents on wage-earning women. Doubled number of sections and coverage of women of color from first (1976) edition.

Berlin, Ira et al., eds. *Freedom: A Documentary History of Emancipation*. New York: Cambridge University Press, 1982– .
A magnificent multivolumed project annotating and publishing documents from the Freedman's Bureau Records. Good material on African American women.

Buhle, Mary Jo and Paul Buhle, eds. *A Concise History of Woman Suffrage: Selections from the Classic Work of Stanton, Anthony, Gage, and Harper*. Urbana: University of Illinois Press, 1978.
A well-edited, useful compendium.

Cashin, Joan, ed. *Our Common Affairs: Documents on Antebellum Southern Women*. Baltimore, Md.: Johns Hopkins University Press, 1996.
Well-annotated and richly illustrated collection of white women in the Old South.

Cott, Nancy, ed. *Roots of Bitterness: Documents of the Social History of American Women*. New York: Dutton, 1972.
A very thoughtful and interesting collection of documents demonstrating issues of domesticity and women's inner reflections.

Dublin, Thomas, ed. *Farm to Factory: The Mill Experience and Women's Lives in New England, 1830–1860*. New York: Columbia University Press, 1981.
An excellent primary collection of letters and other materials tracing women's lives in the early factories of New England.

DuBois, Ellen, ed. *Elizabeth Cady Stanton and Susan B. Anthony: Speeches, Writings, and Correspondence*. New York: Schocken, 1982.
A useful collection, well edited by a leading suffrage scholar.

Foner, Philip, ed. *Women and the American Labor Movement: From Colonial Times to the Eve of World War I*. New York: Free Press, 1979.
A stellar collection of primary documents. Minimal annotation, but a heroic amount of material assembled.

Frost, Elizabeth and Kathryn Cullen-Dupont, eds. *Women's Suffrage in America: An Eyewitness History*. New York: Facts on File, 1992.
Combines overview narrative with primary source documents.

Katz, Jonathan, ed. *Gay American History: Lesbian and Gay Men in the U.S.A.: A Documentary*. New York: Meridan, 1992.

A wonderful, pioneering work.

Norton, Mary Beth, ed. *Major Problems in American Women's History: Documents and Essays*. Lexington, Mass: D. C. Heath, 1989.

A guide to diversity and continuity within American women's experience.

Rawick, George, ed. *The American Slave* [Works Progress Administration Narratives]. 41 vols. Westport, Conn.: Greenwood, 1977.

The rich treasure trove of interviews with ex-slaves conducted during the 1930s. Organized by state volumes.

Sterling, Dorothy, ed. *We Are Your Sisters: Black Women in the Nineteenth Century*. New York: Norton, 1984.

Combines annotated primary source documents, including journals, letters, newspaper accounts, diaries, and autobiographies with photographs.

Walters, Ronald, ed. *Primers for Prudery: Sexual Advice to Victorian America*. Englewood Cliffs, N.J.: Prentice-Hall, 1974.

An out-of-print but not out-of-date collection.

SECTION V. JOURNALS, ARCHIVES, PROJECTS

A. Periodicals

1. Primary Sources

Atlantic Monthly
Christian Herald
DeBow's Review
Godey's Lady's Book
Harper's Weekly
Leslie's Illustrated Times
Southern Literary Messenger

2. Secondary Sources

All She Wrote. Honolulu, Hawaii: YWCA of Oahu, University YWCA, 1981– .

A newsletter focusing on Hawaiian women.

The Ethnic Woman. New York: The Ethnic Woman, 1977– .
A journal on the issues of ethnic women.

Feminist Issues. New Brunswick, N.J.: Transaction Periodicals Consortium, 1980– .
A useful women's studies journal.

Feminist Studies. College Park, Md: Feminist Studies, 1970– .
A refereed journal in the field; lots of American women's history.

Feminist Teacher. Bloomington, Ind.: Feminist Teacher Editorial Collective, 1984– .
A good journal published by a collective.

Gender and History. New York: Oxford University Press, 1989– .
British journal.

Harvard Women's Law Journal. Cambridge: Harvard Women's Law Journal, 1978– .
Often publishes important articles on women's history.

Heresies. New York: Heresies Collective, 1977–1993.
Useful journal; good on racial issues.

Journal of Women's History. Bloomington: Indiana University Press, 1989– .
A refereed journal of women's history.

Off Our Backs: A Woman's News Journal. Washington, D.C.: Off Our Backs, Inc., 1970– .
Newsletter.

Quest: A Feminist Quarterly. Washington, D.C.: Quest, Inc., 1985– .
Social science journal.

Signs: A Journal of Women in Culture and Society. Chapel Hill: University of North Carolina Press, 1975– .
Leading interdisciplinary journal with lots of women's history.

The Women's Review of Books. Wellesley, Mass.: Wellesley Center for Research on Women, 1983– .
Leading review of record in women's history.

Women's Studies International Quarterly. New York: Pergamon, 1978–1981.

Some useful articles.

Yale Journal of Law and Feminism. New Haven: 1989–.
Important legal pieces on American women.

B. Archives

1. African American Women

Atlanta University: Robert W. Woodruff Library, Negro Collection, Atlanta, Ga.
Cullen-Jackman Memorial Collection: Miscellany
Nellie Towns, in George Alexander Townes Papers, 1851–1956

Bennett College: Thomas F. Holgate Library, Greensboro, N.C. 1873–
Afro-American Women Collection
Bennett College Records, 1873–
Vertical File Collection

Bethune Museum and Archives: 1318 Vermont Ave., NW, Washington, D.C.
Unprocessed Collections

Chicago Historical Society: North Avenue and Clark Street, Chicago, Ill.

Detroit Public Library: Burton Historical Collection, 5201 Woodward Ave., Detroit, Mich.

DuSable Museum of African American History: 740 E. 56th Place, Chicago, Ill.

Fisk University Library: Special Collections, Nashville, Tenn.

Indiana Historical Society: 315 W. Ohio St., Indianapolis, Ind.
Black Women in the Middle West Project Papers

Library of Congress: Manuscript Division, Washington, D.C.
Mary Church Terrell Papers, 1886–1954

Minnesota Historical Society: Archives and Manuscripts, 345 West Kellogg Blvd., St. Paul, Minn.
Hallie Q. Brown Community House Records, 1861–1960s

Morland-Spingarn Research Center: Manuscript Division Founders Library, Howard University, Washington, D.C.
Mary Ann Shadd Cary Papers, 1844–1884
Anna J. Cooper Papers, 1881–1958
Gregoria Fraser Goins Papers, 1843–1962

Angelina Weld Grimké Papers, 1887–1958
Anita Thompson Dickinson Reynolds Papers, 1850–1980
Myra L. Spaulding Papers, 1892–1922
Mary Church Terrell Papers, 1888–1976
Sara A. Turner Collection, 1866–1901
Washington Conservatory of Music, Harriet Gibbs Marshall Papers, 1887–1966

Schomburg Center for Research in Black Culture: New York Public Library, 515 Malcolm X Blvd., New York, N.Y.
Conrad and Tubman Papers, 1893–1941
Lyons and Williams Papers, 1830–1957
National Association of Colored Graduate Nurses Papers

Tuskegee University Archives: Hollis Burke Fissell Library, Tuskegee, Al.
Juanita Gilmore Brewster Papers, 1800–1970
Margaret Murray Washington Papers, 1896–1925

University of Illinois at Chicago: Circle Library, Manuscript Division, The Library, P.O. Box 8198, Chicago, Ill.

University of Louisville: Oral History Center, Department of History, Belknap Campus, Louisville, Ky.

Wayne State University: Walter P. Reuther Library, Archive of Labor and Urban Affairs, Detroit, Mich.

Western Reserve Historical Society: 10825 East Blvd., Cleveland, Ohio
Ladies Society of Brocton, Ohio Papers, 1866
L. Pearl Mitchell Papers, 1875–1974

2. Southern Women

Alabama State Archives: Montgomery, Ala.
Mary Grace Cooper Collection
Eliza Gould Collection
Bolling Hall Family Collection
Sarah Gayle Haynesworth Collection
Tait Family Collection

Emory University: Special Collections, Woodruff Library, Atlanta, Ga.
Andrew Collection
Cotton Collection
Fort Collection

Hillhouse Collection
North Six-Mile Baptist Church Record Book
Pinckney Family Collection
Stephens Collection
Thiot Family Collection

Georgia State Archives: Atlanta, Ga.
Martha Baldwin Collection
Boulware Family Collection
Butner Family Collection
Chunn-Land Family Collection
Few Collection
Lee Collection
McCall Collection

Georgia Historical Society: Savannah, Ga.
Allen Collection
Berrien Collection
Blanche Collection
Bull-Morrow Collection
Burroughs Collection
Cohen-Hunter Collection
Floyd Collection
Forman-Bryan-Screven Collection
Fraser-Couper Collection
Gilbert Collection
Gordon Family Collection
Greene Collection
Harris Collection
Houston Collection
Seaborn-Jones Collection
Keith Collection
Lebey-Courtney Collection
McDonald-Lawrence Collection
Mackay Collection
Mackay Family Collection
Morgan Collection
Mulford Collection
Potter Collection
Rogers Collection
Savannah Free School Collection

Telfair Collection

Historic New Orleans Collection: New Orleans, La.
Phelps Collection
Boze Diary, Henri de Ste. Geme Collection

Huntington Library: Pasadena, Calif.
Baldwin Family Collection
Brock Collection
Postlethwaite Collection

Library of Congress: Manuscript Division, Washington, D.C.
Brodeau Collection
Clinch Collection
Stephens Collection
Washington Collection
Wilson Collection

Louisiana State University: Manuscript Division, Baton Rouge, La.
Bowman Collection
Ellis-Farrar Collection
Evans Collection
Marston Collection
Montgomery Collection
Reynes Collection
Weeks Collection
Williams Collection

Mississippi State Archives: Jackson, Miss.
Amelia Collection
Archer-Finlay-Moore Collection
Burrus Collection
Dunbar Collection
Howell Collection
Hunt Collection
Montgomery Collection
Pride Collection
Robinson Collection
Eunice Stockwell Collection
Wade Collection
Watts Collection
Wilson Collection
Worthington Collection

Radcliffe College: Schlesinger Library, Cambridge, Mass.
   Hooker Collection
   Somerville-Howorth Collection

Tulane University Library: Manuscript Division, New Orleans, La.
   Brenan Collection
   Cochran Family Collection
   Colcock Family Collection
   Copeland Collection
   Eliza Gould Collection
   Gurley Family Collection
   Charles Colcock Jones Collection
   Ker-Texada Collection
   McConnell Family Collection
   Lise Mitchell Collection
   Weeks Collection

University of North Carolina: Southern Historical Collection, Wilson Library,
   Chapel Hill, N.C.

Contains literally hundreds of paper collections too numerous to list, but includes Barrow, Battle, Bulloch, Fort, Graves, Hawkins, Jones, Lenoir, McBee, Milligan, Mordecai, Person, Pettigrew, Quitman, Randolph-Yates, Ruffin-Meade, and Strudwick Family Papers, as well as individual collections for, among others, Susan Nye Hutchinson, Mary Hunter Kennedy, Caroline Laurens, Catharine McFarland, Miriam Moses, Charlotte Porcher, Louisa Rogers, Rebecca Street Sketch and Mary Stubblefield.

Duke University: Manuscript Department, William Perkins Library, Durham,
   N.C.

Another mammoth collection indispensable to anyone working on southern history or southern women in the nineteenth century. Includes papers of Elizabeth Blackwell, Maria Carr, Ann Coleman, Eleanor Douglas, Kate Edmond, Elizabeth Fitzhugh, Mary Fraser, Amanda Gardner, Amelia High Jeffreys, Ann Reid Lovell, Harriot Horry, Louisa Sills, Ann Smith and Cornelia Storrs.

See also:

College of William and Mary: Swem Library, Manuscript Division, Williamsburg, Va.

Colonial Williamsburg Foundation: Williamsburg, Va.

North Carolina Archives: Raleigh, N.C.

South Carolina Historical Society: Charleston, S.C.

South Carolina State Archives: Columbia, S.C.

University of South Carolina: Caroliniana Library, Columbia, S.C.

University of Virginia: Manuscript Department, UVA Library, Charlottesville, Va.

Virginia Historical Society: Richmond, Va.

Virginia State Library: Richmond, Va.

3. Suffrage

Library of Congress: Manuscript Division, Washington, D.C.
  Papers of the National American Woman Suffrage Association
  Papers of the National Woman's Party 1913–1920, The Suffrage Years

Mississippi Department of Archives and History: Jackson, Miss.
  Belle Kearney Papers
  Lily Wilkinson Thompson Papers

Radcliffe College: Schlesinger Library, Brattle Street, Cambridge, Mass.
  Dillon Collection of Suffrage Material
  Susan B. Anthony Papers
  Mary Ritter Beard Papers
  Beecher-Stowe Family Papers
  Charlotte Perkins Gilman Papers
  Inez Haynes Irwin Papers
  Alma Lutz Papers
  Doris Stevens Papers
  Anna Kelton Wiley Papers
  Mary Winsor Papers

Smith College: Sophia Smith Collection, Northampton, Mass.
  Jane Addams Papers
  Mary Ritter Beard Papers
  Margaret Sanger Papers
  Alice Morgan Wright Papers
  Suffrage Scrapbooks

University of California, Berkeley: The Bancroft Library, Oakland, Calif.
  Anne Henrietta Martin Papers
  Mable Vernon Papers
  Suffragist Oral History Project Interviews:
    Sara Bard Field
    Burnita Shelton Matthews
    Alice Paul
    Jeannette Rankin
    Rebecca Hourwich Reyher
    Mabel Vernon

Huntington Library: Pasadena, Calif.
  Ida Husted Harper Papers
  Sonia Hovey Papers
  Maude Anthony Koehler Papers
  Alice Park Locke Papers
  Maria Severance Papers
  Una Richardson Winter Papers

SECTION VI. ELECTRONIC RESOURCES

Web Directories, Indexes, and Search Engines

The Internet can provide a wealth of information in both online accessible files that can be printed right off the screen or downloaded into your own computer and identifiable archival resources available at research centers throughout the world. But confusion abounds with imprecise references to "directories," "indexes," and "search engines" as one begins the task of mining the Internet. In addition, newcomers to the Internet may find references to "gophers" as well as search programs such as "ARCHIE" and "VERONICA." Before the advent of search engines, indexes, and directories, gopher files were developed as a means of archivally storing topical information, generally as text files. ARCHIE and VERONICA were programs developed to search gopher files. It may be useful to investigate gopher files, but the best place to begin Internet research is using one or more of the following available sites.

Whether websites identify themselves as search engines, directories, or indexes is less important than the fact that they all operate virtually the same way—they compile lists of resources based on keyword search inquiries. The first four sites might best be defined, however, as "search engine search engines," for the simple reason that they seek out other search engines in completing the keyword inquiry.

Finally, the degree of success one has in finding resource information depends heavily on both how precise and how broad the keyword inquiry is. Multiple inquiries using different keywords or keyword combinations will frequently produce very different sets of results.

HyTelnet
  galaxy.einet.net/hytelnet/HYTELNET/html

Internet Sleuth
  www.isleuth.com

MetaCrawler
www.metacrawler.com

SavvySearch
guaraldi.cs.colostate.edu:2000/

AltaVista
www.altavista.digital.com

Excite
www.excite.com

HotBot
www.hotbot.com

Infoseek
www.infoseek.com

Lycos
www.lycos.com

WebCrawler
www.webcrawler.com

Yahoo!
www.yahoo.com

Government and Law Search Engines, Directories, Indexes

Lexis/Nexis
www.lexis-nexis.com/

Thomas (Legislative Information)
thomas.loc.gov/

U.S. Patent & Trademark
www.uspto.gov/

Pay-for-Service Research Websites

Research-It
www.iTools.com/research-it/research-it.html

WWW Virtual Library
vlib.stanford.edu/Overview2.html

Women and History Websites

American Women's History: A Research Guide
Middle Tennessee State University.
http://frank.mtsu.edu/~kmiddlet/history/women.html

This is an especially useful website that is frequently updated and connects the user to a wealth of information under six different headings: American women's history; research guide; general reference and bibliographic sources; subject index to research sources; state and regional history sources; finding primary sources; and finding books, journal articles, and theses. Particularly useful is the Bookmark Page, which will connect to dozens more useful sites.

Digital Women's Collections online
http://scriptorium.lib.duke.edu/women/digital.html

Primary source documents—both actual representations and transcriptions—are being put online at this innovative and important resource. See also the *Women's Collection* at http://www.odyssey.lib.duke.edu/women/

Documenting the American South: The Southern Experience in Nineteenth-Century America
http://metalab.unc.edu/docsouth/

Bibliographic and online primary materials—diaries, memoirs, slave narratives, autobiographies, and more.

H-Net: Humanities and Social Studies online. Michigan State University.
http://www.h-net.msu.edu

The primary resource site for inquiry. H-Net contains more than one hundred scholarly lists and networks, including area studies (Latin America), topics (Anti-Semitism or Slavery), and of special interest: H-Women (Women's History); H-SAWH (Women and Gender in the United States South); H-Minerva (Women and War, and Women and Military).

H-Net is an international network of scholars in the humanities and social sciences with a common objective of advancing humanities and social science teaching and research. Among H-Net's most important activities is its sponsorship of one hundred free electronic, interactive newsletters ("lists").

Subscribers and editors communicate through electronic mail messages sent to the group. These messages can be saved, discarded, downloaded to a local computer, copied, printed out, or relayed to someone else. H-Net lists reach more than 60,000 subscribers in more than 70 countries. Each week advertisements for job opportunities are posted on the list, as well.

List messages are held in archives and can be searched by keyword to obtain information and to follow the "thread" of a discussion more than the course of days, weeks, months, or years.

The networks commission original reviews of books, articles, software, and museum exhibits. Subscribe to H-REVIEW for these, and visit the review website: http://www.h-net.msu.edu/reviews.

Harvard University. Cambridge, Massachusetts.
http://www.harvard.edu

Excellent source for bibliographic research. Harvard's HOLLIS search system allows the user to download information using TELNET, and e-mail to a designated address.

Institute for Research on Women and Gender. University of Michigan.
http://www.umich.edu/~irwg

Particularly useful for information on current research projects, but this will take the user to other sites as well.

International Institute of Social History. Amsterdam, Netherlands.
http://www.iisg.nl/~womhist

Excellent resource; gets the user to a variety of sources and materials including the Z39.50 gateway to dozens of resource sites.

Library of Congress. Washington, D.C.
http://www.loc.gov

Opens up the Library of Congress and all its wonders. Find almost any book citation you need, often with a brief description; download information through TELNET or e-mail information to yourself. Reference sites to archives, special collections, government documents, museums, manuscript collections, some online resources.

National Woman's History Project
http://www.nwhp.org

A wealth of information and site referrals, including a monthly-updated schedule of current events and projects available state by state and nationally.

New York Public Library
http://www.nypl.org

This site will allow the user to locate books in the collection; download bibliographic material; view some online books and documents; and connect to the vast resources of the library, including the research libraries, catalogs, and indexes (CATN.Y.P), international resources, exhibitions, and an extensive women's studies collection.

Viva Link
http://www.iisg.nl/~womhist/vivalink.html

A complete listing of journals of women's studies.

Women's International Center
http://www.wic.org

Overall not as useful as some of the other sites, but the WIC does have a (limited) collection of biographical sketches on notable women, accessible online.

CD-ROMs

Cinemania 98. Microsoft Corp., Belvedere, Wash.
http://www.microsoft.com

Bill Gates turned his minions loose, and they produced a comprehensive film resource. Contains film credits, cast, synopsis, reviews, and awards. In addition there are hundreds of biographies of the principals in the industry, from actresses and actors to directors and producers to cinematographers and costume designers. This film archive extends back to the earliest days of film production, including *Birth of a Nation*.

Women's Resources International. National Information Services Corporation, Baltimore, Md.
http://www.nisc.com

Women's Resources International is an interdisciplinary collection of nine important files containing more than 127,000 records, including: women's studies abstracts; women's studies databases; a bibliography of European women from 1610 to the present; a four-file collection from the Women's Studies Librarian, University of Wisconsin; a bibliography of women of color and southern women, 1975 to the present; and a bibliography on women's health and development.

SECTION VII. NOVELS AND FILMS

A. Novels

Baym, Nina. Woman's Fiction: *A Guide to Novels by and About Women in America, 1820–1870*. Ithaca, N.Y.: Cornell University Press, 1978.

An enlightening and valuable guide to women's literature in the nineteenth century by a leading literary scholar in the field. Accessible and perceptive.

Mott, Frank Luther. *Golden Multitudes: The Story of Best Sellers in the United States*. New York: Macmillan, 1947.

A good companion to Baym, above.

1. Primary

Alcott, Louisa May. *Little Women*. 1871.

Baum, Frank. *The Wonderful Wizard of Oz*. 1900.
Broughton, Rhoda. *Red As a Rose Is She*. 1870
Child, Lydia Marie. *Letters from New York*. 1843.
Chopin, Kate. *The Awakening*. 1899.
Crane, Stephen. *Maggie, A Girl of the Streets*. 1896.
Dreiser, Theodore. *Sister Carrie*. 1900.
Evans, Augusta J. *Beulah*. 1859.
Gilman, Charlotte Perkins. *The Yellow Wallpaper*. 1901.
Jackson, Helen Hunt. *Ramona*. 1884.
Sidney, Margaret. *Five Little Peppers and How They Grew*. 1880.
Southworth, Mrs. E.D.E.N. *The Hidden Hand*. 1859.
Stowe, Harriet Beecher. *Uncle Tom's Cabin*. 1852.
Warner, Susan. *The Wide, Wide World*. 1850.
Wilson, Harriet. *Our Nig*. 1859.

2. Secondary

Cather, Willa. *My Antonia*. 1918.
Mitchell, Margaret. *Gone With The Wind*. 1936.
Morrison, Toni. *Beloved*. 1987.
Wharton, Edith. *Ethan Frome*. 1911.

B. Films

The Age of Innocence (1993). Michelle Pfeiffer, Wynona Ryder, Daniel Day-Lewis. Director: Martin Scorcese; producer: Barbara de Fema.

Adaptation of Edith Wharton novel of manners and mores among New York's late nine-teenth-century social elites who value the orderly transfer of wealth above all.

The Bostonians (1989). Vanessa Redgrave, Christopher Reeve, Jessica Tandy. Directors and producers: Ruth Prawer Jhabvala, Ismail Merchant, and James Ivory.

Adaptation of Henry James's intriguing novel about feminism and women's fate in turn-of-the-century Boston.

Daughters of the Dust (1991). Adisa Anderson, Barbara-O, Cheryl Lynn Bruce, Cora Lee Day, Cornell Royal. Director: Julie Dash.

A lush portrait of the clash between Sea Island culture in coastal South Carolina and urban black life in this haunting, lyrical film about late nineteenth-century African American life.

Days of Heaven (1978). Brooke Adams, Richard Gere. Director: Terrence Malick; producers: Bert and Harold Schneider.

A compelling story of itinerant farm labor and rural life in the early twentieth century—reflects rural values and gender issues from an earlier era as well.

Friendly Persuasion (1956). Dorothy McGuire, Gary Cooper, Anthony Perkins. Director and producer: William Wyler.

Based on the Jessamyn West novel; the film portrays the struggle within a farm family when the Civil War tests Quaker beliefs in conflict with patriotism.

Gone With the Wind (1939). Vivian Leigh, Clark Gable, Olivia deHavilland, Leslie Howard, Hattie McDaniel (Academy Award, Best Supporting Actress). Director: Victor Fleming; producer: David O. Selznick.

Margaret Mitchell's much beloved but romanticized tale of the "lost civilization": the Old South.

Heartland (1979). Conchata Ferrell, Rip Torn. Director: Richard Pearce; producers: Michael Hausman and Beth Ferris.

Set in turn-of-the-century Wyoming and based on actual diaries of pioneer women. *Heartland* is an excellent film both for the depth of character development and its unsentimental view of the almost overwhelming isolation of the frontier.

The Heiress (1949). Olivia deHavilland (Academy Award, Best Actress), Montgomery Clift. Producer and director: William Wyler.

Set in 1850, this adaptation of Henry James's novel *Washington Square* tells the story of a young woman rejected by her father who grows from a docile victim to a strong, rational adult.

Little Women (1994). Susan Sarandon, Wynona Ryder, Claire Danes. Director: Gillian Anderson.

Louisa May Alcott's story of a mother and four daughters in nineteenth-century New England.

McCabe and Mrs. Miller (1971). Julie Christie, Warren Beatty. Director: Robert Altman; producer: David Foster.

A meandering but effective meditation on life on the early frontier. Christie is particularly compelling as an opium-smoking prostitute.

INDEX

AASS. *See* American Antislavery Society

Abbott, Edith, 3, 99, 180

Abbott, Grace, 99, 180

Abolition movement, 51–52; American Antislavery Society, 52, 113, 141–42, 175; and beginning of women's rights movement, 112–14, 116–17; Child, 51, 81, 112, 142, 158, 182, 222; chronology, 222, 223; Grimké sisters, 51, 112, 141–42, 175–77, 222; Harper, 81, 178–79; Kemble, 183; opposition to, 187–88, 206; and religion, 51, 56, 116; resources, 246–47; Shadd, 155–56; Stowe, 80–81, 188, 206–7; Tubman, 80, 211–12. *See also* Abolition/women's rights conflict

Abolition/women's rights conflict, 117, 169–70, 205; abolition movement split, 52, 223; chronology, 223; and Civil War amendments, 64, 87–88, 120–22, 192–93

Abortion, 107–8, 139; chronology, 224; historiography, 11–12; resources, 267

Abortion in America: The Origins and Evolution of National Policy (Mohr), 11–12

Acquaintances Old and New, Among Reformers (Brown), 155

Activism. *See* Abolition movement; Moral reform; Social reform; Woman suffrage

Adams, Abigail, 25, 39, 165

Adams, John Quincy, 51

Addams, Jane, 98–99, 132, 139–40, 173, 180, 204; chronology, 229; resources, 283, 290

Advocate of Moral Reform, 49, 143

AERA. *See* American Equal Rights Association

AFL. *See* American Federation of Labor

African American education, 44, 129; chronology, 221, 222, 224; and Crandall, 163–64, 222; during Civil War, 86, 168–69, 224; Reconstruction, 47–48, 86, 88, 89, 143

African Americans: and abolition movement, 80, 117; birth rates, 19, 102; and Catholicism, 58; Civil War role, 85, 86, 168–69, 196, 207–8, 211, 212; Cooper, 44, 162–63; domestic service, 74; Great Migration, 192; historiography, 14–15; and labor movement, 120; lynching, 122–23, 163, 191, 213, 230; and Reconstruction, 88–89; religion, 55–56, 57–58, 88; resources, 255–56, 297–98; segregation, 128, 191; sexual exploitation, 88–89; and sexual purity ideal, 102; suffrage, 87–88; and woman suffrage, 117; women's clubs, 88, 95–96, 179, 191–92, 209, 213; and women's rights movement, 117; working women, 32, 92, 129, 130. *See also* African American education; Enslaved African Americans; Free blacks; *specific people*